States of Delinquency

AMERICAN CROSSROADS

Edited by Earl Lewis, George Lipsitz, George Sánchez, Dana Takagi, Laura Briggs, and Nikhil Pal Singh

States of Delinquency

*Race and Science in the Making
of California's Juvenile Justice System*

Miroslava Chávez-García

UNIVERSITY OF CALIFORNIA PRESS
Berkeley · Los Angeles · London

University of California Press, one of the most
distinguished university presses in the United States,
enriches lives around the world by advancing
scholarship in the humanities, social sciences, and
natural sciences. Its activities are supported by the UC
Press Foundation and by philanthropic contributions
from individuals and institutions. For more information, visit www.ucpress.edu.

University of California Press
Berkeley and Los Angeles, California

University of California Press, Ltd.
London, England

Library of Congress Cataloging-in-Publication Data

Chávez-García, Miroslava, 1968-
    States of delinquency : race and science in the
making of California's juvenile justice system /
Miroslava Chávez-García.
        p. cm.
    Includes bibliographical references and index.
    ISBN 978-0-520-27171-5 (cloth : alk. paper) —
ISBN 978-0-520-27172-2 (pbk. : alk. paper)
    1. Juvenile justice, Administration of—
California—History. 2. Minority youth—California—
History. 3. Juvenile delinquents—California—History.
4. Crime and race—California—History. 5. Eugenics—
California—History. 6. Whittier State School (Whittier,
Calif.) 7. Preston School of Industry (Ione, Calif.)
I. Title.
    HV9105.C2C43 2012
    364.3609794—dc23

                                    2011033524

Manufactured in the United States of America

21 20 19 18 17 16 15 14 13 12
10 9 8 7 6 5 4 3 2 1

In keeping with a commitment to support environmen-
tally responsible and sustainable printing practices, UC
Press has printed this book on Rolland Enviro100, a
100% post-consumer fiber paper that is FSC certified,
deinked, processed chlorine-free, and manufactured
with renewable biogas energy. It is acid-free and
EcoLogo certified.

To my children, Eliana Aliyah García and Evan Abraham García, and to the youths in this study. Thank you for your inspiration.

The publisher gratefully acknowledges the generous support of the Anne G. Lipow Endowment Fund for Social Justice and Human Rights of the University of California Press Foundation, which was established by Stephen M. Silberstein.

Contents

Illustrations

Acknowledgments

This book represents the collective effort of the many people who shared their knowledge and spared their time in helping me weave these stories. Among those who played critical roles is the brilliant Alexandra M. Stern, whose guidance, patience, and generosity in the early stages of this project steered me in the right direction. Norm Skonovd, a sociologist, professor, and employee of the Department of Corrections provided great insight on the Fred C. Nelles School for Boys (formerly Whittier State School) and piqued my curiosity in searching for more details and nuances of the institution. Equally supportive and adept colleagues who provided significant feedback at various points include Sunaina Maira, Tony Platt, Vicki Ruiz, and Steven S. Schlossman.

I am particularly grateful to those colleagues who took time from their busy schedules to hear and/or read parts of my work and provide feedback. They include Sasha Abramsky, Al Camarillo, Ernesto Chávez, Nathaniel Deutsch, Marta Gutman, Anne Meis Knupfer, Sunaina Maira, Paula Moya, Tony Platt, Vicki Ruiz, Norm Skonovd, Alexandra M. Stern, and Rashad Shabazz. I also had the great fortune of participating in several important symposiums on eugenics, imprisonment, and delinquency, including "From Eugenics to Designer Babies: Engineering the California Dream," held at California State University–Sacramento in 2005; "Incarcerations and Detentions," organized at the University of California–Los Angeles in 2010; "Writing Policing and Punishment into Modern U.S. History," held at Rutgers University in 2010; and "Juvenile Delinquency in Comparative (East-West) Contexts," organized at Humboldt University in Berlin, Germany. Those experiences—and the individuals who participated—contributed to this project by helping me to think in new ways about delinquency, youth, race, and science. Thank you, too, in particular to Alex Wellerstein, a graduate student at Harvard University, who shared his writing and resources on Sonoma State Home.

In creating this work, I also had the opportunity to collaborate and share resources with many other smart colleagues who have taught me a lot about race, class, gender, psychology, eugenics, and juvenile justice. They include William "Bill" Bush, William "Bill" Deverell, Yvette Flores, Milmon Harrison, Laura Mihailoff, Natalia Molina, Tamara Myers, Judith R. Raftery, Eddie Salas, and Geoff Ward. David M. Hernandez merits particular praise for his fabulous suggestion for the title of this book.

My colleagues and former students also deserve a million thanks for their support throughout this process. My colleagues in the Chicana/o Studies Department at UC Davis merit praise for their patience in allowing me to steal time away from teaching and service to focus on my research. Lorena Marquez, a former doctoral student and recent Ph.D., warrants *mil gracias* for her unflagging support and generous ear. Many undergraduate students at UC Davis also contributed to this project. Research assistants Liliana Madrid, Dominique "Niki" Windberg, and Lydia Werner found important newspaper articles, tracked down old essays, and photocopied dozens of eugenics fieldworkers' case files. My step-daughter Alejandra "Alex" García also gave up some of her summer to assist me in the archives searching state prison records. Thank you to all of you.

None of this work, of course, would have been possible if it wasn't for the generous archivists who put up with my incessant requests. Those most deserving of my gratitude are the archivists at the California State Archives in Sacramento, California, where I spent a number of years collecting data. Thank you to Melodi Andersen, Sydney Bailey, Jeff Crawford, Stephanie Hamashin, Linda Johnson, Genevieve Troka, and Rebecca Wendt, among all the other friendly faces at the State Archives. Archivists at the Amador County Archives; the American Philosophical Society Library, particularly Charles Greifenstein; the Bancroft Library, particularly Theresa Salazar; the California State Library; the University Archives at the California Institute of Technology; Special Collections at the University of California–Los Angeles; Special Collections at Stanford University; and the Southern California Regional Library also deserve recognition for their assistance. A particular thanks goes out to John Lafferty, a retired librarian from the Preston School of Industry, who took time out during his retirement to meet with me in Sacramento and share his insights and work at Preston. Finally, Roberto Delgadillo, a librarian at Shields Library at UC Davis, deserves much praise for his attending to my every research need. Roberto, for instance, located an important court case that appears in Chapter 4.

Equally significant are those institutions that provided invaluable support to carry out and, ultimately, finish this study. Funding for research came from UC Davis, Office of Research; UC Davis, College of Letters and Science, Humanities, Arts, and Cultural Studies; UC Davis Humanities Institute; and the University of California Institute for Mexico and the United States (UC-MEXUS). A year-long faculty fellowship at the Center for Comparative Studies in Race and Ethnicity (CCSRE) at Stanford University not only allowed me the opportunity to meet new colleagues and share my work but also to plow through writing and finishing the book. Thanks, too, to CCSRE Executive Director Elizabeth Wahl for her patience.

I also had the wonderful opportunity to share my work with the residents of Whittier, California, whose history is inextricably linked to the Fred C. Nelles Correctional Facility (Whittier State School). For facilitating that exchange, I thank Julie Collins-Dogrul, a professor at Whittier College.

I was fortunate, too, to visit the grounds of Nelles Correctional, though the institution has been closed since 2004. For allowing me the opportunity to tour the site, I thank Norma Fong-Mori, John Day, and other officials working the Department of Corrections and the State of California. I first learned of the plans to raze Nelles Correctional from Mike Sprague, a newspaper reporter at the *Whittier News* who keeps close tabs on that place. Through him, I had the great chance of meeting Frank Aguirre, a former inmate whose story appears in the epilogue. Frank, in turn, is responsible for keeping me honest about this project. Frank's interest and commitment to this project runs deep, perhaps deeper than I realize. Our frequent e-mails and phone conversations reminded me that this project is not about the past but about the present and the future as well.

With much appreciation I thank my editor, Niels Hooper, Eric Schmidt, and the American Crossroads series editors at the University of California Press, particularly George Sánchez, my former advisor at UCLA, William "Bill" Deverel, and Laura Briggs, for supporting this project and bringing it to fruition. Nothing brings me more satisfaction than getting these stories out into the public.

Finally, I would like to acknowledge my family, who helped me put my work in perspective and remind me of the most important things in life. Ebers García, my spouse, I thank for his brilliance and speed with the photos that adorn this book; my children Eliana, 7, and Evan, 5, I thank for making me write quicker than I ever have; and to Alex, 20, I thank for her support. I dedicate this book to Eliana, Evan, and to the youths in this book, for whom I feel a great responsibility. To my children, I feel responsible for helping to craft their futures; to the youths in this work, I feel responsible for recounting their past. I hope I have done all of them some justice.

Introduction

In the last three decades, the proportion of Latino and African American males eighteen years of age and under in the juvenile justice system has climbed remarkably in relation to white or Euro-American males. This is true particularly for young males residing in some of the most populous states, including New York, Texas, and California. Statistics from around the country indicate that youths of color comprise 38 percent of the population, yet they make up a whopping 72 percent of incarcerated juveniles. Advocacy groups such as the W. Haywood Burns Institute report that, at all stages of contact with the juvenile justice system, minority youth face discrimination. For instance, they are more likely than whites to be arrested, assigned higher bail amounts, given stiffer sentences, and transferred to adult court. The sources of these disparities are not yet clear although it is known that poverty, poor schooling, cultural and language barriers, racial profiling, and deep-rooted mistrust of the police, courts, and corrections in communities of color have contributed to the overrepresentation of racial and ethnic minorities, particularly males, in the juvenile justice system.

Our knowledge of the relationship of cops, courts, and corrections, on the one hand, and of youths and communities of color, on the other, is sparse and more so when it comes to understanding the historical underpinnings of that mistrust. Our greatest insight on Latinas and Latinos and Mexican Americans, specifically, comes from the World War II era and the criminalization, racialization, and pathologization of *pachucos* and *pachucas* (or zoot suiters) in the 1940s. These were young, U.S.-born Mexican Americans who felt out of place both in American society as well as in their Mexican-born parents' cultural milieu. To distinguish themselves as neither wholly American nor Mexican, they adopted a youth culture that included sporting distinctive styles of dress (namely, the drape or zoot suit), donning a pompadour hairstyle, and speaking a unique language (*caló*, or pachuco slang). In attempting to carve out their identity, they affronted notions of American patriotism and invited frequent assaults, particularly by United States servicemen stationed on the West Coast in Los Angeles on temporary leave from duty. Those tensions reached a peak in June 1943, when rioting broke out across the city. The police, however, did little to ameliorate the situation. When called to quell the disturbances, the cops stood by idly and only stepped in after the beatings of youths had ended—to arrest the youngsters.

The judicial system treated the pachucas and pachucos no better. With little evidence, judges and district attorneys often prosecuted them to the fullest extent of the law. A year earlier, in the Sleepy Lagoon trial of 1942, in which nearly two dozen boys were tried for the unsolved murder of another youth, José Díaz, who had died after an altercation at a party all the youths had attended, the court not only convicted seventeen defendants for crimes they did not commit but also identified them as inherently—biologically—criminal and menaces to society. At the trial, "expert" witnesses testified that the boys' Indian or Aztec heritage naturally shaped their need to draw blood. The young pachucas caught up in the court case were similarly characterized, though the justice system impugned their sexuality and morality in particular. Police and judges as well as members of the media and public identified them as female gangsters as well as prostitutes. When arrested in the Sleepy Lagoon affair, they faced harsher consequences than the males. For their involvement in the case, a handful of girls ended up in the Ventura School for Girls, California's only female state reformatory, where they endured indeterminate sentences under a repressive regime. The males, whose convictions were later overturned on appeal, gained their freedom after two years of imprisonment, but the girls languished behind bars until their maturity, twenty-one years of age.[1]

The Sleepy Lagoon incident and zoot suit riots of the early 1940s, while telling of the racism, sexism, and violence Mexican American youths encountered, limit our understanding of the ways in which youth of color have been criminalized, racialized, and pathologized in history. The over-emphasis on the 1940s as fundamental in shaping the nature of relations between nonwhite youths and the broader juvenile justice system—identified here as the network of police, courts, and corrections as well as the private and public institutions designed to handle wayward youth—has led to a distorted understanding of the origins of the their criminalization, racialization, and pathologization. In California, that process dates back to the turn of the twentieth century, specifically the Progressive Era, when ideas and ideologies about the promise of science and scientific research to resolve most social problems, including juvenile delinquency, took hold in the emerging juvenile and criminal justice systems in the United States. New approaches to determining and preventing the causes of juvenile delinquency—defined loosely as antisocial behavior and criminal acts committed by youths under the age of eighteen—as well as ideas about creating a well-ordered and efficient society had profound implications for youths of color who ended up in facilities for delinquent, dependent, or otherwise unwanted youth. *States of Delinquency* demonstrates that many of these young people faced long terms of incarceration as well as physical, sexual, and likely psychological harm.

States of Delinquency examines and analyzes the experiences of youths of color in California's emerging juvenile justice system in the nineteenth and early twentieth centuries. The focus is on young Mexicans, Mexican Americans, and African Americans, the largest ethnic and racial minority groups who ended up at the principal correctional facilities (or reformatories) in the state: Whittier State School for Boys, located in Whittier, California; Preston School of Industry, in Ione, California; and the Ventura School for Girls, originally established as the California School for Girls within Whittier State School and later relocated to Ventura, California. The narrative opens with a broad overview of the ideologies and practices guiding the treatment of wayward or unwanted youth in mid-nineteenth-century California, paying close attention the rise of state institutions in the 1880s and 1890s—effectively replacing the family and community—as a means to handle such youngsters. The study then closes in the early 1940s with the statewide reorganization of the juvenile correctional system that followed in the wake of the suicides of two Mexican American youths in 1939 and 1940, respectively. The book interrogates how the application of science and scientific research as well as the latest theories of delinquency, intelligence, and heredity in the emerging fields of psychology, education, eugenics, and criminology had criminalized, racialized, and pathologized incarcerated youths of color, rendering them "defective delinquents." *States of Delinquency* demonstrates that, despite the marginalization of young people of color and their families, they found ways to contest state policies and practices and did so in creative ways.

This book uses the lives of individuals or groups of individuals to demonstrate how the application of science and scientific research as well as the latest theories of delinquency, intelligence, heredity, and race intersected and shaped the experiences of children and youths of color who, for various reasons, ended up caught in the web of the juvenile justice system.[2] As these stories attest, children and youths had little say in the state policies and practices designed to control and contain them. Indeed, structural forces operating at the state level and permeating public and private spaces were beyond the understanding and reach of young people. However, these same youngsters—often alongside their families—found creative ways to negotiate and contest institutionalization and did so at all stages of their confinement. Yet for some children and youths survival meant acquiescing to state interventions and leaving it up to state officials, such as reform school administrators, state leaders, and scientific researchers, as well as the public to meet their needs, though they often fell short of doing so. Instead, they neglected and ignored state institutions until their conditions had deteriorated significantly or tragedies struck, such as the suicides in 1939 and 1940.

Beginning in the early 1900s, when conditions at Whittier State School took a turn for the worse after only twenty years of operation—with rampant physical and sexual abuse, excessive corporal punishment, meager state funding, and neglect—state and reform school officials employed scientific researchers to develop effective programs aimed at redeeming delinquent, dependent, and otherwise unwanted youth and transforming them into productive male citizens. To do so, the researchers applied the latest theories and tools in the emerging fields of psychology, education, social work, eugenics, and criminology to administer hundreds, more likely thousands, of physical, psychological, and intelligence tests as well as fieldwork studies on the youths' families, home environments, and communities of origin. The goal: to classify, sort, and segregate state wards along a continuum of normalcy to degeneracy. In the process, scientists identified a disproportionate number of Mexican, Mexican American, and African American youths as feebleminded and criminally minded offenders whose genetic or racial stock was the root cause of their deficiencies. Though the researchers argued that neither delinquency nor criminality was inherited or passed from parent to offspring, they believed that closely associated dysgenic traits, including feeblemindedness, psychopathic constitution, excitability, nomadism ("the tendency to wander"), and "weakened . . . self-control," almost always ensured criminal behavior. It was no matter that most Mexican-origin youths who took the tests or responded to the fieldworkers' questionnaires often had little command of the English language or that most of the African Americans and Mexican Americans as well as some ethnic Euro-Americans who performed poorly on the exams and queries had substandard or no schooling at all. Current scientific thought held that identified intelligence and related physical deficiencies resulted from inherited and genetic differences, not from cultural biases inherent in the investigative process. Reform school officials used the findings, in turn, to transfer the mentally deficient to state hospitals or other institutions for their confinement, permanent care, and, ideally, sterilization. In the process, the reformatories were transformed into social laboratories in which to carry out social experiments aimed at dealing not only with juvenile delinquency but also race betterment. Ultimately, the process of weeding defectives and improving the race—largely understood as the Nordic American race—was intimately tied to biological determinism and nation building at home and across the globe, particularly in the post-1898 era.[3]

The faith in intelligence, psychological, and physical examinations to sort and create a well-ordered and strong society as well as the belief in eugenics, the ideology of race betterment through selective breeding as first developed by Francis Galton in the nineteenth century, was not unique to state reformatories or the emerging juvenile or criminal justice systems in California. Rather, contemporary political leaders and social reformers in the Golden State turned to leading thinkers across the United States and Europe to gather ideas and borrow models from which to craft the most promising and cutting-edge scientific approaches to preventing and determining the causes of juvenile delinquency and of other similar social ills that threatened the moral fabric of society. The work of H. H. Goddard, the director of the Vineland Institute in New Jersey and major proponent of the Binet-Simon intelligence test in the United States, for instance, had piqued the curiosity of state officials working with delinquents in California, as did the studies carried out by Charles Davenport and Harry Laughlin of the Eugenics Records Office (ERO) in Cold Spring Harbor, New York. Davenport not only ran an institute where he and Laughlin disseminated ideas and practices through lectures, scientific papers, and training manuals but also trained primarily young, college-educated, white, middle-class women and a few men to conduct eugenics-based research on families and communities throughout the country. This research consisted of tracking the presence of dysgenic traits across at least three generations of individuals and family members in order to draw links among intelligence, criminality, and sexual deviancy, among other dysgenic traits. Such work interested state officials and reform school administrators in California, prompting them, under the leadership of Fred C. Nelles, to hire leading psychologists and education specialists at Stanford University as well as eugenics fieldworkers to carry out research in the newly established Department of Research (later, the California Bureau of Juvenile Research, the self-described West Coast representative of the ERO) at Whittier State School.[4] The ultimate goal was to determine the causes of delinquency and develop prevention, intervention, and treatment models.[5]

Californians turned to the latest thinkers and practitioners not only in the fields of psychology, education, social work, eugenics, and criminology but also in the juvenile justice system. For that, they looked to Illinois, specifically Chicago's juvenile court, the first tribunal for minors established in the United States, in 1899. In Chicago, the juvenile courts, probation officers, and juvenile halls also regularly tested youths detained for some malfeasance or for the simple fact of being dependent and having no one to care for them. Judges in Illinois used those exams, in turn, to determine the fate of youngsters as productive and reproductive members of society. Similar ideas and practices across the United States as well as in Germany, France, and England served as models for Californians, for the European investigators had conducted dozens of studies on the relationship among intelligence, criminality, heredity, and, to some extent, ethnicity.[6]

Rather than simply apply the latest trends in juvenile justice or mimic the latest beliefs in eugenic thought in the United States and abroad, state leaders in California crafted home-grown ideologies and practices about the nature of and solution to juvenile delinquency, race betterment, and, ultimately, nation building. The need to develop regionally specific approaches to delinquency, race, and empire building was largely due to the increasingly diverse racial and ethnic population of the Golden State. California, unlike most regions throughout the United States with the exception of Texas, had a racially mixed population of Euro-Americans, Mexicans, Mexican Americans, and African Americans, along with fewer numbers of Asians and Native Americans; the Euro-Americans also comprised significant ethnic communities, namely Italians, Portuguese, Greeks, and Spaniards, among others. Rather than relying on a black-white binary to demonstrate the results of biometric and other scientific examinations, researchers formulated a nuanced yet problematic under-standing of intelligence and racial differences, with whites on top, blacks in the middle, and Mexicans on the bottom. In between the rungs, ethnic Americans occupied various positions either slightly above or below that of Mexicans and Mexican Americans. This structure, though shifting slightly in form and nature, shaped the researchers' and state officials' thinking about racial, ethnic, and cultural hierarchies as they pertained to intelligence and delinquency and guided their policies and practices in state institutions.

The scientific researchers, state officials, and the many public and private men and women invested in California's juvenile justice system at the turn of the century would emerge as part of a larger trend of an increasingly professional, bureaucratic class of workers in the United States concerned about their rapidly changing environment. In the late nineteenth and early twentieth century, the growing urban professional class became increasingly concerned about the effects of rapid industrialization, urbanization, and immigration and the significant changes to the urban environments such as increased crowding, demands for services, and competition for resources, which created tensions and a sense of disorder. To address these social ills, many young professionals turned to science and scientific thought and focused their attention on developments in the behavioral and social sciences as well as in medicine. Through these fields, they believed professionally trained and educated individuals had the power to bring efficiency and order to an increasingly chaotic environment. While this process excluded the numerous volunteers who often had filled positions in the police force, the courts, and corrections in the nineteenth century, it gave young professionals, many of them single, middle-class women such as the eugenics fieldworkers, the opportunity to develop skills and command authority in their jobs and job sites, which were often communities composed of mostly ethnic and racial foreign-born families with native-born children. Ultimately, it was these men and women, the Progressives, who carried out much of the day-to-day work with youths of color and their families and communities in the early twentieth century.[7]

The Progressives' concern with the changing environment reflected larger significant population movements to California and the West more broadly. As jobs in the agricultural, railroad, and mining sectors expanded in the Southwest and as cheap sources of labor from China, Japan, and southeastern Europe dried up, thousands of Mexicans immigrated to the United States and to California in particular in search of jobs and stability; many of them fled there during the violence of the Mexican Revolution, a civil war that drove nearly 10 percent of the Mexican population north. African Americans as well as white Southerners also increasingly called California their home in the early twentieth century. In the late 1910s and early 1920s, World War I and its aftermath spurred the migration of African Americans and poor whites from the South. Not everyone supported migrants or immigrants, particularly the virulent immigration restrictionists who believed in the biological inferiority of racially impure or mixed persons, especially Mexicans and other immigrants. The power and reach of anti-immigrant forces was so great that it resulted in increasingly strict immigration policies and migration polices to California in the early 1920s. Viewed as a burden by white society, many migrants and immigrants, including children and youths, were returned to their regions of origin during times of economic downturns, such as the Great Depression that rocked the country in the 1930s. Despite the unwelcoming reception, African Americans, many of them youths traveling alone, as well as Mexicans made their way west on freight trains and settled in California with extended family members, establishing new and expanding old communities. The growing number of ethnic and racial minority youths in burgeoning cities and counties, such as Los Angeles and Alameda, clashed with more frequency with police and became entangled in the network of institutions that made up the juvenile justice system.

As many youths experienced, the doctrine of *parens patriae* gave the state the legal right to assume control of a minor if the parents could not or were unfit to do so; thus, it gave state institutions power over all children and youths identified as delinquents (those eighteen years and under who broke the law or customs as established by the white middle class) or dependents (those eighteen and under without guardianship and in danger of becoming delinquent). As wards of the state, youngsters were placed in alien environments such as reform schools and state hospitals where they or their next of kin had little say or control over their immediate or long-term future. A parent who had his or her child committed to a state reformatory and later had a change of mind and wanted the child released could not simply take that child home: the state had the ultimate authority in determining such children's needs.

Despite such power imbalances, youths and their families found ways to challenge the ideologies and practices of the state institutions. Drawing on anthropologist James Scott's construct of the "weapons of the weak" to explore the larger meanings of "everyday"—rather than formal, organized—forms of resistance by youths, this book shows that young inmates in particular employed what few resources they had at their disposal. Like the Malay peasants in Scott's study, the incarcerated youths dragged their feet, feigned a lack of interest in the testing and research, and disrupted classrooms and other settings in the reformatories. In at least two reported instances, boys took back control of their lives by committing suicide rather than continuing in state detention. Though they were extreme, such measures ultimately brought statewide attention to the needs of incarcerated youths in California. While most incidents appeared to be of little consequence, the actions demonstrated the will of a relatively powerless group of young people to challenge the terms of their incarceration as well as the state's process of criminalization, racialization, and pathologization.

Youths also demonstrated their opposition to the institution by escaping or attempting to escape from the reformatories. In some cases, when necessity called for it, youths organized in multiracial and multiethnic groups to escape; in others, when more drastic means were necessary, they employed violence, feigned illness, and in others ways managed to escape. Attempting to escape, considered to be among the most serious offenses, was a grave matter—if caught, escapees were subject to harsh punishments including whippings and solitary confinement in cold, dark, and dungeonlike rooms. For a time, administrators eased these policies, especially during the height of Progressive experimentation and reform in the 1910s and 1920s. Much along the lines of Michel Foucault's history of the evolution of disciplinary practices in the correctional system, state officials discontinued or discouraged the use of the whip to castigate the body in favor of solitary confinement to discipline the mind. Rather than placing youths in dank holes, the officials built "lost privilege" cottages where they confined the young people to reflect on their mistakes and shortcomings. At Whittier State School, the shift in disciplinary practices occurred with the arrival of the ardent progressive Fred C. Nelles in the early 1910s. Nelles banned the use of the corporal punishment and adopted the loss of privileges regime. Over time, Nelles's experiments would decay, especially following his death in 1927, when the state curtailed funding, the public grew apathetic, and administrators and staff alike winked at the harsh treatment of incarcerated youths. Eventually, conditions deteriorated so badly that two Mexican American boys committed suicide.[8]

Recovering the historical experiences of youths in general and of youths of color in particular who were identified as delinquent, dependent, or defective and confined to state institutions poses many challenges. First, notions of gender, sexuality, and immorality and beliefs about the ability of male and female delinquents to reform and reenter society have nearly erased the historical presence of a significant majority of the females confined to the Girl's Department at Whittier State School and, later, the California School for Girls, established in 1913. As the records indicate, state officials paid much less attention to the females than the males, for they believed that the girls—the majority of whom were incarcerated for sex-related "crimes," whether victims or not—were tainted and shamed for good, whereas males, many of whom had committed seemingly minor infractions such as petty theft, had the ability to reform and return to society as productive members. For these and other reasons, the record keeping for the girls in the state reformatory system was poor at best and nonexistent at worst. The records detailing the boys' experiences, on the other hand, are rich qualitatively and quantitatively across the first fifty years of the reformatory's history—specifically, at Whittier State School. This study, therefore, focuses primarily on boys and less on girls, all of whom were confined to the California (and after 1916, Ventura) School for Girls.[9]

States of Delinquency faces a second obstacle in recovering the youths' histories, namely, their status as minors and prisoners. Put simply, the youths' incarceration in state institutions obscures their experiences, for they had little, if any, social power in or outside the state and larger society, which gave them few opportunities to voice their motivations and aspirations as well as their fears and desires. Significant insights about the youths' sentiments and reasoning *do* appear in juvenile county court records, but those documents are difficult to procure, if available, due to poor record keeping as well as privacy laws. The youths' status as minors and the use of state hospital records also preclude this work's disclosing their identities, though in cases where their full names were made public, such as in newspaper reports, the boys' information is disclosed.[10]

A third barrier to gleaning their experiences is the youths' dependent status in the family and larger society, as young people—much like today—were often ignored and objectified. A fourth layer that obscures the voices of young people of color—namely, the Mexican, Mexican American, and African American youths—was their social, economic, and political marginalization in the larger society, like their adult counterparts at the turn of the twentieth century. The youths' limited literacy or lack of ability to write or read in English or Spanish is a fifth challenge in finding sources detailing their experiences, for few left written records. Finally, *States of Delinquency* recognizes a sixth difficulty in writing such a history: while reform school and state hospital records and other similar state-generated sources *do* exist, the institution's (and state's) interests—and not those of the individual or collective community—are best represented, and the texts reflect the values and ideologies of the state. The sources, therefore, illustrate the larger inequalities shaping the imbalanced power relations between the youths and state representatives.

Despite the limitations of the source materials, reviewing the documents a second and third time and reading them "against the grain"—against the beliefs of state representatives and other white, middle-class professionals—allows for the youths' voices, actions, thoughts, and agency to emerge, albeit in limited yet significant ways. This approach is used when examining some 8,000 inmate case histories from Whittier State School—kept in large dusty volumes at the California State Archives—that are used extensively for this study. Dating from the 1890s to the 1940s, the case histories provide a richly textured profile of the youths who ended up at Whittier, some of whom were later transferred to other institutions. The records are both quantitative and qualitative in nature, illuminating the gender, racial, ethnic, class, age, and regional background as well as the personal, educational, and familial histories of most inmates. Inmate case files for Preston and Ventura are woefully less complete and less detailed than those available for Whittier. Thus, Whittier State School forms the basis of this study with Preston and Ventura serving as comparative points of reference.

The case files are complemented by a diverse and rich set of primary sources including over two hundred social case histories—carried out by eugenics fieldworkers at Whittier State School's Department of Research (later, the California Bureau of Juvenile Research)—of male inmates in the 1910s and early 1920s. These records are significant for they not only provide insight on major environmental, psychological, and biological influences shaping the boys' young lives but also detail the fieldworkers' eugenicist ideologies and practices as they affected male youths across race and ethnicity in California. This study relies on thousands of other records as well, including San Quentin Prison and Folsom State Prison registers, dating from the 1850s to 1940s; authorization forms for the sterilization of patients in California state hospitals; institutional reports; hospital admission ledgers; official letters to and from imprisoned youths and state officials; local and regional newspapers reports; and photographs and oral histories.

Taken together and read in creative ways, the sources offer significant insight on the youths' agency and the structural constraints shaping their daily lives. The documents detail, for instance, the extreme measures boys took in attempting to break out of the school as well as the punishments and abuses they often suffered at the hands of other inmates, staff, and administrators. The inmates' performance on intelligence, psychological, and physical tests and their removal to (and eventual sterilization at) state hospitals appear in the documents as well, demonstrating the uses and abuses of science and scientific research in the early twentieth century. Reports of sexual abuse by staff and other inmates, though most often these incidents went unreported or were distorted to hide their widespread practice, also appear and indicate not only significant power differentials but also the willingness of reform school officials to ignore such practices.[11] Collecting and analyzing case studies, then, allows this study to recover individual as well as collective experiences of troubled youths of color and the ways in which their lives intersected with the broader juvenile justice system in California.

The book is organized chronologically and thematically and uses the personal and collective narratives of people—youths as well as adults—to tell the larger story of how notions of youth, delinquency, race, and science shaped the early juvenile justice system in California. Chapter 1 opens in the nineteenth century and examines briefly the experiences of Arthur C., an incorrigible Mexican American boy whose only crimes were running the streets and being an economic burden to his family, to explore the changing ways Californians dealt with troubled youths in the 1800s. Initially, in the early 1800s, Californians, primarily Native, Spanish, and Mexican-origin peoples, used the family and community to deal with recalcitrant youth such as Arthur C. That approach began to change, however, following the American conquest in 1848 and California's statehood in 1850. Thereafter, the growing public—which was predominantly Euro-American—took an increasingly grim view of the rising numbers of children and youths roaming community and city streets, causing disorder and disrupting neighborhoods, local businesses, and city projects. Rather than have individuals and families deal with the issue at the local level, they advocated the use of private and public institutions to handle delinquents and dependents. When those places proved wholly insufficient to meet the demands of increasing numbers of youths, the public called on the state to resolve the matter. State officials, in turn, looked to what they considered the latest or "modern" state-run reform schools, like those scattered across the United States, Europe, and Latin America, to confine and control troublesome youths in California. The establishment of such institutions in California, they argued, would also contribute to the Golden State's transformation from a largely rural region to an increasingly urban and modern state. Yet rather than use the most recent models, such as those found in Massachusetts that focused on reforming the individual in a homelike setting, Californians turned to an archaic, often called brutal system that paid little attention to individual needs and extended the state's power over troublesome youngsters. The transformation from the use of familial and local-level institutions to the use of state-run organizations to handle recalcitrant youths ushered in a period of punitive institutionalization.

Twenty years later, under the administration of Fred C. Nelles, significant changes came to Whittier State School. Chapter 2 uses the life story and legacy of Fred C. Nelles, Superintendent of Whittier State School from 1912 to his death from pneumonia in 1927, to examine how reform school administrators in California and across the country used science and scientific research to transform archaic, dysfunctional reformatories into premiere modern institutions of juvenile reform and citizenship building. Whittier led the state and arguably the nation in research into juvenile delinquency. Nelles did so by calling on scientific researchers trained in the latest tools and techniques for identifying, preventing, and treating the causes of delinquency not only to curb criminality but also to create productive citizens and promote race betterment. In the process, he built an exemplary reform school and advanced research institution— a nationally and internationally recognized social laboratory. Nelles's success with rebuilding and implementing new policies and practices took a toll, though, on the most vulnerable children and youths at Whittier State School, primarily the impoverished, poorly educated racial and ethnic minorities. Under his administration, Mexicans, Mexican Americans, and African Americans in particular were disproportionately identified as mentally defective and feebleminded youth who needed permanent care and ideally sterilization.

Nelles and his staff of researchers did not carry out this work alone. Rather, they relied on an army of scientific researchers, staff, and ordinary people to poke and probe the youths' intellectual, psychological, and physical abilities and disabilities in order to sort the disabled from the able—the defective from the normal—and to evaluate their social outlook or prognosis as members of society. Chapter 3 focuses on the role of eugenics fieldworkers in criminalizing, racializing, and pathologizing youths, particularly Mexicans, Mexican Americans, and African Americans and their families, as feebleminded individuals who, along with other defectives and low-grade individuals around the country, posed a menace to American society. Using the work of Mildred S. Covert, one of two fieldworkers who carried out more than half of the 200 interviews with Whittier State School boys (I found no similar records for girls), the chapter examines the fieldworkers' training, tools and techniques, and ideas and ideologies used in evaluating the youths and their families. It shows that they drew on nineteenth-century beliefs about race, ethnicity, and gender to explain and draw conclusions about the nature of Mexican, Mexican American, and African American youths and their families as largely defective, feebleminded individuals who needed low-skilled work that involved constant supervision at best, or permanent care and sterilization at worst. *States of Delinquency* demonstrates that, despite the power imbalance between fieldworkers and their clients, the Mexican, Mexican American, and African American youths and their families managed to challenge the prejudices rampant in scientific thought and the larger society.

The scientific practices of fieldworkers such as Mildred S. Covert and the psychologists employed by Fred C. Nelles had a real, long-term impact on the children and youths—as well as their families and friends—who ended up at Whittier State School, which had the most vigorous scientific research program of the three reformatories in the state. Chapter 4 uses the experiences of Mexican American siblings Cristobal, Fred, Tony, and Albert M. to examine the process through which troublesome and otherwise unwanted youths were sorted, classified, and transferred among juvenile justice institutions across the state. Unlike their Euro-American counterparts, wayward youths of color who ended up at Whittier State School were more likely to be criminalized, racialized, and pathologized as deviant and defective boys needing further institutionalization and, ultimately, sterilization. To demonstrate these processes, the chapter begins by exploring the process through which youngsters like the four brothers were caught up in the web of the juvenile justice system in California. Next, it examines the daily experiences of the boys at Whittier State School, including the process of testing and investigating the boys' home and community, demonstrating how and why researchers disproportionately identified youths of color as feebleminded and pathologized them as racially and criminally deviant. Finally, it examines how and why the youngest brother, Albert, was sterilized but not his older brothers, even though they were all identified as feebleminded. The chapter compares his experience with that of the thousands of other youths in California who were also sterilized in the 1920s and 1930s. No matter that Albert's parents refused to provide consent for the surgery, state hospital administrators used a little-known provision in the law allowing them to sterilize their patients without parental or guardian consent.

Though few records remain detailing the extent of the scientific research carried out at the Preston School of Industry, and even fewer for the California/Ventura School for Girls, enough published primary sources survive to piece together a comprehensive history of what took place at Preston at the height of the research in the 1920s as well as in the first fifty years of its history. Chapter 5 details the experience of Otto H. Close, superintendent at the Preston School of Industry from 1920 to 1945, to examine how he turned the school around from a largely archaic, brutal reformatory to an efficient and well-regarded system in the 1920s, relying on the model of testing and segregation introduced and used extensively at Whittier State School. The chapter demonstrates that, despite the promising outlook for Preston in the 1920s and early 1930s, by the late 1930s the industrial school had stagnated, becoming a military-style penitentiary with little vocational training and few educational programs. At the root of the school's decline were administrative complacency, state neglect, little oversight of the day-to-day operations, and scant public support. By the early 1940s, state officials agreed that a new vision for the treatment of youthful offenders was needed at Preston, and they removed Close to an administrative post in Sacramento in the early 1940s, thereby ending his twenty-five year administration at the reformatory.

The troubles that plagued Preston in the 1930s and early 1940s, though significant, paled in comparison to those that emerged at Whittier State School in the same period. Chapter 6 uses the lives and deaths of Benny Moreno and Edward Leiva, Mexican American boys who committed suicide in the isolation unit of the Lost Privilege Cottage in 1939 and 1940, respectively, to explore the decline of Whittier State School. Once hailed as a world-class institution, Whittier had fallen into gradual disrepair after Nelles's death in 1927 and, especially, after the stock market crash of 1929. The chapter explores how political rivalries, severe cutbacks in state support, gross neglect, incompetent leadership, and an informal code of silence resulted in the deplorable conditions—including widespread physical and sexual abuse—that contributed to the deaths of the two boys. The boys' deaths were not in vain, however. Rather, they triggered a series of lengthy and controversial investigations that blew the lid off the reformatory and the larger Department of Institutions (responsible for the reformatories' administration), resulting in the reorganization of juvenile corrections and establishment of the Youth Authority in 1941. By 1943, the Youth Authority had assumed control of Whittier State School, Preston School of Industry, and the Ventura School for Girls and promised an individualized program—not unlike that established years earlier by Fred C. Nelles—attendant to the needs of California's most troubled youths, increasingly the youths of color.

The stories weaving the fabric of this book are in many ways partial and, as noted earlier, at the mercy of the records left for posterity or those that survived natural and man-made disasters as well as shoddy record keeping. The Epilogue, "Recovering Youths' Voices," explores the silences that we have to contend with in the recovery of voices and the writing of histories of young people, particularly of the young people of color confined to the California state institutions, and what happened to them before, during, and after institutionalization. Using the oral history of a formerly incarcerated Mexican American man, Frank Aguirre, the Epilogue explores the problems and possibilities in using oral histories to recover the histories of incarcerated youths and youths of color, many of whom now predominate in state-based, juvenile justice systems across the United States. The Epilogue also explores what became of Frank Aguirre as well as other former reform school inmates once they left their respective reformatories. While many of the males ended up in city jails and state prisons in California and across the country, others married, formed families, and led productive lives, despite the odds against them.

Indeed, as the youths of color in this study experienced, the process of racializing, criminalizing, and pathologizing loomed large in their young lives, for it shaped their daily lives as well as their future experiences in and outside the juvenile justice system and formed a legacy that we still live with today. Understanding and reversing the results of that legacy are just some of the basic goals we can work toward accomplishing if we aim to intervene in the lives of the young people who are locked up behind bars with little hope for the future. Only then can we engage significant sectors of the male youth population, particularly the Mexicans, Mexican Americans, and African Americans who today make up significant proportions of the incarcerated population and an increasingly tinier segment of the youth in higher education and other places of promise for young people today.

CHAPTER 1

Building Juvenile Justice Institutions in California

In 1891, Arthur C., an eleven-year-old Mexican American boy from San Francisco, found himself at Whittier State School, a newly established reformatory in Southern California designed to house delinquent and dependent youths between the ages of ten and eighteen. Under California law, delinquents were those convicted of a crime or those who had, in other ways, violated middle-class norms of society, whereas dependents were those who lacked parental supervision and support, and were in "danger" of leading "an idle and immoral life."[1] Like many parents, Arthur's father, Henry C., had committed his son to the reformatory on a charge of vagrancy, suggesting that Arthur refused to obey his father's orders to attend school or stay off the streets. More likely, though, Arthur's commitment to Whittier resulted from his father's inability to maintain the boy, for he had already spent time at the San Francisco Aid Society, a private, state-subsidized organization designed to assist needy children and their families. When the Aid Society could no longer assist the boy's family, Arthur's father sent him to Whittier, expecting relief. Apparently, it worked, for he remained a state ward for six years. Yet for Arthur life was not well behind the walls of the institution.

In his stint at the reformatory, Arthur incurred the wrath of the administrators for blatantly breaking the rules. In 1894, for instance, he escaped and was punished harshly with a strap as a result. Later, a staff member placed him on the "guard line"—standing at attention for an hour or more—for disobeying orders. Although he was regarded as bright, officials nevertheless viewed Arthur as a troublemaker, a reputation he would not shake for years. Indeed, a few months after his discharge from Whittier State School, Arthur ran into trouble with the local authorities. Picked up for burglary and believed to be too old for the reformatory, he was sent to San Quentin State Prison, California's oldest prison established in the early 1850s. After that, Arthur was released but soon ran into trouble again and ended up in Folsom State Prison, opened in 1880. Eventually, Arthur was released, and little else is known of what became of him.[2]

Arthur's on-again, off-again contact with state institutions, though typical of many of the youths who ended up at Whittier State School at the turn of the twentieth century, differed significantly from the experiences of similarly troubled youths who lived only a few decades earlier. Prior to the founding of Whittier State School, families and local communities took much of the responsibility for the care and control of boys and girls such as Arthur C. Prior to the American conquest in 1848, parents, extended family members, and other members of the community dealt with recalcitrant as well as needy children. Under Spanish colonial and Mexican republican rule, from the 1770s to the early 1850s, *Californios* (Spanish-speaking settlers and their descendants) relied on the family, extended kin, and community networks to care and control youngsters. California Indians, on the other hand, had their own methods of rearing children and dealing with the troublesome in particular. Native peoples in the region used a flexible, loosely structured family and community-based system for keeping the young in line.

For many decades prior to statehood in 1850, Californians of varying cultural, ethnic, and racial origins relied on the family and community to raise, socialize, and, if necessary, discipline youngsters who went astray. Yet by the late 1850s and 1860s, as rates of youthful crime increased—or at least behavior deemed criminal rose—Californians, most of them recently arrived Euro-Americans and Europeans, pressured state representatives to deal with the perceived growing menace to society. State leaders, in turn, took a long, hard look at prison policies and practices around the United States and across the globe to find alternatives that would, at the same time, modernize the relatively young state in the care and control of its population. State officials proposed several cutting-edge approaches, but in the end they adopted less-costly outdated methods, which led to the institutionalization of children and youths, a process that had special implications for ethnically and racially marginalized youngsters such as Arthur C.

Using Arthur C.'s experience as the culmination of a larger process begun decades earlier, this chapter traces the formation of the modern-day juvenile justice system in nineteenth-century California and its impact on Mexican, Mexican American, and African American young people, in particular, and compares it with that experienced by Euro-American and European youngsters. It focuses on the ways in which late eighteenth- and nineteenth-century Californians—Native Americans, Spaniards, Mexicans, and Euro-Americans—handled children who threatened the stability of the family, community, larger region, and, later, the state. Beginning with the Spanish conquest and colonization of California, the chapter explores the experiences of troublesome youths in the Native, Spanish, and Mexican periods and shows the significance of parents, extended family members, and community members in dealing with them. The discussion then probes in detail the approach of Euro-Americans and Europeans in handling the same youngsters and shows that, despite the availability of innovative models across the country and the world, Californians adopted an archaic system. By the 1880s and 1890s, the previous methods for caring and controlling youngsters gave way to an outdated and punitive structure that had long-term effects in shaping the modern-day juvenile justice system in California.

TROUBLESOME CHILDREN IN CALIFORNIA'S NATIVE, SPANISH, AND MEXICAN ERAS, 1770S TO THE 1840S

The Native peoples who inhabited present-day California in the eighteenth and early nineteenth centuries were culturally and linguistically diverse and held a variety of beliefs and practices, particularly when it came to childrearing and dealing with youngsters who, in some way, threatened the stability of their communities. Among most California Indian tribes, parents had primary authority over children, defined as individuals who had not yet reached puberty. Boys and girls who had reached manhood and womanhood, respectively, on the other hand, were treated as adults, subject to one or more chiefs who, in turn, led the tribe collectively.[3]

To prevent children from misbehaving, parents and relatives related moral stories and legends, which at the same time taught them the religious laws and codes as well as the social and supernatural sanctions that came with them. The oral narrative of Delfina Cuero, an elder and descendant of Native peoples in the Mission San Diego region, the Kumeyaay, for instance, relates many of the customs the young had to follow.

According to Cuero, the Kumeyaay instructed boys to bathe frequently and to stay away from a pregnant woman or one menstruating. If male children failed to do so, "it would ruin [his] hunter's eyesight and he couldn't find rabbits," thereby threatening his ability to feed the family and sustain the larger tribe.[4] To discourage children from eating certain plants or fruits, likely poisonous, the Kumeyaay warned that they would grow hair, which they believed was a "big sin."[5] The contemporary letters of Hugo Reid—a Scottish immigrant who arrived in California in the early 1800s and later married Victoria Bartolomea Comicrabit, a Native woman from a notable family in Southern California—indicate that parents also taught their children to respect elders and siblings and to reciprocate the kindness and generosity of others, particularly when it came to food because sustenance was scarce.[6]

Some neighboring tribes, on the other hand, invoked mystical beings to keep children in line. The Gabrieleños, natives of the Mission San Gabriel region, for instance, taught their children the precepts of Chinigchinich, a god they revered as the creator, while the Cahuilla Indians, south of the mission, invoked the supernatural power of Tahquitz, who used his force "mischievously and lecherously" upon those who transgressed community norms.[7] Other peoples warned of dire consequences if children—or adults, for that matter—carried out offensive acts. The Pomo of the Northern California region, for example, warned children to behave themselves for fear of poisoning or witchcraft by anonymous members of the community. A member of the same family could poison another for some wrongdoing. The Pomo attributed sicknesses and deaths to poisonings and thus took great pains to avert such spells upon them or members of their family or community. Unruly boys in particular who refrained from heeding such warnings received little training and were not allowed to pick up any wealth in the form of beads or baskets.[8]

By all accounts, Native peoples in California rarely used corporal punishment or other means of physical force to socialize or reprimand the young for breaking rules. Ruby Modesto, a desert Cahuilla medicine woman from the present-day Coachella Valley, affirmed that physical punishment was unknown until the arrival of the Europeans. "We talked to our children, and if necessary shamed them into behaving. Whipping is new, since the white man," Modesto stated.[9] Elders of the Concow Maidu, a tribe situated near the Feather River northeast of Sacramento, also reported that "physical punishment or abuse of children . . . [was] virtually inconceivable."[10] To control antisocial behavior, they warned children of supernatural consequences. In Gabrieleño society, Hugo Reid

observed, "whipping was never resorted to as punishment" and "robbery was never known among them. Murder was of rare occurrence,"
yet, he conceded, it was "punished with death."[11]

Contemporary eyewitness accounts told from the perspective of Spanish missionaries, though biased, agree that corporal punishment was used
infrequently to discipline California Indian children. In the 1813–1815
interrogatorio, a questionnaire the Spanish colonial authorities issued
to the new world—specifically, asking priests to describe Native culture—
the friars decried the seemingly lax parenting techniques of the indigenous peoples. Friars at the missions of San Gabriel, San Juan Capistrano, and San Luis Rey, established in Southern California in 1771,
1776, and 1798, respectively, harshly criticized local natives—most of
them Gabrieleño and Dieguño or Kumeyaay—for failing to educate
and correct their children along the lines of Spanish ideologies and practices. In Spanish colonial society, male heads of households had the
obligation to admonish their dependents, including children, when they
transgressed patriarchal authority as well as any other Spanish customs
and laws. Fathers sometimes chastised, imposed corporal punishment, or
in other ways forced their children to obey religious and secular teachings. The California natives held vastly different practices.

When the California Indians showed little understanding of or interest in following or inculcating European gender and family values, the
Spanish priests believed that natives lacked the initiative, judgment, and
morals to rear their children. The friars at Mission San Miguel, for instance, expressed disdain of the seeming overindulgence bestowed on
Native children. "Toward their children they show an extravagant love
whom they do not chastise," one wrote. At Mission San Antonio, founded
in 1771 along the central coast, the priests too believed that the excessive
love the Native parents devoted was "a vice[,] for the majority lack[ed]
the courage to punish their children's wrongdoing and knavery."[12] At
Mission San Gabriel, the religious officials reported that the natives cared
for their children so much "that we might say they are their little idols."[13]
In only one report did priests provide an alternative view of Native childrearing practices, and that came from Mission San Diego friars José
Sánchez and Fernando Martín. They reported that local indigenous
peoples "love[d] their children extremely" and educated them: "when
the children [did] wrong the parents admonish[ed], reprehend[ed] and
even punish[ed] them."[14]

The majority of representatives of the Spanish crown, however, expressed few kind words toward the Native peoples' parenting. Fray

Gerónimo Boscana, a Spanish-born missionary who spent nearly fourteen years at Mission San Juan Capistrano, from 1812 to 1826, for instance, held many of the same prejudices as his contemporaries and wrote about them at length. Boscana criticized Native parents for not instructing young-sters in the arts, making them "ignorant of all useful knowledge to keep them from idleness."[15] Instead, he said, they taught them only how to make the bow and arrow, to procure game, and to defend themselves against enemies. He admitted, though, that they sometimes imposed harsh measures, particularly when children failed to follow religious beliefs. "The perverse child invariably was destroyed, and the parents of such remained dishonored."[16] How frequently this occurred—the taking of troublesome child's life—is unknown, as are the reasons for killing a "per-verse" child; few if any sources verify such practices. Boscana's observa-tions, though questionable, are telling of the missionaries' larger rationale for practically enslaving California Indians in the mission system.

The limited use of corporal punishment when dealing with trouble-some youths among California Indians is explained, in part, by the larger goals of the judicial process among Native peoples. Vine Deloria Jr., in his account of the American Indian legal system, explains that the goal in resolving conflicts was "to ensure restitution and compensation [rather] than retribution" as in European custom. Councils, whether villages, tribes, or bands, headed by charismatic chiefs "looked to custom and precedent" as well as larger community values to handle discord. Rarely, did they develop new laws. Thus, wayward children and young people whose behavior threatened individuals or the collective good likely received punishment in line with previous generations' notion of mediation.[17]

The oral traditions of Native peoples as well as the observations of European contemporaries suggest regional differences in disciplining troublesome Native children. Corporal punishment appears to have been more common in places such as the northern New Mexico–southern Colorado region. There, elders rather than parents meted out penalties when legends or stories proved insufficient. Among the Jicarilla Apache, grandmothers most often corrected the young. Further south in central Mexico, Aztec parents rather than grandparents used "rigorous corporal punishment" and sometimes forced idle children to "breathe acrid fumes of a fire in which red peppers were burning."[18]

Whether in California or the larger Southwest, Native peoples' cus-toms and beliefs in handling misbehaving youngsters largely gave way to European ideologies and practices with the conquest and colonization of the region in the late eighteenth and early nineteenth centuries. Though many indigenous tribes managed to retain key aspects of their cultural traditions, most suffered displacement, death through disease and violence, and severe deprivation. In the colonial world, Spanish priests had ultimate authority over Native peoples, adults and children alike, and particularly those whom they managed to lure into the mission system. The friars derived this power over Christian Indians—*neófitos* (neophytes)— from a 1773 Spanish decree issued by the Viceroy Antonio María de Bucareli y Ursúa, the highest civil and military representative of the Spanish crown in New Spain. That decree granted them the exclusive rights to train, educate, govern, and punish neófitos except in cases where blood had been spilt. In capital cases, the colonial authorities in Mexico City made the final decisions. The priests had much less authority over non-Christian Indians—or *gentiles*—who managed to elude the Europeans and remained on the periphery and independent of the mission system. In general, priests saw themselves as the literal and figurative fathers of neófitos, whom they believed to be ignorant and childlike and took it upon themselves to punish when necessary. Whether Native children were orphaned or not, the Spanish priests acted as their surrogate fathers and often trained them as apprentices or used them as manual laborers, exploiting them in the process.[19]

Missionaries such as those at Mission San Gabriel in the 1810s, Luís Gil y Taboada and José María de Zalvidea, for instance, regularly used the whip to chastise Native peoples, young and old alike, who refused to learn the Spanish language or follow European notions of time, labor, and leisure.[20] Other transgressions ending in punishment included running away and taking mission cattle, grain, or other basic staples. Father Junipero Serra, the founder of Mission San Diego, admitted to the deep-rooted practice of using the whip in California: "That spiritual fathers should punish their sons, the Indians, with blows (*con azotes*) appears to be as old as the conquest of these kingdoms."[21]

Whippings, contemporaries observed, were not only commonplace but also excessive. Zalvidea, according to Hugo Reid, "must assuredly have considered whipping as meat and drink to the [neófitos], for they had it morning, noon, and night."[22] Lorenzo Asisara, a Costanoan Indian and neófito from Mission Santa Cruz, verified that some Spanish priests or their Indian assistants (*alcaldes*) seemed to relish using the lash. Asisara explained that Ramón Olbés, a priest who spent three years at Mission Santa Cruz from 1818 to 1821, was "very inclined to cruelly whip. He was never satisfied to prescribe less than 50 lashes, even to the little children of 8–10 years he would order 25 lashes given at the hand of a strong man, either on the buttocks, or on the stomach, when the whim would enter him."[23] Native children at other missions doubtless experienced similar punishment as well, for Olbés had served six years at Missions Santa Ines, Santa Barbara, and San Luis Rey before moving to Santa Cruz.

Girls as well as boys faced punishment when they transgressed Spanish teachings. Young women who escaped from the missions, specifically from the *monjerios* (nunneries), which were often large, crowded rooms used to house, protect, and control the sexuality of young females in preparation for Christian marriage, faced harsh punishments.[24] According to Eulalia Pérez, a long-time *llavera* or key keeper at Mission San Gabriel, the mothers of these same girls were also punished.[25] María Solares, an ancient Chumash woman (reportedly ninety years old), would years later say that her grandmother had been "*un esclava de la mission* [*sic*]," a slave of the mission. "She had run away many, many times," Solares recalled, "and had been recaptured and whipped till her buttocks crawled with maggots."[26]

Contemporary supporters of the mission system, such as Governor Pablo Vicente de Sola, dismissed complaints of excessive punishments. Rather, he claimed, "The padre imposed the chastisement on the culprit as a father would upon his children, . . . [and] when administered, consisted of from twelve to fifteen strokes." In reality, he said, it "was better suited to children six years of age than to adults." To underscore the relatively mild nature of the scolding, he said, "most of the Indians who received it did so without crying out."[27] Fermin Francisco de Lasuen, also an apologist of the mission system, denied the use of severe methods. "It is never ordered to give anyone more than twenty-five lashes and with an instrument incapable of drawing blood or of causing notable contusions," he noted; "the treatment given the Indian is very gentle."[28]

Years later, Eulalia Pérez, a witness to the punishments doled out at the missions, challenged Padre Lasuen's characterization. She noted that the punishments imposed to recalcitrant neófitos included the stocks and confinement to a cell. "When the crime was serious," she said, "they would take the delinquent to the guardhouse. There, they would tie him to a cannon or to a post and whip him twenty-five times or more, depending on the crime. Sometimes they would put them in the stocks head first. Other times they would put a shotgun behind their knees and tie their hands to the gun." "It was very painful," she admitted. Such practices undoubtedly continued throughout the 1810s and 1820s with the end of Spanish rule and onset of Mexican governance in 1821. The dismantling or secularization of the mission system in the 1830s finally ameliorated such practices among the friars but not among the broader *gente de razón* (Spanish-speaking, settler) society.

Secularization of the mission system—carried out from about 1833 to 1840 by Mexican secular authorities who were interested in divesting the church of its properties and power in the region—brought significant changes to the lives and customs of Native Californians, including Christian neófitos and gentiles. After Mexican officials shut down the missions and distributed the land primarily to the Californios—despite the Spanish intent to return the land to the neofitos—most Native peoples fled east to the interior, taking refuge with independent tribes in the mountainous or desertlike regions, while others stayed near local Spanish-speaking settlements—*pueblos* (towns), *ranchos* (large land grants), and former missions—working as common laborers and domestics, where they eked out minimal subsistence. Native Californians—the young and old alike—who remained in or around the pueblos were subject not only to the Mexican system of justice but also to the patriarchal ideologies and practices shaping the gente de razón communities.[29]

The treatment of troublesome Native children after the end of Spanish rule and the mission system is sketchy, for few sources detail their experiences or transgressions as well as the consequences of their actions. In general, the documentation for the Mexican period portrays Indian children, boys and girls, more often as victims of assaults rather than as perpetrators of such crimes. Apparently, parents, guardians, and employers of Native children handled any indiscretions by their dependents on their own terms and within the confines of their own homes and families rather than bringing them to the attention of the local authorities, who they largely distrusted. Spanish-speaking officials, on the other hand, rarely took notice of Native children who committed misdeeds, unless their actions in some way threatened *Californio* society. In such cases, local leaders exercised their authority to the fullest extent of the law. In cases in which that power was questioned, they even turned to the highest authority in the region, the governor, to maintain that control.[30]

Native children accused of committing crimes not only faced the formal legal structure, specifically, criminal charges, but also justice outside the law—namely, the whip—as they had during the Spanish period. Indeed, the practice of flogging Indians in the Mexican era was so severe that, in 1833, Mexican Governor Echeandia issued orders for the local authorities in San Diego to halt the "arbitrary flogging, imprisoning, and outraging of neófitos."[31] The secular priests in Los Angeles also claimed that residents mistreated former neófitos, likely the young as well as the adult, punishing them with public whippings.[32]

In contrast to Native American youth, who often faced the lash, Mexican youngsters in Mexican California rarely experienced the same for similar offenses. Nevertheless, like neófito children and youths, they remained subject to patriarchal figures of authority, namely, older Mexican males. In Mexican law and custom, a male head of household held authority over any unmarried children until his son or daughter's marriage or twenty-fifth birthday. Fathers who neglected or failed to keep their children in line were sometimes forced to defer their power to the local authorities, especially when young people's indiscretions were threatening not only to patriarchal authority but also to the community's stability. In such instances, fathers as well as local leaders reprimanded the minors, reminding them of their place in society. The authorities treated young males and females differently, however, especially in cases involving sexuality, revealing the double standard used in judging such matters in Mexican California. In contrast to males, Spanish-speaking females, youths as well as adults, who violated norms of society by engaging in sexual activity deemed inappropriate—such as sex before marriage—faced severe sanctions. To protect or hide the shame of a female who transgressed sexual norms, patriarchs sometimes placed them in *casas de honor* (honorable homes) or banished them from the community. Even victims faced such consequences, revealing the gender discrimination in sexually based crimes.[33]

THE TREATMENT OF UNRULY YOUNGSTERS IN THE AMERICAN ERA, 1850s TO THE 1890s

In the aftermath of the United States–Mexico war of 1846 and American conquest in 1848, the method of disciplining wayward children and youths shifted from a largely familial and community-based system of care and control to a state-run, penal-like system. This occurred with the imposition of new Euro-American political, economic, social, cultural, and legal frameworks in California, particularly the shift from the Spanish civil law to the English common law as well as the introduction of the doctrine of *parens patriae* (state power over the guardianship of individuals) and the English language in the 1850s, all of which brought devastating consequences to Californians of all ages and particularly to Native peoples and their children. It was these changes, along with migration of Euro-Americans and immigration of Europeans to the Golden State, that altered the landscape forever.

The American conquest and the rapid transformation to a Euro-American, Protestant, capitalist society in the second half of the nineteenth century proved most destructive to indigenous peoples and children as well, who were, for all intents and purposes, disenfranchised and overrun quickly throughout California, especially in the northern part of the state with the discovery of gold in 1849. Word of that find led thousands of Euro-American migrants from the Midwest and East Coast and Europeans from Ireland, Germany, and France—as well as Latin Americans from Mexico, Chile, and Peru—to make their way to the region. Between 1846 and 1850, thousands of Euro-Americans and Europeans came to region, seeking riches as well as the laborers necessary to make their fortunes possible. In that same period, the number of Native Californians dropped from some 80,000 to 20,000 as a result of violent clashes with Euro-Americans throughout the state and continued losses through European diseases and impoverishment. To many Euro-Americans, the Native Americans who survived the decimation were the ready supply of workers they needed. To harness the labor of "cooperative" Native peoples—the uncooperative ones they simply exterminated or ran off—Euro-American lawmakers crafted a series of policies and practices aimed at controlling Native peoples, the young and old alike, particularly those identified as lawbreakers.[34]

Among the first order of business of the new state legislature in 1850 was the passage of the Act for the Government and Protection of Indians, a highly discretionary law criminalizing Native Californians, regardless of age or gender. Section 20 of the Act, for instance, held that any unemployed Indian, regardless of age, "found loitering and strolling about, or frequenting public places where liquors are sold, begging, or leading an immoral or profligate course of life shall be liable to be arrested on the complaint of any resident citizen."[35] Once arrested under such charges, local-level justices of the peace—who had authority over Native peoples, the young and old alike—had the right to "hire out such vagrant[s] within twenty-four hours to the best bidder" for up to four months.[36] In short, unemployed, homeless, and otherwise poverty-stricken California Natives not only faced jail time but also forced servitude. In Los Angeles, where they had a similar city ordinance, California Indians were sold to the highest bidder, akin to a slave market, according to Horace Bell, a contemporary resident.[37]

. The Act of 1850 not only criminalized and indentured Native Californians but also granted ordinary citizens—primarily Euro-Americans and Europeans—considerable power over the young and old alike. Section 14 of the act, for instance, allowed any white employer—presumably including California-born Mexicans, identified as "white" under the Treaty of Guadalupe Hidalgo of 1848 that ended the United States–Mexico war of 1846—to arrest any Indian found guilty of a crime punishable by a fine. Payment of that penalty and any court costs assured the employer access to the Native person's labor. In return, the white employer provided food, clothing, and humane treatment, a provision likely rarely enforced. Indeed, Native peoples had little, if any, recourse against whites who abused or harmed them in other ways. Section 6 of the same Act held that "in no case shall a white man be convicted of any offense upon the testimony of an Indian or Indians."[38]

Native children suffered in specific ways under the new law, for it subjected them to indentured servitude, even though they had committed no criminal or delinquent act. Section 3 of the Act of 1850, for instance, allowed nearly any white person to obtain custody of Native children as long as the parents or friends of the parents granted permission or consented to do so before a justice of the peace. Under the law, boys remained with their employer until the age of eighteen and girls until fifteen, with both males and females having the right to basic clothing, food, and care. Any inhumane treatment—as decided by whites—was punishable by a $10 fine.[39] Overnight, American law essentially turned Native children into indentured servants at best and slaves at worst. A decade later, in 1860, the law was amended slightly to include a provision requiring the training of Indian children in trades, husbandry, or other employment in order to make them efficient and potentially self-sustaining laborers. The 1860 amendment also made it easier to acquire child laborers and keep them longer, for potential employers no longer needed the expressed permission of parents or friends—before a justice of the peace—to do so. As long as the interested party convinced the court that they had received permission from the parents or friends, they could take that child. And they could now do so for longer periods of time. If the minor was a male, the employer could keep him until he turned twenty-five; if the child was female, the age was slightly lower, twenty-one. The immediate and long-term outcome was the increased kidnapping and abuse of Native children and youths. Sherbourne F. Cook estimates that between 3,000 and 4,000 Indian youngsters faced forced removal from their parents and communities.[40] The practice was so notorious, recalled Elsi Allen, an elderly Pomo woman living in the early twentieth century, that her "mother used to hide [her] . . . because [they] had heard of Indian children who had been kidnapped."[41] In the process, many youngsters labored under harsh working and living conditions and likely perished in the process.

Native children who managed to survive their circumstances and resist the laws by running away, defending themselves against any abusive employers, or in other ways challenging whites, were subject to varying degrees of punishment in and outside the courts. Those who challenged the laws and ended up before a tribunal faced the full brunt of the legal system, even though California made special provisions for children less than fourteen years of age. According to the Act Concerning Crimes and Punishments, passed in 1850, youths—presumably whites—fourteen and under could not "be found guilty of any crime," though judges had the ultimate discretion to decide if the child "knew the distinction between good and evil" and to try the youngster as a minor or an adult.[42] Not surprisingly, Native youngsters were treated as adults, for several of those fourteen and under charged with and convicted of felonies ended up at San Quentin State Prison.[43] Prison registers reveal that in the 1850s, 1860s, 1870s, and 1880s at least eleven California Indian boys and one Indian girl were sent to the harsh, labor-intensive environment of San Quentin. They included Ysabel, a thirteen-year-old Indian girl from Contra Costa county convicted of manslaughter in 1856, along with Antonio Peralta, a twelve-year-old from Los Angeles County sentenced for burglary in 1878.[44] Ysabel, who measured an inch shy of five feet, had the distinction of being the youngest female—across ethnic and racial lines—and Peralta one of the two youngest Indian males sent to San Quentin in the first forty years of the prison's history.[45]

Once at San Quentin, Ysabel and Peralta as well as all other inmates were segregated along gender lines, with the small group of females residing in small units above the main offices of the prison and males occupying the remainder of the penitentiary. According to an 1868 investigation, women were "strictly secluded from all others" and not allowed to leave the building except for a weekly two-hour break in the yard when the men attended religious services.[46] Male inmates of all ages, on the other hand, such as Peralta, convicted of murder, rape, grand larceny, and other similar crimes, labored and socialized in the main yard and slept in one of three main buildings. Young convicts such as Peralta and Ysabel likely faced many of the same dangers incarcerated children and youths in early nineteenth-century New England encountered in the prisons, asylums, and poor houses of that period: physical abuse, sexual assault, and moral corruption. Indeed, the San Francisco *Daily Alta California* reported in 1868 that San Quentin inmates "instructed each other in the fine arts of robbery, pocket picking, theft, burglary, and doubtless murder."[47] Unlike many prisons in the eastern United States, however, which often excluded Native Americans and other non-whites (namely, African Americans), San Quentin admitted inmates of all racial and ethnic backgrounds, though administrators segregated them throughout the day and night. California Indians, African Americans, and Chinese prisoners, for instance, ate and slept in separate quarters.[48]

Native children and youths identified as criminal, while sometimes confined to San Quentin, rarely ended up in "child-saving" institutions designed primarily for the care and control of Euro-American and European youngsters, who formed part of the larger population that increasingly dominated the state in the late-middle to late 1800s. Moreover, cultural and racial prejudices as well as ideologies about who was worthy of a childhood and of receiving assistance dictated that Native Californians—barred from civic participation and from citizenship more generally—would be excluded. Only years later, in the 1890s and 1900s, with the advent of special boarding schools in California aimed at Americanizing Indian children and youths, were these youngsters institutionalized in any significant way.[49]

Indian children and youth in California were not only excluded from state-supported child-saving institutions but also faced the wrath of individuals who took the law into their own hands. Though it is difficult to quantify the daily incidents aimed at punishing or controlling Native youngsters in the early American period, it is evident that Native Americans in general faced extreme violence and attacks from newly arrived Euro-Americans and Europeans who saw them as savage and uncivilized peoples who needed taming at least and exterminating at worst. Native peoples, the young and old alike, who wronged Euro-Americans faced significant retribution. Former Southerner and slave owner Cave Johnson Couts, for instance, had a small army of workers with Indian peoples among them employed at his Rancho Guajome, near San Diego, and he regularly imparted his own sense of justice on recalcitrant laborers. Couts seemed to take special interest in punishing Indians, adults and children alike, who ran away while still indebted to him or who had in other ways affronted his sense of honor and pride. Couts regularly whipped them, sometimes with rawhide *reatas* (whips), or shot at them with his revolver, killing some in the process.[50]

California-born and immigrant Mexican children and youths who broke laws or in other ways violated social norms of behavior in American California faced extralegal justice less frequently than their Native American counterparts, for Spanish-speaking peoples had access to political power generally denied to Indians. Under the Treaty of Guadalupe Hidalgo of 1848, Mexican-origin peoples who chose to remain in the territory had all the rights of citizens, including due process of law. In reality, however, most experienced a dual system of justice, one for Euro-Americans and the other for Spanish-speaking peoples. The courts reflected this system, for those accused of crimes rarely had a Spanish-speaking lawyer, access to a jury of their peers, or an interpreter. The result was that the criminal justice system of the second half of the nineteenth century made it nearly impossible for Californios and Mexicans—or California Indians, for that matter—to receive fair or adequate trials. Violent race warfare in the aftermath of the war, particularly between Californios and Mexicans on the one hand and Euro-Americans and European immigrants on the other, exacerbated contentious encounters with the authorities and more frequently with Euro-American and European vigilantes. In the process, significant numbers of non-white peoples, youths among them, ended up in county jails and the state prisons.[51]

The San Quentin prison registers indicate that Californios and Mexican immigrants made up a disproportionate number of those committed to the prison in the 1850s, 1860s, and 1870s, even though they made up an increasingly smaller fraction of the larger California society (Table 1). At San Quentin, inmates of Mexican origin comprised 16 percent of the inmates in the 1850s, 14 percent in the 1860s, and 9.5 percent in the 1870s. In contrast, in the 1850s, the 7,500 Californios and estimated 25,000 newly arrived Mexicans from Sonora who resided in the state constituted about 8.5 percent of the 387,500 residents in that decade, indicating that twice as many were locked up than resided in the larger population. Central and South American immigrants made up another 4.5 percent of inmates in the 1850s, though they represented an even smaller portion than their Mexican counterparts in the larger California populace. Euro-American migrants and Europeans immigrants, in contrast, made up about 355,000 residents, or 92 percent of those in the state in the 1850s, yet they made up only about 72 percent of those behind bars in that same decade. By the 1860s and 1870s, increased migration of Euro-Americans and Europeans to the region relegated Spanish-speakers to an even smaller fraction of the populace—a mere 4 percent in the last decade—yet peoples of Mexican descent continued to be overrepresented in the state prison.[52]

TABLE I MEXICAN-ORIGIN/SPANISH-SPEAKING PRISONERS IN
SAN QUENTIN IN THE 1800S

	Years		
Region of Origin	1851–59 (%)	1860–69 (%)	1870–79 (%)
California	4.7	7.2	6.5
Mexico	11.5	7.0	3.0
Central/South America	4.5	1.9	0.6

SOURCE: San Quentin Prison Registers (microfilm), Department of Corrections
Records, F3717, California State Archives, Sacramento, California, 1851–1939.

Californio and Mexican youths, those sixteen and under, fared significantly worse than their elder counterparts, for they were grossly overrepresented at San Quentin (Table 2). In the 1850s, Spanish-speaking
youths, including one Chilean, made up 63 percent (17 of 27) of youngsters sixteen years of age and under locked up at the penitentiary. In the
1860s, the proportion fell to 36 percent (9 of 25), though they were still
in disproportionate numbers. In the 1870s and 1880s, as the proportion of the Spanish-speaking population decreased (in relation to Euro-
Americans and Europeans), so did their figures in the prison. In the 1870s,
they decreased to nearly 18 percent (17 of 96) and down to 13 percent
(13 of 103), respectively, yet they continued to be overrepresented. Euro-
American and European youths, on the other hand, remained under-
represented throughout the same period. They made up 22 percent (6 of
27) of young convicts in the 1850s, 28 percent (7 of 25) in the 1860s, 52
percent (52 of 96) in the 1870s, and 76 percent (79 of 103) in the 1880s
even though they comprised the overwhelming majority of the youths
in the Golden State. The figures demonstrate that Californio and Mexican immigrant youth—all of them male—were more likely than male
youngsters of all other ethnic and racial backgrounds to be tried, convicted, and imprisoned in the state penitentiary in the nineteenth century.[53]
    Besides Spanish-speaking youths, the only other racial and ethnic group
to see significant rates of imprisonment was the Chinese. A largely immigrant population, the Chinese filled demands for cheap labor critical
to the expanding economy of the Southwest. In the 1850s, when the Chinese constituted a tiny fraction of the state populace, not a single young
person was incarcerated. In the next ten years, increased Chinese immigration as well as blatant hostility, racism, and violence brought on

TABLE 2   YOUTH (16 YEARS AND UNDER) PRISONERS IN SAN QUENTIN

	Years			
Region of Origin	1851–59 (%)	1860–69 (%)	1870–79 (%)	1880–89 (%)
California/Mexico/Latin America	63	36	18	13
United States/Europe	22	28	52	77
China	0	15	25	5
Other (Native, African American)	15	21	5	5

SOURCE: San Quentin Prison Registers (microfilm), Department of Corrections Records, F3717, California State Archives, Sacramento, California, 1851–1939.

by competition over labor with Euro-Americans saw a sharp rise in Chinese boys at San Quentin. In the 1860s, they constituted 15 percent (4 of 25), while in the 1870s they made up a whopping 25 percent (24 of 96), exceeding the proportion of Mexican-origin youths. By the 1880s, however, the proportion of Chinese youths fell precipitously to 5 percent (5 of 103), likely due in part to the decreasing numbers of Chinese-origin peoples, young and old, as a result of the recent passage of the Chinese Exclusion Act in 1882 and the aging of the population.[54]

Youths confined to San Quentin had a tough life, particularly the youngest inmates who labored alongside older males in the dirtiest, back-breaking jobs. Spanish-speaking youngsters, including Antonio Lugo, a fourteen-year-old California-born Mexican boy at San Quentin, likely assisted in brick-making, the main staple of Mexican and Mexican American inmates. Chinese and Native youths, on the other hand, had charge of the laundry. If any of these inmates attempted to escape, as a group of Spanish-speaking convicts did in a massive breakout in 1859, they faced guards "armed with Henry rifles and six-shooters" with orders to bring back escapees dead or alive. Those captured and returned to the penitentiary faced a whipping, sometimes receiving up to fifty lashes, which was followed by chaining and imprisonment in a dungeon.[55]

Although many Spanish-speaking youths ended up in San Quentin, some of the more fortunate went to the San Francisco Industrial School. Founded in 1858 for the "detention, management, reformation, education, and maintenance" of children and youths leading an "idle and immoral life," the school admitted youngsters from across the state and country, even though it was run by the city.[56] For that work, the state funded them partially with annual sums up to $5,000, while private citizens contributed another significant amount. Lauded as exemplary, the school nevertheless suffered a series of scandals in the 1860s and 1870s over its reported misuse of funds, leading to decreased support from the state. A few years later, trouble erupted once again, particularly with the integration of male and female wards, forcing them to segregate and transfer the girls to the Magdalen Asylum, a private Catholic institution established in 1858 for wayward or "fallen" girls—those deemed sexually immoral—in San Francisco. Despite those difficulties at the Industrial School, the work at the institution expanded significantly over the years, leading school administrators to focus exclusively on correctional practices and discontinue placing and supervising children in homes and trades, respectively, as they had done in the past.[57]

While some Spanish-speaking children ended up at the San Francisco Industrial School, others ended up at California's first state-run reformatory, the Marysville Industrial School, located about 55 miles north of Sacramento. Established in 1859, the Industrial School was developed along the lines of an East Coast "House of Refuge" and specifically "for . . . the instruction, employment, and reform of juvenile offenders."[58] At Marysville, advocates argued, unruly youths would be "cared for, housed, clothed, instructed and taught, not alone farming but . . . serviceable trades such as blacksmithing, carpentering, . . . [and] painting." Training in manual labor would not only teach the young inmates the values of industry, morality, and self-sufficiency but also provide sources of revenue for the school.[59] Moreover, the school's rural setting would help keep the children free from devious influences of the urban environment.

Contrary to its design, the Marysville Reformatory attracted no more than forty to fifty boys and girls annually during its six-year history. Mexican-origin youths made up a small yet significant fraction of those admitted. In one year, from November of 1864 to October of 1865, Spanish-speaking youngsters made up about 10 percent (4 of 30) of those sent to the reformatory, while the remainder were Euro-Americans (18 of 30), Irish (4 of 30), French (3 of 30), and Scotch (1 of 30), with no Native Californian—or Chinese for that matter—children or youths appearing on the rolls for that year. Two years later, the proportion of Californio and immigrant Mexican youths increased to over slightly 20 percent (10 of 47), considerably less than the proportion found in the same period in San Quentin (36 percent).[60] Though the identity or experiences of the inmates are unclear, it is evident that most of them, like the other inmates, were males, had lost one or both parents, came from destitute and impoverished backgrounds, had committed few or no crimes, and originated from the surrounding counties in north-central California, which held large Euro-American populations. In time, the school became male-only, as administrators ceased admitting girls for lack of privacy.[61]

Despite the enthusiasm for the reformatory's establishment, support for the institution waned quickly, for few counties could afford the costs of transportation. Instead, they continued to send recalcitrant youngsters to the overcrowded industrial school in San Francisco or ship them off to San Quentin. An 1867 investigation into San Quentin practices, for instance, found sixty-seven boys, twenty years and younger, at the San Quentin penitentiary, a practice the San Francisco *Daily Alta California* criticized: "The large proportion of young men is astonishing, there are several boys of the ages of fifteen and sixteen. We think their reform would be more surely effected and the interests of society . . . by committing youths of such tender ages to the [Marysville] reform school."[62] The state prison, the state board of commissioners argued, was a school of crime, leading many youths to become "*confirmed villains*" (emphasis in the original), a statement confirmed by increasing rates of recidivism.[63]

Those arguments not withstanding, state legislators believed maintaining the Marysville reformatory was too expensive and refused to allocate financial support, forcing its closure by 1868. The remaining youths were sent to the San Francisco Industrial School and to the U.S.S. *Jamestown* at Mare Island, a training ship used to educate troublesome and unwanted youths in nautical experience. That experiment—like the Marysville Reformatory—lasted only a few years. Poor management, questionable conduct, and other administrative difficulties forced its closure. The remaining boys on the ship also ended up at the San Francisco Industrial School.[64]

While some children and youths viewed as disorderly, rebellious, and dependent spent time at poorly funded state-supported institutions such as the Marysville Reformatory, the San Francisco Industrial School, and San Quentin prison, others—particularly Spanish-speaking youngsters— remained with family members in their communities of origin. Though it is difficult to know the way in which the majority of people of Mexican descent, both Californios and Mexican immigrants, preferred to deal with recalcitrant and disobedient children and youths in the post-1850s period, it is clear that they relied on their own familial and community resources to handle their own. In contrast to a significant proportion of Euro-Americans who had spent but little time in the region and had few social networks on which to rely, Californios in particular had deeply rooted family and social networks they could tap, especially in the Southern California region, where they remained in the majority until the 1870s.

Likely, they counted on extended relatives, fictive kin such as *padrinos* and *madrinas* (godfathers and godmothers, relationships forged through baptism), and neighbors to watch over or take in those who lacked parents or immediate relatives to care and control them.

Spanish-speaking members of the community also occasionally backed the establishment of private religious organizations designed to handle the care of disadvantaged and potentially wayward youngsters. In 1855, for instance, local citizens in Los Angeles helped finance the *Institución caritiva de los Angeles*, a girl's orphanage and school run by the Sisters of Charity, an order of Catholic nuns from Baltimore, Maryland. The Sisters oversaw the daily maintenance of the home where they kept primarily Spanish-speaking children whom they taught in Spanish, French, and English. The *Institución* drew its clientele from the neighborhood, as a number of orphaned and school-aged children resided nearby. Other than the *Institución* and a few small parochial schools established in the 1860s, Spanish-speaking communities across the state infrequently turned to institutions to oversee the care and control of youths, for they lacked the resources to establish formal organizations. Since the United States conquest in 1848, Mexican-origin peoples had to deal with increased impoverishment, landlessness, violence, and marginalization, processes that continued for decades to come, making it burdensome for most of them to contribute their meager resources to such a cause.[65]

Euro-Americans and Europeans, in contrast, had the resources and the strength in numbers to support state-run institutions for the care of troublesome and unwanted children. Many of the state's English-speaking newcomers were also familiar with such child-saving institutions, for they hailed from the East Coast of the United States, which had a long history of using asylums, reformatories, and houses of refuge to deal with unruly and unwanted youths. In that region, the presence of "street urchins"—poor children of native-born and immigrant families—running around, unattended and unsupervised, while their parents labored for hours in industry or scavenged for food, coal, and rags, often disturbed and sometimes offended the sensibilities of elite, native-born, Protestant families as well as the growing Euro-American middle class. In California, socially and economically prominent residents believed that, with proper moral and manual labor training, these youngsters could be turned into useful workers and domestics rather than have them end up in adult prisons or almshouses, as they had done since the eighteenth century. The Europeans who settled in California had had a similar approach in dealing with wretched and recalcitrant children and youths in their native countries. Several decades earlier, in the 1840s, Germans had established the Rauhe Haus, while the French erected the Mettray House, "reform-ist" institutions known for their alternative approach to the correction of disobedient and troubled youths. In many ways, Europeans institutions as well as those located throughout the United States influenced Californians in their approach to the reformation of youths, for Golden State officials often looked to them as models for the state's future.[66]

Euro-Americans and Europeans in California not only had knowledge of institutions for troubled and unwanted children and youths but also had the human and financial resources from which to draw on to support those places. Population statistics reveal that, within the first few years of settlement, the English-speaking populace quickly dominated the social landscape, surpassing the numbers of Californios, Mexican immigrants, and Native peoples combined, particularly in Northern California. City censuses for San Francisco, Los Angeles, and San Diego in the aftermath of the American conquest confirm that dominance. In 1850, for instance, Los Angeles and San Diego combined counted about 2,000 residents. Within ten years, the towns expanded significantly, claiming slightly more than 5,000 inhabitants in 1860. A decade later, that figure increased by more than fifty percent to over 8,000 in 1870. A real estate boom and promotion of Southern California as the land of sunshine and health led to the migration of thousands of East Coast and Midwest migrants to the region in the 1870s, increasing the residents living in the two southern towns to 13,820 by 1880.[67]

Northern California's inhabitants, on the other hand, surpassed those in the southern portion of the state. A year after the gold rush, in 1850, San Francisco claimed 34,776 inhabitants, most of them single men between the ages of twenty and forty. A decade later, in 1860, increasing numbers of families, women, and children led to the near doubling of that figure to 56,802. In the next ten years, rapid expansion in the economy, particularly in the sectors of agriculture, industry, and transportation, attracted many more and almost tripled the number of residents to 149,473. By 1880, the city's figure skyrocketed yet again, albeit at a slower pace, almost doubling to 233,959.[68]

The booming Euro-American and European populace as well as the growing agricultural, business, and industrial sectors of the state in the 1870s and 1880s gave rise to a significant white middle class concerned with the growing population of rowdy, uncontrollable, and needy youngsters frequenting unsavory dens of moral turpitude such as saloons and brothels. Until then, the state's attempt to deal with the growing problem of wayward youngsters had achieved limited success. As the demand for the care and control of young people mounted, a handful of organizations—primarily Euro-American and Protestant—offered assistance to the marginalized, particularly orphaned and destitute children of Euro-American origin, while few did the same for non-white youths. Among those who aided English-speaking minors were the San Francisco Protestant Orphan Asylum and San Francisco Roman Catholic Orphan Asylum, established in 1851 and 1852, respectively.[69] Eventually, San Francisco hosted most of the child-saving institutions—seventeen of twenty-eight found statewide, while Los Angeles had a single orphanage for girls.[70]

Within a few years, with the expansion of the economy and rise of the Euro-American and European middle class, private individuals not only aided in the founding of child-oriented homes, asylums, and societies throughout the state but also helped pass a number of reforms aimed at dealing with parental responsibilities and obligations. In the process, these individuals and organizations brought into sharper relief the power of the state—as represented in the police, probation officers, and court judges—over troubled youths and families in California. The Boys and Girls' Aid Society, for instance, founded in 1868 to care for "homeless, neglected, abused, and delinquent children," backed the passage of the Juvenile Probation Law of 1883, a statute enabling municipal and county judges as well superior courts to place wayward youngsters under the watch of private citizens and nonsectarian organizations, rather than in county jails or in the state prison. Though the probation law kept some youngsters away from adults charged with serious crimes and saved counties and the state money by keeping them out of institutions, it reinforced the doctrine of *parens patriae* and expanded the powers of the courts over delinquent and dependent youngsters, a right they would exercise more broadly in the twentieth century.[71]

Like the Boys and Girls' Aid Society, the Society for the Prevention of Cruelty to Children (SPCC), established in 1876, supported legislation aimed at protecting children and youths that, at the same time, increased the state's power over young persons. Among the most influential laws the SPCC helped pass was the 1878 statute, "An Act for the Protection of Children, and to Prevent and Punish Certain Wrongs to Children." That law limited the movements of youngsters sixteen years and under, prohibiting them from begging and from going into a saloon or dance hall unless accompanied by a parent or guardian. It also segregated children and adults while being transported or detained in a criminal proceeding, except in the presence of an official, and granted judges the power to determine when a child might be removed from parental custody—that is, when the state had the right to exercise *parens patriae*. Most of these provisions, which were meant to punish neglectful parents and save children from the evils of society, were largely ignored in the 1870s and 1880s. Only later, in the 1890s and 1900s, did they prove essential in the development and expansion of juvenile justice system.[72]

The SPCC, Boys and Girls' Aid Society, and, to some extent, the San Francisco Industrial School all played integral roles in assuming the responsibility for the care and control of delinquent and dependent youths in California in the late nineteenth century. Yet, as private organizations, they could not keep up with the statewide demand in the 1870s and 1880s—especially among white, middle-class members of society—to deal with increasing criminal activity, as constructed through the law, among youths and adults. State officials, too, decried crime as well as the conditions of the penitentiaries and the presence of youngsters in those places. In 1889, Secretary of State W.C. Hendricks, for instance, claimed that between 1850 and 1880 the proportion of criminals in the larger population had jumped 400 percent and would climb even higher in 1890—to 600 percent.[73] That same year, another state official noted the presence of many boys—between 1,500 and 2,000—who fit the profile for incarceration. "The cry has been coming from the lips of nearly every Judge of every Court in our land," Brainard F. Smith wrote. "'What shall we do with these boys!' Our penitentiaries are filled, not with old criminals, but with young felons."[74] Social reformers also joined the critique. "Will California, whose praises are upon the tongues of visitors from afar, and strangers from the ends of the earth—refuse an appeal for aid to little children, for whom our laws and institutions provide no resource?" asked the Ladies Protection and Relief Society of San Francisco in 1870, an organization dedicated to the assistance of destitute mothers and children.[75]

CALIFORNIA'S PRISON REFORM MOVEMENT AND THE RISE OF REFORMATORIES

By the early 1880s, more forceful opinions forced the legislature to take a long, hard look at penology, or prison policies and practices, as they affected adults and youths in California. For the first time since statehood in 1850, public officials pondered prison management, crime prevention, particularly among minors, treatment of the incarcerated, indeterminate sentencing, and parole. In other regions of the United States, Europe, and Latin America, such matters had long been debated in public and private forums and tested and tried in various institutional settings. In California, legislators initiated such a dialogue in 1884 when they appointed a five-person commission to find ways to "remedy existing evils, improve present conditions, and reform and aid the criminal."[76] The head of the commission and the Secretary of State, W. C. Hendricks, in turn, spent two years visiting reformatories, prisons, and asylums on the East Coast and in the Midwest, meeting with public officials, administrators, and staff. At the same time, he sent a list of questions to reform school superintendents, prison wardens, charity workers, and leading citizens from around the country and across the globe inquiring about best practices.

The move to advance innovative methods for dealing with crime and juvenile crime, though new to the Golden State, was part of a larger effort at reform across the country at the end of the nineteenth century. Sexual purity campaigns, child labor reform, and compulsory education, among many other areas, were some of the ways in which middle-class social reformers sought to effect the care and control of children and youths, most of them part of the growing ranks of the ethnic immigrant, poor, and working classes. Social reformers in California managed to get the legislature to pass a series of laws aimed at serving the interests of their campaigns, yet little was done to enforce many of those statutes, including truancy laws.[77]

The work of the California commission on penology, on the other hand, focused both on investigating and identifying the ideal policies suited for California as well as recommending legislation to implement those practices. Among the main issues the commission studied was prevention of youthful crime. In England, the commission found, the government had a long history of success in using industrial schools and reformatories in dealing with unwanted, destitute children, who often fell victim to criminal tendencies. Illinois state penitentiary officials, on the other hand, stressed formal schooling to the commission, particularly "disciplined education in early life" among the best sources of crime prevention, for they kept youngsters busy and trained them to become hard-working and moral, upright citizens. The commissioners in California admitted that the state had failed miserably in sending children to school. In 1881 alone, over 50,000 children and youths failed to attend any kind of public instruction. Instead, the commission reported, youngsters were "educated in dens of vice and trained in a criminal course whom our school system does not reach."[78] In general, the commission received positive feedback on the use of reformatories throughout the United States, Europe, and Latin America, while some qualified their endorsements by recommending the housing of delinquent and dependent youths in separate institutions.

Though taken seriously, the information received by the state commission was not altogether an accurate or truthful representation of daily operations at institutions across the country and globe. Many administrators, public officials, and charity workers in other regions often distorted the results of their work in order to present models of success with the prevention, intervention, and treatment of crime. Indeed, most of the industrial schools and reformatories were often nothing more than prisons for children. Many implemented extreme forms of punishment, including whippings, isolation in dungeonlike cells, and beatings, while others had disgruntled youths who escaped on a daily basis. Girls seemed to suffer the harshest experiences in these institutions, for they were often locked up more readily and for longer periods of time.[79]

Notwithstanding the brutalities suffered in some of these institutions, the California commission concluded that it was ultimately the responsibility of the state to raise responsible children and youths, particularly when parents or guardians lacked the ability to do so.[80] To carry out its duty, Hendricks recommended that the state develop a program centered on the discipline, education, and labor of youth in a familylike environment alongside peers of their own age, sex, and personal background. The family-plan or cottage system they advocated, though not a recent invention in the United States or Europe, where it had originated and which called for the use of small buildings and the appointment of a house "father" and "mother," appealed to the commission, for the members believed that such a setting would provide youngsters the homelike environment they lacked. More importantly, the separation of youngsters along ages, maturity, and criminal background would prevent the contamination of younger inmates from older, more experienced inmates.

The commission especially recommended the cottage system in the reformation of wayward girls, for it believed it would not only prevent the spread of moral corruption among the virtuous females but also provide them with the special attention they needed to gain the trust of the larger society. Unlike boys, most girls who ended up in institutions for the wayward did so for sexually based crimes, sins not easily forgotten or forgiven, as Euro-American middle-class codes of sexuality enforced strict standards on females while those imposed on males were generally lax. The commission understood the sexual double standard and addressed it plainly. "Society does not look upon the woman who has lapsed from the path of virtue with the same feeling as it does upon the male offender," Hendricks wrote. "To the young man in society," on the other hand, "on proof of evidence of reformation, [society] is willing to extend a helping hand. But the girl with the mark of sin on her brow is denied admittance to those circles in which alone she can find good and virtuous friends." Yet the commission held hope for these girls. "It is fair to assume that by proper means a large proportion of this class can be saved and made good and virtuous wives and mothers."[81]

Ultimately, the California commission's recommendation for establishing state-run reformatories for delinquent and dependent boys and girls—built along the cottage plan, with discipline, education, and labor at its core—was neither progressive nor reformist in nature. Rather, the structure envisioned was conservative, reflective of traditional approaches found in the United States, Europe, and Latin America. Indeed, those institutions merely removed children from their environment and, in the process, only scratched the surface of larger deep-rooted, structural problems facing wayward and needy children and their families. Even the commission's advocacy of individualized, sex-segregated facilities for boys and girls eventually yielded to more pressing statewide financial concerns and waning public support.

Despite the lofty goals envisioned, in 1889 the state established the State Reform School for Juvenile Offenders (later renamed Whittier State School) as a large, congregate, coeducational facility for boys and girls. Created as an institution for the "confinement, discipline, education, employment, and reformation of juvenile offenders in the State of California," the reformatory focused on the needs of male inmates, largely neglecting the females who were housed in a separate building a mile down the road from the main building. Nevertheless, administrators at Whittier were responsible for boys as well as girls, ages ten to sixteen years, who had committed any crime "which committed by an adult would be punishable by imprisonment in the county jail or penitentiary."[82] (Two years later, the age limit was lowered to eight.) The reform school also accepted dependents or youngsters who had committed no crime per se but had been declared incorrigible, morally depraved, and in danger of leading an "idle and immoral life." Rather than create institutions tailor-made to the needs of delinquent and dependent males and females, the reformatory made relatively few accommodations for differences among inmates.[83]

A year after the legislature enacted the statute, the Whittier State School's Board of Trustees continued to advocate for a state-of-the-art reformatory, akin to the most progressive institutions established in other parts of the United States and in Europe. "This is no experiment we are asking you to further aid and endorse. For a half-century these industrial, reformatory homes have been in successful operation in Europe and America," the Board reminded state leaders in 1890.[84] Harvey Lindley, President of the Board, continued, saying the goals were "to save the criminally inclined youth of this State; to take their corrupting influence from our streets; to train and educate them mentally, morally, and physically, so that they will spend their manhood years as farmers, mechanics, and honest laborers, instead of in penitentiaries and insane asylums; to make these boys the bulwark and pride of the State, instead of the burden and shame of our commonwealth."[85]

Those arguments fell on deaf ears, however, and failed to get any traction in the public. All "could not be done at once," state officials claimed.[86] Despite the reluctance to introduce progressive institutions in California and to spend public monies on such places, Commissioner Hendricks took solace in the commission's piecemeal work. "California shall take one step *at least* towards caring for that rising criminal and vicious class who may by proper influences be reformed, but who, if left to their own wild inclinations, will surely become professional criminals" (emphasis added).[87]

Following the establishment of the first reformatory at Whittier in 1889, the legislature established the Preston School of Industry, located near Ione in Amador County, in the northern portion of the California Central Valley. Governed by the State Board of Prison Directors and designated as an "educational institution" for the instruction in manual trades of males eight to eighteen years of age, Preston was established as a large, all-male congregate facility and imposed military discipline, including daily drill and industrial training. Initially, the Director of the Prison Board, Robert T. Devlin, hoped to model the school on East Coast and Midwest reformatories "of the best repute." In the end, though, it resembled a state reform school like those established in states such as Minnesota with its large imposing structure.[88] Like the institution for juvenile offenders at Whittier, Preston admitted boys guilty "of any offense punishable by fine or by imprisonment, or by both" but also took in inmates under eighteen years of age who were serving sentences (other than a life term) at San Quentin and Folsom state prisons.[89] Upon the successful completion of their time at Preston, all inmates had their criminal records expunged. Ultimately, Preston's administrators hoped to produce "inmates for honorable and profitable employment after their release."[90]

Initially, state officials exhibited much fanfare over the reformatories. At the laying of the cornerstone of the State Reform School, Governor R. W. Waterman extolled the state's investment. "Our great and growing population demands that something be done for the little ones, those now growing up amid hotbeds of vice and iniquity," he remarked. "No State in the Union," he continued, "is doing as much for its orphans, poor, and insane as the State of California."[91] The governor's accolades, though impressive, were not altogether accurate, for many states had similar programs and had invested more resources.

The Board of Trustees, appointed by the governor to supervise and govern the reform school at Whittier, and the superintendent, selected by the Board of Trustees in turn to oversee the daily operations, painted a somewhat more realistic picture of public support for the reformatory than the governor, for they understood public's reluctance to fund such an institution. Among the first moves they took was to lessen the stigma associated with reform schools by changing the name in 1891 from the State Reform School for Juvenile Offenders to Whittier State School. Legislators, in turn, supported the measure.[92] To make their case for additional funds, which they knew might be difficult, the Board of Trustees at Whittier assured the governor the money would yield favorable outcomes: "Carefully prepared statistics prove that *90 per cent of the pupils in these* [reform] *schools become good citizens*" (emphasis in the original).[93] In the end, the governor approved the funding, expressing confidence in the reformatory's goals.

The immediate result of the establishment of the reformatories was the sending of fewer delinquent youths to San Quentin and Folsom State Prisons. The prison registers indicate a sharp drop in the number of commitments of youngsters to the state prisons, which were filled primarily with men in their twenties and thirties (Table 3). The registers also show that the trend continued well into the first half of the twentieth century, with Folsom accepting no prisoners sixteen and under and San Quentin taking in a dozen to two dozen at most per decade through the end of 1939, even though a legislative decree in 1907 ordered the removal of all prisoners eighteen years of age or younger. In fact, the first seven wards at Preston were former inmates at San Quentin. Their ages ranged from about seventeen to about twenty-one. After the establishment of the reformatories, youths—sixteen and under—would serve little time in adult prisons, unless convicted of a crime punishable by death or life imprisonment.

TABLE 3   SAN QUENTIN AND FOLSOM PRISON INMATES, 16 YEARS AND UNDER, 1880–1940

Prison	Years					
	1880–89	*1890–99*	*1900–1909*	*1910–19*	*1920–29*	*1930–39*
San Quentin	103	35	31	6	16	11
Folsom	28	18	8	0	0	0

SOURCE: San Quentin Prison Registers (microfilm), Department of Corrections Records, F3717, California State Archives, Sacramento, California, 1851–1939, and Folsom Prison Registers (microfilm), Department of Corrections Records, F3717, California State Archives, Sacramento, California, 1880–1939.

The child-saving institutions adopted by Californians at the end of the nineteenth century as well as a growing body of laws governing the care and control of wayward and troubled youth addressed only half-heartedly the sources of delinquency and dependency in California among youths in general and youths of color in particular. Whittier State School and Preston School of Industry, like the other child-saving institutions for troubled children and youth in California, dealt with problems of troublesome, wayward, and unwanted youngest in the easiest and least expensive way known possible: remove children from their environment, punish parents for failing to keep their children in line, as determined by white, middle-class standards, and place children in institutions, which often did more harm than good. Neither the state nor the courts investigated further or developed a better understanding of why children and youths of various gender, class, ethnic, and racial backgrounds had to beg, dance, gamble, or, as some undeniably did, sell their bodies for a dime. Moreover, rarely did state officials attempt to deal with the larger structural problems of poverty, nativism, racism, and limited schooling, among other concerns, all of which affected poor, immigrant, and racial and ethnic families' ability to care and control their children properly. Rather, state officials blamed and punished those who failed to abide by state policies and practices, which were imposed primarily by the white, Euro-American middle class in power.

Within a matter of decades, the shift from family and community-based care and control of troublesome and unwanted children and youths to that of the state was nearly complete. Families, extended kin, and communities in the early nineteenth century determined how and why as well as when and where young people—particularly Mexicans and Native Americans—were taught to obey and follow community norms, but later state-appointed officials, many of them with little training in the care and control of children and youths, used the state-apparatus to take over a role once allocated to members of the family and community.

To explore the ways in which the state's power expanded over the care and control of youngsters deemed delinquent and dependent, the next chapter examines and analyzes Whittier State School's effort to deal with growing problem of wayward youth in California. It shows how one man, Fred C. Nelles, a leading Progressive, invoked science and scientific research to overhaul a brutal institution and transform it into one of the leading reformatories in the state, across the country, and, arguably, around the globe. That accomplishment was not without its costs. Nelles's policies and practices had serious repercussions for some of the most vulnerable youths at Whittier State School, namely, the Mexicans, Mexican Americans, and African Americans who bore the brunt of early twentieth century innovations in science and scientific research.

CHAPTER 2

Fred C. Nelles

Innovative Reformer, Conservative Eugenicist

A preeminent leader in California's emerging juvenile justice system in the early twentieth century, Fred C. Nelles distinguished himself nationally and internationally for his work as Superintendent of Whittier State School from 1912 to 1927 (Figure 1). Through the use of the latest science and scientific research into the causes of juvenile delinquency, Nelles helped craft innovative policies and practices aimed at unraveling juvenile crime that, at the same time, proved pernicious to those on the margins of society, namely, Mexican, Mexican American, and African American youths. With the support of influential politicians, scientific experts, and members of the public, who, like Nelles, supported eugenicists beliefs, the superintendent transformed a decaying, brutal reform school into a premiere institution admired by many across the country and globe. Nelles's work proved so successful that child advocates as well as public officials throughout the United States sought him out for his expertise. Arguably, within a few years Nelles transformed the field of juvenile corrections in California, eventually gaining the support of even those most stridently opposed to his methods.

Nelles's story is significant to juvenile justice and to California history more broadly for his willingness to challenge the accepted conventions in dealing with troublesome (delinquent) and unwanted (dependent) youths. In the early 1910s, Nelles took a group of largely wayward, impoverished, and marginalized young males (he removed the girls from the institution) and turned them into what he called "manly, productive

HON. FRED. C. NELLES
SUPERINTENDENT
WHITTIER STATE SCHOOL

FIGURE 1. Fred C. Nelles. During his administration of Whittier State School in the 1910s and 1920s, Superintendent Fred C. Nelles transformed the run-down reformatory into a premier institution. A champion of Progressive policies and practices, Nelles used the latest theories in science, eugenics, and race to overhaul the reform school, but at the expense of the most vulnerable boys in the institution. Photograph by Fred C. Nelles School for Boys (Whittier), California State Archives, Office of the Secretary of State, Sacramento, California.

citizens" capable of assuming the challenges of the new century. Nelles's approach included crafting an individualized program using the latest tools and techniques in the emerging fields of psychology, education, social work, eugenics, and criminology to sort, classify, and segregate incarcerated youths along a continuum of normalcy to degeneracy. His approach rested on the basic assumption that the institution's program could only help "normal" youngsters, those who had the capacity of becoming productive and reproductive members of society. On the other hand, those identified as "feebleminded" (unable to develop mental capacities beyond a twelve-year-old child) were considered backward and a threat to Nelles's rehabilitation program. Nelles and his research staff argued that the feebleminded or the mentally defective needed segregation, long-term care, and, ideally, sterilization. To this end, Nelles transferred children and youths identified as defective to state hospitals where most were sterilized as a matter of policy. Those unable to gain admittance to state hospitals were sent to the Preston School of Industry, the juvenile court, or simply back home. In the process, a disproportionate number of youths of color, namely, Mexicans, Mexican Americans, and

African Americans, were identified as feebleminded and criminally minded offenders, and eventually they were institutionalized in state hospitals and elsewhere. Euro-Americans or whites, on the other hand, who were more often classified as normal than the nonwhites, remained at Whittier, which increasingly catered to their needs. Nelles built his program at the expense of the most vulnerable element of the reform school: the poor, illiterate, unschooled, and unwanted ethnic and racial minorities. This led to the criminalization, racialization, and pathologization of youths of color in the early twentieth century.

FROM BUSINESSMAN TO STATE SCHOOL ADMINISTRATOR AND SOCIAL ENGINEER

A businessman and engineer by training, Fred C. Nelles had little knowledge of or experience with reform schools when Governor Hiram Johnson, a leading member of the California Progressive Party, appointed him as the interim Superintendent of Whittier State School in 1912. Nelles, a Canadian by birth and a recent arrival to Los Angeles, came from an established, middle-class family active in social reform in Southern California. Nelles's initial involvement in government came in 1910, at the age of thirty-four, when Governor Johnson appointed him to the first State Board of Control, a statewide committee responsible for overseeing state finance. There, Nelles learned of Whittier State School and the long-standing negative publicity surrounding it. To clean up the school, Governor Johnson dismissed the current superintendent and appointed Nelles in 1912 to take over the management until a permanent replacement could be found. Nelles's Progressive politics and friendship with Johnson doubtless influenced the governor's decision. With little knowledge of what was in store for him, Nelles accepted the post temporarily.[1]

When Nelles arrived at the reformatory, he found "untrained, underpaid politically appointed guards, brutal inhumane treatment . . . [and] unspeakable conditions that made him ill," according to Kenyon Scudder, who later served as the superintendent at Whittier State School.[2] Nelles saw young boys mixing with older males, living in a repressive, "cold, cheerless five-story building with barred windows, . . . surrounded by iron fences and walls."[3] Committed to cleaning up the institution and supported by Governor Johnson, Nelles agreed to remain as the permanent superintendent. Among his immediate goals were humanizing the institution by overhauling the school's outdated practices and changing the staff's attitude toward the boys and girls. Nelles believed that with individualized attention and proper guidance most wards could be transformed and "turn[ed] back into society as useful, law abiding and God-fearing citizens."[4] "I believe there is a chance for redemption of many of the boys and girls who come here and I believe I can help them along the right road," he told the Los Angeles Times his first year in office. Not all youths, however, would benefit from his program.[5]

Nelles's experience at Whittier State School, though unique in many ways, formed part of the larger Progressive social reform movement of the early 1900s. Encompassing a wide range of political, social, and economic interests, the Progressive movement emerged as a consequence of contemporary transformations and fears brought about by rapid industrialization, urbanization, and immigration in major cities across the country. At that time, many urban, white, Euro-American middle-class men and women became worried about the effects of the growing number of foreigners and migrants, many nonwhite, who they believed were overcrowding the cities, work sites, and neighborhoods. To bring about order and stability, Progressive reformers in California, such as Nelles, promoted science, education, and efficiency and argued for the assimilation of millions into the mainstream. Americanization or the whitening of ethnics and racial minorities, they believed, would make the recent arrivals—and their children—productive citizens and workers who would accommodate themselves to industrial and agricultural capitalism's insatiable demand for labor. Progressives also endorsed educational reforms for children, including compulsory public schooling, home economics classes, and kindergartens, and they promoted evening English-language and citizenship courses for adults. Progressives pushed, too, for the rethinking of reform schools, calling for an end to harsh punishments and the use of science and scientific principles to transform delinquent boys into idealized productive white male citizens and delinquent girls into model white women who were respectful, domestic, and marriage oriented.[6]

Nelles's ideas, although relatively new to Whittier State School, resonated with broader beliefs about juvenile delinquency in the developing juvenile justice systems across the state and country at the turn of the twentieth century. Spearheaded by white women's clubs in San Francisco, the focal point of activism was the juvenile court. Californians adopted that tribunal in 1903 with the passage of the Juvenile Court Law, modeling it on those already established in states such as Illinois and Colorado.[7] Influenced by recent developments in psychology, sociology, medicine, and business management, the juvenile courts—although they were not all of one mind—emphasized the rehabilitation of delinquent youth (those who had violated the law or committed a crime) within the family environment rather than prosecuting and punishing them in adult criminal courts and sentencing them to adult jails. Dependent youths (those in danger of becoming delinquents) were subject to the law as well. They included children found begging, gathering, or receiving alms, youths found wandering or otherwise vagrant, and those having no means of subsistence, who were destitute, or whose home was deemed "unfit" as a result of "neglect, cruelty, or depravity" of the parents or guardians. This group also included minors found in the company of reputed criminals (including prostitutes) or in any brothel, saloon, or place where liquor was provided. Any child identified as "incorrigible" or truant was also subject to the law.[8]

Rather than pull wayward youngsters from their homes and dump them in jails and reformatories, as justices had often done the nineteenth century, the California juvenile court law of 1903 provided alternatives for keeping youths in their homes, ideally on probation under the watchful eye of a probation officer. California had introduced "supervised probation" in 1883 as a means of saving the state money by keeping children at home rather than in overcrowded, poorly built jails and prisons meant for adults.[9] It also allowed probation officers—as representatives of the court and the state—to impart moral instruction to boys and their families in the intimate setting of the household. When that approach failed to alter the boys' behavior, judges sent problematic youngsters to private homes, orphanages, and, later, local facilities. As a last resort, justices in the juvenile court committed younger boys and girls of all ages who continuously broke the law or had no one to respond for them to Whittier State School, and they ordered older boys (or those previously committed to Whittier) to the Preston School of Industry.

In California, as in other states, the establishment of the juvenile court meant the expansion of the juvenile justice system, essentially enlarging the reach of the state over youths who ran afoul of community norms. The juvenile court law of 1903—and the state's power—was further strengthened six years later in 1909, when the California legislature set aside funding for probation officers. Prior to that, these officers had functioned on a volunteer basis. The 1909 statute also increased the grounds for asserting jurisdiction over minors, provided for the establishment of detention homes, and set specific procedures for committing youths to Whittier State School or the Preston School of Industry. The law also allowed the court to decide where to send the young people and to determine if they were mentally and physically capable of benefitting from the "reformatory educational discipline" of the reform schools. If not, they sent them elsewhere.[10]

Many local officials were unsatisfied with the law, which they found to be too burdensome and too expensive, so it was amended in 1911 and again in 1915, when it was overhauled to give local jurisdictions— rather than the state—more flexibility in the law's implementation. The shift to local control was offset when that same law expanded the grounds for admitting children, which were established originally in 1903 and expanded in 1909. It added a category for admitting "insane or feeble-minded children," who posed a danger to society and could not be controlled by their parents or guardians. The 1915 statute also increased the powers and duties of probation officers, giving them more authority to supervise children and to assist the court. These changes further expanded the state's power over delinquents and dependents, who were essentially treated the same in the State of California, making them more vulnerable to the state's authority regardless of their transgressions.[11]

In Nelles's view, the boys and girls who ended up at the reformatory would respond more effectively to a familylike environment rather than the prison-style conditions that had predominated during much of the school's history. As early as the 1890s, the Boys' Department of the school had imposed a strict masculine ideal by implementing a military regimen in which the young "cadets" wore military uniforms and drilled on a daily basis. Rather than continue with such practices, Nelles instituted a policy of what he called "friendly cooperation and rehabilitation." At the same time, he changed some of the prevailing gender ideals, at least as they pertained to males. Nelles relaxed and nearly abandoned the military system, instead implementing an honor system in which he trusted boys to follow school policies. Most significantly, he altered discipline and punishment. He did away with the use of guards "armed with guns and clubs" and the so-called Oregon boot, a nine-to ten-pound weight fastened around the lower leg that was commonly used with adult prisoners. According to Nelles, the boot often "cut into the skin and led to sores that sometimes extended into the bone," causing serious and sometimes permanent injury.[12] Nelles proclaimed an end to the use of the guard line, too—a process by which a youth was forced to stand at attention, forbidden to move or speak to anyone for an hour or more. Despite the long-standing pronouncements against flogging inmates, Nelles found that administrators and staff regularly whipped the wards, both boys and girls, sometimes with the infamous cat-o-nine tails, for attempting to escape or being absent without leave (AWOL), an infraction considered among the most serious at the reformatory.

The use of such extreme measures, as Nelles found out, was not a recent development. Rather, they formed part of the school's history. Since the 1890s, staff and administrators at all levels inflicted or threatened to inflict bodily pain to discipline seemingly unruly boys and girls. Adina Mitchell, a member of the Board of Trustees, was one of the few school officials to criticize publicly the ill treatment. In a scathing report issued in 1896, she chastised the school's "obsolete" methods, likening the punishment to "barbarism and a relic of the dark ages which is a disgrace to modern civilization."[13] Superintendents sometimes held strict policies against the use of corporal punishment, yet staff often violated the rules and likely did so with the implicit approval of their superiors. That practice was clearly in use in the 1890s during Superintendent J. B. Van Alstyne's administration, when corporal punishment was banned in the Girls' Department but allowed in the Boys' Department when necessary. Despite Van Alstyne's adamant public opposition, an incident in 1897 indicates that he sometimes turned a blind eye when it occurred.[14]

That year, George D. P., the father of an inmate, accused staff member Charles H. Treat of whipping his son inhumanely with a rubber gasket, a half-inch rubber tube about a yard in length. According to the *Los Angeles Times*, Treat inflicted the punishment after the offending boy and nearly a dozen other boys rioted in their unit or company. At the court hearing, Treat and the other officers involved defended their actions, saying that they had permission from the superintendent: "if necessary to control the boys, use force." The only way to prevent future incidents, Treat reasoned, was to move quickly in imposing punishment. Yet, according to the *Los Angeles Times*, the beating was brutal: "The boy to be lashed was compelled to clasp his hands around an iron post, the tail of his shirt was pinned up to his collar and his trousers rolled down to his ankles. The whipper stood to the left of and behind the boy, wrapped the hose around his hand and laid on the strokes with all his vigor. When the hose struck a boy, it left a mark every time, not only on the back of the legs but on the front also, the tube encircling the limb." After receiving ten lashes, the boys were placed in bare, cement-floor cells where they spent the night without food or water.[15]

After a few days of testimony, the court acquitted Treat, ruling that he deserved censure for using a "savage" and "dangerous" instrument but not for punishing the boy, for that was within his purview. Moreover, the court reasoned, neither Treat nor the other staff members had the time necessary to get the administration's approval before carrying out the punishment and therefore deserved only a verbal reprimand. The court's decision to acquit Treat, though perhaps reasonable under the law, absolved the reform school from the responsibility of treating boys and girls humanely and discouraged similar lawsuits. Not surprisingly, severe punishments continued, with both boys and girls feeling the sting of the lash.[16]

In 1905, for instance, under the stewardship of Superintendent Sherman Smith, a scandal erupted over the punishment of Mabel S., an inmate who had incited an insurrection in the Girls' Department. The *Los Angeles Times* reported that the superintendent ordered his assistant to punish Mabel and her accomplices, which he did by use of a leather strap "three inches wide and twenty-four inches long." In total, he dealt Mabel a total of nine to ten blows on the buttocks through her undergarments while the matron of the Girl's Department observed the punishment. News of the incident triggered a scandal, which led to an internal investigation by the Board of Trustees, who oversaw the management of the reformatory, into mistreatment and cruelty at the school. A year earlier, the *Times* reported, the girl had received another punishment for running away—that time, her hair had been shorn. As a result of the most recent incident, the board forbade male employees from whipping recalcitrant girls or shaving their heads as punishment. Finally, the board ruled that the superintendent had to provide a weekly accounting of the punishments doled out. Despite those reforms, conditions remained the same or, in some cases, worsened.[17]

The final incident that prompted Governor Johnson to dismiss Superintendent Sherman came in 1911. That year, several girls staged a riot, charging the staff with "brutality beating them, inflicting punishments for most trivial things, dungeon confinements, poor food, loss of meals, lack of segregation, and absence of proper medical treatment." The girls' complaints were not without merit. To get into the solitary confinement cells, "girls had to get down on their hands and knees to crawl," Kenyon Scudder recounted years later. "Once in," he continued, "an iron gate was slammed shut and padlocked. The girls received only bread and water. If the girls protested and made noise, they took them out and put them on hooks. They would handcuff the girls to the hooks and let them hang until they passed out or 'cried for mercy.'"[18] In the 1911 riot, one girl claimed she had received "twenty-seven lashes of a whip on her exposed body" for answering back to a teacher, while another reported "seventy licks of the whip" because she refused to identify her accomplices.

"The whip-lash is made of leather," the *Los Angeles Times* reported, "and is usually soaked in water several hours before using," a custom dating back to the institution's early years and practiced in the Boys' Department as well. Eventually the administration regained control, but tensions remained.

When Nelles arrived at Whittier State School the following year in early 1912, he found that in addition to using corporal punishment to discipline wards, past administrators had appointed boys, usually the older and physically stronger ones in their squads, to positions of authority within each unit to keep watch over the others. Essentially, school officials used fifteen- and sixteen-year-old male "sergeants" and "captains" as informants—or cadet monitors—to infiltrate peer groups, create distrust among cadets, and prevent groups of boys from taking collective action against the institution or individuals. Sometimes the boy-officers—assisted by a group of their cronies—abused their power by berating and dominating the more vulnerable boys, particularly by physically and sexually assaulting them. Apparently, school officials did little to check such behavior, particularly the sexual attacks; they recognized that they occurred, and would periodically record the incidents in their internal records.[19]

Nelles worked to outlaw corporal punishment, underground cells, and food deprivation, methods used in reformatories throughout the United States in the eighteenth and nineteenth centuries. Instead, Nelles instituted an honor system in which he entrusted inmates to follow orders independently of administrators' enforcement. Staff placed the wards who refused to follow the new rules in the Lost Privilege Cottage, built soon after Nelles's arrival. In that unit, boys who had committed infractions such as running away could be accommodated in a family setting with regular meals provided to them. There, they carried out their work assignments alone and could not to speak to anyone other than the unit's officer. Young men who failed to follow those orders received only bread and milk until they obeyed house rules. The new regulations, although strict, indicated a shift in the understanding and meanings of masculinity as well as discipline and punishment. Like many of his contemporaries, Nelles sought to inculcate a sense of manliness among the boys that emphasized the values of the family rather than of the military.[20] And, rather than inflict pain or the threat of pain to get boys to behave, he used solitary confinement as a way to discipline the mind and change antisocial behavior, an approach that had been used in prisons throughout the United States and across Europe.[21]

While Nelles modernized policies on discipline and punishment as well as ideals of masculinity at the school, he nevertheless reinforced long-held beliefs about females and femininity. Like many of his contemporaries, Nelles believed that, through training and education, most boys had the ability to reform and to become productive members of society, for the crimes they had committed, mostly petty theft and burglary, left no visible scars and could be considered male youthful indiscretions. Wayward girls, on the other hand, most of whom had been picked up for sexually based crimes were not so easily saved. Reform school officials as well as the public in general believed girls like those that ended up at Whittier State School were morally tainted and unappealing in the marriage market. Boys who committed similar indiscretions rarely suffered the same consequences. The sexual double standard about male and female criminality (or delinquency in the case of minors) and the consistent difficulties that plagued the Girl's Department, largely as a result of the inattention and scant resources provided to the unit, led Nelles to back the placement of the Girls' Department under separate management. Ideally, he wanted the girls sent to a separate institution, a move that had long been advocated by many Progressive female social reformers. Fifteen years earlier in 1896, outspoken trustee Adina Mitchell had urged the expansion and reform of the Girls' Department, which suffered from neglect. Girls, she said, dressed in "rags and tatters," deserved a school of their own because, unlike with boys, the reformation of a girl's character was "more delicate and trying." Along the same lines of thought as Nelles, Mitchell held that such girls were emotional rather than reasonable, so they needed special attention in an institution designed with their interests at heart—namely, domestic training for employment or ideally marriage.[22] Nelles and his staff also argued that removing the girls from the school would also solve the problem of having the Girls' Department so close to the Boys' Department. To avoid any further unsavory publicity and to rid the school of the ill repute of the Girls' Department, Nelles worked behind closed doors with California women reformers to have the girls transferred quickly and quietly to a separate institution.

After a year of much wrangling, the legislature finally passed the bill establishing the California Training School for Girls at Whittier State School in 1913. Along with the school, a new Board of Trustees—composed of all women, the first in the United States—was appointed, and $200,000 was appropriated to build a facility at Ventura on a tract of 125 acres. The funds allowed for the partial construction of the school, and a second appropriation of nearly the same amount enabled the completion of the California School for Girls (renamed Ventura School for Girls in the 1920s). In 1916, about 70 girls and 29 staff members relocated to the new institution, and C. M. Weymann, a former police officer of the women's division of the San Francisco jail, was appointed as its first superintendent. Weymann, a strict disciplinarian, had no plans to change the emphasis on domestic training and moral reform at the new facility, noting that the school wanted "to give the girls an idea of real home life and to teach them to care for a home." Disciplinary measures continued at the reformatory, especially in the 1920s and 1930s under the administration of Olive P. Walton, a physician who was known for her repressive and outdated measures. Not until the 1940s with the appointment Mary Perry did the Girls' School see any significant changes in its policies and practices.[23]

At Whittier, Nelles managed not only to segregate the girls from the boys but also to transform the housing plan from a congregate to a cottage plan, as originally proposed. To many contemporary observers, Whittier State School's congregate system—in which boys of all ages and backgrounds ate, lived, and trained in one main five-story brick building—reflected a "cruel and ugly environment."[24] That scheme, Whittier's board of trustees argued in 1912, invited many problems, for it allowed "every class and gradation of misdemeanants and felons, young and old, vicious and comparatively innocent, [to be] intimately associated in the unrestricted intercourse of their daily lives."[25] To cultivate a reform-friendly environment, school administrators repeatedly called for the building of cottages—small, one-story units, run by a housefather and housemother—which could accommodate several dozen boys of similar ages and experiences. Despite the apparent benefits of that approach, Whittier remained a congregate school for another decade.[26]

Nelles plan for segregating wards also involved removing the older boys, those sixteen years of age and above, who he considered too old and too difficult to reform. The younger boys, he believed, were more pliable. For many years before Nelles's arrival, the school accepted boys as old as twenty-one years or sometimes older, even though the limit was eighteen. And, it occasionally took in younger children, as young as six according to some newspaper reports though the lower limit for children was eight years.[27] The school accepted such wards in special circumstances, when no one else wanted them or could take them in, despite the availability of private homes and orphanages. In the 1910s, Nelles helped draft and pass a law fixing the age to a minimum of nine and maximum of fifteen to ensure he received a group of boys amenable to his program. As a result, any boys sixteen and over were returned to the juvenile court or transferred to Preston School of Industry, which had flexible age limits. Nelles's move did not go unnoticed. In response to their impending move to Preston, a group of older boys at Whittier rioted, "barricading themselves on the top floor of the three story main building," Kenyon Scudder recalled. When they learned the door had been locked, they threw furniture out of the windows. The protests lasted for several days, but Nelles and the staff finally managed to load them on a train and transfer them to Preston in a matter of hours.[28]

In addition to removing older inmates, Nelles focused on working with boys on an individual basis. Like many of his fellow Progressives, Nelles believed that the most effective means of reaching his charges involved one-on-one contact and what he called "character building." To this end, Nelles emphasized vocational training and athletics, which were activities, he noted, "which have helped give to the Y. M. C. A., Y. W. C. A., Hull House, and kindred organizations, the grip they have on the lives of young people."[29] Within a matter of months, Nelles built a reputable athletic program by hiring trained instructors and applauding the efforts of key youths who led the school to victory in many competitions, particularly in baseball, football, and track.

Despite Nelles's successes, support for the changes he advocated took time to cultivate, as many disagreed with his approach. Indeed, Nelles met staunch resistance in the first two years of his administration. Former employees, disgruntled staff, and middle-class, Euro-American clubwomen active in social reform issued particularly scathing criticisms of his ban of corporal punishment and his use of an "honor system," which, Nelles explained, gave the boys a role in running the school.[30] Members of the public also questioned the worthiness of the boys in such a program. "What are we coming to?" wrote on irate reader of the *Los Angeles Times*. "Are we supposed to make dudes out of these kids? They are lucky enough to be at Whittier. Why treat them like millionaires' kids?"[31]

Nelles encountered even more stiff opposition from his peers. Within days of Nelles making his policies understood and his superintendent position permanent, nearly the entire institution revolted. Among the first to protest was Assistant Superintendent Coffin, a strict disciplinarian, who resigned in protest. The Matron in the Girls' Department and at least a dozen other long-time staff members followed suit, charging that Nelles was a political appointee who was "woefully incompetent and misguided." With the disgruntled staff's prodding, girls and boys rebelled by rioting and escaping. When Nelles attempted to quell the disturbance among the girls, they ran him out of the building, shouting and throwing objects. Nelles then rounded up the loudest girls and confined them to cells. News of the "deplorable conditions" in the Girls' Department and the school in general led the Women's Advisory Board, an advisory board made up of Euro-American middle-class social reformers, to carry out an investigation. Though they had no real institutional power, the board proceeded with its inquiry, criticizing Nelles for his secretive nature and lack of experience and training. The superintendent of a girls' school "should be a woman and not a young unmarried man," they concluded.[32] The Board of Trustees looked into the matter as well, especially the escape of nearly 200 boys. Unlike the women's board, the trustees found no irregularities in Nelles's administration. Yet members of the public continued to disagree. "The king can do no wrong!" an individual charged in a letter to the editor of the *Los Angeles Times*. The honor system was not compatible or feasible for use among young boys, the writer continued, and experienced officers were needed. In time, Nelles would fail, and in the meantime, "the state pays," he finished.[33]

Nelles took the widespread resistance to his policies and practices seriously and campaigned shrewdly in the 1910s to gain support. "The substitution of kind, intelligent vocational guidance for former methods of rigid and often inhumane discipline has contributed much to the problem of juvenile reform," he informed the Board of Trustees and Governor Johnson.[34] To prove his point, Nelles noted that many boys paroled or discharged stayed on at the school carrying out responsibilities and receiving employment training rather than leaving the grounds. Another group, he said, had changed their views toward going AWOL. Where once male youths had celebrated peers who fled successfully, characterizing them as heroes carrying out daring escapes, they later saw those same individuals as weak, shameful deserters. "The hero worship of the boy who resisted longest and most vigorously, no longer exists. The most respected boys now are the ones who are making the best records."[35] The number of boys going absent without leave had fallen sharply, he argued.

Nelles's claim of decreasing numbers of boys who escaped was not without merit (Table 4). School records reveal that the frequency of flights among all boys fell considerably during his administration in the 1910s and 1920s from the previous two decades.[36] Following his death, in the late 1920s and 1930s, as conditions deteriorated, due in part to decreased state funding, the numbers of escapes reversed, shooting up significantly.

TABLE 4   ESCAPES AND ATTEMPTED ESCAPES AT WHITTIER STATE
SCHOOL, 1891–1940

Year	Mexican Origin	African American	Euro- American	Total
1890s	49 (17%)	12 (4%)	229 (79%)	290
1900s	53 (15%)	23 (6%)	285 (79%)	361
1910s	27 (10%)	8 (3%)	232 (87%)	267
1920s	31 (15%)	8 (4%)	174 (81%)	213
1930s	155 (20%)	36 (5%)	573 (75%)	764

SOURCE: Inmate History Registers, vols. 98–137 (1890–1940), Fred C. Nelles
School for Boys (Whittier), Youth Authority Records, F3738, California State Archives, Sacramento, California.

To gain more converts, Nelles also took his campaign to the streets,
spreading the news in the local paper about the early gains at the reformatory. In 1914, Nelles informed *Whittier News* about the "hope of new
things in reform work" and the many dramatic improvements at the reformatory. Among them was the positive change in attitude of the boys
toward the school as well as the sentiments of the school's officers toward
the boys. "Boys who have been sent here as incorrigible, are working
industriously and are contented. Boys who have escaped from several
other institutions are staying here because they prefer to stay and earn
their credits, learn their trades, and 'go out right' instead of keeping a
charge hanging over their heads for the rest of their lives. Boys with vicious habits," Nelles continued, "are voluntarily asking for help to get rid
of them. Liars are learning to tell the truth. Thieves are learning to respect
property. Cigarette fiends are fighting to regain their self control." Most
importantly, boys have learned how to "assume personal responsibility
for personal acts and personal character." Staff, too, gave up knocking
down or whipping boys. "We do things differently now."[37]

In 1919, Nelles gave a more intimate appraisal of the school in a talk
before the Men's Club of St. Matthias's Parish, a local church, on the benefits of the cottage system. In 1920, he spoke again before a crowd of 2,500
people at the California Congress of Mothers and Parents Teachers Association on "giving the boy and girl a chance."[38] In 1922, he gave another
speech at the Annual Convention of California Social Work, touted as
one of the leading social work organizations in the country.[39] Later, in
1924, he co-headlined the inaugural meeting of the Southern California
Academy of Criminology, of which he was a member. Nelles, the *Los Angeles Times* reported in covering the event, "has earned a nation-wide

reputation in his work at Whittier, where he has had the support of several State administrations in changing an old-fashioned 'house of correction' or 'reform school' into one of the most successful educational institutions in the country." To allay any lingering doubts, Nelles also brought the Boy Scout troop members from the school, boasting that 80 percent of those graduated from Whittier State School took "their place in society with good jobs, maintaining excellent records as law-abiding citizens."[40] Regardless of the veracity of his statements, Nelles's message made an impact, for many attendees promised to assist his program.[41]

Within a few years, Nelles's campaign as well as his ability to transform a run-down institution and energize demoralized wards and staff earned him a solid reputation among social reformers and the larger Progressive movement in the United States. In 1920, the California governor recognized Nelles's work by appointing him adviser to the State Board of Control, a committee responsible for finances. In that capacity, he visited all state schools and brought their needs to the board's attention. His selection, noted the *Whittier News*, "stands as an example of his executive and administrative ability."[42] That same year, following a long and protracted crisis in management at the Preston School of Industry, Nelles took over as interim superintendent, while his Assistant Superintendent, Karl Cowdery, administered Whittier in Nelles's absence. Nelles welcomed the recognition, for he aspired to the directorship of the Department of Institutions, the administrative unit responsible for the state schools and state hospitals.

IMPLEMENTING SCIENCE AND SCIENTIFIC RESEARCH

Nelles's ability to transform and modernize Whittier State School came from his ability not only to devise effective policies and practices but also to implement the latest scientific research in the study of juvenile delinquency, even if it meant the marginalization of the most vulnerable youths. Like his peers, Nelles had an unshakable faith in the ability of science and scientific methods to solve a host of growing social issues, including juvenile delinquency, which many attributed to the growing number of foreign immigrants and their children. To carry out his goals, Nelles—with the support of the governor, Hiram Johnson—looked to college-educated men trained in the "history of corrective institutions, [and] the development of modern ideas in connection with them" to analyze each boy's case and recommend treatment.[43] For assistance, Nelles turned to Stanford psychologist Lewis M. Terman, a leading proponent of the intelligence

TABLE 5 INTELLIGENCE QUOTIENT (IQ) SCORE AND CLASSIFICATION

Superior	Normal	Dull	Borderline	Feebleminded	Imbecile	Idiot
1.01+	0.92–1.00	0.83–0.91	0.75–0.82	0.50–0.75	0.49–0.30	0.29–0.00

SOURCE: Lewis M. Terman, *The Measurement of Intelligence: An Explanation of and a Complete Guide for the Use of the Stanford Revision and Extension of the Binet-Simon Intelligence Scale* (Boston: Houghton Mifflin, 1912).

testing movement in the United States and an advocate of eugenics. Terman agreed to send J. Harold Williams, his doctoral student and a research fellow at the Buckel Foundation at Stanford University, in his stead to carry out a preliminary survey of boys at Whittier State School, to identify the causes of delinquency and, in the process, complete his dissertation.[44]

To carry out his task, Williams employed Terman's revision of the Binet-Simon Measuring Scale of Intelligence, a standardized intelligence test developed in France in 1908 and later adopted in the United States as modified by Terman. The examination consisted mostly of a series of quizzes, arranged in order of difficulty, involving two- and three-dimensional puzzles and games as well as pencil and paper quizzes. According to Terman, the Stanford-Binet Scale, as it was later popularly known, took into consideration a boy's mental age—that is, his overall score as determined through his performance on the test as well as his chronological or birth age. The difference between the two—the ratio of the mental age to chronological age—determined a child's intelligence or intelligent quotient (IQ). According to the scale (Table 5), individuals with an IQ ranging from 0.50 to 0.75 scored as feebleminded or moron, those whose intelligence would never develop beyond that of twelve-year-old; those between 0.75 and 0.82 were "borderline" feebleminded; those between 0.83 and 0.91 were "dull-normal"; and those 0.92 or above were "normal" or "superior." This meant, for example, that a sixteen-year-old boy who had a mental age of eight-and-a-half years, and hence an IQ of 0.53, fell among the ranks of the feebleminded or moron. In contrast, a fourteen-and-a-half-year-old boy with a mental age of sixteen-and-a-half had an IQ of 1.22, deeming him superior.[45]

The test and its interpretation had major flaws. In administering the survey, Williams, like his mentor, ignored the role of language and education and gave the exam to youths with limited to no English skills or formal school instruction. Williams, Terman, Alfred Binet—the coauthor of the original test—and Henry Herbert Goddard, a renowned psychologist, eugenics advocate, and one of the greatest champions of the exam in the United States, all vehemently argued in the 1910s that the test was largely independent of verbal abilities and language acquisition.[46] Not everyone agreed, however. Grace Fernald, an applied psychologist who had tested girls in Whittier's Girls' Department in the winter of 1912, questioned the men's scientific assumptions. Fernald argued that language, as well as schooling, socioeconomic class, and environment, influenced the testing process and outcome. In her 1916 report on the psychological work at the Ventura School for Girls, she acknowledged that intelligence scales had less value when "children were not thoroughly familiar with the English language."[47] Wayward youth, she stated later, led "very different sorts of lives" from nondelinquents, often dealing with crime, alcoholism, and parental abuse in their homes and larger communities. Delinquents, Fernald believed, "act[ed] rather than talk[ed]."[48]

Other specialists also argued that IQ reflected cultural background and educational achievement rather than innate intelligence.[49] George I. Sánchez, among the earliest and most notable Mexican American intellectuals in the Southwest, voiced continuous opposition in the early 1930s to the use of those tests, particularly with Spanish-speaking and bilingual children. The tests, he said, "fail[ed] to recognize the importance of the fundamental personal, social, and cultural differences of the pupils and of the extremely important question of differences in milieu."[50] Despite those critiques, researchers continued to hold fast to beliefs about inherent intelligence well into the 1930s.

In private and public circles, Williams, Terman, and others, including Goddard, dismissed the critics. "Anyone living in an average environment, even with not a day of schooling, should be able to do the tests," Goddard declared.[51] To counter any claims of biases in the testing carried out at Whittier, Williams argued that the exams evaluated "native intelligence," not "the consequences of opportunity" such as schooling.[52] Although environmental factors influenced the ways in which individuals expressed those deficiencies, "heredity," Williams wrote in 1914, "accounts for about 75 percent of the feeble-mindedness which exists."[53] He believed that the mentally deficient or feebleminded, as well as their offspring, were born that way and had inherited it from their parents or grandparents. Later, many of the researchers, including Williams and Goddard, would modify their stance on the role of language in the testing movement.

After Williams had completed his research at Whittier, he drew two major conclusions that reflected broader beliefs in the scientific community, particularly among eugenicists, about class and crime. First, he found that a significant proportion of delinquent boys—most of whom came from impoverished backgrounds and unstable homes—tested as mentally deficient. Among the 150 boys surveyed, 28 percent were definitely feebleminded, 25 percent borderline feebleminded, 22 percent dull-normal; and 25 percent of average or superior intelligence. Comparing the Whittier boys with ordinary or nondelinquent public school children, Williams found that delinquents had lower intelligence levels than nondelinquents. According to contemporary scientific studies evaluating the mental ability of public school children, 75 percent, a significant majority, tested as having a normal or superior intelligence, while the remaining children were distributed among the dull-normal, borderline, and feebleminded groups. In contrast, only 25 percent of Whittier boys tested as normal, suggesting a strong link between intelligence and delinquency as well as class and crime.[54]

To bolster the connection between mental weakness, poverty, and criminality, Williams relied on the latest national and international scientific writings. Williams noted that U.S. and European investigators had reported a connection between mental deficiency and crime, and that mental weakness had characterized 25 to 50 percent or more of the criminals in their studies. Moreover, such scientific researchers reported a direct correlation between mental weakness (or feeblemindedness) and moral abnormality (criminality and delinquency). To lend further credence to his own work, Williams cited national studies carried out in Ohio, New Jersey, Illinois, Indiana, Massachusetts, Kansas, and Virginia. These reports found that 24 to 79 percent of the studied inmates were feebleminded, similar to the findings at Whittier. Contemporary studies of "degenerate" families, such as Goddard's *The Kallikak Family,* supported Williams's argument about the inextricable links between heredity and feeblemindedness. Surveys of delinquent females supported Williams's deductions as well, and based on that work, he concluded unabashedly, "We are justified in believing that fully half of the professionally immoral women of our towns and cities are feeble-minded."[55]

Williams's second major conclusion from the Whittier State School survey found "marked racial differences among the boys," a core belief among eugenicists who believed in race-based hierarchies.[56] He determined that, while most boys—regardless of race or ethnicity—had a gap or significant difference between their mental and chronological ages, those with the largest differences were youths of Mexican descent, a group that he and the other researchers referred to as "Mexican-Indians," a term underscoring their Native "blood" and their biological racial differ-ence from Euro-Americans because the federal census identified Mexi-cans as "white." In California, according to Williams, Mexican-Indian boys had a six-year difference between their mental and chronological ages; the gap for African Americans was five and a half years and for Euro-Americans three years. This meant that Mexican-origin youth had the largest percentage of feebleminded individuals or morons among them. Indeed, Williams's results indicated that about 60 percent of Mexican-origin youth were feebleminded, while 48 percent of African American boys and 6 percent of white or Euro-American boys tested similarly. Mexican and Mexican American boys also comprised the lowest percentage of youths who tested in the normal range—about 5 percent—while 15 percent of African Americans and nearly 40 percent of European Americans did so. In short, boys of Mexican origin appeared the least likely to achieve the normal range, the most likely to be mentally deficient, and were, according to Williams's line of reasoning, the most criminally minded in nature.[57]

The links among race, class, and crime did not surprise Williams or Nelles. Williams noted, "While Mexicans are usually classified as white, it seems best here to make the distinction on account of intelligence differences probably due to the intermingling of Indian blood."[58] Moreover, he observed that Mexicans and blacks, on the whole, "often contribute[d] to the amount of crime and delinquency in this country."[59] Williams's generalizations about Mexican-origin peoples in particular reflected the growing chorus of social scientists, educators, and advocates of immigration restriction, among others. In the 1920s, the passage of stringent immigration laws called for an end to the "Mexican problem" of inferior, unassimilated, culturally backward, and economically burdensome hordes. Indeed, the connection between the research at Whittier and the national mood on race and immigration was undeniable.[60]

Ultimately, Williams's findings on racial, ethnic, class, and intelligence differences among Whittier's delinquent boys supported the idea of a race-based intelligence hierarchy, with most whites on top, blacks in the middle, and Mexicans on the bottom. This hierarchy varied across regions, however. In Texas, intelligence testers placed African Americans on the bottom, Mexicans in the middle, depending on class and color, and whites on top. In California, the racialization and subordination of Mexicans and blacks, based on inferior biology, was not a new phenomenon. Rather, it stemmed from long-held beliefs about race, blood, and nation that solidified in the nineteenth century concerning the Spanish-speaking peoples and in the seventeenth century for the peoples of African descent.[61] The difference in the early twentieth century was the use of intelligence tests and other biometric measurements to identify youth of color as mentally deficient and to segregate them on that basis.

Curiously, Williams later admitted that racial prejudice aimed at African Americans probably played a role in their criminalization, though he said little else about the role of race and ethnicity in the juvenile justice system. "The colored population of our state school for boys being approximately 15 per cent, while the colored population of California is but one per cent. That delinquency is 15 times as common among negro boys as among white boys suggests either important causal facts among the negroes, or a difference in the attitude of the courts toward this race." While Williams entertained the idea that racism in the courts influenced the future of African American children, he made no similar claim for Mexicans and Mexican Americans. To Williams, they had poor endowment: "Mexican children do not learn readily at school, and few of them ever pass above the third grade." Their inability to catch on in school did not stem from "language difficulties," he noted, but from "low intelligence." "Apparently, the average intelligence of Mexican children in southern California is not greater than three-fourths that of American children. If this is true, nearly one-half of the Mexican children in our schools are feeble-minded."[62]

To weed out such defectives, Williams recommended the segregation and sterilization of mentally deficient boys, a practice that many scientific researchers, eugenicists, intellectuals, and Progressives—including Nelles—also advocated. In Williams's view, feebleminded children and youths needed permanent care and ideally sterilization. Ezra Gosney and Paul Popenoe of the California-based Human Betterment Foundation, a leading organization in the Golden State advocating the sterilization of the mentally unfit, promoted such beliefs as well. Sterilizing the unfit, they believed, protected rather than punished the individual and larger society. "Institutional care," Williams stated, "not punishment, is the only just or rational solution of the problem."[63] Terman, an ardent eugenicist, agreed, saying that the feebleminded should be "segregated during their period of reproduction in order to extinguish the defective strains which now encumber our prisons, reform schools, jails, courts, and public schools."[64] Like his mentor Terman, Williams supported the creation of a state-sponsored sterilization program to contain the reproduction of tainted persons and thus "lighten considerably the burden of crime, alcoholism, prostitution, and pauperism."[65] He continued, "When this policy [of sterilization] has been relentlessly followed for a few generations, the menace of feeble-mindedness will be reduced to about one-fourth its present proportion."[66]

Nelles agreed with Williams's findings and supported his recommendations, urging the regrouping of Whittier's youth along intelligence levels. Unlike Whittier's normal and superior boys, who could reform and reenter society as productive citizens, the "morally diseased," should be "quarantined" with similar individuals, he continued. "Dependents, delinquents, incorrigibles (all with great diversity of age and nationality) associate on terms of enforced intimacy with the moron, the feeble-minded and the epileptic. . . . To attempt to properly care for and train [them] . . . and all the different kinds, nationalities, and ages of boys, in one institution, is not wise." Moreover, by removing deficient boys to proper institutions, they would be sure to "receive scientific, reasonable and effective treatment. That sort of treatment is impossible" at Whittier.[67] Despite Nelles's insistence throughout his administration that the goal of Whittier State School was "to restore . . . boys to normal life" and to teach them values of citizenship, he had little hope for the mentally deficient, significant numbers of whom were youths of color. "Some," he conceded, "cannot be reformed."[68]

Nelles not only advocated the segregation of the so-called mentally deficient but also supported the establishment of institutions with the capacity to maintain and sterilize "morons" (feebleminded individuals) and "idiots"—those deemed to have the mental capacity of a young child. In 1915, Nelles suggested the use of the Girls' Department—once it was vacated by the girls—as such a place. With the support of the Psychopathic Association of Southern California, an influential organization headed by Curtis D. Wilbur, the first juvenile court judge of Los Angeles, Nelles led a legislative committee that sponsored a bill for a school for the "mentally deficient" who could not "safely be permitted to be at large." The only home for the feebleminded in California, the Sonoma State Home for the Feebleminded located in Eldridge in Sonoma County, they reported, was full with 1,100 patients and a backlog of hundreds of would-be patients. The bill called for an educator "skilled in caring for feeble-minded persons" to head the new Southern California Psychopathic Home, which would follow the successful methods employed at Vineland Training School in New Jersey under the direction of Herbert Goddard. The goal was to admit "high-grade defectives"—those who, with some training in basic methods of unskilled labor, could become "reasonably useful members of society," for they threatened normal children in public classrooms and the family structure, as they lacked the ability "to share the family life."[69]

Many prominent Californians supported the move, including professors, judges, and psychologists, all of whom believed morons posed a grave menace to society. Unlike imbeciles and idiots, who were easily discernible in the larger population, the high-grade feebleminded were difficult to identify and posed a grave danger by intermingling and intermarrying and thus tainting the larger society. Grace Fernald, though opposed to the testing methods, echoed the sentiments of her peers when she said that such an institution would allow morons to lead happy lives living among their own kind and learning how to become partially or wholly self-supporting. Despite the support for the institution, the bill failed to pass the legislature largely due to political budget battles.[70]

The defeat of the bill did not mean an end to the development of such an institution in Southern California. Rather, it simply delayed it. That same year, the California legislature appointed members of Whittier's Board of Trustees, Nelles, and two other representatives of the Psychopathic Association to a special committee responsible for investigating and reporting on the viability of establishing the Pacific Colony for the Feebleminded in Spadra, California, an institution advocated by John R. Haynes, a leading physician in Southern California and an ardent supporter of the sterilization of the mentally unfit. All the committee members eventually agreed to its establishment and drafted a report to the legislature recommending its formation. Legislators, in turn, drafted and passed the bill creating the Pacific Colony in 1917, the second state institution for the feebleminded. (The first, Sonoma State Home at Eldridge, was founded in 1889.) The Pacific Colony bill not only established the colony but also recognized mental deficiency as a psychological and social condition that could be accurately measured through science.[71]

As institutions for the feebleminded, the medical superintendents at the Pacific Colony and Sonoma State Home had the legal right to sterilize wards with or without their or their immediate family members' consent, a provision many Californians failed to understand. The power to sterilize was first conferred on state institutions in 1909 when the California legislature passed a law granting those officials as well as the medical superintendents of state prisons the right to sterilize wards with "hereditary insanity or incurable chronic mania or dementia" so long as it improved their "physical, mental, or moral condition."[72] In 1917, the legislature amended and expanded that statute to include any "mental disease which may have been inherited and is likely to be transmitted to descendants," thereby allowing a more expansive and eugenics-based rationale for sterilization. The hospitals did not carry out sterilizations without oversight, however. The State Commission in Lunacy, later the Department of Institutions, had the power to investigate any patient or case identified for sterilization and approve or disapprove of such action, particularly when a family member or guardian refused to provide consent. By the 1920s, most medical superintendents made it a policy not to release any patient without sterilization. According to historian Alexandra M. Stern, by the 1960s nearly 20,000 individuals, "or one-third of 60,000 total nationwide," had been sterilized in California.[73]

At the same time that Nelles worked to establish the Pacific Colony, he also made a great effort to establish a department of "research for intelligent action" at Whittier State School, a unit strongly advocated by Williams and Terman. Ideally, Nelles wanted a scientific institute for social engineering, headed by a psychologist and supported with medical and psychiatric consultants. He also wanted it to facilitate meetings and publications of expert social and behavioral scientists studying the causes of juvenile delinquency in particular and the latest findings in eugenics in general. The department's work would not only benefit those at Whittier, Nelles argued, but also those across the state and nation more broadly.

Within a short period of time, the practice of removing mentally deficient or unwanted boys—many of them youths of color—from Whittier State School resulted in one of Nelles's greatest successes of his program. By 1925, Nelles boasted that merely 2 percent of youths tested at Whittier State School scored as feebleminded or borderline feebleminded, a significant reduction from the 28 percent identified in 1914. The normal and superior made up the overwhelming majority (78 percent) of Whittier boys, he continued, a proportion that surpassed the average public school classrooms. The proportion of superior children increased as well, he noted, from 3 percent to 10 percent. Not coincidentally, the percentage of Mexican, Mexican American, and African American boys at Whittier State School declined significantly. Population statistics show that Mexican and African American boys made up 14 and 9 percent of the population, respectively, in the 1910s; those figures fell in the following decade, and the percentage of Euro-Americans increased from 77 percent in the 1910s to 83 percent in the 1920s (Table 6). Nelles's social engineering—that is, his plan to work with a young, pliable, "more responsive," and intelligent group of boys who also came from superior racial stock—had come to fruition.[74]

TABLE 6 WHITTIER STATE SCHOOL MALE POPULATION ACROSS
ETHNICITY AND RACE, 1891–1940

Decade	Mexican (%)	Black (%)	White (%)	Other (%)
1891–1900	12	4	84	>1
1901–10	11	10	78	1
1911–20	14	9	77	>1
1921–30	10	6	83	1
1931–40	19	9	71	1

SOURCE: Inmate History Registers, vols. 98–137 (1890–1940), Fred C. Nelles School for Boys (Whittier), Youth Authority Records, F3738, California State Archives, Sacramento, California.

The state also supported Nelles's line of reasoning. In 1915, the legislature passed a bill—at Nelles's urging—establishing the Department of Research, which later became the California Bureau of Juvenile Research (CBJR) in 1921, with J. Harold Williams as its director. With "a corps of trained investigators," Nelles believed they could investigate questions pertaining to delinquency, intelligence, and heredity "unbiased, free from personal opinions," and without "sentimental injections."[75] Touting themselves as leaders among Progressives in the research of juvenile delinquency, Williams, Nelles, and their colleagues sponsored meetings and published scientific proceedings in the newly established *Journal of Delinquency*.[76] The department also continued testing all incoming wards at Whittier into the late 1910s and early 1920s and carried out similar surveys at reformatories and detention homes throughout California and the United States.

The ongoing research carried out at Whittier State School and elsewhere led Williams, Terman, and Nelles as well as their contemporaries to harden their views on the links among intelligence, race, class, and heredity and on the role of the feebleminded in society in general. In 1915, Williams argued that the "segregation and sterilization [of individuals such as Whittier boys], both strongly advocated by leading authorities, seem to be the only means at hand."[77] A year later, Terman expanded on those ideas when he published *Measurement of Intelligence,* in which he advocated the sterilization of Mexicans and blacks and the confinement of youths of color to vocational trade training. Feeblemindedness, Terman wrote, was "very, very common among Spanish-Indian and Mexican families of the Southwest and also among negroes":

Their dullness seems to be racial, or at least inherent in the family stocks from which they come. The fact that one meets this type with such extraordinary frequency among Indians, Mexicans, and negroes suggests quite forcibly that the whole question of racial differences in mental traits will be have to be taken up anew and by experimental methods. The writer predicts that when this is done there will be discovered enormously significant racial differences in general intelligence. . . .

Children of this group should be segregated in special classes and be given instruction which is concrete and practical. They cannot master abstractions, but they often can be made efficient workers, able to look out for themselves. There is no possibility at present of convincing society that they should not be allowed to reproduce, although from a eugenic point of view they constitute a grave problem because of their unusually prolific breeding.[78]

Terman remained steadfast in his beliefs, even when broader questions surfaced in the scientific community about the validity of the intelligence tests. These criticisms followed on the heels of the poor performance of World War I army recruits on the examinations. Terman, who had coauthored those evaluations with Robert M. Yerkes, his student and a comparative psychologist, wrote several essays and gave speeches defending the findings. One of the most scathing critiques Terman encountered came in 1922, when, in a six-part series published in the *New Republic,* Walter Lippmann indicted Terman's basic principles and, in the process, dismantled his theories. Terman, in response, fired off a rebuttal, objecting sarcastically to many of Lippmann's points. Lippman did not remain silent but rather replied to Terman's response, suggesting he was "loose-minded."[79] The doubts expressed publicly by Terman's and Yerkes's critics did little, however, to dissuade Whittier's administrators about the legitimacy of the tests and their conclusions about the feebleminded.[80]

Indeed, Nelles's faith in the scientific research as well as his own beliefs in hereditarianism and eugenics led him to go so far as to suggest the testing of all children in California public schools and state institutions. By doing so, Nelles argued, as did Terman, society would prevent delinquency among students in the public schools. Moreover, testing promised efficiency in classifying and segregating pupils into the three main classes of intelligence: average, superior, and inferior. This process would, in turn, allow instructors and administrators to weed out—segregate and eventually sterilize—the mentally incompetent who struggled in school and made it difficult for normal children to learn.[81]

Nelles's proposition for universal testing was nearly realized in the early 1900s when the Preston School of Industry, the California School for Girls, as well as public schools throughout the United States subjected thousands of children to intelligence tests. Public school officials carried out some of the first exams as early as 1913 in Columbia, South Carolina, administering them to African American and Euro-American students. The researchers found the former to be mentally younger, or inferior, compared with the latter. From 1916 to 1929, behavioral scientists, educators, and others carried out over 175 studies on a total of 36,882 participants. The most frequent ethnic and racial groups tested included African Americans, followed by Native Americans, Chinese, Italians, Portuguese, and Mexicans. The results of those exams concluded that Northern European Americans were mentally superior to all others tested. In California in 1918, the Santa Ana School District hired J. Harold Williams to oversee the testing of its mostly Mexican-origin school population, many of whom scored below normal. As a result, school administrators placed these students in remedial classes, providing only nonacademic vocational training as they did at Whittier State School. By the 1930s, school officials throughout the Southwest, including Texas and Colorado, commonly placed Mexican and Mexican American children in manual trade classes.[82]

The use of intelligence tests at Whittier State School and other efforts at individualized study formed part of Nelles's plans to transform the reformatory into a premiere, world-class institution, yet his project was only partially complete. In the scientific world of intelligence testing, the use of fieldwork—carried out by eugenics fieldworkers trained by Charles P. Davenport in New York—was critical to developing a complete picture of the delinquent and potentially defective boys in question. Nelles was aware of the value of fieldwork, and he contacted Davenport, the director of the Eugenics Records Office (ERO), as well as Harry H. Laughlin, the superintendent of the ERO and second in command, and asked them to visit the school and advise him on the latest developments in the field. Through his meeting with Laughlin in California, Nelles secured the services of Karl Cowdery and, several years later, of Mildred S. Covert and Edith Bryant, eugenics fieldworkers. They would perform dozens of interviews on Whittier State School boys. Nelles placed high value on their work, and he later granted Cowdery considerable privileges at the reformatory, even appointing him acting superintendent while Nelles tended to a crisis at Preston in 1920.[83]

Despite the national and international notoriety it brought to Whittier State School and the Golden State more broadly, Nelles's program—which criminalized, racialized, and pathologized youths of color—began to unravel in the early 1920s as a result of political battles and drastic economic cutbacks at the state level. In 1921, Nelles was crushed when California officials overlooked his candidacy for director of the Department of Institutions, a newly established department at the state level that had been organized to administer the juvenile correctional facilities and the state hospitals as one unit. Stunned by that rejection, Nelles took an increasingly grim view of state politics and the CBJR. His relationship with Williams, in turn, became strained. Julia Mathews, a psychologist for the CBJR, informed Lewis Terman that "something seemed to happen to Mr. Nelles" in those months. "It is not easy to analyse just what this [change] was but there came at about this time a sudden, distinct and radical change in his attitude toward Dr. Williams and the Bureau," she said, and the results of Nelles's transformation were "disastrous." Apparently, Nelles had sent Williams a letter sometime in 1921 expressing his "cruel suspicion and repudiation of faith." Nelles, it seemed, believed Williams had thwarted his appointment. Mathews suggested that is reflected "unbalance of mind," and "only Dr. Williams' intense loyalty to their friendship and the work and his almost superhuman determination to see things squarely and in their entirety," allowed him to continue at Whittier. Politics and, increasingly, fiscal constraints, Mathews explained, brought the "tragic" situation to a "crisis."

Indeed, in 1923, with the election of California Governor Friend W. Richardson, the former state treasurer, Nelles faced a drastic reduction in appropriations. The crown jewel in Nelles's scientific program, the CBJR, was hit hard in the process. The state not only cut the bureau's funding, nearly wiping it out, but also provided little for improvements at Whittier State School.[84] The governor's decision, with the legislature's approval, to end much of the research carried out at Whittier State School dealt Nelles a blow. Despite Nelles's attempts to have prominent individuals such as Lewis Terman write letters to the legislature in support of the work at the CBJR, no further appropriation was provided in 1923, and Nelles lost the services of J. Harold Williams as well as the fieldworkers and staff.[85]

The near collapse of Whittier State School's research program began to take a toll on Nelles's health, though he managed to convince Governor Richardson, in 1924, to provide emergency funding to renew the Department of Research. "Whittier present[s] an unsurpassed opportunity for laboratory work," Nelles reminded state officials, with its emphasis on the analysis, diagnosis, and treatment of boys.[86] Nelles continued his program only as a result of volunteer researchers from the University of

California at Los Angeles, Stanford, and Wyoming. The work seemed to pay off, for Nelles claimed that the percentage of feebleminded youths at Whittier continued to shrink from previous years. It decreased from 5 percent in 1924 to 2.2 percent in 1926, which was a result of the identification and segregation of mentally defective youths both at Whittier and, prior to their commitment, in the juvenile courts. Such changes, Nelles noted, led to much success with the boys at the reformatory, for few of them relapsed into delinquency. "Not less than seven out of ten boys coming to Whittier succeed after leaving, and . . . a possible additional 10 per cent are doing fairly well," he said in 1926. Correspondingly, the wards who were youths of color also decreased, according to Nelles. While the institution normally reported the population of Mexican-origin boys at anywhere from 12 to 15 and sometimes more, by 1926, the school reported that only 4 percent of boys were of Mexican origin (although the school's case files suggest that figure was closer to 10 percent). Nevertheless, Nelles's program continued.[87]

The continued fight with state officials in Sacramento and his duties at Whittier State School were apparently too much for Nelles's health, and he was forced to retreat for rest and recuperation in 1925. For two years he languished, while his assistant superintendent took over the school's administration, resulting in the unraveling of Nelles's program. According to Kenyon Scudder, Nelles's successor, the decline of both the school and Nelles himself began with the closure of the CBJR, the loss of Williams and his staff, and the negligible state support. During that time, "the school had necessarily been operated under a strict retrenchment program," Scudder explained.[88] Nelles's weakened state apparently made him vulnerable to infections, which led to him contracting pneumonia and influenza in 1927. Within two weeks, Nelles was dead at the age of fifty-one.

News of Nelles's sudden death not only stunned his most ardent supporters but also dealt a near mortal blow to his scientific program. For three months after his death, the school remained without a permanent superintendent, though the assistant superintendent thought, erroneously, he would be ascending to the post.[89] Much to his chagrin, officials selected Kenyon Scudder, the former vocational director and assistant psychologist at the Preston School of Industry, to take over Whittier State School in August 1927. Colleagues questioned Scudder's ability to handle the task. Scudder said years later that Dr. Jessica Peixotto at Berkeley believed that Whittier State School had nearly killed Nelles, and she wondered about Scudder's own stamina to take on such a grueling position: "What have you done that makes you think you can handle a job that practically killed Fred Nellis? [sic]," she asked him.[90]

In many ways, though, Scudder's appointment at Whittier State School seemed an obvious choice, for he shared some of Nelles's basic principles when it came to dealing with troubled and delinquent youths, though his views on racial and ethnic minorities were less clear. Scudder's plan involved introducing the most recent science-based recommendations in working with juvenile delinquents. "Naturally there are new fields and new scientific methods of approach which will be developed in the administration of the school," Scudder wrote soon after arriving in 1927.[91] Scudder, for instance, believed in prevention programs as an answer to delinquency and also took precautions in selecting staff, as did Nelles; however, Scudder also screened and trained potential staff by giving them intelligence and occupational tests, which had not been done in any consistent manner. Scudder changed some of Nelles's previous policies and practices as well. He eliminated, for instance, Nelles's interest in building champion sports teams as well as star athletes. Scudder believed that such an approach took away from the school's energy and narrowed the opportunities for other boys to participate. Instead, Scudder emphasized intramural athletics.[92]

The scientific research program at Whittier State School, though haphazard since the dismantling of the CBJR, showed signs of renewed life under Scudder's administration with the election of Governor C. C. Young in 1927 and the hiring of Norman Fenton, a psychologist from Ohio University in 1928. In contrast to his predecessor, Governor Young believed government had an important role to play in dealing with the social issues of the day. In fact, Governor Young backed the establishment of a commission for the "study of problem children." That committee, officially named the Commission for the Study of Problem Children, was composed of Kenyon Scudder, Lewis Terman, Miriam Van Waters, and other national leaders who worked with troubled children and youths. With Young in office, the possibility of reviving the CBRJ, under Fenton's leadership, seemed a real possibility, though Fenton had been hired specifically to replace psychologist Ellen Sullivan (who had returned full time to her duties at the University of California at Los Angeles in 1928) and to take over the fledgling Department of Research and the *Journal of Delinquency*.[93] Lewis Terman, who esteemed Fenton as a colleague and friend, was pleased with his appointment. "You couldn't have made a better choice," Terman said.[94]

Notwithstanding the stability Norman Fenton and Kenyon Scudder eventually brought to Whittier State School in the late 1920s, changing economic and political currents brought new waves of change to the school. The onset of the Great Depression in 1929 and the election of Governor "Sunny" James Rolph in 1930 over incumbent C. C. Young unsettled Superintendent Scudder and the school's administration because Rolph introduced a spoils system in the state political process that proved disastrous for Whittier State School. Among Rolph's first moves was to appoint J. M. Toner as the director of the Department of Institutions, who then had the charge of dismissing Scudder. Scudder, however, refused to go, and he even sought the backing of the Board of Trustees, though it had no political power and acted in an advisory mode primarily. Toner disregarded Scudder's attempts to block his dismissal, and he replaced him with a relative unknown: Claude Smith, a former Texas sheriff and Toner's apparent crony. Not surprisingly, "Smith lasted three months," Scudder recalled years later, "to be followed by fifteen Superintendents over the next ten years."[95] Toner then appointed George Sabichi, a medical doctor from Los Angeles, to head Whittier State School. Sabichi's appointment as well as his administration was clouded in mystery, for few records remain detailing his experiences or the developments at the school under his tenure.[96] What seems clear was that his leadership was weak at best.

Orin Bell, the superintendent at Whittier State School from 1947 to 1953, recalled years later that the "Nelles School's" relationship with the city of Whittier greatly deteriorated after Kenyon Scudder's stint as superintendent ended in 1932. The "constant large-scale runaway episodes, with the ensuing break-ins and burglaries, kept neighboring residents in perpetual turmoil. 'Get that prison out of Whittier' was becoming a passion with many good, well-meaning citizens," he explained in an oral interview. Eventually, better and closer supervision, coupled with perimeter security in the form of a fence—which Fred C. Nelles had refused to construct during his tenure, believing it would create a prison-like atmosphere—"became a necessity." Not until years later, when security and supervision increased significantly, did the "community pressures diminish accordingly."[97] By then, state leaders had abandoned Fred C. Nelles's type of Progressive politics and the eugenics-based practices that had led to the criminalization, racialization, and pathologization youths of color.

An innovative reformer and conservative eugenicist, Nelles, like many of his Progressive peers of the 1910s and 1920s, turned to science, scientific research, and eugenics as well as widely held ideas about race, intelligence, and heredity to identify, segregate, and remove so-called mentally deficient boys, disproportionately youths of color. According to the intelligence tests carried out by J. Harold Williams and his peers, youths of color were more likely to be feebleminded and had little, if any, potential for increasing their mental capacities. As such, these young men in particular had little hope of leading normal adult lives and would do best in institutions such as Sonoma State Home or the Pacific Colony for the Feebleminded. The scientists also gave intelligence exams to young males of Euro-American descent, but the majority of them scored as normal or dull-normal, a classification given to those scoring slightly below normal. In contrast with youths of color, the majority of whites were deemed capable and worthy of reformation and citizenship by school officials.

Intelligence testing and sorting of delinquent youths was not the only process through which young men of color, namely, Mexicans, Mexican Americans, and African Americans, were criminalized, racialized, and pathologized. The next chapter demonstrates that the eugenics fieldwork carried out at Whittier State School reinforced popular ideas about intelligence, race, delinquency, and heredity in ways the intelligence examinations could not. The fieldworkers' writings and case histories reveal in rich detail the nature of the ideological beliefs and practices guiding their work as well as the ways in which youths and their families challenged such notions of who was fit and who was not fit to produce and reproduce in the larger society.

CHAPTER 3

Mildred S. Covert

Eugenics Fieldworker, Racial Pathologist

In 1921, Mildred S. Covert, a fieldworker from the Eugenics Record Office (ERO) working for the California Bureau of Juvenile Research (CJBR), a research unit located at Whittier State School, sat down to have an interview with Pedro C., a fifteen-year-old Mexican American boy sentenced to the reformatory for truancy and incorrigibility (Figure 2). The exchange followed a series of intelligence tests that the boy had completed recently at the CBJR and failed miserably. The goal of her meeting with Pedro was to investigate his personal and family history as well as his home and neighborhood environments in order to identify the causes of delinquency and to predict his social outlook. Covert paid closest attention to evidence of dysgenic traits such as feeblemindedness, immorality, or criminality in his early history and the family's background at least three generations back, for she was trained to believe that such "unit characters" were determined biologically and inherited directly from parents to offspring.[1]

Upon completing Pedro's interview, Covert seemed annoyed though likely unsurprised with the findings, for she and her colleagues at the CBJR shared assumptions about intelligence, race, delinquency, and heredity. "The boy's memory," she wrote, "is very deficient; he is unable to remember the names of streets and buildings in the neighborhood where he has lived . . . or to recall dates of events that have occurred in the recent years of his life." The youth's low intelligence, she noted, was manifested in more obvious ways as well. "In talking with the boy," she

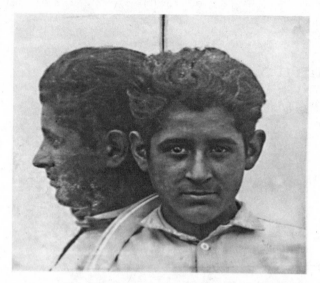

FIGURE 2. Pedro C. Like many Mexican American boys who performed poorly on the intelligence tests administered at Whittier State School, Pedro C.'s family history and home environment were closely scrutinized by eugenics fieldworkers, looking for evidence of dysgenic (inherited) traits, namely, feeblemindedness. Photograph by Fred C. Nelles School for Boys (Whittier), California State Archives, Office of the Secretary of State, Sacramento, California.

noted, "his inferior mentality is at once noticeable." Moreover, according to a former teacher, Pedro was phlegmatic and excitable, that is, he lacked energy and was quick to anger, traits the fieldworkers commonly associated with youths of Mexican origin that suggested an early stage of manic-depressive insanity. In Covert's understanding, her observations and the father's description of the boy as lazy affirmed his feeblemindedness.[2]

Covert's visit to Pedro's impoverished home and unkempt neighborhood further underscored the boy's poor genetic makeup. Like eugenics researchers around the country, Covert believed that feebleminded individuals came from degenerate environments.[3] The furnishings in the home, she said, were "very cheap," and "the children had on the cheapest of ready-made dresses." Outside the home was no better, Covert observed. "The porches and sidewalks were kept in just as slovenly a condition as the interior of the home."[4] The boy's parents appeared equally base to Covert, particularly the mother. In fact, eugenicists believed mothers generally had lower intelligence levels than fathers.[5] The mother "was filthy dirty and slovenly in her dress," Covert reported. "Her hair was sadly in need of combing, having received no attention since she had arisen in the morning." Moreover, she "is quite phlegmatic and shows no animation" and is "probably feeble-minded." The community members fit Covert's general description as well. "Most of the residents are Italians, Mexicans, and negroes. Many are ignorant and practically unschooled."[6]

The rampant deficiencies in Pedro's neighborhood, home, and family notwithstanding, Covert believed the boy's future had a glimmer of hope but only if he escaped his environment. If taught "a trade and placed out in the world on his own responsibility he will undoubtedly be able to adjust himself to industrial life and become self-supporting and a well-behaved citizen," Covert concluded.[7] He should not return home, Covert recommended, for he would continue on the same path of delinquency and later criminality.

Covert's report, though harsh in its assessment of Pedro C., his family, and his community, was typical of the social case histories carried out on of youths of color at Whittier State School in the late 1910s and early 1920s. An examination of 203 surviving social case histories demonstrates the ways in which researchers such as Covert used ideas and ideologies about intelligence, race, delinquency, and heredity to evaluate the present and diagnose the future of Mexican, Mexican American, and African American boys as well as ethnic Euro-American boys.[8] Through this process, Covert and her colleagues participated in the criminalization, racialization, and pathologization of nonwhite youths. Euro-American boys, particularly poor ethnics of southern and eastern European origin, were also studied and often judged as feebleminded but with far less frequency and fervor than the nonwhite boys.

This chapter uses Covert's experiences at Whittier State School to examine the role of science and scientific research—namely, eugenics fieldwork—in linking notions of race, heredity, and delinquency in the making of California's juvenile justice system and its impact on youths of color. The chapter begins with an overview of eugenics fieldwork, tracing its origins and development in Europe and the United States. Next, it examines the fieldwork that Covert and her colleagues carried out in California, paying attention to the development of the CBJR and its role in the state more broadly, and demonstrating how the researchers criminalized, racialized, and pathologized youths of color and their families. Finally, it ends by demonstrating that boys of all ethnic and racial backgrounds as well as their families challenged the scientific researchers' assumptions and conclusions about intelligence, delinquency, heredity, and race. In more ways than one, the boys and their families demonstrated intelligence, strength, and humanity in the face of impoverishment, marginalization, and racism.

THE ORIGINS OF EUGENICS FIELDWORK
IN THE UNITED STATES

Mildred S. Covert's training in eugenics fieldwork occurred in the early twentieth century, as part of the rapid expansion of eugenics-based ideologies and practices across the United States. Eugenics as a science or field of inquiry was originally developed in the late nineteenth century in England by Charles Darwin's cousin Sir Francis Galton, a statistician and the founder of the biometrics movement in England. In 1883, Galton coined "eugenics," which literally meant "well born," a term he used to denote "the science which deals with all influences that improve the inborn qualities of a race" and develops them to "the utmost advantage."[9] Eugenics borrowed from contemporary theories emerging in the fields of plant and animal biology such as neo-Lamarckian theory. Devised by French naturalist Jean Baptiste de Lamarck, neo-Lamarckian theory taught that the environment could alter human heredity—both positively and negatively—and affect any future offspring. Mendelian theory, on the other hand, developed with the rediscovery in the late 1800s and early 1900s of Austrian monk Gregor Mendel's work, posited that characteristics or traits in humans were passed directly from parents to offspring. The rise in popularity of those beliefs, described as Mendelian hereditarianism, dovetailed with Galton's research on talented men and led him to argue that certain traits were innate and not acquired. Galton's work eventually eclipsed neo-Lamarckian theory in the United States and popularized eugenics as better breeding through selective reproduction of the "fit" while preventing the reproduction of the "unfit," as espoused in the doctrines of positive and negative eugenics, respectively. Moreover, eugenicists and their supporters argued that selecting the inheritance and transmission of particular genes or unit characters had the power to prevent the development of "physical, mental, and emotional pathologies" brought on by the introduction of tainted "germ plasm."[10] By the 1920s, Galton's research into eugenics as the science of breeding individuals "good in stock, hereditarily endowed with noble qualities" was accepted as a prestigious science around the world, developing into a scientific movement—albeit with significant variations across time and place—in at least thirty-five countries around the globe.[11]

In the United States, Galton found an ardent supporter in Charles Davenport, a professor at the University of Chicago and Covert's future teacher. On a year-long sabbatical in 1899, Davenport traveled to England to study biometrics under Galton's mentorship and became a proponent of Mendelian theories of inheritance. When he was back in the United States, Davenport worked to establish his own research laboratory for selection and breeding experimentation on animals. To secure funding, he approached the newly established Carnegie Institution of Washington (CIW), whose mission was to "improve mankind." After successfully lobbying the CIW and opening the Station for Experimental Evolution (SEE) at Cold Spring Harbor in New York in 1904, Davenport set his sights on applying Mendelian theories to human beings, believing that a rising number of socially inadequate peoples threatened the nation's moral and social fabric. When the opportunity arose for securing private funding for an institute dedicated to the study of human genetics and eugenics, Davenport managed to secure support from a major donor—Mary Harriman, widow of the railroad magnate E. H. Harriman—who also feared increasing social instability manifested largely as growing crime, immorality, poverty, and alcoholism in expanding urban centers. With that support, Davenport launched the Eugenics Record Office (ERO) in 1910, which eventually joined the SEE as the CIW's Department of Genetics.[12]

The ERO quickly became a hotbed of eugenics advocacy, research, and publication in the United States. To promote their agenda, Davenport and his assistant, Harry Laughlin, a former schoolteacher and ardent biological determinist, focused their energies on advocating their social and legislative agenda across the country and on gathering scientific research on the inheritance and distribution of particular human traits. Beginning in the late 1910s and early 1920s, Laughlin worked diligently at the state and national level drafting and supporting legislation advocating the exclusion, elimination, and sterilization of the unfit, most of them poor, non-Nordic white immigrants. In 1920, Laughlin wrote a model law on eugenic principles and sent it around the country to legislators for use in drafting their own compulsory sterilization laws. Eventually, thirty states adopted aspects of Laughlin's work, passing similar legislation resulting in the sterilization of thousands of persons in state prisons, mental hospitals, and reformatories. Around the same time, Laughlin joined Albert Johnson, the nativist head of the House Committee on Immigration and Naturalization, to call for restricting immigration, particularly from eastern and southern Europe, Russia, and the Balkans. In contrast to the previous immigrants from northern, Nordic European countries, Davenport informed Johnson, these new immigrants, constituted a "genetically inferior stock."[13] During the debates of immigration restriction in the post–World War I era, Laughlin testified before Congress as an "Expert Eugenics Witness," providing three days of testimony on the dangers of continued immigration. The result was the passage of the "first comprehensive restriction law," the Johnson-Reed Immigration Restriction Act of 1924, which curtailed immigration from southern and eastern European and debarred Asian immigration in general.[14] The law also targeted Mexican immigrants, not by imposing quotas but rather by increasing the enforcement of restrictions. Davenport, in the meantime, launched the research arm of the ERO to give prospective students such as Mildred Covert an opportunity to test their talents.

In response to the growing demand for the collection of family histories and pedigrees of medical patients and prison inmates, Davenport set out to train and hire an army of eugenics fieldworkers. In 1910, the same year the ERO opened, Davenport opened the first summer training institute for eugenics fieldwork. Davenport's courses lasted six weeks, and students learned the latest theories and methodologies, including Mendelian law, anthropological approaches to inheritance, the nature of mental traits, and ideas about feeblemindedness, nomadism, criminality, and insanity. Davenport also taught students how to use the various intelligence tests, including the Simon-Binet Intelligence test, and he supplied them with the *Trait Book,* a manual he had developed at the ERO. The *Trait Book* contained hundreds of codes representing various "physical, mental, and social characteristics, behaviours and diseases."[15] Though it was biased and open to subjective interpretation, the publication enabled Davenport to maintain a semblance of scientific objectivity and criteria in evaluating clients. Finally, Davenport provided students with training in "interviewing subjects, conducting investigations, preparing pedigree charts, and interpreting results."[16]

Davenport made sure, too, that summer institute students such as Covert studied the work of leading thinkers in eugenics and related fields, including Lewis S. Terman, author of *The Measurement of Intelligence,* G. Stanley Hall, Terman's mentor and the author of *Adolescence,* an influential work in the late nineteenth century child-study movement, and Herbert Goddard, author of well-known works including *Feeble-mindedness; Its Causes and Consequences* and *The Kallikak Family: A Study in the Heredity of Feeble-Mindedness.* Ultimately, Davenport's goal was to enable students to prepare family histories as complete as those published by Goddard and later by Arthur Estabrook, a fieldworker turned popular writer, in order to publicize the dangers of the reproduction of the mentally deficient and more generally the socially unfit.[17]

From 1910 to 1924, when Davenport's summer institute closed, the ERO trained over 250 fieldworkers or "health officers of the race," most of them—85 percent—women like Covert.[18] Davenport assumed that women rather than men best fit the criteria for fieldworkers because of their "feminine tactfulness" and ability to engage family members, primarily women, in the home.[19] Davenport's preference was for women to study delinquents, imbeciles, and epileptics, while men would work with the vicious and criminal classes. Davenport believed that women, as the weaker sex, were too frail to work with incarcerated and institutionalized males. Regardless of their gender, Davenport required his fieldworkers to have college or university training in related fields of the sciences, including biology, zoology, and psychology. Indeed, most of the women he hired were young and single, educated in women's colleges of the eastern United States. Davenport also expected these students to be "industrious, loyal, [and] discrete" as well as "accurate, confident, [and] systematic" and to have favorable social and interview skills, giving them "the ability to gain the confidence of their informants, demonstrate an interest in their clients, and [be] able to direct conversation."[20]

Ultimately, Davenport sought to produce efficient and productive fieldworkers who had the skills to get their clients to reveal their knowledge—with all of its perceived limitations—as well as their family secrets in order to legitimize the ERO's purpose. Davenport knew, however, that male and female fieldworkers would encounter difficulties in securing such information. To overcome such challenges, Davenport encouraged fieldworkers to seek out family members, friends, and neighbors for their opinions and insights, despite the possibility of inviting rumor and suspicion into the research. Davenport also believed that researchers had the right to "go to the homes of . . . people . . . to make intimate inquiries about their behaviour."[21] In his view, the invasion of privacy was a small price to pay in the battle to improve and ultimately save the race, namely, the Nordic Euro-American race. At the same time, Davenport cautioned student fieldworkers against diagnosing clients and drawing conclusions before completing a history. "A physician would be apt to diagnose and that is what we *do not* want" (emphasis in the original), he instructed them.[22]

Though they had limited training and independence, Davenport and the ERO portrayed the fieldworkers as scientific professionals. According to the *Eugenical News*, a newsletter of the ERO dedicated to the fieldworkers' activities, they earned salaries on a par with other professionals. In the late 1910s, a typical fieldworker such as Covert, for instance, made $60 to $100 a month, which was 70 percent more than nurses, who garnered anywhere from $23 to $75 a month.[23] With such support, fieldworkers spread out across the country in the 1910s and early 1920s, compiling hundreds of social case histories on individuals institutionalized in state prisons, mental hospitals, and reform schools.[24]

The fieldworkers' productivity and stature fell considerably in the late 1920s and 1930s with the growing controversies and increasing rifts within the eugenics movement. In those years, reform eugenicists, many of them medical doctors, criticized the ERO's overtly "racist, class-biased and . . . unscientific claims."[25] An investigation of the ERO in 1937 found much of the work as lacking "clarity, standards of evidence, and scientific objectivity," and the report declared it "useless for genetic purposes." Indeed, in the postwar period the ERO became increasingly aggressive in promoting nativist policies and programs and espousing racist views, and less interested in carrying out research. Eventually, Harry Laughlin's open support of Nazi Germany and his fulminating against the "menace of Mexican immigration" became an embarrassment for the major funder of the ERO, the CIW, leading to Laughlin's early retirement and the transformation of the nationwide program.[26]

EUGENICS FIELDWORKERS AND THE CALIFORNIA BUREAU OF JUVENILE RESEARCH (CBJR)

In California in the 1910s and early 1920s, Mildred S. Covert and Karl Cowdery were among the first ERO fieldworkers sent to work at the CBJR, under the auspices of J. Harold Williams and with the approval of Fred C. Nelles. Touting the CBJR as the western representative of the ERO, Williams followed the ERO's practices and procedures for carrying out eugenics research.[27] To spread the work throughout California, the CBJR established branches and appointed resident psychologists at state institutions, including the Preston School of Industry. In effect, the

CBJR's organizational structure provided researchers with an easily accessible resident-subject population on which to experiment, conduct research, and deepen understandings of intelligence, delinquency, race, and eugenics.[28]

The CBJR's structure, like that of the ERO, was hierarchical and male-dominated. Williams, as the head psychologist, had much of the power at the CBJR, though Nelles too had some say in its operations. Fieldworkers received instructions from Williams, who in turn tested most of the boys, approved all social case histories, and oversaw the training of fieldworkers. That training began in 1920 and consisted of twelve-week seminars as well as one-on-one internships with students, many of them graduates of sociology and psychology from the University of Southern California.[29] Covert as well as Cowdery and a few other lead fieldworkers mentored the students, though they focused primarily on performing much of the day-to-day research. In fact, two-thirds of the dozen or more researchers the CBJR hired and trained in California were much like Covert, that is, college-educated, young, single women. The men, on the other hand, consisted of three males, including Cowdery. The women conducted the majority of social case histories, while the men produced far fewer, demonstrating that the women carried out much of the legwork at the CBJR.

Covert's reports, like those of her coworkers, reflected the scientific model and influence of the ERO. Prior to Covert's arrival in California sometime in the late 1910s, Cowdery and Clark Willis, another fieldworker, carried out most of the initial case studies, which were brief descriptive reports of each boy's history, intelligence, physical tests, and family history. With Covert's arrival and the expansion of the CBJR's personnel and operations in the late 1910s, the reports became increasingly sophisticated, analytical, and judgmental. Indeed, by the early 1920s, Covert and her fellow fieldworkers not only administered "abbreviated intelligence tests"—shortened versions of the Stanford Revision of the Binet-Simon Intelligence Scale—to those they interviewed, but they also paid close attention to a laundry list of details in the boys' personal and family histories, including their mental and physical health, moral character, education, and employment. The fieldworkers concluded the reports by summarizing the boys' causes of delinquency and future prognosis or social outlook. The reports did not end there but also included a list of sources, the individuals who had been consulted in formulating the social case history.[30]

Arguably, the most compelling component of the fieldworkers' social case histories was the family history tree or pedigree chart, which illustrated the biological influence of inherited dysgenic traits. Developed at the ERO and replicated at the CBJR, Covert and her fellow fieldworkers used the trees to map the boys' inheritance across three, preferably four, generations. Every social case history, save the earliest ones, began with the boy's family history tree, displaying multiple generations of offspring, parents, and grandparents with corresponding characteristics or dysgenic traits identified for each individual (see Chapter 4 for an example). If the boy was nonwhite, the fieldworker noted the boys' racial origin or group as either "Mexican-Indian" or "negro" or "colored" (no Asian or Native American boys were identified as part of their study). Covert typically refrained from marking Euro-Americans as a separate race, though in a few instances such youths were identified as "white." Fieldworkers represented male subjects or male family members who had been identified as feebleminded with a darkened square, and they marked feebleminded females with a shaded circle. Those with borderline feeblemindedness, in contrast, had partially darkened circles or squares, while those with a history of institutionalization had an icon of a hand with a pointed index finger pointing toward them or had their corresponding shape (circle or square) underlined.

If the fieldworkers detected any dysgenic traits such as alcoholism, sexual immorality, nomadism, or excitability or dullness—early signs of insanity—they identified those with letters. Persons they judged as alcoholics, for instance, received an "A," while those who were sexually immoral got an "Sx." Covert marked those with excitability, on the other hand, with an "Ex" and those who were feebleminded with an "F." Such identifications of individuals and their place in the family trees enabled Covert and her fellow eugenics researchers to map the influence of heredity in passing defective traits—or positive traits, for that matter—from one family member to the next and thus prove the researchers' scientific contentions about the connection among heredity, intelligence, delinquency, and ultimately race.[31]

The purpose of the fieldworkers' family history tree (as well as the social case histories) was not only to assist in determining the causes of delinquency but also to demonstrate the scientific rigor of the CBJR. In the *Whittier Social Case History Manual*, a comprehensive guide reflecting seven years of research at Whittier State School, the fieldworkers touted their scientific approach and objectivity. "The truly scientific worker," they wrote, "has no theories to prove or disprove, no preconceived notions." They only possess "the scientific point of view." That is, the "ability to accurately describe facts . . . without the interference of personal bias." Fieldworkers, they noted, should also have "good, clean, solid character, with a reasonable amount of common sense, and a strong feeling of responsibility toward the betterment of human nature and social conditions."[32] Moreover, a fieldworker should "consistently report, as accurately as possible, what [s]he sees, hears, and reads" in order to "deepen the richness and accuracy of the complete study" Ultimately, they hoped the rigorous training would, at the same time, lead to the replacement of untrained volunteer workers with scientifically trained workers and to professional respectability, a larger trend emerging in the professionalization of social work and related fields in the early twentieth century.[33]

Despite Covert and her colleagues' claim to scientific objectivity, much of the fieldworkers' research rested on biological determinism, cultural biases, and a host of unverified criteria. Undoubtedly, most of the scientific misconceptions dealing with inheritance and genetics stemmed from the field of eugenics, as reflected in the ERO's guides and training manuals. At the CBJR, Williams and the fieldworkers regularly invoked the use of Davenport's *Trait Book* as well as his coauthored *How to Make a Eugenical Family History*.[34] The CBJR's research was, ultimately, biased against poor nonwhites or Euro-Americans, and immigrants. In evaluating homes and neighborhoods, for instance, Covert and her peers used the *Whittier Scale for Measuring Homes* and the *Whittier Scale for Measuring Neighborhoods*, standardized instruments for evaluating a household's necessities, neatness, size, parental conditions, and parental supervision as well as a neighborhood's neatness, sanitation, improvements, recreational facilities, local institutions and establishments, and the residents' social status. Homes and neighborhoods that scored closest to the maximum of twenty-five points possible (each of the five categories received a maximum of five points) were those that reflected idealized Euro-American middle-class standards of living.

In evaluating individuals, Covert and her colleagues paid close attention to any physical marker of dysgenic traits. J. Harold Williams—who borrowed from Herbert H. Goddard's work—noted that, to the untrained eye, the feebleminded, particularly the "higher grade," were "often normal looking yet their conversation . . . [was] marked by poverty of thought or even silliness."[35] Most high-grade defectives passed undetected in the general population, the researchers argued, making them an acute social menace, for they could easily attach themselves to normal individuals and eventually marry and reproduce, which they did at an alarming rate. "They are the most prolific breeders and constitute the gravest social and moral offenders," affirmed a leading psychologist.[36] Some of the physical markers identified among such boys at Whittier State School included "loosely hanging, protruding lips," "irregular facial expressions," particularly when resting or sleeping, "sluggishness," "insensitivity to cold," and a "colorless and negative make-up" (personality). According to the CBJR researchers, speech defects, nervousness, childishness, and foolishness as well as the "'feeble-minded grin'—the smile of too puerile delight"—were also markers of the defective.[37]

Covert's ability to use an individual's general appearance and manner in detecting feeblemindedness, while efficient, was nevertheless rash. When talking with the boys' parents, fieldworkers often relied on brief conversations to determine whether they possessed any flawed traits. For example, soon after meeting the mother of a poor, Euro-American boy at Whittier State School, Covert criticized the woman's apparent lack of intelligence and judgment: "Mother would not be considered a judge of one's mentality, as she appears somewhat more retarded than the propositus [her son]."[38] In speaking with the younger sister of a Whittier State School boy, for instance, Edith Bryant swiftly judged the girl: "During a few minutes of conversation," Bryant wrote, the little girl "has the appearance of a mentality below normal, but not any lower than borderline, if as low." Bryant would have preferred to give the girl an intelligence exam but noted that the conditions were not ideal.[39]

Fieldworkers such as Bryant and Covert used appearance and manner not only to judge intelligence but also morality. After visiting the home of two Whittier State School boys, for example, Covert suspected the mother, a divorced African American woman, of sexual promiscuity and specifically prostitution, for she entertained too many men, did not work, and lived in "very good circumstances." Admitting she was a "mother of normal intelligence, [and a] pretty smart negress [sic]," Covert nevertheless criticized her morality: "Circumstantial evidence points strongly in the direction of immorality of [the] mother and aunt, who lives there [too] and probably make their living in that way." Covert, however, had little evidence to go on, admitting it was circumstantial.[40] That evidence included the opinion of the probation officer assigned to the case and Covert's own observations of the home. "The field worker," Covert said, "had an opportunity to walk through the apartment and there were several good indications that the mother and aunt were both in the habit of entertaining men in their bed-rooms for questionable purposes."[41]

In instances when Covert and her colleagues could not meet family members one on one, they relied on photographs to make their evaluations.[42] In some cases, the evidence worked to affirm the fieldworkers' suspicions of inherited dysgenic traits. After viewing the photograph of a Whittier State School boy's mother, a Euro-American woman, fieldworker Edith Bryant, for instance, identified her as a "woman of a weak character."[43] Though she had never met the woman, Bryant knew that her fifteen-year-old son, Thomas, was deceitful and had "immoral tendencies with other boys."[44]

Generally, fieldworkers had little understanding of the boys'—and families'—cultural, ethnic, or socioeconomic makeup, for they came from different worlds. Many fieldworkers, including Covert and Cowdery, as noted earlier, originated from middle-class East Coast families, and they had little knowledge of the ethnically and racially diverse peoples they met on the West Coast, particularly the growing population of Mexicans and Mexican Americans. Moreover, the fieldworkers operated in an ideological framework that privileged Euro-American values and customs as well as the authority of science and scientific research. At the same time, they scorned the beliefs and practices of their poor, ethnic, and nonwhite clients, reserving particular antipathy for Mexicans, Mexican Americans, and African Americans, and to a lesser extent the Italians, Greeks, Russians, Spaniards, and other peoples of southern and eastern European descent, all of whom they believed to be biologically and racially inferior to Nordic, Euro-American whites. In fact, Williams's earlier research, *The Intelligence of the Delinquent Boy,* had established a race-based, hierarchical intelligence order, with whites on top, African Americans in the middle, and "Mexican-Indians" on the bottom. Fieldworkers were well aware of those findings, and they used them to inform their research, which contributed to the criminalization, racialization, and pathologization of nonwhite youths of color.[45]

RACIALIZING, CRIMINALIZING, AND PATHOLOGIZING MALE YOUTHS OF COLOR

The social case histories demonstrate the ways in which Mildred S. Covert and her colleagues invoked long-held assumptions and understandings of biological differences—understood as racial differences—among Mexican, Mexican American, African American, and Euro-American youths to develop a system of race-based "typologies." The terms they used to describe boys of Mexican descent included "Mexican type," "cholo type," and "Mexican-Indians." Typologies used to refer to boys of African origin were "negro type," "nigger type," or "big coon type," similar to those epithets established decades earlier in the Southern and Northern states to remind African Americans of their status first as slaves and later as former slaves, to keep them in their place, subservient to whites.[46] The fieldworkers used these typologies, in turn, to describe a host of perceived cultural and biological characteristics shared by non-white boys of color as well as their families. The researchers rarely devised or invoked similar typologies or models to refer to Euro-Americans, particularly those of Nordic descent, though occasionally they made special references to some youngsters of eastern and southern European ancestry. In dealing with boys of Mexican and African origin, the researchers most commonly used the race-based typologies to infer subnormal or low intelligence, as determined by the Stanford Revision of the Binet-Simon Intelligence Scale. In many ways, the research process confirmed what Covert and her colleagues already knew or believed they knew about youths of color at Whittier State School.

The fieldworkers' convictions about the links among intelligence, race, heredity, and delinquency among nonwhite boys were so firmly ingrained that when a youth of Mexican-descent challenged their beliefs—mainly by performing well on the intelligence tests administered at the CBJR—they found ways explain away the results. For example, Covert's colleague, Julia Mathews, a psychologist for the CBJR who was employed at the Preston School of Industry, could not believe that eleven-year-old Victor R. (Figure 3), a Mexican American boy, had performed exceedingly well on the intelligence examination; his intelligence quotient (IQ) 1.15 or 115 percent (with an IQ 1.0 or 100 percent defined as normal) was rated "superior." "That fact that he is classified so high," Mathews said, "was due to the effect of practice and probably coaching, which his test showed."[47] Moreover, she continued, "it is interesting to note that in spite of his fluent English and talkative tendency he has a vocabulary only equal to that of a [nine] year old child."[48] Mathews clung to her line of reasoning even though the staff members she interviewed at Whittier State School believed Victor was "clever" and "brighter than the average boy." To explain his performance in scientific terms, Mathews reasoned that he was not your typical Mexican. Rather, she said, "Victor is on the whole an American type rather than a Mexican-Indian type."[49]

Mathews was not alone in her assessment of Mexican and Mexican American youths' intelligence. When Karl Cowdery and Willis Clark

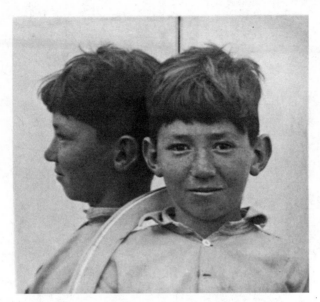

FIGURE 3. Victor R. Eugenics fieldworkers could not believe that this boy, Victor R., a Mexican American, had a "superior" intelligence, as indicated by the results of his examinations. Rather, they believed the outcome was a result of "practice" and "coaching." Photograph by Fred C. Nelles School for Boys (Whittier), California State Archives, Office of the Secretary of State, Sacramento, California.

encountered Mexican and Mexican American youths who demonstrated higher-than-expected aptitudes for boys of their race, they expressed surprise yet remained steadfast in their conclusions. In an interview with Manuel C., a fourteen-year-old Mexican American boy, Karl Cowdery noted that he "seem[ed] intelligent for a Mexican," while Willis Clark observed in another similar situation that Jesus G., the thirteen-year-old Mexican boy he interviewed, was "above average for general intelligence for his race, [yet] would pass for normal in that respect any where."[50] In other words, Clark and Cowdery held that peoples of Mexican descent in general had lower levels of intellect than the dominant population, namely Euro-Americans.

In interviewing the family members of Mexican and Mexican American youths, Covert, like her fellow fieldworkers, discounted evidence of extraordinary intelligence. Covert and the others assumed that parents, siblings, and even distant relatives of delinquent Mexican-origin boys who had tested poorly had low intelligence levels at best and were

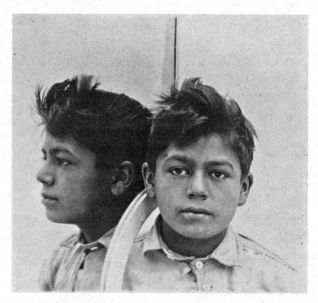

FIGURE 4. John A. Identifying John A. as "feebleminded,"
eugenics fieldworkers guessed that his family members were
defective in intelligence as well. His sister, Irene, for instance, was
deemed a "moron" for refusing to speak with eugenics fieldworker Mildred Covert. Photograph by Fred C. Nelles School for
Boys (Whittier), California State Archives, Office of the Secretary
of State, Sacramento, California.

defective at worst. After meeting the family of John A. (Figure 4), a Mexican American Whittier ward classified as feebleminded, Covert decided
his younger sister Irene, who refused to speak with her, was "probably
of moron intelligence." The girl's "reasoning," she wrote, is "very poor."
Irene had some redeeming qualities, Covert admitted, for she was "quiet
and quite clean in her personal appearance, although lacking in ordinary courtesy and refinement." Apparently, she lacked the social attributes and decorum expected of Euro-American middle-class girls.[51]

Even when family members of Mexican and Mexican American boys
incarcerated at Whittier State School had special skills, fieldworker Covert
and the others took little notice. Willis Clark, for instance, was barely impressed with the language skills of eight-year-old Josephine T.—the little
sister of a Whittier State School boy, fourteen-year-old Pedro T.—who fa-
cilitated Clark's interview of the family. Acting as an interpreter, she trans-
lated questions from English to Spanish and responses from Spanish
to English. Essentially, she served as a cultural broker between the sci-

entific researcher and the family. Willis, though, granted the child little credit, saying simply, "brighter than the average Mexican child of [the] same age."[52]

Covert was less understanding than fieldworker Clark in assessing children who used both the Spanish and English languages. When visiting the home of a thirteen-year-old Mexican American Whittier boy, Louis A. P., Covert characterized his four-year-old sister Lucy as mentally deficient because of her "code switching," that is, her tendency to shift between Spanish and English and her reticence in speaking to Covert. "She talks very little and when she does talk it is a combination of English and Spanish." From this interaction, she judged as her as below average.[53] Doubtless, Covert's beliefs were reinforced by the prevailing view among eugenics advocates that individuals—usually immigrants—who could speak little English after living in the United States for a number of years were morons. Fieldworker Helen Cook, for instance, assessed the parents of fifteen-year-old José F. as "probably both of inferior intelligence" because they could not speak English even though they had lived in the United States for over ten years.[54]

According to Covert and her fellow researchers, having a low mentality did not place Mexicans and Mexican Americans at a decided disadvantage as long as they stayed among their own kind. If they did so, they had little to fear. Negotiating Euro-American society, on the other hand, was a losing battle. In evaluating and predicting the future of Henry P. (IQ 0.54), a thirteen-year-old boy of Mexican and English ancestry who had scored poorly on the exams, fieldworker George Brammer warned of his future pitfalls in Euro-American society. "A complication is brought in by this boy being a half-breed," Brammer stated. "If he remained under Mexican competition, he should be able to succeed fairly well, but if he attempts to live with white competitors, his inadequate mental endowment will place him at a decided disadvantage. He is definitely feebleminded according to the standards of our [Euro-American] society."[55] Covert made similar comments about the outlook of Ernest S. (IQ 0.65), a fifteen-year-old Mexican American boy also identified as defective. Though Ernest S. had low intelligence, Covert believed that if he "were to be compelled to compete on equal terms with the general [Euro-American] public he would undoubtedly fail, but having chiefly his own race to deal with, the prognosis is more favorable."[56]

Covert and her coworkers held many of the same beliefs about African Americans that they had about Mexicans and Mexican Americans. Covert described Nathan M., for instance, a sixteen-year-old African

American Whittier State School boy who had scored "moron" on the Stanford Revision of the Simon-Binet Intelligence Scale, as being "of average [low] intelligence for his race." Nathan's defective powers, however, posed no disadvantage, she noted, for many African American men led their lives that way, laboring as unskilled workers. "Although we believe in our classification of this boy (moron) is justified by his low mental level, there are nevertheless men of his race (negro) and his intelligence who are able to make their living and support families." Farm work was best suited for "one of his mental level."[57] Nathan's mother had similar mental endowments, Covert surmised. When the mother volunteered insight about her son's development, Covert scoffed at the advice. She "would not be much of a judge of one's mentality," the fieldworker quipped, "being rather feeble herself."[58]

When Covert and the other researchers encountered African American boys who defied race-based hierarchies, they described these youths as anomalies, just as they did with their Mexican counterparts. Among the highest scoring boys in the reform school's history was twelve-year-old John W. P., an African American boy with an IQ of 1.27 or 127 percent. "This is the highest intelligence quotient ever found at Whittier State School," Williams informed fieldworker Bryant, who investigated the case. "The vocabulary . . . is nearly superior adult . . . higher than many college students attain." Not everyone agreed with those findings, however. The Whittier State School staff doubted the test results, calling them "erroneous." However, a second test two years later confirmed the earlier findings. "He is still one of the brightest boys in the School of any race and has developed intelligence since the last test," Williams remarked. "The whole test, as well as the previous test, indicates genuine superior intelligence and should denote superior development and ability." Along with intelligence, the boy had better than average refinement, observed the researchers, "using little slang in speech and his thoughts being rather free from unrefined ideas." Moreover, Williams and the fieldworker continued, the boy has "self-respect" and his "personal habits [are] clean. He is apt to be profane, but does not smoke, although he did at one time."

Despite his refinement and intellectual superiority, the researchers identified a dysgenic trait in John W. P. that they often associated with African Americans and, to some extent, with Mexicans and Mexican Americans. The boy, they found, suffered from "racial inertia" or laziness. John's sluggishness is "evident in both mental and physical reactions and has led to the notion that he is mentally weak." "He is not a keen thinker, but slow and lazy intellectually," said Williams. "He is, however, more tractable and less conceited than the average negro. Neither has he the average negro's idea of self-importance." "He should be taught to cultivate a mental 'drive' of which he is fully capable," Williams concluded.

Bryant, who took much interest in the case, agreed. "John is definitely lazy. The racial inertia is present in him in both mind and body. Much of his misconduct is traceable to his intellectual and physical inertia," she observed.[59] The boy's supervisors at Whittier State School agreed. They characterized him as lazy, careless, deceitful, and insolent. Bryant was baffled, she noted, that his behavior did not reflect his intelligence.

John W. P.'s racial inertia was no trivial matter. Rather, the researchers took the character trait seriously, believing it undermined his intellectual capabilities and future promise, despite the intelligence tests. "It is seriously to be feared that the racial inertia with which john [sic] is unduly endowed will prevent anything more than average in a very mediocre if not entirely menial occupation," Bryant noted. "Can it be that his extreme inertia, which characterizes mental and physical acts alike, has so operated as to make him too indolent to exert himself to inhibit natural predatory instincts?" Bryant wondered. "Can it be that mental inertia could be responsible for his doing the nearest and easiest thing and thus be responsible for his thiefts [sic] and deceit?" Yes, she answered, implicitly. The culprit: Heredity.

The father's side of the family, she noted, "shows a strain of persistent thievery, which in all probability, has come down to the propositus. The paternal aunt . . . is also lazy." "Thus," the fieldworker concluded, John inherited "the tendency to theft from her, coupling it with a superior intelligence," which was not enough to deter him from "predatory inheritance," despite his "superior home care and training." "Prognosis is unfavorable. It is difficult to be believe that John will so overcome his laziness, deceit and 'sticky fingers' as to become a true social asset." Biology, she concluded, had overridden environment, preventing any future potential success resulting from his intelligence.[60]

John's racial inertia fit neatly with the race-based typologies developed at the CBJR, for the researchers considered temperament, or "prevailing mood," as a sign of excitability or insanity, an inherited dysgenic trait. Temperaments most often associated with African American youths were those characterized as phlegmatic or simply, as in John W. P.'s case, slow and lazy. Fieldworker Covert described eleven-year-old Oscar K., for instance, an African American boy with a near normal intelligence quotient of o.99, as not only "probably above average for his race" but also "a little more lazy than average for his race." According to the disciplinarian at the Whittier State School, Oscar K. wasted time and engaged in frivolity while working in the print shop of the reform school.[61] Fourteen-year-old Joe F., Covert noted, an African American boy who had the "perpetual darky grin," "worked only the way the average darky boy does. He was rather lazy and had to be watched."[62] Covert characterized Douglas W., a twelve-year-old "no account, shiftless niger [sic]," as being cruel and mischievous as well. It is "impossible to get any work out of him," Covert declared. "He was just born lazy."[63] His chief supervisor agreed to some extent but tempered his views on the boy's potential for violence, saying, "he is just the 'swamp niger type', not malicious and not good for much [sic]."[64] The boy's home fared no better: Covert described it as the "usual shiftless negro type of home."[65]

Covert and her colleagues' views of African American boys were not surprising given the long-held, gender-specific, race-based stereotypes that dated back to slavery in the U.S. colonial period of Africans and African Americans. They were considered inherently lazy, stupid, inferior, and animalistic, and proponents of the slave system used these designations to justify their enslavement and subhuman treatment of peoples of African descent. Later, following emancipation and passage of the Thirteenth, Fourteenth, and Fifteenth Amendments to the Constitution in the nineteenth century, Southern whites used those same ideologies as well as the convict lease system, the courts, violence, rape, intimidation, threats, and many other dehumanizing tactics to dismantle Reconstruction, to control the freed Black population, and to segregate African Americans in employment, schools, and many other sectors of society. In the twentieth century, Jim Crow segregation and many of same beliefs about African Americans persisted and were used to explain their menial position in the social, economic, and political structure of the country and their increasing presence in reformatories and prisons in California and throughout the United States.[66]

Researchers in the twentieth century described the temperament of "Mexican-types" or "Mexican Indians" similar to that of African Americans. In addition to phlegmatic, slow, stubborn, and lazy temperaments, Mexican-origin boys had "inferior energy."[67] Drawing on decades old ideologies about Mexican-origin peoples, most Euro-Americans viewed them as a base, racially mixed—of Spanish, Indian, and some African ancestry—"mongrel" people. In the nineteenth century, only "Spanish" or seemingly "white" females—women and girls—of the upper landed classes were considered to have any redeeming qualities, particularly as potential mates for European and Euro-American men who might provide ready access to property and other economic resources. And indeed many European and Euro-American men married such women in the 1800s in the Southwestern region of the United States. In general, though, most Americans believed the conquest of Mexico in the United States-Mexican War of 1846 was justified, and they held that it underscored the Mexican people's racial and cultural inferiority. In contrast, proponents of the "Anglo-Saxon" or Nordic Euro-American race believed they descended from a racially pure Teutonic or Aryan people whose superior modes of life would eventually eclipse those of the lower orders. It was these understandings of Mexican-origin peoples that influenced the eugenics researchers' views of Mexicans and Mexican Americans.[68]

In her analyses, fieldworker Covert and her colleagues drew upon these ideologies and stereotypes to make sense of both Mexican and Mexican American boys and African American boys' histories. Covert characterized Mexican-origin Luis A. P., for instance, as slow, sly, and untrustworthy. "He has all the characteristics of the Mexican race, is suspicious when among others than his own people," she reported. The trade instructor at Whittier State School agreed, saying, "He is deceitful, sneaky and not to be trusted out of sight."[69] Willis Clark described Havier V., a thirteen-year-old Mexico-born boy, in a similar way, noting he did "everything in a 'sleepy' fashion. He is rather lazy and indolent."[70]

To Covert and the researchers in general, Mexican-origin boys' lazy demeanor was also rooted in their biology, specifically their Indian ancestry. In evaluating Jacob V., a thirteen-year-old Mexican American, Covert said that he "doesn't take much interest [in work], [and] does not realize the value of learning a trade." He "is just a boy and his mind is more on play than work. The Indian nature is very strong," she concluded, and "he would love to roam around the hills with a gun."[71] Covert and fellow fieldworkers often described the parents of Mexican youths in similar manner. Covert depicted twelve-year-old John A.'s mother, Angelina A., whom Covert had never met, as "a woman of very ordinary ability. Not progressive, but of the negligent, course [sic] type of 'Cholo.'"[72]

When Covert and her fellow researchers met Mexican and Mexican American boys who challenged their ideologies, they explained the findings as unusual and not typical, much as they did when describing unusually bright African American boys. Joe M., for instance, a fifteen-year-old Mexican American boy diagnosed as "one of our lower grade Mexican boys intellectually," had a "better disposition and more active temperament than characterize[d] his social and racial group," Covert noted.[73] Sixteen-year-old Armando T., like Joe M., also surprised Covert, for he was not only "average-normal and unusually intelligent for his race" but also "active; especially noticeable in view of his race and [borderline] intelligence."[74]

African American boys also defied Covert's and the other researchers' assumptions about refinement and race. Nine-year-old Edward B.'s "cooperation," for instance, "was marked and refinement [was] unusual for one of his race," observed Williams during the testing process. "He should react well to training, [and] should be given a thorough schooling [at Whittier State School]," Williams recommended in an unusual move, for he rarely, if ever, gave such orders when dealing with African American or Mexican and Mexican American youths. Edward's mother, Jennie S.—who had taken him in as an infant (his biological mother, Minnie G., gave him up to her)—surprised Covert as well. "In intelligence Mamie [sic] would probably rate dull-normal," Covert surmised, "although she makes an exceedingly good impression in conversation, expressing herself well without the exaggerations and crudeities [sic] common to her race."[75]

The race-based typologies used to render boys of African and Mexican descent in the reports not only included behavioral attributes but also physical characteristics. In portraying the appearances of many boys, the researchers explicitly described their bodies, particularly their facial features. Fieldworker Covert described Jacob V., for instance, the thirteen-year-old Mexican American boy with the Indian tendencies as described earlier, as "a typical Cholo type of boy." He "has straight black hair, brown eyes, [and] thick regular shaped lips," and his "eyes slant inward to a slight extent; particularly noticeable is the fact that they are usually bloodshot, a condition which he seems to have inherited from his mother." Jacob's nose, she continued, "is quite broad and nostrils quite wide open. [His] cheek bones [are] high, suggesting some Indian descent. [And, his] ears project outward from the head."[76]

Equally important to Covert and other fieldworkers in describing the boys was their skin color or pigmentation. Fred G., a thirteen-year-old Mexican boy identified as feebleminded and "of average intelligence for his race," not only had "black hair, brown eyes" like Jacob V. but also the "usual dark skin of the Mexican-Indian," reported Covert.[77] Mexican boys of mixed racial ancestry were characterized similarly, especially when they looked like Thomas D., a nine-year-old Mexican American boy. Thomas's "father is white," Covert said, "his mother Mexican-Indian with some negro blood. The boy is of Mexican type, save for his wavy hair, thick lips, and grey eyes."[78] In other words, "Mexican types" had straight hair, thin lips, and presumably dark eyes.

Covert and her colleagues used alternative terms and classifications to describe Mexican and Mexican American youths as well as adults who defied the typologies. Covert described the mother of Victor R., a Mexican American boy, as "Spanish" for her light skin and apparent intellect, characteristics atypical of women of Mexican descent. The mother, Covert explained, was "born in Mexico" and "says that she is Spanish." Covert seemed to believe her, for she described "her skin [as] much fairer than the average Mexican-Indian with whom we come in contact." "Although she has not learned the English language which one would almost expect her to have done after living here for twenty-five years, she, however, seems much brighter than the mothers of our Mexican boys."[79]

The fieldworkers' descriptions of African American physical types were equally explicit yet more disparaging in their meaning and tone than those used for Mexicans and Mexican Americans. Covert and her coworkers referred to large—tall and heavy—African American boys as "big negroes," likely in reference to late nineteenth-century fears of the "New Negro" and of seemingly oversized African American males who threatened Euro-American society in general and Euro-American women in particular. As Leon Litwack and many other scholars have described, after African Americans had obtained their emancipation in 1864, gaining equality before the law and the right to vote—as guaranteed with the passage of the Thirteenth, Fourteenth, and Fifteenth Amendments to the Constitution—images of menacing, sexualized black males circulated in the South and throughout the United States to instill fear among Euro-Americans of "race rule" as well as the rape of Euro-American women and contamination and subordination of the white race. The threat of the New Negro—in contrast and in reference to the safe "Old Negro" bound in chains during slavery—remained in the minds of many Americans in the early twentieth century, even in California where the African American community remained fairly small, compact, and potentially nonthreatening. Their alleged threat was palpable in the way Covert and the remaining fieldworkers and researchers at the CBJR described young black males, most of them the grandchildren of former slaves and the products of Jim Crow segregation.[80]

Fieldworker Covert described fifteen-year-old Walter J., for instance, as "a large strong negro boy, almost of gigantic proportions, although only slightly taller than average" with "the 'big nigger' appearance."[81] Julius J., like Walter, "shows the usual 'big coon' features," noted Covert. He had "broad nostrils, thick heavy protruding lips and his profile shows strongly the negro type face. See [the] photograph," Covert implored the reader. He also had "very dark skin."[82] Nathan M., the sixteen-year-old African American boy described earlier, Covert also believed resembled "the usual big featured negro type—broad nose, big thick lips, chin somewhat receding." His "eyes [are] inclined to be blood-shot most of the time," with skin "quite badly pimpled," she said.[83]

Though Covert and the other researchers usually reserved the "big type" epithet for African American boys like Nathan M., the girls did not escape the designation. In describing Nathan's younger sister, fifteen-year-old Florence, Covert wrote, she "is the 'big coon' type—large features and a very dark skin. She is inclined to be rather sullen and non-communicative." Likely, she refused to speak with Covert when questioned.[84]

Covert and her fellow fieldworkers not only developed typologies for evaluating African American, Mexican, and Mexican American youths but also graded the boys' home and neighborhood environments, which researchers believed contributed to delinquency. According to J. Harold Williams, social workers and the public in general supposed that juvenile delinquents came from "poor home environments." "There is a relation between the social quality of homes and the social quality of the people who live in them," Williams wrote in the 1920s.[85] Such beliefs doubtless influenced Covert and the other fieldworkers' views of the homes and neighborhoods they visited, as when Covert visited Pedro C.'s "filthy" home, described earlier. Karl Cowdery's visit to ten-year-old Paul B.'s home confirmed his beliefs about "typical negro homes." The home, Cowdery said, was "not very clean, but [had] fair order and arrangement. [The] front yard [was] well kept, but back-yard [appeared] disorderly with boxes, rubbish, etc., and a poor excuse for a garden in one corner." The "care given [to the household was] probably average for [a] negro home," he concluded. The "Negro section" in which they lived, he continued, included a "few low-grade whites [and] mostly illiterate[s]" with "low moral standards."[86]

To the fieldworkers, the homes of Mexican and Mexican American youths were no better or worse than those of their African American peers. When visiting the home of four Mexican American brothers who ended up at Whittier State School, Covert seemed mildly surprised. "The [r]ooms and doors [were] screened for flies," Covert noted. And the "rooms [were] unusually clean for [a] Mexican family. Everything [was] in order. Good arrangement of furniture."[87]

Cleanliness was, nevertheless, relative across racial and ethnic lines. When visiting the home of another Mexican family, Covert noted that the "interior of home [was] cleaner than most Mexican homes and yet under our [Euro-American] standards [it] would not be considered clean." The "rooms [were] screened and floor swept, but little soap and water [was] used," suggesting that the place appeared clean but in reality remained dirty.[88] Through such findings, Williams asserted years later in a history of the CBJR, "racial differences were found [in] the median [home] score for the Whites, Negroes, and Mexicans."[89] Simply, the shabbier the home, the lower the intelligence of its inhabitants. "Home conditions," asserted Williams, "are affected by race, nativity, and the relationship and occupation to the principal wage-earner."[90]

In contrast to their analyses of Mexican, Mexican American, and African American youths, fieldworkers infrequently invoked notions of race and ethnicity in their assessment of Nordic Euro-Americans—boys and their adult family members—as it pertained to their personal experiences, homes and neighborhoods, physical appearance, temperament, and intelligence. Indeed, in only once instance did they mention the ethnicity of a Euro-American family of Nordic descent; rather, they spent more time on those of southern and eastern European ancestry, revealing the researchers' beliefs about the differences of race and ethnicity as applied to heredity, intelligence, temperament, and physique. In explaining fifteen-year-old William V.'s temperament and overinhibition, for instance, which was described as "almost pathological," fieldworker Bryant invoked the boy's Italian origins to explain his "extreme reticence." William was born in the "Province of Novara, in the extreme north of Italy," Bryant explained. "This is more as might be expected, as the south[ern] Italians are far less phlegmatically inclined." Logically, she reasoned, southern Italians had excitable moods, while the northern peoples had "sullen" and "stubborn" dispositions.[91] In contrast to Italians, the researchers believed the southern Irishmen and women had jolly, genial, and generous temperaments and, at times, aggressive tendencies as well as the "quick Irish pride."[92] Slovenians, on the other hand, had "that calm quietness common among Slavs," and Armenians had "clannish" inclinations.[93]

Russians, comparatively, had "peasant type" homes. Thus, the household of John S., of Russian ancestry, was far from "American ideals of health or cleanliness," rating a "one," the lowest score on the scale. The interior had a "greasy atmosphere," fieldworker Brammer said, with "soiled clothing lying around or hung on walls." Plus, it had an "indiscriminate arrangement" of furnishings. The boy's "parents [were] both well-meaning, it appear[ed]," Brammer conceded, "but doubtless socially feeble-minded, [for] they have not adapted themselves in any way to the customs or language of the United States."[94] The Swedish, in contrast, fieldworker Bryant remarked in the one instance in which the ethnicity of a Northern European family was mentioned, were "hyper-religious," "law abiding and quiet," and "very industrious as might be expected from their race."[95]

Typologies of southern and eastern European peoples, though developed to some extent, paled in comparison to those used to render Mexican, Mexican American, and African American peoples. The markers "Mexican types" and "negro types," to name a few, conjured a host of perceived long-standing, race-based, biological differences among Mexicans, Mexicans Americans, African Americans, and Euro-Americans. But youths of Mexican and African origins and their families found ways to resist the fieldworkers' beliefs and practices, thereby challenging the pernicious stereotypes that were being employed to marginalize and eventually subjugate them.

CHALLENGING THE SCIENTIFIC RESEARCH AND RESEARCHERS' TYPOLOGIES

In more ways than one, boys of Mexican and African descent as well as their family members challenged and resisted Covert and her fellow researchers' assumptions about their intelligence, temperament, and physical appearance, among many other qualities. Throughout the interview and testing process as well as during the home and neighborhood visits, the youths and their relatives demonstrated what James Scott has called "everyday forms of resistance." Just like the peasants in Scott's study, unplanned and unorganized defiance—demonstrated through "foot dragging, dissimulation, desertion, false compliance, pilfering, feigned ignorance, slander, arson, [and] sabotage" as well as "passive non-compliance, subtle sabotage, evasion, and deception"—characterize the ways in which the youngsters dealt with the adults in positions of power as well as the institutions shaping their daily lives. Alone, everyday forms of resistance do little to change power relationships or the nature of institutional structures, but taken together they have the potential to rattle those in power. Contrary to the researcher's ideas and ideologies about delinquent youths of color, the boys had intellect, creativity, leadership, and compassion as well as many other human qualities.[96]

Ernest S., a fifteen-year-old Mexican American boy, for instance, identified as feebleminded (IQ 0.69), was among the most cunning of Mexican-origin youths, for he used his perceived "babyish or girlish actions" to keep "him from being suspected" as the culprit in sticky affairs such as stealing money from the schools he attended. "He is vastly more clever than any boy who has been in Castelar [Parental] School for [the last five] years," said the former principal of Ernest's continuation school. "Ernest is exceptionally wily, when caught red-handed he is wise enough to tell the truth." Moreover, "Ernest is very sly and a good actor," the principal continued, he "had [stolen] money and had given it to several boys to hold for him. He is deeper than his looks indicate."[97]

Ernest used his talents in more ways than one. While in school, Ernest had caught the attention of Nellie Jonas, a Euro-American teacher at the Macy Street School who not only defended his actions but also seemed infatuated with him. That teacher, "whose husband was in France," Cover reported, "bought clothes for him, took him out in her car, [and] had him out to her house for dinner." "When Ernest first entered the school," Covert continued, "she wrote him notes of an endearing nature which finally ceased because [school officials] could not permit a friendship of that type." Jonas "seemed to have a peculiar fondness for young Mexican boys," Covert stated after a visit to her home, and she "noticed many pictures of Mexican boys in her home."[98] To the fieldworker and to other officials as well, the teacher's interest in Ernest was improper and baffling. Ernest, however, took advantage of that relationship, for she provided him with the material support that he lacked at home, although she never contributed to the well-being of his larger family who was in dire economic circumstances.

Like their Mexican counterparts, the African American boys also found ways to circumvent the unequal power relations by manipulating their superiors both at the reformatory and in the CBJR investigations. Oscar K., for instance, one of the few (6 of 33; 2 percent) African American boys the fieldworkers rated as "normal" (IQ 0.99), was unhappy working in Whittier's print shop, a training program coveted by many boys and reserved only for older, promising boys, most of them Euro-Americans. To leave the unit, Oscar dragged his feet, disregarded instructions, and in other ways misbehaved and invoked 'everyday forms of resistance.' When Covert learned that Oscar wanted out of the print shop and into the dining room, she asked him to explain. "'Printing was lazy work,' Oscar replied, 'because one sat down to it all day and he preferred to do work in which one exerted themselves a little more.'" Staff misunderstood Oscar's ploy, however. The print instructor had interpreted Oscar's resistance as a sign of mental weakness. "Oscar did not have enough mentality to remain in the print shop," the teacher stated. He "was inclined to be frivolous. [He] would not apply himself. Did not try, but wasted his time." The disciplinarian at the school also misread Oscar's motives. "A little more lazy than average for his race," he said. In spite of the staff's interpretation, Oscar's tactics eventually worked: he was transferred to the dinning room and kitchen, areas usually staffed by African American, Mexican, and Mexican American youths.[99]

Oscar K.'s resistance was only one of the ways in which boys challenged the reform school officials and the researchers. Another approach the youths took in voicing or expressing their desires was to disrupt the fieldworkers' investigations by failing to follow instructions, feigning ignorance, and generally acting disinterested. Walter J., for instance, a fifteen-year-old African American boy, showed little concern with the testing process or with pleasing the researchers. He scored relatively low (IQ 0.82), J. Harold Williams reasoned, not because he lacked the ability but "because of [his] lack of cooperation or desire to succeed." He is "the most disinterested boy who has been examined for some time." Williams observed that the examinations appeared to bore Walter, for the boy only paid attention "when he wanted to or was particularly interested in a problem. [He] showed no interest whatever in his success in any test or in the examination as a whole. His intelligence level, [sic] is really higher than his intelligence quotient would indicate," Williams admitted.

Walter's resistance annoyed Williams because it disrupted the broader scientific research aims of the CBJR. Walter "is very egotistical; [he] boasts of his work, his standing, and his intimacy with the officers [at Whittier]," Williams stated. However, Williams later admitted that "in refinement he is superior. [His] speech, personal appearance, and neatness, all show considerable effort on the part of the boy."[100] Walter's lack of interest in the testing process does not suggest that he underestimated the significance of the exams or interviews; in all likelihood, he had a reasonable understanding of the research and gained some satisfaction in redirecting the researchers' goals.

Despite the pernicious stereotypes and harsh treatment they encountered, the youths managed to hold onto the care and compassion they felt toward their parents, siblings, and friends. Covert's research and that of her coworkers, though generally casting aspersions on Mexican, Mexican American, and African Americans boys, also revealed the youths' humanity, innocence, and helplessness in a world governed largely by adults who were failing to look out for their best interests. John A., for instance, the preteen Mexican American boy mentioned earlier, expressed pain and pity for his father and anger toward the juvenile court judge who ignored his father's pleas. The incident began sometime in early 1920, when a public school nurse suspected John of having tuberculosis, a deadly disease considered a dysgenic trait in the 1910s and 1920s. The boy was quarantined in a hospital, but after six days John "became home-sick and ran home." He told the researcher that he had left because he "didn't like it at the hospital because I had to go bed at noon and nine o'clock at night. Mr. Welsh, [a probation] officer, told me that I must go to school. After a week they took me back to the hospital. [But] I ran home again. Then Mr. Kramer, the sheriff, took me to jail. I was there a week and lived on bread and coffee." John's father, upset over the boy's imprisonment, appeared in court to protest to the judge. "My father felt bad," John explained to the fieldworker, "and told the judge I had done nothing but run away, and that other boys can steal and nothing is done to them." His father's pleas had little effect on the judge: "My father cried," John continued, "but the judge would not notice him."[101]

The researchers, like judges, frequently misunderstood and ignored the youths' care and concern for their loved ones. John A., for example, was belittled for his familylike relationship with the elderly woman who had cared for him. "Soon after his own mother's death," Covert explained, "his father put him to live with a woman whom [he] always [spoke] of as 'the little old lady.'" "The child does not know her name, but he speaks of her with great reverence," Covert noticed. "He says that he had often gone to bed hungry while living with her, but 'the little old lady' did not know it; he would not wound her feelings by asking for more food, he knew she had given him all she could afford." On another occasion, Covert later learned, John expressed tenderness for the house-matron at Whittier State School when she became ill. "This attention and concern about the comfort of others is sincere," Covert said, for "he does not look far enough ahead to hope to gain by it." Yet, she concluded snidely, John "reminds one of a dog, grateful for the least attention."[102]

Despite the researchers' interpretation of the boys' motivations, the boys not only expressed tenderness for family members but also for friends and peers. Not everyone welcomed such relationships, especially when they crossed social and racial lines. When Nathan M., an African American boy, for instance, wrote love letters to Euro-American girls, school officials and the researchers became incensed, offended by intimate communication across racial lines. Even in places such as California, with seemingly more pliable black-white race relations than in the Eastern and Southern states with their deeply rooted legacies of race prejudice, crossing the black-white color line for intimate purposes was socially unacceptable and sometimes grounds for reprisals. Moreover, marrying across color lines was forbidden legally: nineteenth-century statutes in California forbid persons of African descent as well as other nonwhites from marrying "whites."[103] Doubtless, Nathan knew of the taboos of entertaining and expressing interest in white girls, for he had been suspended from his previous school for allegedly writing a note to a white girl.

At Whittier, Nathan's affinity for Euro-American girls persisted, despite warnings from the staff and administrators. A supervisor noted that he had seen Nathan "making himself rather obnoxious in the presence of white girls." The supervisor, wrote Covert, "fully predict[ed] a 'neck tie' party for him, rather than a natural death," suggesting the boy's future lynching. Nathan "has to be watched all the time as there is nothing he wouldn't stoop to do," the supervisor said.[104] Nathan's actions indicate that he either gave little thought to the consequences or was purposely challenging the rules. Either way, he willingly continued to pursue white girls and, in the process, to transgress dominant views of race relations.

Boys like Nathan M. were not the only ones who demonstrated the wherewithal to confront the scientific researchers' assumptions about race, delinquency, and heredity—their families did as well. Indeed, the youths' siblings and parents resisted the intrusive nature of the fieldwork investigations carried out at the CBJR. Nathan M.'s younger brother, for instance, indicated his displeasure with Covert when she tried to take his picture during one of her home visits: "When the field worker took his picture," she said, "he stuck out his tongue." Covert was not amused. He "is dirty and is just growing up like a little animal," she retorted indignantly.[105]

The mothers of the Mexican, Mexican American, and African American boys at Whittier State School also challenged the researchers. Cristobal M.'s mother, Marguerita, for instance, eyed fieldworker Covert suspiciously when she appeared at the front door. Initially, after Covert was let in (or let herself in—it is not clear), the mother refused to speak to her or answer any questions, indicating only that she was busy with laundry. Covert was perhaps not too surprised; she knew Cristobal's mother was a tough customer. Prior to her visiting the family's home, the probation officer had informed Covert that Marguerita was known to "cuss officers out" and was "cranky and obstreperous." Covert found her a more amiable woman, yet nonetheless reticent. "She is a typical Mexican woman," Covert said. She "speaks no English and says that she cannot read or write in Spanish. It was some time before she was quite convinced that the visit of the field worker was of a friendly nature."[106]

Although Cristobal M.'s mother eventually did let her guard down and cooperate with Covert, Mrs. Agnes R. F., the stepmother of an Irish American boy, successfully kept another fieldworker at bay for two days, despite the researcher's adamant insistence on entering the home to survey the surroundings. Edith Bryant's determination to investigate the home stemmed from her interest in understanding the boy's motivation for aiding in an elderly woman's murder, the crime that had landed him at Whittier State School. Because the boy had tested within the normal range (IQ 0.92) and demonstrated no visible signs of feeblemindedness, the researchers believed the clues for his crime were rooted in heredity and his home environment. Bryant, however, struggled in getting information from Mrs. R. F., describing her as a "fiery," "typical red-haired Irish woman" with "a most determined jaw," rarely "vacillating," "extremely stubborn," and having the "Irish love of an argument."[107]

When Mrs. R. F., who was the caretaker of at least seven children, met Bryant, she questioned her intentions in snooping around the house and refused her admittance, despite Bryant's persistent efforts. After several failed attempts to enter the home, Bryant left to obtain more support: the police.[108] When Bryant returned with a policeman, she did not bother to try to enter the front door—she walked straight to the rear of the house and "entered the kitchen without ceremony." Mrs. R. F.'s defiant attitude, according to Bryant, broke down in front of the officer and shifted quickly to fear. Crying, Mrs. R. F. said to them that "everyone was always 'coming and making trouble for her and writing her up in the papers[.]'" After ten minutes of listening to Mrs. R. F. vent her frustrations, Bryant said she finally managed to console her and then when about her work of inspecting the children, home, and neighborhood.[109]

Upon completion of the inspection, Bryant seemed outraged. "The atmosphere and condition of this home make the latter an utterly unfit place in which to bring up children," Bryant declared. "It is the worst home visited by the writer [Bryant]." She had hoped to "give Mrs. [R. F.] a short scale intelligence test," but "this was, obviously, out of the question." Bryant continued, "She is not a good mother; her discipline is lax and often times entirely absent," and the home was "vicious," too. After that unflattering indictment of Mrs. R. F. and her home, Bryant concluded that environmental conditions, along with heredity, ultimately removed "all real individual responsibility" from her stepson as an accomplice to murder. Thus, the boy was allowed to remain at Whittier State School rather than endure an adult criminal trial that would likely have landed him in San Quentin Prison with the other minors convicted of murder.[110]

Mrs. R. F. finally succumbed to state authority, but the dozens of boys such as Pedro C. who was described at the outset—Mexicans, Mexican Americans, and African Americans—and their families endured poking and probing by the CBJR and found ways to challenge Mildred Covert and her fellow fieldworkers' beliefs about the relationship among intelligence, heredity, delinquency, and race. Those same youngsters could not, however, overturn the prevailing ideas and ideologies held by the researchers or by the CBJR about nonwhite youths of color in particular. For the researchers and the state officials who employed them, science in the form of intelligence tests and fieldwork developed in the CBJR and modeled from the Eugenics Records Office training confirmed their beliefs about low intelligence and the presence of dysgenic traits among boys of Mexican and African descent, rendering them mentally and socially inferior to their Euro-American peers. Although Covert and her colleagues also characterized Euro-American boys of southern and eastern European descent as subpar compared with Nordic Euro-Americans, the scientific researchers viewed nonwhite boys of color in the least favorable light, effectively criminalizing, racializing, and pathologizing them.

As the next chapter demonstrates, the results of the scientific research carried out by Mildred Covert and her colleagues had far more pernicious and long-term consequences than simply rendering typologies and cementing long-held stereotypes about youths of color. For many—for dozens of delinquents identified as feebleminded and hundreds and thousands of nondelinquent California youths labeled mental defectives—it meant sterilization, regardless of their own or their family's wishes. Chapter 4 examines how youths identified as delinquent and mentally defective would eventually end up in the state home for the feebleminded where they were sterilized, often after the state had overridden or ignored their families' protests.

CHAPTER 4

Cristobal, Fred, Tony, and Albert M.

Specimens in Scientific Research and Race Betterment

In the late 1910s, Cristobal, Fred, Tony, and Albert M., Mexican American brothers between the ages of fifteen and nine, found themselves in frequent trouble with the law for skipping school and carrying out petty thefts in the community of Redlands, a town near the San Bernardino Mountains of Southern California. After repeated offenses, the officer representing the juvenile court of San Bernardino County placed the older boys, Cristobal and Tony, in the Detention Home, a modern day juvenile hall, expecting that it would straighten them out. On the contrary, the boys refused to follow the rules and ran away, though the authorities eventually caught and sent them home with their parents' likely pledge that the boys would stay out of trouble. That approach failed to have any affect, however. After repeated run-ins with the authorities and warnings from the judge, the court sent the eldest, Cristobal, to Whittier State School in 1917, the last stop for troublesome youths. Cristobal's confinement did not scare his younger brothers straight; they kept getting into trouble, which, in 1919, earned both Fred and Tony a one-way ticket to Whittier as well, with Albert, the youngest, following two years later in 1921.[1]

Within a year of their arrival at Whittier State School, the four brothers, like most wards admitted in the 1910s, 1920s, and 1930s, received a battery of tests from scientific researchers intent on evaluating their intelligence as well as their physical health and vocational fitness, among other things. Next, fieldworkers trained in the latest eugenics fieldwork methodologies investigated the boys' family history, heredity, and home and neighborhood environment by interviewing the boys, their family members, and anyone who could speak to their personal makeup and experiences. The scientific researchers at the school held that, taken together, the findings from the visits, interviews, and examinations would not only help determine the causes of delinquency but also predict the boys' social outlook or fitness as members of society. If classified as "fit," the youths remained at Whittier and were assigned to appropriate housing, work, and instructional units. If determined "unfit"—a broad category encompassing those identified as feebleminded, insane, and disabled—they were sent to state hospitals for permanent care and, ideally, sterilization, as sanctioned by California's compulsory sterilization laws.

Like a significant proportion of young Mexican, Mexican American, and African American males at state reformatories throughout California, the siblings performed poorly on the intelligence tests and showed little promise in the eugenics fieldworkers' investigations. Curiously, even though all four brothers were identified as feebleminded, reform school authorities sent only one—the youngest, Albert—to Sonoma State Home for the Feebleminded for sterilization. Why was Albert M. and none of his older brothers sterilized? What was it about him, Whittier State School, or Sonoma State Home that led to his sterilization? Though the details behind Albert's removal to Sonoma remain a bit unclear, he was institutionalized at a time when medical superintendent Fred O. Butler, the hospital's infamous doctor who performed more procedures than any other state hospital administrator in California or across the country (Figure 5), was willing to take an increasing number of delinquent youths. Generally, Butler disliked accepting delinquent youths from Whittier State School and other reformatories around the state because he believed they were too rowdy and disrupted his larger program. Ironically, Butler preferred to take in primarily nondelinquent youths and adults, despite eugenicists' and his own claim of the need to contain "defective delinquents." Nevertheless, Butler's willingness to accept Albert M. resulted in the boy's sterilization, despite the family's opposition.

Using the childhood experiences of Cristobal, Tony, Fred, and Albert M., this chapter examines the process through which troubled youths—such as these four brothers—ended up at institutions such as Whittier State School and eventually state hospitals for the feebleminded where some of them would be sterilized "above and beyond" their family's consent. We will analyze their experiences before, during, and after

FIGURE 5. Fred O. Butler. Former
Sonoma State Hospital Medical
Superintendent Fred O. Butler at
the age of 87, commemorating the
seventy-fifth anniversary of the
institution in 1966. As Medical
Superintendent at Sonoma from
1918 to 1949, Butler oversaw the
sterilization of thousands of
patients, many of whom (or their
guardians on their behalf) had
refused the procedure. California
state law, nevertheless, allowed state
officials such as Butler to sterilize
state mental hospital patients with
or without their consent. Photograph
by Department of Mental Hygiene,
Mendocino State Hospital Records,
California State Archives, Office of
the Secretary of State, Sacramento,
California.

institutionalization to shed light on the social, economic, legal, medical, and ideological influences shaping their young lives. This discussion will demonstrate how thousands of young people, significant numbers of them ethnic and racial minorities such as Albert M., were sterilized because they had diseases and disabilities believed to threaten the larger society. Not all families consented to their children's sterilization; by the 1930s, increasing numbers of California families, Albert M.'s clan included, challenged the Golden State's effort to sterilize their sons and daughters, most of whom belonged to the most vulnerable sectors of society. Ultimately, however, the families had little authority and could not triumph over the legal apparatus and medical machinery of California. Not until sterilization laws were rewritten in the 1950s was the state forced to respect the wishes of individuals and their families.

EMERGING COMMUNITIES OF COLOR AND THE EXPANSION OF THE JUVENILE JUSTICE SYSTEM

Coming of age in the early twentieth century, Cristobal, Fred, Tony, and Albert M. lived in a period in which the Golden State witnessed

TABLE 7   POPULATION GROWTH IN LOS
ANGELES AND SAN FRANCISCO, 1850–1930

Year	Los Angeles	San Francisco
1850	1,160	34,776
1860	4,385	56,802
1870	5,728	149,473
1880	11,183	233,959
1890	50,000	299,000
1900	102,000	343,000
1910	319,000	417,000
1920	577,000	507,000
1930	1,238,000	634,000

SOURCE: Robert M. Fogelson, *The Fragmented Metropolis:
Los Angeles, 1850–1930* (Berkeley: University of California
Press, 1967), 21, 79.

dramatic transformations in its social, economic, political, medical, and institutional as well as ethnic and racial landscapes. Unprecedented urbanization, industrialization, migration, and immigration, which had begun in the mid-nineteenth century and then picked up again in the late nineteenth century, transformed largely rural areas into growing and bustling metropolises. The real estate boom and "boosterism" of the 1880s—in Southern California in particular, where the boys originated—encouraged the migration of thousands of Midwest and East Coast residents to the region in search of healthier conditions and better economic fortunes. The real estate crash in Southern California in the 1890s, which left many investors reeling from their losses, temporarily slowed the pace of migration, but it quickly recovered. By the 1900s, Los Angeles was one of the fastest growing cities in the United States, with its population approaching and exceeding that of San Francisco, which had been the most populous city in California since the 1850s (Table 7).

The early 1900s also witnessed the unprecedented expansion of the Mexican and Mexican American population. Thousands of Mexican immigrants—such as the four brothers' Sonora-born mother, Marguerita V.—migrated to California as a result of increased impoverishment and landlessness of Mexicans in Mexico, a byproduct of Mexican President Porfirio Diaz's economic policies, the onset of the Mexican Revolution of 1910, and the expansion of the southwestern capitalist economy and demand for cheap laborers in mining, railroad, and agribusiness. The arrival of tens of thousands of Mexican immigrants, *los*

TABLE 8   POPULATION OF MEXICO-BORN MEXICANS
IN CALIFORNIA

1900	1910	1920	1930
8,086	33,694	88,771	191,346

SOURCE: Arthur F. Corwin, "Quien Sabe?: Mexican Migration Statistics," in *Immigrants and Immigrants: Perspectives on Mexican Labor
Migration to the United States*, ed. Corwin (Westport, Conn.: Greenwood Press, 1978), 100, 110. The figures do not include U.S.-born
Mexicans.

recién llegados (recently arrived), expanded the long-time Mexican-
origin communities throughout California and the larger Southwest. In
1900, for instance, the number of Mexican-born Mexicans constituted
slightly over 8,000 (Table 8). Within ten years, that population nearly
quadrupled, increasing to 33,694, and it continued to expand significantly. By the end of the 1910s, an estimated one-tenth of Mexico's
populace had migrated *al otro lado* (to the other side), with many set-
tling throughout the state and beyond its borders. The migration of
many Mexican Americans from other parts of the United States—such
as the boys' father, Alejo M., born in Texas—also meant that in the 1920s
the numbers in California rose to 88,771 and in 1930 to 191,346. By the
1930s, the Mexicans residents who had been born in Mexico and in the
United States numbered 368,013. The arrival of many Euro-American
peoples—single individuals as well as families—and of a smaller yet significant proportion of African Americans from around the country, many
impoverished and looking for shelter, food, and work, created a situation
in California that politicians and concerned Euro-American residents increasingly viewed as taxing on state coffers and straining to resources in
general.

The increasing numbers of impoverished people of all racial and ethnic
backgrounds roaming city streets and transgressing the Euro-American
middle-class societal norms worried the well-established Californians
and those in positions of power who were protecting their interests. The
creation of the state reform school system—as well as the expansion and
sophistication of the juvenile justice system generally—in the late nineteenth and early twentieth centuries was in response to the growing
demand for the state to take action to deal with the growing problem of
juvenile delinquency as well as dependency. In the past, some youngsters who committed infractions went to city jails. In 1900, for instance,
Pedro D., the older half-brother of Cristobal, Fred, Tony, and Albert,

TABLE 9   SAN QUENTIN AND FOLSOM PRISON INMATES, AGE 16 AND UNDER, 1880–1939

Prison	Year					
	1880–89	*1890–99*	*1900–1909*	*1910–19*	*1920–29*	*1930–39*
San Quentin	103	35	31	6	16	11
Folsom	28	19	7	4	0	0
Total	131	54	38	10	16	11

SOURCE: San Quentin Prison Registers (microfilm), Department of Corrections Records, F3717, California State Archives, Sacramento, California, 1851–1939, and Folsom Prison Registers (microfilm), Department of Corrections Records, F3717, California State Archives, Sacramento, California, 1880–1939.

who was their mother's son from a previous union, was placed in the Redlands city jail—the only facility for adults and youths—at the age of seven for reportedly "burglarizing a sporting goods store."[2] At the same time, the courts continued to send some young people sixteen years of age and under to San Quentin and Folsom State Prisons, though that trend began to fall by the wayside. Indeed, from the 1890s through the 1930s, the number of child inmates at San Quentin and Folsom fell from 131 to 11. The decreasing rate was most dramatic at Folsom, which stopped accepting minors in the 1920s (Table 9). At best, these children ended up at institutions for minors; at worst, they landed at San Quentin.

Fortunately, like most youthful offenders sent to Whittier State School at the turn of the twentieth century, Cristobal, Fred, Tony, and Albert M. escaped state prison as a result of their relatively young ages, the availability of juvenile detention, and their relatively light crimes, which were treated as "status offenses." Those infractions usually implied vaguely defined behavior that was seen as evidence of incorrigibility, such as begging, hanging out with immoral companions, and wandering the streets late at night after curfew. For males, status offenses most frequently involved petty theft; for females, a status offense involved engaging in any unsanctioned sexual activity, regardless of whether they were victims or perpetrators of the act or acts.[3] California was not unique in its treatment of female delinquents, potential delinquents, or dependent youths. In the Progressive era, girls often received harsher punishments than boys for sexually based crimes, even though girls were a smaller proportion of the youngsters confined at reformatories.[4] At Whittier State School, girls made up no more than 622 (20 percent) of the 3,000 youths sent to Whittier State School from 1890 to 1913, the year the California School for Girls was established and the girls were transferred to that institution. Indeed, across the United States, the juvenile courts were more likely to prosecute girls for "precocious sexuality" than for any other crime, and they infrequently granted girls any leniency. Rather, any perceived or real sexual activity outside of marriage resulted not only in harsher sentences but also higher rates of incarceration for females than for males.[5]

The four brothers, though an ethnic minority at Whittier State School, formed part of the school's growing Mexican and Mexican American population (Table 10). In the first two decades, from the 1890s and 1900s, Mexican-origin boys were a relatively small group at Whittier, 12 to 11 percent, respectively; however, they were overrepresented in terms of the greater population: Mexicans and Mexican Americans accounted for about 6.5 percent of the population in the state in the early 1910s.[6] In the 1910s and 1920s, their numbers at the reform school increased slightly to 14 percent, leveled off, and then decreased slightly to 10 percent, likely in response to Superintendent Fred C. Nelles's program of segregating and transferring youths identified as feebleminded to other institutions and the state's order for the deportation of immigrants and migrants from California state institutions to their countries or region of origin. The growing population of Mexican-origin boys in the 1910s also caught the attention of Nelles. In 1915, he claimed that Mexican-origin boys constituted 40 percent of the school's population, an exaggerated figure.[7] In all likelihood, Nelles inflated the proportion of boys of Mexican-descent at Whittier State School to sound the anti-Mexican, anti-immigration, restrictionist alarm heard throughout the United States about the growing numbers of unwanted Mexicans. Eventually that alarm turned into the passage of restrictive immigration legislation in the 1920s and to the repatriation of several hundred thousand people of Mexican descent to Mexico in the late 1920s and early 1930s.[8]

The presence and population of girls from across racial and ethnic lines reflected those of their male counterparts. From 1891, the opening of the facility for males and females, to 1913, the year the state segregated the school along gender lines and transferred the girls to the California School for Girls, Euro-American girls formed the largest group of inmates at 82 percent (513 of 622), followed by girls of Mexican-origin at 12 percent (75 of 622), and girls of African-descent at 5 percent (34 of 622). Those figures indicate that the numbers of Mexican and Mexican American girls, in particular, at Whittier State School were disproportion-

TABLE 10   WHITTIER STATE SCHOOL MALE POPULATION ACROSS RACE/
ETHNICITY, 1891–1940

Year	Mexican (%)	Black (%)	White (%)	Other (%)
1891–1900	12	4	84	>1
1901–10	11	10	78	1
1911–20	14	9	77	>1
1921–30	10	6	83	1
1931–40	19	9	71	1

SOURCE: Fred C. Nelles School for Boys (Whittier), Youth Authority Records, F3738, California State Archives, Sacramento, California.

ate to their larger representation in the state. African American girls were also overrepresented at the school, for African Americans represented a tiny minority up until the 1920s.[9]

At the same time, the number of Mexican American and Mexican male youths at Whittier began to increase dramatically, particularly in the 1930s, nearly doubling to 19 percent, despite repatriation efforts. Orin Bell, a former superintendent at the reformatory, indicated that the incarceration of Mexican-origin boys grew rapidly in the 1940s to 25 percent, while another contemporary observer, Ben B. Lindsey, an advocate of the juvenile court movement in the United States, indicated that during his time at the reformatory in the early 1940s they made up to one-third or 33 percent of the population. The Mexican population around the state was far smaller, however, indicating an increasingly disproportionate rate of confinement among Mexican and Mexican American youths in the 1940s, a trend that had originated years earlier.[10]

The population of African Americans sent to Whittier State School, though about half that of the Mexican and Mexican American boys, was also disproportionate to their overall numbers in the state. From 1890 to 1940, black boys constituted between 4 and 10 percent of the Whittier State School population, yet they made up less than 1 percent of the statewide population in the early 1910s.[11] Even in places like Los Angeles, where they had a considerable presence as compared with their overall numbers across the state, their proportion was much smaller than found in the institution. Statistics from Los Angeles indicate that they numbered 1,250 in 1890, 2,131 in 1900, 7,599 in 1910, 15,579 in 1920, and 38,894 in 1930, or about 2 to 3 percent of the city's populace.[12] According to Orin Bell, by 1947, their fraction in the school had

TABLE 11   MALE YOUTHS (AGE 16 AND UNDER) AT SAN QUENTIN, ACROSS RACE/
ETHNICITY, 1880–1939

Year	Mexican	Black	White	Chinese	Native	Total
1880–89	13	2	79	5	9	103
1890–99	2	1	29	0	3	35
1900–1909	2	1	26	1	1	31
1910–19	0	0	0	1	0	6
1920–29	5	1	10	0	0	16
1930–39	3	2	6	0	0	11

SOURCE: San Quentin Prison Registers (microfilm), Department of Corrections Records, F3717, California State Archives, Sacramento, California, 1851–1939.

jumped to 15 percent, likely as a result of increased African Americans in the region as well as the steady rise of incarceration rates for youths of color in general.[13]

The incarceration of Euro-Americans, on the other hand, as compared with their nonwhite peers, experienced a downward trend at Whittier from 1890 to 1940. In the 1910s, Euro-American boys made up 77 percent of the school's population, while they made up nearly 93 percent of the larger state population.[14] Though their proportion increased slightly in the 1920s to 83 percent, it fell to 71 percent in the 1930s and, according to Orin Bell's observation, fell again to as low as 60 percent in the late 1940s. Rather than end up at Whittier for their delinquent behavior, many of the Euro-American boys who ran into trouble likely ended up in forest labor camps, which were established in California in the 1930s and 1940s to deal with out-of-state transients such as these youths. Unlike boys of color, the state provided white boys the opportunity to reenter society more quickly. Thus, over time, fewer Euro-Americans ended up at Whittier State School and African Americans, Mexicans, and Mexican Americans increasingly filled those spaces.[15]

In contrast to Euro-Americans as well as African American and Mexican American youths, the least represented children and youths at Whittier State School included Chinese, Filipino, Puerto Rican, and Native American youngsters. They made up from less-than-one to one percent of those sent to the reformatory in any given year in the first fifty years of the school's history. Their sparse numbers is explained, in part, by their relatively small population in California and by their confinement in alternative institutions, such as Indian boarding schools, including the Sherman Institute in Southern California, aimed at stripping their cultural values

TABLE 12 MALE YOUTHS (AGE 16 AND UNDER) AT FOLSOM, ACROSS RACE
AND ETHNICITY, 1880–1939

Year	Mexican	Black	White	Chinese	Native	Total
1880–89	2	0	23	3	0	28
1890–99	1	0	13	4	1	19
1900–1909	1	3	3	0	0	7
1910–19	0	1	3	0	0	4
1920–29	0	0	0	0	0	0
1930–39	0	0	0	0	0	0

SOURCE: Folsom Prison Registers (microfilm), Department of Corrections Records, F3717, California
State Archives, Sacramento, California, 1880–1939.

and customs. Chinese youngsters, too, who at one point—in the 1860s
and 1870s—ended up in disproportionate numbers at San Quentin Prison,
no longer made up a significant proportion of the youthful offender population. The prison registers demonstrate that their figures decreased over
the decades, especially at San Quentin and Folsom; by the 1890s, only a
single boy would end up at a state prison every ten years until the 1920s,
when none were admitted (Tables 11 and 12).

While the racial and ethnic makeup of the population at Whittier
State School changed over time, the experience of institutionalization
prior to their incarceration at the reformatory remained the same. Indeed, the majority of youngsters at Whittier, including the four brothers, had histories of bouncing among various asylums, detention halls,
orphanages, and detention homes in California and across the country. Cristobal, Fred, Tony, and Albert M., for instance, at one time or
another spent time at the San Bernardino Juvenile Detention Home;
two of their older half-brothers, their mother's sons from a previous
marriage, Alexandro and Reginaldo D., spent nearly three years each
at the Sherman Institute.[16] Although this institution was reserved for
Native youths, many Spanish-speaking boys of Mexican and Puerto Rican origins ended up there as well. Many of these homes, orphanages,
and private institutions, though perhaps well intentioned, carried out
downright harsh and inhumane practices, often neglecting to provide for
their wards.[17]

Not surprisingly, most of the children and youths like Cristobal, Fred,
Tony, and Albert M., who shared histories of institutionalization, came
from similar backgrounds. Indeed, the majority of those sent to Whittier
State School came from Southern California and lived in working-class
or impoverished households in which one or more parents or guardians

were gone or missing as a result of death, divorce, or desertion.[18] For most of their young lives, Cristobal, Fred, Tony, and Albert, for instance, lived in a female-headed household with little consistent parental care and inadequate support. To support the family, their mother, like many Spanish-speaking women, took in laundry; other women would sew clothes or leave the household to secure paid employment. In the process, such women were forced to leave their children at home alone for up to twelve hours or more every day of the week except Sundays. If these mothers were fortunate, their children were watched by an older child or a grandparent. Working long hours for meager wages, whether outside or inside the home, left these women little time to monitor their children's whereabouts or companions. The stress of working to support the household was compounded by the likelihood of unwanted attention from the local authorities, usually probation officers or police officers. Marguerita V. learned this early on with her eldest sons, before the other four came under scrutiny. Those officers often watched the activity of single-parent homes closer than they did two-parent households, as they were anticipating immoral or potentially criminal behavior. Indeed, Mary Odem's work on delinquent girls in California demonstrates that any questionable activities, particularly among single mothers, brought swift attention from the authorities.[19]

Conditions in the brothers' household—described at one point by Mildred S. Covert, the eugenics fieldworker investigating their home, as "filthy"—changed considerably after one of Alejo M.'s older sons, Francisco M., a child of the father's previous marriage, died in combat in France during World War I. Fortunately for the family, Francisco M. had life insurance valued at $10,000. As a result, the household received between $65 and $100 a month from the insurance, allowing them to pay for a six-room bungalow with a porch and a yard as well as plenty of food, adequate clothing for the children, and other essentials for the family. The father nevertheless continued to run afoul of the law, as did the boys, which left the mother and older children to care for the younger ones.[20]

Unstable homes, such as that experienced by the four brothers, were not only shaped by economic and family circumstances but also by differences of acculturation. Acculturation or cultural adaptation, identified by place of birth, played a significant role in the young lives of those children and youths of Mexican descent who ended up at Whittier State School. Youngsters of Mexican origin who were born and raised in the United States, like Cristobal, Fred, Tony, and Albert M., were more likely to end up in the reformatory than their Mexico-born counterparts. Indeed, from 1890 to 1940, California-born Mexican boys constituted roughly 63 percent of all boys of Mexican origin at the reformatory, while those born in Arizona, New Mexico, Texas, and other parts of the United States made up another 14 percent of the Mexican-descent population at Whittier. In other words, more than three-quarters—77 percent—of the Mexican-origin youths were American born, while the remainder (23 percent) were immigrants. Apparently, cultural adaptation, such as learning the English language and picking up values and customs from the American-born children and youths they met at school or in their neighborhood, influenced the likelihood that Mexican American youngsters would engage in "delinquent" behavior. No doubt the nature of the Mexican immigrant population as well, which was composed of a significant number of single individuals rather than families with children, led to the number of American-born (rather than Mexico-born) children predominating in the reformatory, resulting in a generation of young Mexican Americans coming of age at Whittier State School in the first half of the twentieth century.[21]

The majority of the African American boys who ended up in the reformatory, in contrast, had not been born in California or nearby southwestern states. Rather, many originated from the South. Though they were relatively few in number in California in the 1890s, from 1900 to 1920 African Americans, including young people, migrated steadily and increasingly to the state, especially to urban areas such as Los Angeles and Alameda. In Los Angeles, the population of blacks rose nearly sevenfold, from 2,131 in 1900 to 15,579 in 1920. By 1930, their numbers had more than doubled to 38,894. A fifteen-year sample taken from the Whittier State School case files reveals that about 46 percent, a little less than half, came from states such as Missouri, Georgia, and Texas, and usually they had arrived by riding the rails undetected and in impoverished conditions. With or without their families, many of the African American youngsters who migrated did so in search of adventure or opportunity, fueled by the real need for economic survival, improved race relations, and social stability.[22]

Euro-Americans confined to the reformatory, like the African Americans, were nearly evenly divided in their regional origins. A sample taken from the Whittier State School case files in late 1910s and the early 1920s indicates that slightly less than half, or 44 percent, of Euro-American whites had been born in California; the majority had migrated to the region. Apparently, young Euro-American migrants were more likely than their California-born counterparts to engage in behavior that brought them unwanted attention from the local authorities. Having recently migrated with or without their families and lacking a well-established network of extended family members and friends or home life and economic support doubtless contributed to the likelihood that such youths would run into trouble and come in contact with the juvenile justice system. This was especially true during the Great Depression, which saw the migration of thousands of Midwesterners and Southerners, among others, to California. Years later, Karl Holton recalled the scale of that migration: "Well, we had ten and twelve and fourteen thousand kids a day in Los Angeles, dropping off of those rails, and no place to go." Most had no employment or money, Holton added, making for a tense situation, especially with the local police.[23]

DAILY LIFE AT WHITTIER STATE SCHOOL

Once caught in the juvenile justice system and ordered to Whittier State School, youths had to contend with daily life at the reformatory. The regimen and routine varied significantly in the first fifty years and depended largely on the policies and practices guiding the reformatory. Prior to the 1910s, before Fred C. Nelles's tenure, Whittier was known for its antiquated methods of punishment and correction. In the 1910s, following Nelles's arrival, the school reflected the philosophy behind Progressive political thought, which embraced science and efficiency in creating a well-ordered society after the cultural, ethnic, and racial biases of the day. By the late 1920s and early 1930s, after Nelles's death and when the state curtailed funding, Whittier State School's program declined significantly, neglecting the needs of most inmates, regardless of their racial and ethnic background.

The youths' personal profiles also shaped the course of their stay at the reformatory, and ultimately their future lives. A boy or girl's race and ethnicity, class or economic status, gender, sexuality, and age as well as the child's personal history, educational level, and language ability, for instance, all played a role in the ways in which he or she was studied, classified, and sorted within and across the institution.

The great variety of personal experiences notwithstanding, it is clear that in the first two decades of Whittier States School's administration—during the time the four boys' older half-brothers Reginaldo ("Ray"), Alexandro, and Pedro D. were sent there in the 1890s and 1900s—the reformatory generally imposed and enforced strict policies; many in the media and the public characterized the institution as a prison for children. When new inmates arrived, school officials expected all admits, both males and females, to divulge their family history, including their parents' names, marital status, occupations, and drinking habits among other information. They passed a thorough physical or medical inspection, and they were quarantined up to three months to prevent the spread of infectious ailments such as tuberculosis, which were sometimes rampant. The period of isolation, though difficult for the children and youths who found themselves away from the company of their immediate family members and friends, was meant both to transition the youths into the institution and to protect the others from diseases.[24]

Girls faced questioning like the boys but also were either asked about or investigated for any sexual activity. The records are silent on the process through which the girls' sexuality was interrogated, but it is likely they underwent a pelvic examination, as many institutions for wayward or orphaned girls in California and throughout the United States regularly carried these out as part of their programs. In the juvenile court of Alameda County, for instance, girls were tested because, according to the researchers there, "a very large percentage of the girls are mentally abnormal and are cases of sexual abnormality, while a larger percentage of the boys are before the court due to less serious causes such as an excess of boyish spirit."[25] The boys received no invasive examination of their bodies, though they too were checked for venereal diseases. If afflicted with syphilis, as was common, inmates received weekly Salvarsan or arsenic and mercury treatments, which were effective in the early stages of the disease but also painful and prolonged. If the syphilis remained untreated, paresis—which eventually deteriorated the heart, nervous system, and other organs—would set in, and ultimately death ensued.[26]

After their medical inspection, the new wards received their rations. Boys who entered the school in its early years, such as Alexandro, Pedro, and Reginaldo D., received undergarments and shoes with a plain blue shirt and pants—as well as a drab, olive-green military uniform that they wore during the military drills carried out two to three times a week—and the girls received one or two plain gingham dresses. No more clothing was provided, and school officials expected the cadets to care for their uniforms, for supplies were limited. Any tears or other mishaps were repaired in the Girls' Department, where they mended and sewed school uniforms as needed. This practice not only helped to keep the costs down, but administrators boasted that it also instilled domestic values and prepared the girls to be good housekeepers and wives when they left the school. Boys, on the other hand, manufactured the shoes and other supplies. Later, during Nelles's administration in the mid-1910s and 1920s, the administrator eased the militaristic nature of the school, and young inmates donned khaki-colored trousers and white or blue shirts.

Like all youths across the decades, soon after arriving at Whittier State School, the four siblings, Cristobal, Fred, Tony, and Albert M., had their photograph taken as part of the state's larger effort to regulate its deviant population during and after their stay in state-run institutions. From the 1890s to the 1940s, newly admitted youths had their likeness captured by sitting facing forward with a mirror resting right on their shoulder in order to make sure their ears and any marks or scars appeared in the image. The boys were then turned sideways for a side or lateral view. Initially, in the 1890s, Whittier photographed the girls as well, but by the early 1900s the school ended that practice, likely because of the shame associated with female incarceration, which usually marked them as sexually deviant. Later, in the 1910s, with Nelles's appointment and changes in the policies and practices at the reformatory, school officials used the photographs to show the literal transformation of youths from juvenile offenders to accomplished male citizens: wearing new suits and shoes, carrying suitcases, and ready to conquer civilized society. Nelles's practice of providing "before" and "after" reform photos, though common in many similar institutions across the country, lasted only a few years. After he fell ill in the mid-1920s, funding was curtailed, and the practice ceased.[27]

Life at Whittier State School in the 1890s and 1900s, prior to Nelles's arrival in the 1910s, was generally mundane and harsh. Boys, for instance, lived in the three-story, main administration building. They rose every morning at 6:00, washed their faces, marched downstairs to breakfast, ate their morning meal of gruel and water, and then went to school for a few hours or to work at their trade until lunchtime, when they received a slightly more satisfying meal. When finished, the boys who had not received any schooling went to their class assignments, while the others went to work. At 5:00, they had a light supper then went to bed for lights out at 7:00. The girls roomed in the Girl's Department, which was housed in a three-story, single building nearly a mile from the main administration building. The girls followed a similar daily pattern, but they received little schoolroom instruction; instead, they focused on learning domestic chores such as cooking, laundering, and sewing. In the evenings, the staff allowed some entertainment, though the girls' division often lacked games or other supplies to entertain themselves. Occasionally, the girls would watch silent movies; for special events, they entertained officials visiting the schools with songs, poetry, and music. The boys, on the other hand, regularly marched and drilled for visitors. Occasionally, fortunate inmates received letters from home and hosted personal visits from family members.[28]

Soon after arriving at Whittier, most youths learned quickly that they needed to develop survival skills to contend with the older, larger, and stronger inmates, who often used physical force to gain and maintain power in the reformatory. The reform school records, though fragmented, are peppered with dozens of references to physical and sexual assaults committed by dominant boys upon the younger, weaker ones.[29]

Beginning in the mid-1910s, reform school administrators—largely under the direction of Fred C. Nelles—altered radically the philosophy and practices at the school. Among the most significant changes were the implementation and use of science and scientific tools, namely, the intelligence quotient (IQ) test—the Stanford Revision of the Simon-Binet Intelligence Test—and eugenics fieldwork to study the causes of delinquency and to determine the youths' fitness for Whittier State School. Nelles's main interest was to determine whether incoming wards had the ability to reform and eventually become productive members of society. If they did not—if they were identified feebleminded and carriers of other dysgenic traits besides delinquency, such as immorality and alcoholism—they would be segregated and ultimately transferred to an institution for permanent care and ideally sterilization. When the child selected for sterilization was a male, the doctor performed a vasectomy (by closing the vas deferens); when the child was a female, she received a salpingectomy (the removal of one or both fallopian tubes). Doctors believed both procedures to be "safe and simple" and less painful to the patient than the operations that had been performed in the nineteenth and early twentieth centuries. (Salpingectomies were, however, more risky and dangerous than vasectomies.) By limiting the reproduction of the feebleminded, scientists believed society would be protected from potentially violent, destructive, and incompetent individuals.[30]

When the four siblings were given the IQ tests in the late 1910s, the results determined that all were feebleminded. Cristobal, the eldest and the first of the boys tested in 1917, scored the poorest on Stanford Review with an IQ of 0.54, marking him a moron at best and "certainly greatly inferior to average [twelve] year old children" at worst, according to

J. Harold Williams, the school psychologist. Cristobal, Williams concluded, was "very inferior, 'probably defective.'"[31] Two years later in 1919, Cristobal's younger siblings, Fred and Tony, at the ages of thirteen and eleven years, respectively, took the examinations as well and did slightly better, earning IQ scores of 0.75 and 0.70. Fred and Tony nevertheless earned designations as borderline feebleminded and moron, respectively.[32] Finally, two years after Fred and Tony, Albert the youngest was tested at the age of eleven in 1921, shortly after he was admitted to Whittier. He earned a slightly lower score—an IQ of 0.67—than Fred and Tony, yet he managed to outperform he eldest brother Cristobal. To the researchers, Albert was nevertheless a common moron like his siblings.[33]

Despite the boys' limited schooling and English-language skills, Williams believed the boys' scores reflected their native intelligence; Williams and his contemporaries argued that the exams were independent of education and language skills. "There is no indication that [Cristobal's] poor performance," he said, "is due to any language difficulty."[34] In analyzing Albert's results four years later, the assistant psychologist at the California Bureau of Juvenile Research, Julia Mathews, came to similar conclusions, though she acknowledged that the boy's language ability played a limited role in the process. Albert has a "language handicap," she admitted, "but not sufficient to account for failure in digits, counting backwards, similarities, dates, etc."[35]

Following the examination process with the psychologist, Cristobal, Tony, and Fred met with fieldworker Mildred S. Covert, who investigated their family history, childhood experiences, and neighborhood conditions. From her investigations, Covert rendered a less-than-flattering interpretation of the family's history. The entire family—made up of the half-brothers, Alexandro, Reginaldo, and Pedro D., the father, Alejo M., the mother, Marguerita V., the youngest, Albert, and two older sisters— were "naturally" criminal and immoral, Covert stated.[36] The half-brothers, she indicated, had a long history of delinquency, for they had spent time at Whittier State School and other institutions, while the father was a thief, a drunk, and criminally irresponsible for refusing to provide the state-mandated support to his former wife and for selling liquor. In Covert's view, the mother and two older sisters had none of the best morals either, for they engaged in questionable relations. The mother was not married to the boys' father; she was still married to her previous spouse, whom she left because of his excessive drinking. One of the sisters, in Covert's assessment, was likely a prostitute because she "bleached her hair or dyed it red [and] use[d] a large amount of paint and ha[d] the appearance of one who tried to appeal to men for questionable purposes."[37]

Albert arrived two years later at the reformatory and worked with Zelda Moss, another fieldworker of the California Bureau of Juvenile Research (CBJR). When it came time for Albert's assessment in 1921, at the age of twelve, Zelda Moss described him as no worse or better than his brothers. Albert's IQ of 0.67, for instance, was only slightly lower than Fred and Tony's and slightly higher than Cristobal's.[38] However, unlike his siblings, Albert was identified as a likely candidate for commitment to a state hospital for the feebleminded. The reasons: His "information [was] poor," wrote Moss, "[he] [d]oes not know [his] birthday, nor birthplace." Moreover, she said, "in conversations he presents an unquestionably feeble-minded attitude. Has childish interests, responses and attitude," all telltale signs of a moron, according to scientific researchers of the day. "In [the] school room," Moss continued, "he learns with difficulty and it is doubtful whether he will retain what little he has learned." To underscore his deficiencies, Moss recorded his difficulties with the English language. "When asked what he wanted to do in the future," wrote Moss, "he replied, 'I want to be a bakery.'" Her findings: Albert "is likely to prove a case for permanent institutional care . . . [and] should be able to do farm work well if placed in a simple environment."[39]

Curiously, while Moss denigrated Albert's abilities, she idealized his physical appearance: "Albert is exceptionally nice-looking for his class," Moss observed, seemingly infatuated. "He has long, wavy black hair; low forehead; black eyebrows, and long eyelashes; dark brown, dreamy eyes; small nose; chiseled lips; small mouth; and good teeth; dimple in chin; round, full cheeks; and normal sized ears. He is small and compact in build." Covert rarely, if ever, used similar language to describe any boys; if anything, the scientific researchers and their informants often used unflattering terms for the feebleminded, describing them as having unusual earlobes, low foreheads, and widely spaced teeth, among other "stigmata" associated with mentally defectives.

Despite the glowing terms she had used to describe Albert's physique, Moss denigrated his intelligence and his family's history of delinquency, feeblemindedness, sexual immorality, and alcoholism. Those traits were, apparently, sufficient for Whittier State School officials, with the consent of the juvenile court, to send him to Sonoma State Hospital where he was accepted and eventually sterilized in 1927, despite his family's opposition. Unfortunately for Albert and his family, California law granted the state discretionary power to override the family's resistance to the procedure, a fact many Californians failed realize.[40]

SEGREGATING, TRANSFERRING, AND STERILIZING DELINQUENT YOUTHS

Albert M.'s sterilization raises two central questions. Why did state officials sterilize Albert but none of his older brothers (Figure 6), even though they too were identified as feebleminded or borderline feebleminded delinquents with poor heredity? And what was it about Albert that led to his sterilization? Ironically, Cristobal had an even lower IQ, yet reform school officials simply paroled him in 1920 and officially discharged him a year later in 1921. That same year, Whittier administrators also paroled his younger brothers, Fred and Tony, and removed them from the reform school's rolls in 1922 and 1924, respectively. Changing attitudes and approaches to dealing with the increasing menace of the feebleminded in California and the larger United States in the late 1910s and early 1920s seem to have led state officials to sterilizing Albert against his family's desires.

Albert M.'s sterilization at Sonoma State Hospital, while unethical and shameful, was not criminal or uncommon among Whittier State School inmates in particular or among children and youths in California in general. Whittier State School case files as well as the authorization or consent forms for the sterilization of patients in California state hospitals indicate that many youths from Whittier State School, the Preston School of Industry, and the California/Ventura School for Girls were sent to state medical institutions from the 1910s through the 1940s and beyond where they were sterilized with or without their families' consent, as allowed by state law. Under California's compulsory sterilization laws, first enacted in 1909 (two years after the first of several dozen sterilization laws were passed around the country), medical superintendents of any state hospital or the resident physician of any state prison, "in consultation with the superintendent of state hospitals and the secretary of the state board of health," had the authority to "asexualize" a patient if it improved their "physical, mental, or moral condition."[41] Four years later, legislators, who found the law too vague, broadened it considerably; they repealed and replaced it in 1913. Alexandra Stern points that under the new statute any inmate "afflicted with hereditary insanity or incurable chronic mania or dementia" could, upon order of the State

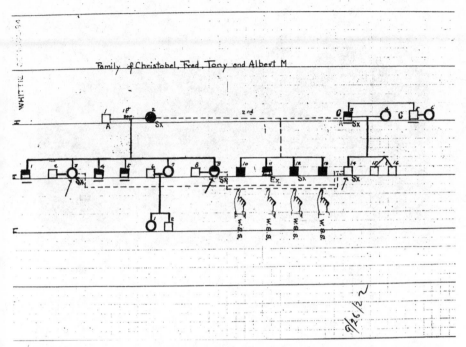

FIGURE 6. Family History Tree. Eugenics fieldworkers completed "family history trees" or charts—such as this one mapping Albert M.'s family history—to map the inheritance of dysgenic traits across three generations. The hands are pointing to Albert M. and his three siblings, all of whom were institutionalized at Whittier State School. Courtesy Eugenics Records Office records, American Philosophical Society Library, Philadelphia, Pennsylvania.

Commission on Lunacy—later, the Department of Institutions—be sterilized with or without their consent.[42]

A few years later, Stern points out, the law was updated again, broadening it even further by removing the "hereditary" requirement. Indeed, the law of 1917 altered the grounds for sterilization from a "hereditary insanity or incurable chronic mania or dementia" to a "mental disease which *may* have been inherited and is *likely* to be transmitted to descendants" or "perversion or marked departures from *normal* mentality or from disease of a syphilitic nature" (emphasis added).[43] Essentially, the new law provided medical superintendents with wide discretion in defining feeblemindedness, perverse behavior, and normal mentality. In short, nearly every patient admitted to a state hospital was a candidate for the procedure. Legislators were likely cognizant of the broad powers bestowed on physicians and thus included provisions protecting the

FIGURE 7. Sonoma State Home. A postcard from the early 1900s shows Sonoma State Home, later renamed Sonoma State Hospital, as it then appeared. In subsequent decades, thousands of patients identified as "defective" or in other ways disabled were sterilized here as allowed under California law, regardless of the patient's or the family's consent. Courtesy Alex Wellerstein, Personal Collection.

doctors against lawsuits and emphasizing the protective—rather than the punitive—nature of the law.[44]

The state law as well as the nationwide promotion of sterilization as the answer to the menace of the feebleminded led to the quickening pace of such procedures in California. The procedures began as a small stream in the 1910s, estimated at a few hundred to no more than 1,000, but they grew into a torrential flood by the 1920s and late 1930s, peaking in 1939, though eventually they would slow in the early 1950s with the rewriting of state laws. Within a few years of the law's third overhaul in 1921, 2,248 patients (among them, Albert M.)—accounting for over 80 percent of all procedures nationwide—had been sterilized in primarily two institutions in California: Sonoma State Hospital (Figure 7) and Stockton State Hospital. Eight years later, the number of patients sterilized nearly tripled to 6,250. In total, from 1909 to 1979, the year legislators finally repealed the law in California, over 20,000 patients were sterilized, accounting for over one-third of the 60,000 sterilized around the country. The per capita rate of sterilization in the Golden State was also among the highest across the nation well into the 1940s.[45]

Albert M. arrived at Sonoma State Home at a time when the pace of sterilization of the unfit—the feebleminded, insane, and disabled, among others—had increased significantly (Tables 13 and 14). A statistical analysis of the children and youths (those aged twenty-one and under) who were sterilized at all state hospitals from 1921 (the earliest date of the authorization forms) to 1940 demonstrates that primarily Sonoma State Hospital and secondarily the Pacific Colony for the Feebleminded in Spadra—established in 1917 and opened in 1927 after many delays—sterilized an increasing number of young people. By 1940, more than half (55 percent) of all youths sterilized in California state hospitals underwent surgery at Sonoma State Hospital; nearly one-fifth (18 percent) ended up at the Pacific Colony in Southern California. The remaining young patients were spread among state hospitals across the state, including Norwalk State Hospital and Patton State Hospital, located in Southern California; Napa State Hospital, Agnews State Hospital, and Mendocino State Hospital, situated in Northern California; and Stockton State Hospital and Camarillo State Hospital, found in Central California. Those places, with the exception of Sonoma and Pacific Colony, focused on mentally ill individuals who had been diagnosed with ailments such as dementia praecox (schizophrenia), manic depression (triggered by various circumstances, apparently including giving birth), psychosis (insanity), epilepsy (believed to induce violence, deteriorate the mind, and lead to greater social ills), sexual perversion (homosexuality), and syphilis (or paresis, a result of syphilis) and those who had disabilities of various kinds, including blindness, deafness, and physical deformities such as clubfeet.[46]

Equally significant as the liberalization of California state sterilization laws in the 1910s were the ideologies and practices of the medical superintendents overseeing the procedures, particularly at Sonoma State Home, where most of the young people were sterilized. Arguably, without the vision of a single figure, Fred O. Butler, the medical superintendent at the Sonoma State Home, it is likely the scale of sterilizations would have been much smaller. When first established in 1884 as the California Home for the Care and Training of Feeble-Minded Children, officials at Sonoma focused on providing children who could not be cared for at home with a warm and supportive environment in which they would be prepared to become useful members of society. Wendy Kline and James W. Trent observe that a shift took place in the approach to dealing with the feebleminded in the early 1900s. Increasingly, superintendents

TABLE 13   STERILIZATION OF YOUTHS (AGE 21 AND UNDER) ACROSS STATE
HOSPITALS, 1921–1940

| Hospital | Years | | | | Total |
	1921–25	*1926–30*	*1931–35*	*1936–40*	
Sonoma	552	686	739	843	2,820
Pacific Colony	0	151	387	371	909
Patton	87	147	206	168	608
Stockton	79	66	40	148	333
Norwalk	33	37	24	53	147
Napa	8	60	70	51	189
Agnews	1	0	49	69	119
Mendocino	1	24	6	4	35
Camarillo	1	0	0	14	15
Total	762	1,171	1,521	1,721	5,175

SOURCE: "Sterilization Authorizations and Related Documents for Patients Admitted to California State Mental Institutions," Department of Mental Hygiene (Health), State of California, Sacramento, California, Reels 114–121 (1921–40).

shifted their focus from protecting their patients to protecting society, for feeblemindedness became more commonly known as an inheritable disease. The popular writing of Herbert H. Goddard, including *The Kallikak Family*, further convinced much of the public of the growing threat of tainted "germ plasm" and inheritance of dysgenic traits. Within a few years, the burden of the feebleminded became the menace of the feebleminded. Despite warnings, William Dawson, the Sonoma State Home superintendent, refused to implement the new law; by 1918, the hospital had sterilized a mere twelve patients. Although he was not opposed to the procedure, Superintendent Dawson believed that sterilization would lead to increased promiscuity and prostitution. Segregation, he believed, was preferred.[47] Dawson's untimely death in 1918 paved the way for his former assistant, Fred O. Butler, an ardent eugenicist, to take over as the medical superintendent and reverse Dawson's policies and practices.[48]

Soon after assuming office at Sonoma State Home, Butler opened the doors to a significant number of patients identified as defective or feebleminded, and he quickened the pace of sterilization. Within a few years, the hospital's population rose by 50 percent, "making it the fastest-growing public institution in the state," according to Wendy Kline.[49] In an interview many years later, Butler confirmed the urgency of his early work:

TABLE 14   STERILIZATION OF YOUTHS (AGE 21 AND UNDER) ACROSS STATE
HOSPITALS (%), 1921–1940

Hospital	Years				
	1921–25	1926–30	1931–35	1936–40	Average
Sonoma	72.0	59.0	49.0	49.0	55.0
Pacific Colony	0	13.0	25.0	22.0	17.5
Patton	12.0	12.5	13.5	9.8	11.7
Stockton	11.0	6.0	2.6	8.5	6.3
Norwalk	4.0	3.0	1.6	3.0	2.7
Napa	0.1	5.0	4.6	2.9	3.5
Agnews	0.1	0	3.0	4.0	2.3
Mendocino	0.1	2.0	0.1	0.1	0.7
Camarillo	0.1	0	0	0.1	0.3

SOURCE: "Sterilization Authorizations and Related Documents for Patients Admitted to California State Mental Institutions," Department of Mental Hygiene (Health), State of California, Sacramento, California, Reels 114–121 (1921–40). The percentages and averages in Table 14 are based on the figures presented in Table 13.

I proposed at our first board meeting, when asked what I had in mind to do for the improvement of mental retardation in California, I said that . . . we should start the program of sterilization. . . . The board approved it providing I got the approval of other departments in Sacramento including the governor. I obtained their approval, and started within three months doing sterilization, with the idea that we would get social service workers to help in planning and training, so by 1919 we were placing patients out, by giving them jobs, or letting them return home after they had been sterilized.[50]

Many applauded Butler's work, including the California State Board of Charities and Corrections and the Commission in Lunacy. National leaders of the eugenics movement hailed the efforts of the Golden State as well. "To California must be given the credit for making the most use of her sterilization laws," said Harry Laughlin, the Eugenics Records Office Superintendent. "The history of the application of these statutes shows an honest and competent effort to improve 'the racial qualities of future generations.'"[51] Many Southerners—public health officials, state hospital administrators, and legislators—acknowledged those efforts, too, using California as a model for their own purposes.[52] Doubtless, Butler felt further reassured with his program with the outcome of the 1927 United States Supreme Court case, *Buck v. Bell*, which ruled that sterilization was an acceptable public health measure to halt the reproduction of "imbeciles." That decision, as Edward J. Larson has found, led to the resurgence of sterilization laws across the country in the late 1920s and 1930s.[53]

Throughout California and around the country, Butler wrote, lectured, and advocated for the sterilization of the unfit, underscoring the benefits to the individual and larger society. Butler, like his contemporary John R. Haynes, a physician and member of the leading eugenics societies, including the American Eugenics Society and Human Betterment Foundation, pushed for the "asexualization" of every patient prior to their discharge, believing it made sense financially and eugenically. Even patients with "normal" intelligence levels, as determined by the IQ scale, did not escape the operating table. The IQ "is not necessarily a criterion to a person's real mental condition but . . . a guide," Butler assured Harry Lutgens, Director of the Department of Institutions in 1936.[54] Rather, the patient's overall health, as determined by the medical superintendent, is what mattered, he said, ensuring him wide latitude in sterilizing patients. In many ways, Butler sold eugenic sterilization as not only a panacea for social ills of nearly every kind but also a restorative or therapeutic procedure beneficial to the defective or diseased body. By the end of his twenty-six year tenure at Sonoma State Home, he had performed 1,000 sterilizations and "supervised a total of fifty-four hundred," more operations than any other medical superintendent in California.[55]

Butler's program of eradicating the menace of the feebleminded included a significant number of youths from different racial and ethnic backgrounds. Authorization forms for sterilization in California state hospitals demonstrate that, although Euro-American or white youth made up the majority of those sterilized, racial and ethnic minorities— namely, Mexicans and Mexican Americans—made up an increasingly disproportionate number or percentage of those patients (Tables 15– 17). In the first half of the 1920s, Mexican-origin youth comprised 15 percent of the young people sterilized in that period; by the second half of the 1930s, the peak of sterilization, they made up 21 percent, a far larger proportion than elsewhere in the state. When other young racial minorities—African Americans, Native Americans, Chinese, Japanese, and Puerto Ricans—are added together with the young Mexican and Mexican American population that was sterilized, the percentage of nonwhite youths increases significantly. As a whole, 25 percent of the youths sterilized at the height of sterilization in the late 1930s were racial and ethnic minorities.

Butler's sterilization campaign targeted boys and girls nearly equally, even though he was increasingly concerned with what he saw as the growing promiscuity among white, working-class females. Wendy Kline argues that Butler's program was aimed particularly at containing the

TABLE 15   STERILIZATION OF YOUTHS (AGE 21 AND UNDER) ACROSS RACE
AND ETHNICITY, 1921–1940

| | Years | | | | |
Race/Ethnicity	1921–25	1926–30	1931–35	1936–40	Total
Mexican	116	187	252	365	920
White	624	979	1239	1270	4,112
Other	15	36	52	68	171
Total	755	1,202	1,543	1,703	5,203

SOURCE: "Sterilization Authorizations and Related Documents for Patients Admitted to California State Mental Institutions," Department of Mental Hygiene (Health), State of California, Sacramento, California, Reels 114–121 (1921–40).

TABLE 16   STERILIZATION OF YOUTHS (21 AND UNDER) ACROSS RACE
AND ETHNICITY, 1921–1940

| | Years | | | |
Race/Ethnicity	1921–25 (%)	1926–30 (%)	1931–35 (%)	1936–40 (%)
Mexican	15.4	15.5	16.4	21.3
White	82.6	81.6	80.3	75.0
Other	2.0	2.9	3.3	3.7

SOURCE: "Sterilization Authorizations and Related Documents for Patients Admitted to California State Mental Institutions," Department of Mental Hygiene (Health), State of California, Sacramento, California, Reels 114–121 (1921–40).

TABLE 17   STERILIZATION OF YOUTHS (AGE 21 AND UNDER), WHITES
AND NONWHITES, 1921–1940

| | Years | | | |
Race	1921–25 (%)	1926–30 (%)	1931–35 (%)	1936–40 (%)
Whites	82.6	81.6	80.3	75.0
Nonwhites	17.4	18.4	19.7	25.0

SOURCE: "Sterilization Authorizations and Related Documents for Patients Admitted to California State Mental Institutions," Department of Mental Hygiene (Health), State of California, Sacramento, California, Reels 114–121 (1921–40).

"female moron." The authorization forms from the 1920s and 1930s demonstrate, however, that the proportion of males to female hovered near 50 percent in the 1920s and 1930s (Tables 18–20), though the figures for female sterilizations likely climbed in the 1940s. Alex Wellerstein also finds that, overall, more males than females were sterilized in California; however, across the country, as Philip Reilly and others argue, more females than males were sterilized after 1928.[56] More significantly, when studying sterilization rates for males and females across racial and ethnic lines, the rates of sterilization for boys and girls of Mexican descent, in particular, increased over time, while those of whites decreased accordingly. The percentage of Mexican girls, for instance, grew from 13 percent in the first half of the 1920s to 20 percent by the late 1930s. Mexican-origin boys also made up a disproportionate percentage of the male inmate population, but their proportion fluctuated over the twenty-year period. In the 1920s, their proportion fell slightly from 17 to 16 percent and then again in the early 1930s to 13 percent, the lowest among any group. Yet within the next five years, those figures rose sharply to 22 percent, a near 10 percent point gain. That jump was likely due, in part, to the growing visibility of young Mexican American youths, particularly the zoot-suit wearing *pachucos* and *pachucas*, whose distinctive dress, language, cultural expressions, and seemingly delinquent and immoral tendencies brought them increased unwanted, unwarranted attention in the late 1930s in the police precincts, the juvenile courts, and the media. That attention culminated in the "zoot suit riots" and the Sleepy Lagoon Trial of the early 1940s. Whatever the precise reasons for the institutionalization and sterilization of these youngsters, it is clear that race and ethnicity played significant roles in criminalizing, racializing, and pathologizing them as defective.[57]

Notwithstanding the significant proportion of young Mexicans and people of color sterilized in California, the numbers of delinquent youths such as Albert M. being sent from state reformatories were far smaller than anticipated by many, among them state reform school administrators. Despite the scientists' and the scientific researchers' descriptions of the delinquent youths identified as "defective" as an ideal population for permanent care and sterilization, the consent forms indicate that only a small number from Whittier State School, Preston, and California/Ventura School were sterilized in the 1920s and 1930s (Table 21).

However, the figures for the sterilization of delinquent youths are higher when the Whittier State School registers and the Sonoma State

TABLE 18   STERILIZATION OF MALE AND FEMALE YOUTHS (AGE 21 AND UNDER),
1921–1940

Gender	Years			
	1921–25	*1926–30*	*1931–35*	*1936–40*
Female	361 (48%)	664 (55%)	794 (51%)	831 (49%)
Male	394 (52%)	538 (45%)	749 (49%)	872 (51%)
Total	755	1,202	1,543	1,703

SOURCE: "Sterilization Authorizations and Related Documents for Patients Admitted to California State Mental Institutions," Department of Mental Hygiene (Health), State of California, Sacramento, California, Reels 114–121 (1921–40).

TABLE 19   STERILIZATION OF YOUTHS (AGE 21 AND UNDER) ACROSS RACE,
ETHNICITY, AND GENDER, 1921–1940

	Years				Total
	1921–25	*1926–30*	*1931–35*	*1936–40*	
Mexican females	48	100	152	169	469
White females	309	547	616	631	2,103
Mexican males	68	87	100	196	451
White males	315	432	623	639	2,009
Total	740	1,166	1,491	1,635	5,032

SOURCE: "Sterilization Authorizations and Related Documents for Patients Admitted to California State Mental Institutions," Department of Mental Hygiene (Health), State of California, Sacramento, California, Reels 114–121 (1921–40).

TABLE 20   STERILIZATION OF MALE AND FEMALE YOUTHS (AGE 21 AND UNDER)
ACROSS RACE AND ETHNICITY (%), 1921–1940

	Years				Average
	1921–25	*1926–30*	*1931–35*	*1936–40*	
Mexican females	65.0	8.5	10.0	10.0	9.0
White females	42.0	47.0	41.0	39.0	42.0
Mexican males	9.0	7.5	7.0	12.0	9.0
White males	42.5	37.0	37.0	39.0	40.0

SOURCE: "Sterilization Authorizations and Related Documents for Patients Admitted to California State Mental Institutions," Department of Mental Hygiene (Health), State of California, Sacramento, California, Reels 114–121 (1921–1940).

TABLE 21   STERILIZATION OF DELINQUENT YOUTHS (AGE 21 AND
UNDER), 1921–1940

Institution	Years				
	1921–25	1926–30	1931–35	1936–40	Total
Whittier	14	15	17	22	68
Preston	9	4	8	4	25
California/Ventura	9	11	12	4	36
Total	33	30	37	26	126

SOURCE: "Sterilization Authorizations and Related Documents for Patients Admitted to California State Mental Institutions," Department of Mental Hygiene (Health), State of California, Sacramento, California, Reels 114–121 (1921–40).

Home admission ledgers are considered as well (Table 22). (Unfortunately, few, if any, equivalent registers exist for Preston and the California/ Ventura School for Girls.) The remaining records show that in the 1910s—a period the consent forms do not cover—through the 1940s, an additional 131 youths from Whittier State School, 26 from the Preston School of Industry, and 9 from the California/Ventura School for Girls were sent to either Sonoma—the only hospital with a locked detention unit—or the Pacific Colony. It is impossible to verify whether these 166 youths were, in fact, sterilized because no consent forms or equivalent evidence remains proving their sterilization. However, Butler's compulsory sterilization program at the Sonoma State Hospital—where the majority ended up—and Preston Superintendent O. H. Close's admission in 1923 that "we have no authority to sterilize [but if] . . . they are sent to Sonoma they are sterilized" suggests strongly that most of these youths eventually faced the operating table as well.[58]

Why, then, were so few of the "feebleminded" delinquent boys or girls sterilized? Why were many of them excluded from such medical procedures when they constituted ideal patients according to the eugenicists? In all likelihood, Superintendent Butler's reputed disdain for delinquents drove him to limit them, when possible, from his institution. Years later, former Whittier State School Superintendent Kenyon Scudder stated that Butler often rejected delinquents as patients, complaining that they were too rowdy, escaped often, and were generally beyond the control of the staff—points that Butler later confirmed as well. Despite Butler's ardent policies and practices for the sterilization of the unfit, feebleminded delinquents proved too unwieldy. Rather than follow through with his eugenic design and run the risk of disrupting his operations at

TABLE 22 TRANSFERS OF DELINQUENT YOUTHS (21
AND UNDER) TO STATE HOSPITALS, 1890S TO 1940S

	Whittier	Preston	California/ Ventura	Totals
Total	131	26	9	166

SOURCE: Sonoma State Hospital, "Register of Applications, 1884–1949,"
9 vols., Sonoma State Hospital Records, Department of Mental Hygiene Records, F3607, California State Archives, Sacramento, California. All names
were double checked against the sterilization authorization forms to ensure
no individual was counted twice.

Sonoma State Home, Butler preferred to exclude them for fear they would antagonize his patients and derail his larger program. As a result, "defective delinquents" were less likely to end up at Sonoma and more likely returned to the juvenile court, along with an explanation of their status as "morons," "too low mentally," or "too defective."

Butler also rejected defective boys on the grounds of overcrowding, explaining that the hospital's waiting list had grown several hundred patients long and could not accommodate the young patients from the reform schools. In some cases, young patients waiting for admittance to the hospital were placed in the care of surrogate parents until they could be accepted. In other cases, would-be admits simply waited until they could be received. Apparently, the increased acceptance of sterilization as a cure-all approach led to the hospital's backlog. Early on, some researchers reported a waiting list of up to 400 to 500 potential patients.[59]

Changing policies and practices of the reformatories also influenced the number of delinquent youths ultimately sent to Sonoma and the Pacific Colony. Whittier State School registers indicate that a significant number of male youths identified as mentally deficient or defective were sent to the Preston School of Industry rather than Sonoma or Pacific Colony for sterilization, for state laws had eased the removal of such boys to places like Ione. According to the 1915 amended juvenile court law of California, the superintendents at Whittier and Preston had the legal right to exchange wards between their institutions at their own discretion and with little oversight from the state, a practice they implemented frequently.[60] Those same administrators could not commit boys to state hospitals so readily, however. A California law passed in 1917 held that superintendents of state reformatories needed a juvenile court judge's permission to transfer minors to state hospitals, and that determination

TABLE 23   STERILIZATION OF DELINQUENT YOUTHS (AGE 21 AND UNDER)
ACROSS RACE AND ETHNICITY, 1921–1940

	Years				
	1921–25	1926–30	1931–35	1936–40	Total
Mexican	7	5.	3	10	25 (19.5%)
White	26	22	33	19	100 (77.5%)
Other	0	1	1	2	4 (3.0%)
Total	33	28	37	31	129

SOURCE: Sonoma State Hospital, "Register of Applications, 1884–1949," 9 vols., Sonoma State Hospital Records, Department of Mental Hygiene Records, F3607, California State Archives, Sacramento, California; and Inmate History Registers, vols. 98–137 (1890–40), Fred C. Nelles School for Boys (Whittier), Youth Authority Records, F3738, California State Archives, Sacramento, California.

could not occur immediately, for the justice also weighed the opinions of the reformatory's board of trustees as well as those of parents and relatives. Ultimately, however, the judge made the final decision.

Rather than rely on this long and complex process to transfer unwanted defective youths to Sonoma or Pacific Colony, Whittier State School Superintendent Fred C. Nelles simply got rid of them by paroling them as soon as they turned sixteen years of age or by sending them to Preston.[61] Paroling defective or otherwise unwanted inmates from Whittier State School or transferring them to Preston produced faster results for the reformatory than segregating them to the state hospitals. Rather than working exclusively toward broader eugenics-based ideas and practices, Nelles preferred to speed the modernization and transformation of his reformatory into a first-class institution by dispensing with those who threatened his program, sending as many boys as possible to Sonoma or the Pacific Colony. Thus, many boys escaped the operating table as a result of bureaucratic delays.

Though relatively few delinquent youths such as Albert M. ended up at state hospitals where they were sterilized, a significant proportion of those young people were nonwhite. Whittier State School case files and the Sonoma State Home admission ledgers indicate that delinquent youths of Mexican origin in particular made up one quarter (25 percent) of all children and adolescents transferred from state reformatories to state hospitals for sterilization. The population of Mexican and Mexican Americans in California, on the other hand, remained far below their proportion at Sonoma State Home, which indicates that youths of Mexican origin—

TABLE 24   TRANSFER OF DELINQUENT YOUTHS (AGE 21 AND UNDER) FROM
REFORMATORIES TO STATE HOSPITALS ACROSS RACE AND ETHNICITY, 1890S
TO 1940S

	Whittier	Preston	California/ Ventura	Total
Mexican	27	4	1	32 (19.3%)
White	95	22	8	125 (75.5%)
Black	7	0	0	7 (4.0%)
Other	2	0	0	2 (1.2%)
Total	131	26	9	166

SOURCE: Sonoma State Hospital, "Register of Applications, 1884–1949," 9 vols., Sonoma State Hospital Records, Department of Mental Hygiene Records, F3607, California State Archives, Sacramento, California; and Inmate History Registers, vols. 98–137 (1890–40), Fred C. Nelles School for Boys (Whittier), Youth Authority Records, F3738, California State Archives, Sacramento, California.

regardless of their IQ—were disproportionately being identified as defective delinquents who were in need of permanent care and sterilization in Sonoma or the Pacific Colony (Tables 23 and 24).

CHALLENGING STERILIZATION AND TAKING ON THE STATE

Albert M.'s institutionalization and eventual sterilization, like that of other youths across the state, did not go unnoticed. His parents, like many others, objected to the procedure and refused to provide consent. However, under California law the family members or legal guardians had little say in the matter; the state—in the form of the medical superintendents of state hospitals in consultation with members of the Commission in Lunacy or the Department of Institutions—had ultimate power to sterilize a patient, a power few Californians understood. In 1940, for instance, near the height of sterilizations, Alfred Urback, a former placement officer at Whittier State School, testified in a statewide investigation into abuse at the reformatory that reform school officials often neglected to obtain permission for the procedure. "I know of cases of enforced sterilization," Urback stated, "in which consent of the parents of the boys forced to undergo operations had not been obtained."[62] Contrary to Urback's beliefs, the medical superintendents, Fred Butler and his staff in particular, did not need the parents' permission, though Butler often made an attempt to ask the parents or guardians for consent. If they objected, Butler made repeated attempts (not just once or twice, but sometimes three times) to gain their consent.[63] Parents and guardians opposed to the procedure sometimes had no choice but to agree, especially when Butler threatened them: he sometimes warned parents and guardians that their loved ones would only be released if they consented to the procedure, a tactic that proved successful and was admired by his peers. According to Paul Popenoe, "Dr. Butler has always had a strong weapon to use in getting consents for sterilization by telling the relatives that the patient could not leave without sterilization."[64]

When Butler or his staff failed to persuade family members to consent, Butler almost always went "above and beyond" for permission. In such instances, he communicated with the director of the Department of Institutions (earlier, the Commission in Lunacy, and later the Department of Mental Hygiene). Butler's requests for familial consent were essentially pro forma because he knew that he—and his staff, who rarely opposed him—had the state's backing and ultimate authority to order and carry out the medical procedure. Butler's attempts to gain permission from family members, some of whom he believed to be morons and feebleminded, were, as Alex Wallerstein has suggested, extra insurance to protect himself and the institution against any future or possible legal action. In fact, John R. Haynes, as a member of the California State Board of Charities and Corrections, a position he held from 1912 to 1923, raised thousands of dollars to build a fund to protect medical superintendents from prosecution.[65] The attempt to gain consent was also an apparent measure of goodwill, though ultimately it was disingenuous and a farce, as Alexandra Stern has argued, for Butler had no intention of releasing inmates without sterilizing them.[66]

Butler's compulsory sterilization campaign was not a one-man production. Rather, he had the support of local institutions and individuals running public and private agencies focusing on public health and welfare. Public health officials, probation officers, and often juvenile court judges were quick to assess youths as feebleminded and to recommend sterilization. When family members objected, local officials used similar rationales (as did Butler) to recommend proceeding with the operation. In one case, a health officer from San Francisco explained one man's opposition to his son's sterilization as evidence of ignorance: "Mr. S. [Benito's father] is, of course, an ignorant, unintelligent Spanish man and it is impossible to convince him of the value of the operation for sterilization either for his son's protection or for that of society."[67]

Despite Butler's promotion of sterilization as an effective prevention, intervention, and treatment program for feeblemindedness as well as a number of other related ailments, his program attracted increasing negative attention, especially in the late 1930s when the pace of sterilizing patients reached an all-time high. The consent forms indicate that few, if any, family members challenged orders for sterilization in the 1920s, but in the next decade the protests increased dramatically. In the 1920s, a mere six families—three Euro-American, two Mexican and Mexican American (among them Albert M.'s), and one African American—refused sterilization. In the 1930s, those figures increased sharply to 115 families of various racial and ethnic backgrounds. They included families of sixty Euro-Americans, forty-five Mexicans and Mexican Americans, five African Americans, two Puerto Ricans, two Chinese, and one Japanese. Many other families also protested the procedure by simply refusing to respond to the written request for consent. When a parent or guardian failed to respond, the state hospitals sent social workers to investigate the home. No doubt some of the families who did not respond had simply moved away or did not have a home where they could be located; others, however, ignored the request in the belief that by doing so their child or nephew or niece would not be sterilized. Among those who ignored the requests were thirty-nine Euro-American, twenty-six Mexican and Mexican American, and six African American families.[68]

Although many families of different ethnic and racial backgrounds refused to provide consent for sterilization, the records indicate that Mexicans and Mexican Americans, such as Albert M.'s family, were among the most likely to refuse. Indeed, the number of Mexican and Mexican American families who protested sterilization (forty-five) came close to that of Euro-Americans (sixty), even though the youths of Mexican origin made up a fraction—22 percent—of those young people sterilized.

The 1927 refusal of Albert M.'s family to provide authorization went largely ignored, as did the nearly all the refusals, even though some were repeated, emphatic denials. Butler's rationale for disregarding the protests of family members was his belief that the parents, like their children, were feebleminded and ignorant of the benefits of sterilization. In commenting on one Mexican family's opposition to the sterilization of their eighteen-year-old son, Butler informed Harry Lutgens, the Director of the Department of Institutions—who had ultimate say in the matter, but rarely opposed Butler or the other medical superintendents—that their ignorance coupled with their low-grade racial stock made it imperative to proceed with sterilization. The boy's mother, he explained to Lutgens in 1936,

> is a native of Mexico. His father is dead. He was also a native of Mexico. They come from a racial stock of Mexicans and Indians. We have written to the mother regarding sterilization and have received three refusals. However, we feel that the refusals were due to ignorance of the importance of such an operation and oweing [sic] to the fact that he has an IQ of only 53, we feel he should have the operation, taking into consideration his criminal tendencies. We therefore request your approval, over and above the three refusals from the mother.[69]

Doubtless, Butler held Albert M.'s family, which Covert and Moss had identified as defective and immoral in some way, in equal disdain. "The relatives of this boy [Albert M.]," he informed the Director, "refused permission for sterilization but we feel he should be [sterilized before release]."[70] Apparently, Butler's request was enough for the state to grant authority for the procedure, for it was carried out without further incident.

It is unclear precisely why Albert M.'s family resisted the procedure—the details of their concerns were not recorded—but many other families of Mexican origin resisted on religious grounds. In 1940, the mother of a Mexican American boy who had been a former inmate at Whittier State School and Preston School of Industry, challenged Butler's efforts to sterilize her son because her Catholicism preached against sterilization. The state had transferred her boy, characterized as a "habitual run-away, [who] practices sex indiscretions," to Sonoma State Home because he "could not adjust" at the reform school, a vague yet commonly used explanation to justify the segregation of delinquent boys to state hospitals. When he was committed, the mother explained that her son had "been a constant source of trouble to her since his father's death in 1930." When she was pressed to sign the consent form to sterilize her son, however, the mother flatly refused, "stating that it [was] against her religion (Catholic)." Butler, however, was undeterred and moved ahead with the planned surgery, noting that the boy's heredity was marred with dysgenic traits. The boy's father had died of tuberculosis, Butler reported, and was a "chronic alcoholic." After discussing the family's resistance during the hospital's regular clinical conference, a monthly meeting with the hospital staff, Butler and his staff agreed to seek permission above and beyond the family's consent. "It was agreed in conference that notwithstanding the mother's refusal he should be sterilized before he elopes [escapes] from the Institution," Butler informed Dr. Aaron Rosanoff, Director of Institutions, in his request for authorization. Presumably that was sufficient to meet the criteria, and the boy was subsequently sterilized.[71]

The families who opposed sterilization on religious grounds received minimal sympathy from Butler or the other medical superintendents. Even the involvement of the Catholic Church, which was vehemently opposed to sterilization in California and around the country, did little to sway state hospital officials or halt the procedures.[72] The grandmother of a nineteen-year-old Mexican American girl learned this lesson in 1935. When Butler asked the grandmother for permission to sterilize her granddaughter, the grandmother went to her local priest to ask for advice. His response: Do not allow it. When she told Butler of her decision, Butler simply ignored her, informing Lutgens, the Director of Institutions, that they would be proceeding without the grandmother's consent because the girl was feebleminded. Shortly thereafter, Lutgens granted Butler permission.[73]

Many Mexican families sought assistance to defend their reproductive rights not only from the Catholic Church but also from the Mexican consulate in Los Angeles, an organization that had long defended the Mexican and Mexican American community in the region. The Mexican consul's office was well known to *mexicanos* in Southern California for protecting their interests during the campaign to repatriate the residents of Mexican origin, including the American-born citizens, during the Great Depression of the late 1920s and early 1930s.[74] In later years, the consulate continued to work for the Spanish-speaking residents; in 1940, it responded to a family's request for assistance in halting the sterilization of their nineteen-year-old Mexican American daughter.

According to the medical doctor at Pacific Colony, where the girl was confined, the girl was "a mental defective, a sex delinquent, [and] an habitual run away" whose parents had no control over her. When they were approached repeatedly for permission to sterilize her, the parents refused. "On numerous occasions," the "operation has been discussed with the mother and father separately, as well as together," Elizabeth Hoyt, the medical doctor at Pacific Colony informed the superintendent, Thomas Joyce. "They have opposed sterilization on religious grounds," Hoyt continued, and they even had sought the assistance of the Mexican consul, who, in turn, had contacted the institution, affirming the parents' resistance. Unfortunately, the Mexican Consulate was misinformed of the parents' legal rights, telling them that the procedure would not take place if they opposed it. Even when the medical officials at the Pacific Colony learned from the family's "spiritual advisor" that "a Mexican boy wished to marry the girl but would not do so if sterilization was done," they moved forward. Doubtless the girl opposed the surgery as well, for the mother informed the physician that "the operation would make [her] crazy."[75] Representatives of the state, however, were not interested in fulfilling personal choices that might compromise or menace the health of the larger society: the girl was sterilized shortly thereafter.

Despite the repeated attempts of families such as Albert M.'s to fight for the reproductive rights of their children and family members, they had a difficult, if not downright impossible, battle against the state. This nearly insuperable challenge was played out in the late 1930s when Sara Rosas García, the mother of a young Mexican American girl identified as feebleminded at Pacific Colony and a candidate for sterilization prior to her release, challenged the constitutionality of Department of Institution's decision and ultimately its right to sterilize her daughter against her consent (the father was no longer living). When García took her case to the lower court, the tribunal ruled against her, prompting her appeal of the case. When she appealed, the Appellate Court upheld the ruling on a technicality, arguing that the case lacked sufficient evidence as grounds for the suit. However, all three justices of the Appellate Court did not agree with that decision. Justice J. White dissented, arguing that the Department of Institutions—an administrative board—wielded too much power in determining a patient's future; he argued that the Department of Institutions violated the "process of law clause of the federal Constitution." The Department of Institutions, in other words, he wrote, "is clothed with absolute unrestricted power to sterilize." He continued:

> In my opinion, the grant of such power should be accompanied by requirements of notice and of hearing at which the inmate might be afforded an opportunity to defend against the proposed operation. To clothe legislative agencies with this plenary power, withholding as it does any opportunity for a hearing or any opportunity for recourse to the courts, to my mind partakes of the essence of slavery and outrages constitutional guaranties [emphasis added].[76]

Notwithstanding Justice White's strong opposition, Pacific Colony, as empowered by the Department of Institutions, proceeded with the girl's sterilization. Not until the 1950s, when lawmakers revamped the sterilization laws, did the number of Californians such as Albert M. who were victimized by the law reduce significantly. In that decade, sterilizations dropped by 80 percent, and by the 1960s, less than half a dozen of the operations were performed.[77]

The experiences of Albert M. and his brothers before, during, and after confinement at Whittier State School demonstrate how changing policies and practices in the network of the juvenile justice system in the early twentieth century worked together in pernicious ways to criminalize, racialize, and pathologize youths of color. Although Albert's older brothers Cristobal, Tony, and Fred were all identified as feebleminded or borderline feebleminded delinquents with a common spurious family history, they managed to avoid sterilization because they were incarcerated at Whittier State School during a period in which state hospitals had not yet fully launched their campaign to sterilize defectives. The youngest sibling was not so lucky. From his early childhood of living with older half-brothers who had been in constant trouble with the local authorities for their youthful indiscretions, to his early teen years of avoiding the same officials for the petty thefts and truancy that he and his siblings committed, Albert M. could not evade the power of the state in the early 1920s.

Albert M. was not alone: thousands of delinquent youths and young people in general in the late nineteenth and early twentieth centuries suffered marginalization, discrimination, and abuse at the hands of powerful authority figures. White, middle-class, urban reformers, science-minded professionals, and Progressives helped shape state policies and practices, thus sealing the fate of children and youths viewed as troublesome social menaces. Progressives believed that defectives, in particular even if they were children, threatened to unravel the fabric of larger society, which was already undergoing significant stress as a result of rapid immigration, urbanization, and industrialization in the nineteenth and early twentieth centuries. Within a few years, youths of seemingly questionable intelligence—particularly ethnic and racial minorities—became ensnared in Progressive reforms of the juvenile justice system, which was intent on bringing order and efficiency in the name of scientific progress, race betterment, and nation building. Progressive policies became a double-edged sword, both figuratively and literally, that wounded and permanently scarred some of the most vulnerable members of society.

Youths at the Preston School of Industry, as the next chapter demonstrates, faced many of the same experiences as the young people at Whittier State School and the California/Ventura School for Girls. Yet in many ways Preston suffered a much more turbulent history, settled only by the appointment of Otto H. Close, perhaps Preston's most well-known superintendent. Chapter 5 examines Close's twenty-five year career at Preston, to permit a nuanced understanding of both the school's sordid past and the benefits gained from the implementation of science and scientific principles in the school's administration. Notwithstanding the improvements at the industrial school in the 1920s, Close's increasing neglect and delegation of his duties to staff turned Preston into a harsh, military-style institution with few opportunities for educational or vocational advancement by the late 1930s, leading it to becoming essentially a prison for juvenile offenders.

CHAPTER 5

Otto H. Close

Promising Leader, Complacent Bureaucrat

In 1920, Otto H. Close, a principal at San Juan High School in Sacramento, California, pondered a difficult decision: whether to leave his post and accept a job as superintendent at the beleaguered Preston School of Industry in Ione, a state reformatory for males between the ages of eight and twenty-one, situated about 40 miles southeast of Sacramento. After a sustained series of crises in leadership in the late 1910s and years of mismanagement and overcrowding at Preston, state officials tapped Whittier State School Superintendent Fred C. Nelles in 1920 to find the school a suitable leader. After interviewing many candidates, Nelles approached Close on the recommendation of J. Harold Williams, Whittier State School's psychologist and the director of the California Bureau of Juvenile Research. Close's belief in vocational education and his training in education at Stanford University, where he and Williams had first met, made him an ideal choice. Content with his job and with no experience in corrections, Close declined the offer. Undeterred, Nelles convinced Close that, as an educator and a citizen, he should visit the school and make any recommendations. Apparently the visit and the prospect of transforming the school impressed him: three weeks later, he agreed to take on the work, chalking it up to divine intervention. Close knew little, however, of what was in store for him.[1]

When Close finally arrived as superintendent at Preston, he encountered a host of long-standing troubles. Unlike Whittier State School, which was at the height of its scientific research program, Preston lacked basic necessities, including the buildings, housing, and equipment necessary to maintain properly an industrial school. Preston also suffered from a lack of leadership. Since the school's doors had opened in 1891, continuous turnover among administrators and staff as well as charges of physical and moral cruelty had marred the school's reputation. Close had to contend with other inherited scandals as well. The school's weak and ineffectual parole system was another concern because the school had infrequently monitored its parolees. For years, Preston had languished in the shadow of Whittier's nationally and internationally acclaimed program, which had left Preston to become a dumping ground of sorts for the unwanted, incorrigible, and older boys from Whittier and the juvenile courts around the state.

Notwithstanding those challenges, Close overhauled Preston's administration and daily activities as well as its public image within the first few years of his tenure. Under Nelles's mentorship, Close reinstated and transformed the outdated military-based discipline and routine as well as the haphazard nature of the scientific research that had been carried out in previous years, enabling him to implement a segregation program similar to the one in use at Whittier. In time, a significant number of the youngsters labeled feebleminded or morons were sent to Sonoma State Home for the Feebleminded or the Pacific Colony for the Feebleminded. A disproportionate number of them were youths of color or racial minorities—Mexicans, Mexican Americans, and African Americans. Despite its transfer program, weak state support plagued Preston, hampering its vocational programs. In the succeeding decades, the initial enthusiasm for Close's administration at Preston waned, which left the reformatory to become a largely ineffectual program, doing little more than housing youths in a prisonlike environment.[2]

This chapter examines the sordid trajectory of one of the Golden State's earliest and most notorious reformatories, the Preston School of Industry, with Otto H. Close's twenty-five year career in California's early juvenile justice system as a focus. It begins by tracing the reform school's early history, from its foundation in the 1890s through Nelles's takeover in 1920, focusing on the school's difficulties with securing adequate facilities, the highturn over among its administrators, the excessive punishments and sexual assaults, and its failure at self-government. Next, we will examine the ways in which Close—with Nelles's mentorship— transformed the institution in the 1920s, paying close attention to how he secured the confidence of the staff and inmates. We will look at the scientific program he instituted and how it affected the lives of delinquent youths, particularly the Mexicans, Mexican Americans, and African Americans identified as defective. Finally, the chapter discusses how, despite the promising outlook for Preston in the 1920s and early 1930s, the place stagnated by the late 1930s, becoming a military-style penitentiary with little vocational training or education provided to young inmates. At the root of the school's decline were administrative complacency, state neglect, and scant public support. By the early 1940s, leading officials in juvenile corrections agreed that Preston and the entire juvenile correctional system were overdue for a new administration and a new vision for the treatment of youthful offenders, which led to Close's removal in 1945. By then, it was clear that what had once been a ray of hope for new leadership had transformed into negligent care for some of the Golden State's most troubled male youths.

CLOSE'S ENCOUNTER WITH THE DEPRESSING KIND: THE EARLY YEARS AT PRESTON

When Otto H. Close arrived at Preston in 1920, he found a neglected facility largely in disrepair and a disorganized staff that was split over leadership, methods of discipline, and day-to-day policies and practices for dealing with the inmates. Among the most noticeable aspects of Preston were the overcrowded conditions and the lack of facilities to house the youths in buildings according to their ages and offenses, a system of segregation established at many reformatories and industrial schools throughout the United States.[3] The insufficient housing was not a recent development at Preston; rather, it dated to the early days of the school's establishment. Indeed, the Board of Trustees, which took over the institution's governance from the Board of Prison Directors (which originally had administered Preston) had made repeated requests to complete and expand the school to meet the growing needs of the region; however, when the first inmates arrived at Preston in 1894 after two years of delay, they found most of the buildings were unfinished with the exception of those devoted to the administration and to trades education. Superintendent E. Carl Bank, a former reform school administrator from the East Coast hired in 1892, echoed the board's urgency, adding that Preston filled an important role in the state by caring for and controlling the increasing number of abandoned and unwanted young males. Because these youngster had limited supervision at home, Bank stated, they took the opportunity to run rampant on the streets, engaging in petty crimes and disrupting the larger community.[4] The local authorities, in turn,

would pick up the most rowdy, haul them into the police court or before a justice of the peace, then either return them home on probation
or send them to a private or religious institution. It was when no one
could care for them or control them any longer that they would end up
at Whittier State School or Preston. In cases where youths had committed a crime punishable with life imprisonment or death, they would end
up one of the two state prisons, San Quentin (1850) or Folsom (1880).

Conditions at Preston improved little, despite Bank's requests to expand the school to accommodate future inmates. Superintendent Bank
insisted that the school needed additional funds for a dining room, com-
missary building, hospital, powerhouse, and a double cottage. Designed
to house relatively small groups of boys along similar ages and background
in each unit, the double cottage was, nevertheless, a compromise on the
cottage plan envisioned at the school's founding. Yet that unit, Bank said,
would be cheaper to construct and maintain than two separate buildings.[5]
All these improvements, Bank wrote in his report in 1894, deserved attention, despite the popular belief that reform schools were nothing more
than schools of crime. "The percentage of those reformed is large . . ."
Bank argued, "a fact which is now known by actual experience and observation, and proven by statistics" (though he provided no such figures).
"The good which is accomplished cannot be estimated and the saving to
the State cannot be calculated in figures." He continued, "There is no more
worthy charity—there can be no better investment."[6] To combat the prem-
ise that Preston was nothing more than a prison for juveniles, he reiterated,
"punishment does not form any part of the scheme."[7]

Bank's speech, though eloquent, did little to move the hearts or pock-
etbooks of bureaucrats at the state's capital. Rather, the legislature appropriated limited funds every few years and passed the responsibility
of constructing the school on to the administrators, who in turn placed
it on the backs of the imprisoned youths, who over the course of a few
years made thousands of bricks and constructed many of the buildings
at the reformatory. Preston officials felt no qualms about putting the
youths to labor, remarking it afforded "practical education," though it
was more akin to slave labor. In fact, for several decades, the boys carried
out many of the school's construction projects, including the first of two
cottages completed in 1911.[8]

Nearly twenty years after Bank's appeal, by the time Otto H. Close
came on board in 1920, he had to confront not only the long-standing
problems of insufficient housing, infrastructure, and funding at Preston,
but also the inconsistent staffing and leadership as well as the internal

conflicts and controversies over corporal punishment and physical and sexual abuse. These difficulties had led to the replacement of five superintendents within a twelve-year period.[9] The first superintendent, Carl Bank, had faced a series of public scandals when he was accused of extravagance, autocratic methods, and "undue severity" with the inmates. Staff members who opposed his tactics told the press that boys at Preston led bleak lives. Only a handful of boys, the staff charged, received any industrial training; instead, the majority spent long hours at chores, often with little to eat. Bank took the critiques in stride, noting that disaffected staff, the attacks on management, and the investigation by the legislature were "a common experience for a new public institution." Rather, he assured the public, relations between the staff and the inmates were "very pleasant." Bank's spin on internal affairs notwithstanding, he was forced to give up the position in 1896.[10]

The succeeding superintendent, E. S. O'Brien, faired no better. In fact, his tenure was worse than Bank's and was characterized by mismanagement and abusive practices. As soon as he arrived, the *Los Angeles Times* reported in 1897, nineteen staff members resigned in protest, and about half a dozen of boys escaped with the help of disgruntled staff.[11] The departure of those employees did little to ease tensions; the remaining staff, the Board of Trustees, and the superintendent wrangled over internal matters, including the treatment of inmates. Several staff members claimed O'Brien paddled boys into "insensibility and until blood ran down their backs." At times, he also reportedly rubbed "salt into the lacerated flesh to add to the intensity of the pain." The *Los Angeles Times* called for an end to such practices, for "radical reform or abolishment of the school." Before any of that could happen, O'Brien resigned—prior to completing his first year in office.[12]

O'Brien's successor, D. S. Hirschberg, who emphasized military discipline and strict conformity, lasted only slightly longer at two years. He too was accused of abusing youths and of allowing abuses by staff to continue unabated. Thomas B., a Euro-American youth, spent four years at Preston during Hirschberg's administration from 1901 to 1905; years later, he told researcher Dexter A. Clement that the Preston administrators used the lash in its various manifestations. One instrument, he recalled, was a large table-tennis paddle soaked in water, which was used to strike the boys. Another was a "cat-o-nine tails," a whip of nine strands, each ending in a knot. Thomas also said that school officials would punish boys for breaking minor rules, including talking to girls while the school's band was on a trip—an offense for which a boy received five lashes. An escape from Preston, considered among the gravest offenses, would result in "ten lashes per day for ten days plus confinement in the administration building (the Castle) tower in a cell for those ten days." Inmates also faced punishment for talking after 9:00 in the evening and smoking on the grounds, transgressions for which they would receive one to ten lashes. In extreme cases, Thomas B. said, recalcitrant boys at the school were "handcuffed to an iron rig set in the cement cutting across the road from the Administration building," a practice that continued until 1917.[13]

Hirschberg not only condoned the physical beating of inmates but also did relatively little to check heinous sexual practices. When Hirschberg first arrived at Preston in 1898, the reformatory had only one bathroom for use by all boys, "an evil" that "required no expert to discover," he admitted. To deal with the problem, he allocated funds for the building of a second water closet or bathroom in the company or unit for the younger boys. To minimize contact between older and younger boys—and, at the same time, decrease the sexual assaults—Hirschberg also oversaw the construction of two double cottages that would hold "families" of fifty boys with similar ages and backgrounds. The goal was to segregate inmates and keep them in their own sleeping quarters, schoolrooms, and playgrounds, thus minimizing socialization among youths of varying levels of maturity. The new facilities—and subsequent cottages built in later years—provided little real change. A couple of years after his arrival at Preston, the *Los Angeles Times* and *Sacramento Bee* reported that seven boys at Preston had assaulted another boy, presumably in a sexual attack, leading to his hospitalization. According to the *Los Angeles Times*, such assaults occurred frequently at Preston. "Older boys run the school," the paper reported, "debauching the younger ones and making it a school of crime and degeneracy." Some boys also became victims of sexually transmitted diseases contracted at the school, the newspaper continued. For the lack of oversight in the assault against the young boy, Hirschberg was charged with neglect. The *Sacramento Bee* also alleged that sodomy was practiced regularly at Preston, right "under the nose of the superintendent" who did little to stem it. According to John F. Lafferty, the latter news article "caused a storm of protests," leading to Hirschberg's resignation.[14]

Following Hirschberg's departure, C. B. Riddick, a strict disciplinarian, assumed the post and implemented changes quickly, earning him a solid reputation in the press. His accomplishments included the construction of a cottage and separate school for the youngest boys who were viewed as potential victims—namely, for sexual assault—of the older and stronger boys at the reformatory. Riddick's tenure, though generally favorable, was brief: he lasted only a year longer than Hirschberg and left office in 1903 for reasons that remain unclear. The rapid turnover of administrators slowed, however, when the Board of Trustees hired William T. Randall for superintendent. Randall, a medical doctor, was praised in the press and official reports for his work, but he too left the school after only six years. When he departed in 1909, he had lasted longer than any other superintendent at Preston, though few details of his administration remain. C. H. Dunton, a businessman and long-time member of the Preston Board of Trustees, followed Randall, functioning as the interim superintendent until a suitable replacement could be found.

Despite his temporary position, Dunton overhauled the school and made changes that few of his predecessors had been willing to make. To deal with overcrowding, he released nearly a hundred of the four hundred boys, an unprecedented number of inmates. The recent surge in the population at Preston had occurred as a result of the age limit (fifteen years) on new admits to Whittier State School, which had forced Preston to absorb the inmates of sixteen years and older who were no longer eligible for Whittier. Dunton held the office no more than three years; state officials replaced him in 1912 with Calvin Derrick, a nationally known and experienced reform school administrator.[15]

Like Fred C. Nelles's appointment at Whittier State School that same year, Calvin Derrick's hire came directly from Governor Hiram Johnson's office. Both Governor Johnson and Reverend Rennison, a member of the Board of Trustees, pledged their support for Derrick, who supported many of the same Progressive methods used to reform wayward and troublesome youths. As the former superintendent of the George Junior Republic at Freeville, a well-known institution founded by William R. George, Derrick had managed an innovative and successful plan of self-government—a program that allowed inmates to administer part of the institution. In light of previous administrations, Derrick's appointment held the greatest promise for Preston, as Close recalled years later in an oral interview, because it brought national attention to the fledgling industrial school.[16] Derrick's tenure at Preston, though promising in some ways, lasted but a few years. State officials in New York offered him a prestigious post at Sing Sing Prison, which he accepted.

Even during Derrick's administration, which boasted enlightened Progressive policies, erring boys, particularly those who escaped, could not avoid punishment. Like at Whittier State School in its early years, some of the harshest punishments awaited youths who escaped or attempted to escape from Preston. Boys who went AWOL (absent without leave) during Derrick's administration received up to thirty lashes, according to the *Sacramento Bee* in 1915, with a whip or sap measuring thirty inches in length and two and half inches wide, an instrument that reportedly "ripped open" the "flesh of young boy inmates."[17] Years later, Kenyon Scudder, an employee during Derrick's administration, said that the sap also had a "black handle with a leather wrist thong . . . so it could be swung with both arms with terrific force."[18] As he recalled, the use of that instrument was nothing short of torture. On one occasion while Scudder was away, his wife—who lived with him at Preston in a room situated above the basement in the main building—overhead a lashing and the "screams of pain" coming from the basement where escapees and disciplinary cases were kept. She "felt sick with horror and fright," Scudder said. "She could hear them [the boys] begging him [the detail officer] not to strike again. It had been terrible."[19] The lash "was supposed to break the lad's spirit," yet, Scudder admitted, it was largely ineffective in deterring bad behavior.[20]

Punishments proved so heinous during Derrick's administration that it led Frank C., an Italian American boy, to commit suicide in 1917. In a suicide note he left for his mother, Frank wrote: "I did six months in Preston and I nearly died of the beatings they gave me. There is a little bad in every woman and every man and you know [mother] that I told [juvenile court] Judge Murasky I was sick and needed treatment and wanted to go to the state hospital at Stockton. What more did he want?" "They ought to investigate that school [Preston]," he implored. "Where is your Society for the Prevention of Cruelty to Children? Why don't they investigate?" He continued, "They say [the school] is good, but it isn't. I learned all the clever stuff about robbery, burglary and crime in the Preston School of Industry—Preston School of Ruination."[21] Frank's suicide and his suicide note, though indicting the policies and practices at the school and larger juvenile justice system, brought little attention to the reformatory and led to few changes. Instead, the state attributed Frank's death to mental illness beyond their control.

Boys at Preston during Derrick's administration not only had to contend with excessive abuse from officers but also from peers who took advantage of the weak and powerless. Such was the experience of many boys during Derrick's self-government plan, which he touted taught "self restraint, obedience, manliness, and good citizenship."[22] When Derrick first introduced the self-government program at the reformatory, Governor Hiram Johnson supported it, though many others questioned the use of such an approach with "much older . . . more seriously delinquent" youths at Preston than those found at the George Junior Republics around the country, where the plan of government was originally implemented.[23] Self-government was essentially the ability of groups of inmates or companies to elect their own governing body, including a president, legislators, and justices, and to draft a constitution and pass their own laws as well as to prosecute those who committed infractions and pass sentencing. Eventually four companies of boys at Preston adopted the plan, though one later discarded it, and the remainder joined as a union, holding a convention where they pledged allegiance to the Preston School Republic. In time, Scudder, as the resident psychologist, observed that self-government became quite sophisticated, especially when the reform school boasted "two houses of parliament, several chiefs of polices, judges, a chief justice, and all nine members of the supreme court."[24]

Initially, self-government proved successful and drew much enthusiasm and applause from the public and politicians alike, including Governor Hiram Johnson who visited the school pledging his support.[25] Within a few years, however, self-government became an elaborate and complex system in which a few individuals had much of the power, making the system vulnerable to graft and kickbacks. The president, for instance, had wide latitude in government, for he oversaw the cabinet and committees, led the military, appointed all officers and commissions, issued pardons and reprieves, made all proclamations, and had the veto power on all laws passed by the congress.[26] Some boys were "imprisoned" in the makeshift prison the boys devised or punished in other ways by the senior members of the republic. Though the program spiraled out of control and corruption invaded the cadet-run government, the administration lauded it in the biennial reports, claiming it functioned as a useful method for "social re-education," allowing young males to reenter society as educated, civic-minded, manly citizens. For his own part, Derrick had little reason to heed the growing concerns at Preston, for he was on his way to a more prestigious position at Sing Sing Prison in New York, leaving J. L. Montgomery, a member of the Board of Trustees, in his stead. Montgomery could not muster the forcefulness for overseeing the self-government plan. Within the year of Derrick's departure in 1918, the Board of Trustees ended the program, calling it a failure.[27]

Abusive practices not only characterized the self-government plan under Derrick's administration but also the policies on AWOL. Boys who escaped or attempted to escape faced the real possibility of death:

Derrick allowed guards to use firearms to hunt down those who absconded. In 1917, for instance, officers wasted little time in pulling their guns to stop an escapee in his tracks. In December, reported the *Los Angeles Herald*, a boy "escaped from the institution and [gave] a sensational chase in which he swam a swiftly-flowing, snow-fed river three times in one night and ran from two officers who were shooting at him while he ran." Notwithstanding the flying bullets, "he escaped and ha[d] never been heard from since."[28]

Apparently the practice of arming guards and shooting at inmates continued at Preston following Superintendent Derrick's departure in 1918. Assistant Superintendent J. L. Montgomery, who had taken over the school's helm temporarily, was later permanently administering the school in 1919 when a guard shot and killed Samuel G., an African American boy who had escaped along with another boy. The shooting death and multiple state investigations into the matter—including the Board of Trustees' censure of the "inexcusable" event—brought the school to a breaking point, according to Kenyon Scudder. Without Derrick's strong personality to administer the school and the staff, Preston began to "crumble," Scudder recalled. "The boys," he said, "were restless and disturbed" and "a depressing atmosphere" shrouded the school. The onset of World War I, Superintendent Montgomery's frequent departures, and the Board of Trustees' clashes with Montgomery over the use of corporal punishment also added much anxiety and strain to the school. Some boys, for instance, clamored to leave the reformatory, and several went AWOL to join the war effort, while staff worried about the draft and also considered resigning their posts to enlist voluntarily. Samuel G.'s death, the controversy over the use of corporal punishment, and the strain on the school eventually sent Superintendent Montgomery packing—it had been uncovered that he was away from the institution when the shooting death occurred. Following Montgomery's departure, Scudder, his temporary assistant, was left in charge until a suitable replacement could be found. When the Board of Trustees offered Scudder the permanent position, he refused, citing inexperience. In all likelihood, Scudder's reluctance stemmed from his unwillingness to take on the troubles plaguing the school, which he witnessed firsthand.[29]

With few options available for Preston's leadership, the Board of Trustees called on former Superintendent E. Carl Bank to resume his old post, for he reportedly "never experienced any trouble in handling the boys" during his tenure at Preston decades earlier, despite media reports to the contrary. Bank, believing it would be a relatively easy appointment, accepted the board's offer, not realizing that the school's population had changed dramatically from the 1890s. Rather than dealing with fifty or so boys, as he did in the 1890s, in the late 1910s he had to contend with nearly 500 boys. A few months into his administration, Bank was unable to meet the challenges under the new rules, which included the banishment of corporal punishment, a move the Board of Trustees had spearheaded, fought, and won after the widely publicized scandals had emerged on the severe treatment of some boys. Scudder reported that when the boys learned that the school had abolished such punishment, "pandemonium followed. Without orders, they [the boys] broke ranks, shouting and surging toward the box [officials]. Caps were thrown into the air. They crowded around, a chattering mob, trying to express its feelings."[30] When Bank attempted to reinstitute the lash, the paddle, and other tools and techniques to punish inmates, Governor William Stephens and a member of the Board of Trustees reprimanded him and others who supported its use.[31] Not satisfied, Bank subscribed the services of J. B. Sears, a professor of education at Stanford University, to investigate—and justify—the merits of punishment at the school. Not surprisingly, Sears concluded that it would be wise to use "in extreme cases, after other means have been tried and have failed."[32] Notwithstanding those findings, the governor and his supporters refused to allow it, and the board issued a formal resolution in 1920 abolishing the practice, leading Bank, in turn, to hand in his resignation in protest.[33]

CLEANING UP PRESTON SCHOOL OF INDUSTRY

Without leadership at Preston and in a state of crisis, the State Board of Charities and Corrections, the agency responsible for the oversight of state reformatories, stepped in and called on Fred C. Nelles to fill in as interim superintendent and to find an ideal candidate for taking command at the Preston School of Industry, no small feat given the school's history.[34] After speaking with and interviewing nearly two-dozen candidates, Nelles pursued Otto H. Close at the recommendation of J. Harold Williams, the psychologist at Whittier State School and director of the California Bureau of Juvenile Research (CBJR). Close was an ideal candidate, Williams argued, because he had extensive experience in education and vocational trade training, though much of it was with adults and not with delinquent youths. Close, who initially balked at Nelles's request, finally agreed to take on the challenge, reportedly deciding with his wife that they had a "higher" spiritual calling in taking the position, which was forty miles away yet a world apart from what he had known.

When Close finally arrived in 1920, he encountered an impressive, prisonlike environment. According to Kenyon Scudder, who spent a few years there prior to Close's tenure, Preston was a "barren . . . old-school prison type" in need of "repair. Built in 1893, [it] represented a type of architecture long discarded. Institutions, in those days, were built on the theory that all should be housed in one building. . . ." However, "the institution had long outgrown the main building and now spread itself over the hill and down the surrounding slopes, but the old building still housed two companies of cadets, and most of the personnel."[35] Along with having to contend with outdated buildings, Close had to deal with incompetent, restless staff, many of whom were poorly educated and unprofessional. "They were apt to be sadistic, slovenly individuals, and quick to use harsh discipline," Close recalled years later. He could not, however, fire them, for he had no competent candidates willing to replace them. Apparently, not all personnel at the reformatory faired so poorly. The school had many dedicated men and women, Close explained in his memoir, local recruits—many of them related by kinship—who worked hard and honestly, and he used them to develop a core of reliable personnel at the school, though they too generally lacked training and education.[36]

As Close learned quickly, implementing new policies and practices, particularly the ban on corporal punishment, and gaining the trust of his employees were difficult. Even after the Board of Trustees and the governor endorsed the ban, employees as well as administrators continued to carry out abusive practices. In the late 1910s and early 1920s, for instance, the staff and the public feared many of the boys, so they treated the youths harshly, apparently to gain and maintain the upper hand.[37] Soon after arriving at Preston, Close had to deal harshly with a guard who had abused a boy excessively for escaping. "A Mexican lad," Close reported, "just at dark, broke and ran from a line of boys and was caught by an officer just as he was about to go through a barbed wire fence. When the boy was brought to the detail office, I saw him. He had a gash in the back of his head." Close was suspicious. "I measured the length of the gash . . . [and] I called the officer to my office and asked to see his pistol. (Some of the group supervisors at that time carried pistols, a practice that we later stopped.)" He recalled, "The length of the butt of the pistol was the same as the cut on the Mexican lad's head. The officer at first denied hitting the boy, but later when confronted with all the facts admitted it. He was discharged for unnecessary brutality and rough-ness, but made threats of retaliation through his political friends." The guard apparently never followed through, for Close remained at Pres-ton for many years.[38]

Close also had to contend with the critical opinions and commentaries of the public and political establishment. Many members of the local com-munity clamored for the construction of a fence around the reformatory—which was originally built on an open plan—to stop escapees. Prevent-ing escapes, Close later admitted, especially with the population of six to seven hundred inmates in the 1920s, was nearly impossible—they always had about twenty-five to fifty boys who went AWOL.[39] Local residents also called into question the vocational training of delinquents, believing it was neither "useful [n]or relevant." Instead, they felt the boys should suf-fer for their crimes: "Life should be unpleasant and distasteful . . . in order to make the stay in the institution as uncomfortable as possible."[40] Pres-ton's visitors, both private citizens and state officials, held similar views about who was worthy of receiving state-funded aid. When they saw the training and housing provided to Preston boys, they remarked it was su-perior to that of boys in their communities and accused the school of ex-travagance and pampering "bad boys."

Close not only battled with locals and politicians, he also struggled with the state to gain much needed resources. Nowhere was this more apparent to Close than with medical care. The school reportedly lacked sufficient medical doctors for even the minor care of the youths. When the State Board of Charities and Corrections investigated Preston's med-ical facilities in 1920 after allegations of medical neglect, the Board re-ported, "with regret it must be stated that the medical care and treatment of the boys in the school is at a low ebb." The school, for instance, failed to isolate or treat boys with venereal infections and allowed "young, untrained boys to puncture veins and give vaccines," presumably to other boys.[41]

The scientific research program at Preston also lacked attention, es-pecially as compared with the one at Whittier State School. At Whittier in Southern California, state leaders supported the establishment of the Department of Research, which later became the CBJR, and they allowed for the hire of leading psychologists as well as eugenics fieldworkers from across the country to study "problem" children and youths. Re-searchers at Preston, on the other hand, carried out similar scientific stud-ies but did so on a smaller scale and kept their findings to the institution. During Calvin Derrick's tenure, for instance, he launched a modest yet

seemingly respected program of science and scientific research at Preston
to develop effective prevention, intervention, and treatment programs for
delinquent youths, many of whom he—as well as his contemporaries—
believed were feebleminded or mental defectives. Doubtless, Derrick derived his assumptions about Preston's population from the proliferation of
national and international studies on delinquency and criminality, many
of them with ties to eugenics ideas and ideologies, which documented the
relationship between antisocial behavior and mental deficiency. Using the
then current estimates of defective persons in criminal institutions around
the United States, Derrick guessed in the late 1910s that, among the current population at Preston of 400 inmates, they had at least 20 percent (80
boys) of inmates identified as normal, 60 percent (240 boys) subnormal
and mentally defective, and 20 percent (40 boys) vicious and incorrigible.
Derrick admitted that his estimate was not based on science or "scientific
segregation" but rather was an educated guess of what they would find
once they carried out investigations. If the boys were segregated along age,
offense, and mental capability, he observed, training and results at the reformatory would be more effective than what they had.[42]

Derrick was not alone in his estimation of the proportion of mentally
defective youths at Preston. The parole officer also believed that feeblemindedness was rampant at Preston and that it affected the boys' ability
to succeed while on parole. "The tendency [of the courts] is to send us
a great many who are weak minded. Our feeble-minded institutions
are over-crowded, and as boys who are weak mentally, are easily made the
tools of crafty criminals, we are receiving a very large percentage of these,
who, while in some ways are more easy to manage, are most difficult to
prepare for citizenship, where they are expected to be economically independent."[43] Most such boys, he said, could not find a job when paroled.
"I feel free," he said, "in saying that at least 25 per cent of the boys in
Preston School are away [sic] below the normal, mentally." Boys paroled
from George Junior Republic, he said, in contrast, found success after
their stint in the reformatory. Those institutions, the George Junior Republics, had a choice of inmates, the parole officer explained, saying, they
"will not accept the moral pervert, the mental weakling, and the criminally insane." Preston, he said, "must accept what is sent to us and do the
best we can."[44]

To identify and separate what they called "harmless" boys from "vicious" delinquents, Derrick collaborated with the University of California, offering residential fellowships to graduate students interested in
working in a "real-life laboratory" and with delinquent boys in state

custody.[45] Derrick especially wanted the student researchers to explore "sex irregularity, as expressed in unnatural crimes as sodomy or masturbation."[46] Derrick, like many of his contemporaries, held that sexual deviance—in this case, defined primarily through homosexuality—was a dysgenic trait and an expression of mental deficiency. In fact, sexual "perversion" or engaging in an immoral sex act with another ward was considered among the most offensive transgressions.[47] To carry out his plan, Derrick hired three researchers from Berkeley in the fall of 1913 to carry out the work. Shortly after arriving, they tested the boys using Herbert Goddard's Revision of the Binet-Simon Measuring Scale of Intelligence (rather than Lewis Terman's Stanford Revision, for reasons that remain unclear). Fred Allen, one of the researchers, tested 100 newly committed boys and found that only 25 percent were normal, while the remaining 75 percent was in some way backward or defective, findings similar to those later identified by J. Harold Williams at the CBJR. The outcome of the testing was likely not surprising and confirmed many of their suspicions about the link between mental deficiency and delinquency, for they believed that mental defectives, particularly "the moral imbecile, the sexual pervert, and the incorrigible defective," required segregation.[48] Further testing of those same boys revealed that a significant proportion—37 percent—were feebleminded. Using those results, they posited that nearly 30 percent of the current larger population of Preston—which had yet to be tested—was likely defective, too. H. H. Herrick, another of the young researchers, went further in guessing that all boys at Preston likely fell into one of three groups: the normal boys estimated at 23 percent of the population, the mentally and morally weak at 48 percent, and the hopelessly morally depraved and vicious at 29 percent.[49]

The scientific research under Derrick's administration, though limited, proved sufficiently productive to be continued for the next two years. By 1915, Fred Allen had tested 588 boys to probe deeply the relationship between delinquency and feeblemindedness. Allen's group of boys was not a randomly selected scientific population, he admitted, for it included fifty boys who had been chosen for their apparent "marked mental deficiency," though exactly what criteria he used is unclear.[50] Despite that bias, Allen found that "the middle and high grade morons constitute a very heavy percentage" of the population at Preston.[51] Indeed, about 63 percent of the boys were scored at the ten- and eleven-year level, indicating feeblemindedness—which suggested that most of these boys had little reasoning or judgment, making them susceptible to delinquent and other immoral tendencies. Their high- and middle-grade status made them even more dangerous, the researchers noted, for they were able "to cover up their true mental condition by the glib use of language." The ability to "pass" made the high- and middle-grade feebleminded particularly menacing to society, scientific researchers argued—including Henry H. Goddard, a leading proponent of the testing movement—because such people could easily marry and reproduce defectives, who would in turn taint and ultimately undermine a well-ordered society. In contrast to the high- or middle-grade defectives, the "lower" types of feebleminded were more easily identifiable and more likely to be segregated in an institution prior to embarking on any delinquent careers. The early identification of most lower grade defectives helped to explain, the researchers reasoned, why few of them appeared at the school. Yet, they noted, it remained critical to test and remain vigilant of the borderline feebleminded persons, for their degeneracy was not fully evident or expressed but dangerous nonetheless.[52]

The researchers' findings at Preston seemed to prove what many in the scientific community—including Fred C. Nelles, J. Harold Williams, Lewis Terman, and eventually O. H. Close—suspected: a direct link between feeblemindedness and delinquency. Soon after the researchers publicized their findings in the late 1910s, the *Sacramento Bee* published an article on their work: "Twenty Per Cent of Ione Boys Normal." By default, then, the remaining 80 percent was subnormal in varying degrees. "The average age" of the boys, the *Bee* reported, "is 17 and average mental age is eleven, the educational standing being equivalent to the fifth or sixth grade in the public school." A great majority of Preston boys, the investigations suggested, lacked the capacity to mature beyond the age of young school children and necessitated close attention and supervision.[53]

Unlike many scientific researchers investigating the relationship between criminality and intelligence, the graduate students agreed that language—in this case, English skills—played a significant role in the research process. For several years, Henry H. Goddard and many of his colleagues argued that language had minimal bearing on the outcomes of the exams. Yet a growing number of researchers, including those at Preston as well as Grace Fernald, a psychologist working with female inmates at the California School for Girls, believed otherwise. In a subsequent study, the University of California researchers purposely excluded about a dozen foreign-born youths, including Mexicans, Portuguese, Italians, and Germans, "whose ignorance of the English language made it difficult to examine them."[54]

Despite the limitations of the examination process, the student-investigators at Preston identified 35 percent (135 of 382) of the inmates admitted from July 1914 to January 1916 as feebleminded and considered 20 percent (77 of 385) to be normal, with the remainder somewhere in between. To further substantiate the significant proportion of mentally defective youths in that sample, they compared those findings with the examination results carried out on boys who entered Preston in the subsequent six-month period from January 1916 to July 1916. In the latter exams, the researchers tested 149 boys, once again excluding at least seven foreign boys for their lack of proper English-language skills. Among the tested boys, 39 percent (58 of 149) scored within the feebleminded range.[55] The significant proportion of mentally defective youths at Preston, the researchers noted, was due in part to the juvenile courts' difficulty in having them sent to Sonoma State Home instead. Indeed, for many years Sonoma State Hospital Medical Superintendent Fred O. Butler refused to admit "defective delinquents" as patients, arguing they disrupted his program.[56]

The scientific research carried out at Preston in the 1910s, though thin compared with the work carried out at Whittier State School, not only allowed the investigators to make links between mental deficiency and delinquency but also between feeblemindedness and race and ethnicity. Among the 382 boys examined from July 1914 to January 1916, for instance, the researchers confirmed that 30 percent (42 of 135) boys identified as feebleminded were foreign-born Mexicans, Portuguese, Italians, and Germans. According to their findings, 73 percent (8 of 11) of Mexicans, 70 percent (7 of 10) Portuguese, 64 percent (16 of 25) of Italians, and 11 of 23 (48 percent) Germans were defective. How many American-born ethnic and racial minorities tested equally poor is unclear, for they made no mention of ethnic and racial differences among the Preston inmates born in the United States.[57]

The researchers also determined that youths of Mexican descent, in particular, were more likely to commit serious crimes, usually those involving bodily injury such as murder. Their explanation: there was a higher percentage of feeblemindedness among Mexicans as compared with other racial and ethnic groups. Preston records for 1918 backed up those general beliefs, for they indicated that youth of Mexican descent were more likely than other ethnic or racial groups to be charged with murder. Of the ten murder cases charged against boys at Preston, Mexicans reportedly committed 60 percent (6 of 10) of those crimes. Boys of Mexican origin in general were also more likely than their peers to be charged with violent crimes and less likely than their peers to be released on parole.[58]

A boy's race and ethnicity and his inability to speak the English language not only reflected his intelligence, as determined by the researchers, but also his education and home life. As investigators discovered and most reform school officials acknowledged, most of the delinquent youths identified as "morons" had little formal education and few employment skills. Feebleminded boys, the researchers found, were most interested in and best suited for manual, unskilled labor such as farming as an occupation, whereas those identified as normal generally eschewed such labor. The feebleminded boy's desire to take up manual labor made sense to the researchers. "The work does not overtax their mental capacities," one of the graduate researchers reasoned; "it builds them up physically, it offers considerable variety, and places them in an environment which is not conducive to criminal activity."[59] The researchers held that the feebleminded were also more likely than the average delinquent boys at Preston to have poor and inadequate home conditions, to have had previous institutionalization, and to have failed on probation. The home conditions of the overwhelming majority (80 percent) of boys at Preston, they found, were marked by death, divorce, or desertion and were tainted by immoral parents, similar patterns found at Whittier State School, the California School for Girls, and other reformatories across the country.[60] "They came from broken homes, poverty, and distress and many had been reared by their parents to steal and lie," Scudder later observed about the youths at Preston.[61] In 1916, the *Oakland Tribune* reiterated those beliefs when it noted that "thirty-five per cent of the boys [at Preston are] . . . feeble-minded, but 19.4 per cent are normal." Feeblemindedness, the *Tribune* observed, "was most prevalent among Mexicans, Portuguese, Italian and German children," those with the "worse" home conditions found among the inmates at Preston.[62]

Once they completed their investigations, the researchers issued a series of recommendations to Derrick's administration, including the reorganization of the Preston School of Industry, arguing that such an approach was needed to handle the increasing number of boys identified as feebleminded. The staff at Preston, however, balked at those suggestions. In contrast to Whittier State School, where the CBJR had considerable respect and was influential in the reformatory's operations, the staff at Preston under Derrick's administration largely ignored the researchers' findings. To convince the employees of the merits of their suggestions, the Berkeley students spoke at length with the staff about the benefits of the scientific work. Knowledge of the boys' mental ability and their special needs, the researchers repeated, played a central role in the classrooms and trades school as well as in the administration of housing and parole placement. With "many of the shiftless ones and low grade mental defectives [at Preston], there can be very little hope of success," they argued.[63]

Like his staff, Superintendent Derrick resisted the researchers' recommendations, except for one: segregating the feebleminded. In 1915, Derrick sanctioned the removal of twenty of the "most seriously defective cases," "whose low and unbalanced mental conditions caused them to stand out as misfits in the other companies," to a recently built, cottage-sized unit.[64] Hugh Montgomery, his assistant and later the succeeding superintendent, justified the segregation of those youths, arguing it was for their own protection, as they were vulnerable to other inmates. The boys, most of whom were of Mexican, Italian, Portuguese, and German descent—were not only marked as social outcasts but also as constant disciplinary menaces and "sexual perverts." A similar group, consisting of sixteen boys of "high grade feeble minds [sic] and the lowest grade morons," were placed in an alternative unit, Company M, in the old band room situated above the printing office. One of the Berkeley researchers directed the unit, and a cadet captain chosen from among Preston's most trusted boys—a feature of the cadet monitor system—was placed in charge of their daily activities. In Company M, the boys received harsher treatment than other Preston inmates: they were forced to perform hard manual labor, take cold showers, and report their every move. The staff watched them closely, especially at night, to prevent what were called "perverse sex habits." Such an approach, the researchers argued, not only protected the larger population but also saved these inmates from the "immoral advances of older and more vicious boys."[65]

Initially, Company M received accolades from the administration. When Company M boys worked together, Fred Allen noted, they accomplished a significant number of tasks, earning them a reputation as the "hardest workers in the school." Scientific researchers such as J. Harold Williams believed that the feebleminded were adept at completing simple, routine tasks under supervision, similar to those carried out by unskilled manual laborers. If they were left unsupervised, however, it meant trouble—a line of thinking that led Superintendent Derrick to exclude the youths identified as feebleminded from his self-government experiment. Because they were viewed as lacking self-control, responsibility, and discipline, they were barred from joining the Preston Republic, for Derrick feared they might "wreck it." The feebleminded have an "insatiable appetite for trouble," Preston officials explained.[66] However, the researchers found that in Company M among defectives of their own kind, the boys were "cheerful, talented, and capable of leadership." Overnight, Allen boasted, the troublesome boys had been transformed into well-behaved youths.[67]

Despite the accolades for the company, trouble was brewing. Within a few months of the company's establishment, the atmosphere had changed. Many of the boys, Fred Allen admitted, clamored to leave the unit and the stigma associated with it, for everyone understood the special status assigned to the cadets in the company and the derision that accompanied it. Other Preston boys called them the "Mutt" Company or the "Goofie Gang," according to Kenyon Scudder.[68] Contrary to the researchers' beliefs about the feebleminded and their happy disposition, the boys in the unit became increasingly resentful of their assignment and the taunting from other Preston boys, leading all to ask for reassignment.

The growing problems with the company and the administration's refusal to place them in the larger population eventually led reform school officials to disband the unit and send most of those boys to Sonoma State Hospital for their segregation and eventual sterilization, a policy carried out with vigor during Medical Superintendent Butler's administration.[69] The transfer of the defectives to Sonoma was lauded on all fronts, for it meant the expulsion of exceptional problem cases. "The . . . elimination of these cases from the School has been the best solution for the most irresponsible of these mental cases."[70] To maintain a minimal number of defective boys at Preston, interim Superintendent Montgomery discouraged state institutions from sending them to the reformatory, arguing that they lacked adequate educational facilities to handle them. Few heeded his plea, however; the number of boys identified as feebleminded continued to rise, particularly during O. H. Close's administration.[71]

Indeed, intelligence tests carried out shortly before Close's arrival in 1920 determined that the number of boys identified as mental defectives had risen. In 1918, the newly appointed psychologist at Preston, Dr. Warren Brown from the University of California, and his student, Kenyon Scudder, examined 300 boys' intelligence levels as well as their personal and family histories, determining that the proportion of "normal" or "dull normal" had decreased from 47 percent (determined two years earlier, in 1916) to 35 percent. In other words, the proportion of less-than-normal boys had increased in relation to their normal peers. The researchers explained the higher number of defectives at Preston as

being a result of the juvenile courts' preference not to send boys identified as "normal" to the reformatory but rather to place them in alternative care, namely, private institutions such as foster homes, orphanages,
and other places for unwanted children and youths. The onset of World
War I, the researchers continued, also decreased the presence of normal
youths among the ranks of the delinquents who ran into trouble with
the authorities, for they believed many of the "best and brightest" had
been sent into service.

The proportion of borderline boys, considered subnormal but not
feebleminded, also increased at Preston from previous years. In 1916,
they made up 17 percent of the population, while in 1918 that figure
nearly doubled to 32 percent. That proportion worried Preston officials,
for they believed such individuals, when released into the larger society,
drifted into crime easily and failed on probation because of their limited
capacities in work and social life. "Defectives" also constituted a significant portion of the population in 1918—32 percent—which was doubtless a worrisome finding.[72]

Superintendent Derrick agreed with Dr. Brown's suggestion of return-
ing defectives to the juvenile court for alternative solutions, for such
youths "are destined to be failures here."[73] Derrick's suggestion, though
reflecting a practice Superintendent Fred C. Nelles carried out at Whittier
State School, was never enforced. In fact, the Board of Trustees disbanded
the scientific research program altogether soon after Derrick's departure;
they requested Dr. Warner Brown's resignation and abolished the post
of the psychologist in 1919.[74] Kenyon Scudder, the assistant psychologist
who had carried out much of the work at Preston while Dr. Brown provided his consultant services from Berkeley, resigned as well to enlist in
the war effort in early 1920. E. Carl Bank, the newly appointed superintendent, then appointed Dr. Proctor, a psychologist, to carry out intelligence testing on a part-time basis, namely, the weekends, and followed up
with Nelles's offer for assistance from Whittier State School. However,
none of these arrangements were apparently followed through; Bank's
tenure ended quickly as a result of the controversy over corporal punishment. By the time Close arrived at Preston in 1920, the scientific research
program and any vocational training were practically nonexistent. It
"never reached Preston at all, you see," Scudder said years later, and "less
than a third of the boys" received any vocational instruction, "a deplorable condition."[75]

Nevertheless, when Close arrived, he followed Nelles's lead and attempted to build a program of scientific research at Preston. To do so,

he visited Stanford University and conferred with Dr. Ellwood Cubberley, head of the Department of Education, as well as with Dr. Lewis M. Terman, a long-time supporter of the research at Whittier State School. Dr. Cubberley suggested individualized, practical training—or vocational and trade training—in the classroom, while Dr. Terman advised diagnosing boys in a clinic prior to their assignments. Close agreed with most of their suggestions; in response, he asked his friend J. Harold Williams to work with him in staffing a branch of the CBJR at Preston. Williams responded by providing the part-time services of Julia Mathews, a psychologist, and Willis Clark, a sociologist and eugenics fieldworker, both of whom worked for the CBJR. Close recalled that among the first things the researchers accomplished was the examination of the seemingly obvious cases of mental deficiency, followed by an examination of those who appeared on the verge of psychosis or insanity. From that work, Mathews, Clark, and Close identified the mentally defective boys and transferred them to the Sonoma State Home for segregation and, likely, sterilization.

Indeed, Sonoma State Home admission ledgers indicate that from January 1920 to January of 1922 the Preston School of Industry transferred eight boys to the hospital. Kenyon Scudder, as the interim assistant superintendent, oversaw the transfer of four of those boys, and the part-time psychologist Julia Mathews admitted one. (It is unclear who oversaw the transfer of the remainder.) When Close came on board, the Board of Trustees granted him the power to "transfer any feeble minded boys to the Sonoma State Home, [yet only] after conferring with Dr. [Fred O.] Butler."[76] Close said years later in his memoir that officials at Preston also sent "badly disturbed" boys or those they considered potentially insane or suffering from some disease such as dementia praecox (schizophrenia) to Stockton State Hospital for diagnosis and observation.[77]

The process of transferring Preston youths identified as feebleminded to Sonoma State Home did not slow but rather sped up later in 1921 with the creation of the Department of Institutions, which replaced the State Board of Charities and Corrections (and before that the Commission in Lunacy) with oversight of the state hospitals and juvenile corrections. After 1921, the director of the Department of Institutions had the power, in consultation with the superintendents, to facilitate the transfer of wards among the state hospitals and juvenile facilities without interference from the courts. Preston's Board of Trustees, which no longer had authority over the superintendent, also endorsed Close's ability to transfer "any feeble minded boys to the Sonoma State Home, after conferring with Dr. Butler."[78] These powers allowed Close—and Superintendent Nelles at Whittier and Superintendent Olive P. Walton at the California (later, Ventura) School for Girls, for that matter—to transfer any delinquent youths identified as defective to a state hospital or home with Butler's approval and relatively little oversight. Through that process, from March to September 1922, Close transferred twenty-six boys identified as "moron" or "borderline moron" to Sonoma State Home for their confinement and ultimately sterilization. The majority of those young males sent to Sonoma were sixteen to twenty-three years of age, though it is unclear which ethnic and racial groups were represented as only a few had ethnic and racial identifiers. Five of the twenty-six, for instance, had Spanish surnames, indicating Mexican or Latin American origins; the remainder are unknown, for few records remain indicating their origins and backgrounds.[79]

Though the records fail to disclose the youths' ethnic and racial profiles, they indicate that Close carried out a real coup, for Butler rarely admitted delinquents. According to Kenyon Scudder, the juvenile courts sent "many feeble-minded boys to Preston because it was so difficult to get them into the Sonoma State Home for the Feeble Minded. The waiting list for the latter ran into the hundreds and the Home did not like to take delinquent boys. So many were coming to Preston they created a serious problem."[80] Contrary to eugenics designs, Butler preferred not to accept criminals and delinquents, a point he reiterated in 1931 when he informed an official with the Public Health Department in San Francisco that "we dislike to take those with a criminal record."[81] Butler's acceptance of the Preston boys in the early 1920s was an exception, rather than the rule. Nearly all those boys were sterilized, a process Close confirmed in an interview in 1923: "We have no authority to sterilize. If they are sent to Sonoma they are sterilized."[82]

By the late 1920s and 1930s, however, Close had transferred few, if any, other boys identified as morons to the Sonoma State Home or the Pacific Colony for the Feebleminded, which finally accepted patients in significant numbers in 1927. Why Close sent so few Preston boys to Sonoma or Pacific Colony remains unclear. Close had another option for dealing with defective boys and that was to return them to the juvenile court—as Nelles often did—where a judge could then decide to commit them to a state hospital or send them elsewhere, including back to their home. That was not a sure-fire process to see to these boys' institutionalization in a state hospital, according to Scudder. "The only way we [at Preston] could transfer the more serious cases to the State Home was to return them to the Juvenile Court for commitment. This was difficult to do and often misfired," he said, with no other explanation. The Sonoma State Home Admission Ledgers indicate that Close did, however, send one boy successfully to Sonoma in 1937, while the sterilization authorization records demonstrate another four former Preston inmates also made their way to Sonoma in the 1930s.[83] Apparently no other Preston youths ended up at Sonoma or the Pacific Colony, though Close and his assistants complained repeatedly in the 1920s and 1930s about the presence of defective delinquents at Preston.[84]

Indeed, in 1924, a few years after he had arrived at Preston, Close remarked that 25 percent of the boys were feebleminded.[85] Six years later, a researcher investigating the role of intelligence, truancy, and delinquency at Preston reported an even greater proportion of potentially feeble-minded youths, a finding that reinforced Close's beliefs about the school. Of the 300 boys V. Pierpont Husband studied in 1930, the majority was below average in intelligence. "This very large proportion of cases below the normal, together with a considerable number at the lower border of normal, indicates a predominating mental deficiency which is highly significant as a contributing factor in both truancy and delinquency."[86] Husband, like many other anti-immigrant "restrictionists" around the country, felt the source of the youth and nation's "moral decay" was foreign immigrants: "The influx of the foreign element under America's generous 'open door' policy has brought an admixture of racial stocks that is disrupting our national solidarity, and throwing into discord our former ideals of thrift and orderly living." The foreign element at Preston—which Husband estimated at 50 percent—was a threat as well, he argued; the majority (30 percent) were of Mediterranean descent, the minority (18 percent) of Spanish/Mexican origins, and the remainder (2 percent) made up of unknown origins. The school's official reports indicate that Mexicans constituted an even higher proportion than Husband's estimate, at 20 percent in the 1920s, and African Americans made up less than half at 8 percent.[87]

Apparently, Close did little else to check the proportion of Italian, Mexican, Spanish, or other "foreign element" at Preston in the 1920s and 1930s. Rather, the population of foreign youths continued to expand, particularly the youths of Mexican origin. In 1928, Close remarked that Mexicans constituted the largest group among them. Doubtless, that proportion continued to climb, as did the populace across the state. The number at Preston ballooned from 450 in 1920 to 700 by the early 1940s. To handle these youths, Close advocated a "scientific approach" that resulted in "classification, segregation, counseling, active work and train-ing programs" for youths. At the same time, he admitted, "an occasional removal of mentally disturbed and a few very low grade feebleminded types to mental institutions" was also in order. Thus, for nearly twenty-five years, Close oversaw a large, racially and ethnically mixed popula-tion of delinquent males.[88]

BENIGN NEGLECT AT PRESTON SCHOOL OF INDUSTRY

Though the majority of youths identified as defective at Preston—as well as those at Whittier State School and the California School for Girls—were spared from Sonoma State Home's sterilization program, they had to contend with their daily reality, namely, harsh reform school policies and practices at an underfunded, neglected institution. According to a 1923 undercover investigation by Leon Adams, a reporter with the *San Francisco Daily News,* the reformatory was nothing more than a "school of crime." In an eleven-part series, Adams—who had passed as an inmate at Preston—criticized the institution for "graduating" professional crimi-nals rather than reforming juveniles. One of every twenty-five prisoners at San Quentin, Adams reported, had been at Preston at one point in their careers. Many of those released, he continued, had been let out "only to commit other crimes." Ninety of one hundred Preston boys "who are released end up in a state institution, and only [two] of [one hundred] who are taught a trade follow those trades after they are released."[89]

Adams not only criticized the reform school's failure to rehabilitate boys but also the punishments that recalcitrant boys suffered. Close's program for dealing with troublesome inmates was inhumane, according to Adams. It eschewed corporal punishment and relied on disciplining the mind. Ad-ams reported that boys who failed to follow rules at Preston were stripped of their clothing, and given scant covering, meager meals, and little to no bedding—then were placed in solitary confinement in one of six damp, dark cells in the basement of the main administration building. "Terrible punishments that impair mentality and physique are administered by offi-cers who are unable to control the youths they guard unless they make an example of every offender," he wrote. Adams's criticism of Preston did not end there, for he also blasted the presence of abusive guards, inadequate food and supplies, and outdated equipment as well as poor pay and low morale among Preston staff.

In the end, though, Adams's criticism was directed at the State of California—specifically, the governor and state officials for their neglect of the school. In the process, he absolved Close and his staff of Preston's shortcomings. "Friend W. Richardson in his 'economy budget' has reduced the appropriation for food and clothing and instruction for boys at Preston," wrote Adams. The reporter said little, in comparison, about Superintendent Close's personal role in the school's administration. Nevertheless, Close worried about the public fallout and censure that would result from the lengthy series.

Close chose not to respond directly to the public allegations, saying only in confidence to a colleague that, contrary to the reports, he believed Preston was more than a custodial holding tank or prison. He believed it did, in fact, reform boys. "There is a very decided change in many of the boys after training, and many go out with cleaner thoughts, with ambition, and a desire to make good rather than see how 'hard' they can be, which is the ambition of many when they arrive."[90]

Despite Close's firm beliefs about the boys' ability to reform and his larger attempts to clean up Preston, he retained the much maligned monitor system. That set up, which involved the use of older senior or captain cadets—usually the stronger and more ruthless fighters of a company or unit—to monitor and keep other inmates in line under the supervisor's orders, was especially despised by the boys for its tendency to lead to abusive and corrupt practices among the wards. The practice was first organized during Derrick's administration, and Close continued it, giving specific cadet captains a great deal of power over their peers. An escapee from Preston confessed to Kenyon Scudder sometime in the late 1910s that the system was indeed rampantly abusive. The supervisors did not run the companies, he said: "it's those tough thugs they select as Captain or Lieutenant—any kid who can lick every other boy in the company. I took all I could [from them], and blew my top. That's why I don't want to go back. I know they are laying for me and I'm afraid it only means more trouble." Scudder believed the boy, saying, "I could sympathize with his position for I too had witnessed the results of the vicious monitor system at Preston. . . . It is my strong conviction that no inmate in any institution, either for juvenile or adults, should ever be given power or authority over any other inmate."[91] Notwithstanding the criticism, the system remained in use well into the late 1950s, long after Close's tenure had ended.[92]

Close's steady, albeit mediocre, program of rehabilitation, which included vocational trade training, scientific research, and military instruction, declined in the late 1920s and early 1930s, particularly with the onset of the Great Depression and drastic reductions in state appropriations. Admittedly, few details remain about the impact of the Great Depression on the school in general and the boys in particular. The records providing insight on the boys' experiences at Preston in the early twentieth century are woefully incomplete. What is clear is that the national and international downturn in the economy brought increased pressure to the already strained reformatory. Most visibly, the number of inmates increased significantly as a result of the migration of young, single males from other parts of the United States who had come to California looking for work and a means of survival. Those young vagrants clashed with the police and other members of the community, leading to their detention and ultimately their incarceration in Preston, where they helped increase the population to well over seven hundred inmates.[93] The crowded conditions at the school plus continued reductions in expenditures further crippled the reformatory. During Governor Richardson's first year in office, for instance, his budget officer, Nellie Pierce, slashed Preston's monthly budget by $2,000, forcing Close to lay off the assistant superintendent, the educational director, parole officers, and six group supervisors.[94]

Curiously, when the Osborne Association visited Preston in 1939 as part of its nationwide survey of institutions for delinquent youths, it had nothing but praise for the school and Close. Doubtless, O. H. Close's membership on the Osborne Association's California advisory committee influenced their evaluation of Preston and its administration. The association, for instance, lauded Close as an "outstanding administrator" and called Preston's program excellent, noting it had "developed one of the most effective programs" in the United States. Preston is the only reformatory, the report continued, that "seeks through planned, organized means to guide and train older youths through the use of adequate trade training facilities and experienced personnel." Moreover, it continued, the psychology department is "better organized than any similar department of the state institutions for delinquent juveniles on the Pacific Coast." Plus, "there are special classes for mental defectives and a sincere attempt seems to be made to provide them with an appropriate program within the institution's general framework of activities." The association concluded, "There is nothing to suggest a correctional institution."[95] The association did, however, observe that many of the personnel had little training in professional fields and suggested the hiring of a trained psychologist and other staff to provide adequate assessment of the inmates. It also recommended that the school do away with some of its antiquated approaches, including the credit system, silence bench, and use of the "V" mark on shoes to track potential escapees.[96]

Despite that praise, by the early 1940s and the United States' entry into World War II, which further diverted attention from the reformatory and juvenile corrections in general, conditions at Preston had deteriorated significantly, and Close's job was on the line. Reform school officials were lax in their duties, according to one researcher, sometimes performing operations on the boys without the parents' notice and often keeping boys in horrible conditions in the detention unit.[97] An investigation by the California Tax Payers' Association in 1945 also found significant recidivism rates among boys, raising questions about the institution's efficacy. According to the Tax Payers' Association, Close had released 250 boys in 1929 considered to be among the most "promising." By 1939, at least 69 percent of those inmates had been arrested at least once, and nearly half (49 percent) had been sentenced to state prisons. "It is obvious," wrote the California Taxpayers' Association, "that the present program has not retrained the boys; in fact it may possibly have done them serious damage. Far too large a portion of these youth have continued in criminal ways after release."[98]

Years later in an oral history, Karl Holton, the Chief Probation Officer in Los Angeles (and later the first director of the Youth Authority), recalled that many working in juvenile corrections resisted change in the early 1940s—especially at Preston, which "had been running under same superintendent for [2]2 years." He said, "Many of those people had worked their entire lifetime there." Most had little education, meager salaries, and had personal connections to the school: "They were all interrelated." Firing anyone was difficult, for it created unrest throughout the institution.[99]

Holton also had little positive to say about Close's program of scientific research. "Psychology, psychiatry, social work was a lot of apple sauce," he charged. "They rather reluctantly accepted the fact that the school program ought to be improved and that the teacher ought to have the chance to go to teacher's institutes." When the state started bringing in people to help with training, "almost open rebellion" ensued, particularly among Preston staff, "although the superintendent [Close] was presumably on our side (I think actually he was, but not in any effective fashion)."[100]

Ultimately, Holton's solution to improving conditions at Preston included removing Close, giving him a job in the recently established Youth Authority office in Sacramento, and placing a "man out there [at Preston] whom we could depend upon to do something, Bob Chadrow [Chandler]."[101] Holton moved quickly in making the changes at Preston, knowing the staff would resist vehemently. Sure enough, within a few days of

Close's removal, the staff incited the boys to run away and called the media to bring attention to the events taking place at the school. Holton admitted that he knew the conditions would lead to a blowup at the school, which would then allow him to "clean house"—which he did when a riot of 400 boys ensued. According to Holton, as a result of those events, Preston received much attention, and an ad hoc legislative committee even traveled the forty or so miles from Sacramento to Ione to investigate. The end result was that they managed to oust many long-time staff, and in the process received a "larger appropriation than ever before."[102] Some of that funding was used, in turn, to train staff under Chandler's new administration, which was a conspicuous change after Close, according to George Tonzie, an employee at Preston from about 1933 to 1948. During Close's administration, the staff received little training, had little knowledge about how to deal with boys, and were unprepared for resolving racial conflicts such as those that erupted in the early 1940s among Mexican "'zoot suit' groups and gang members" and between Mexicans and whites.[103] Those episodes were particularly challenging because they involved a large inmate population: in the 1930s, the school had had a population of 500 boys, but by the mid-1940s the number had ballooned to well over 1,000.[104] Change was slow, nevertheless. According to Kenyon Scudder, it took the Youth Authority another eighteen years to clean up Preston, namely, to get rid of incompetent staff, construct modern facilities, and implement innovative policies and practices—including giving "boys academic and vocational classes by teachers accredited by the State Department of Education."[105]

Alfred Deutsch, a journalist known for exposing harsh conditions in state institutions who had visited numerous reformatories throughout the United States in the early 1940s, also had little positive to say about Preston. "Preston, by law, was maintained under military discipline, with the discredited 'cadet and monitor system' in full employ," he wrote. The buildings reflected the drab conditions at the school. "The double-tiered prison cell blocks for boys undergoing punishment—known as Company G—were among the most depressing I saw anywhere." That unit had nearly fifty boys with the "tougher ones" in a special cell block, in "isolation and under all-day silence rules. They ate three meals a day consisting of a baked meat-and-vegetable cake." He said, after he tried it, "It looked like and tasted like a mud pie." The cell block had no furniture, and the boys slept on the floor. Equally inhumane was Company S, the segregation unit, he said. It was "a small cluster of buildings enclosed by a steel-wire mesh fence about 13 feet high for very disturbed boys, chronic runaways, homosexuals and others representing a serious morale problem. It looked like a concentration camp, and that was the name given it by the Preston boys."[106]

After visiting the new and much lauded diagnostic center of the Youth Authority, established at Preston for screening and assigning delinquents to proper programs and institutions, Deutsch pronounced the unit impressive only on paper. In reality, the diagnostic center was surrounded by a depressing atmosphere: "an old building with about 100 boys and with a well-trained psychologist who was grossly overworked, unprovided [*sic*] with any adequate staff, forced to fight off the indifference and even hostility of other Preston officials." The place was starved for attention, he said, despite the public statements lauding the establishment of the Youth Authority and reformation of the juvenile justice system in the Golden State. Little change, it seemed, had come to the juvenile correctional system in California.

Alfred Deutsch's exposé of conditions at the Preston School of Industry, the Tax Payers' Association report, and statements from numerous state officials who had intimate knowledge of that institution reveal that, over the course of twenty-five years, Otto H. Close's administration had gone from promising to largely ineffectual and in many ways incompetent. Hired in 1920 to turn around the reformatory, Close succeeded in bringing basic changes to the school, including getting rid of corporal punishment, garnering local public support, instituting a semblance of training for a limited group of youths, and overseeing some scientific research that often criminalized youths of Mexican descent and to some extent African Americans and those of eastern and southern European descent. Close turned a blind eye to the larger problems plaguing the reformatory and apparently did little to call attention to the needs of the school, such as maintaining a staff of trained professionals for vocational trade training and primary and secondary education. Doubtless, the state's inability and unwillingness to provide funding, particularly during severe economic crises such as the Great Depression, contributed to Close's inability to improve conditions. State neglect and staff incompetency combined with Close's complacency led to declining conditions at the Preston School of Industry in the 1930s and 1940s.

Preston was not the only reform school in California to suffer from decline and decay in the 1930s and 1940s. Nowhere was the deterioration of the juvenile justice system more apparent than in the southern portion of the state at Whittier State School. Once hailed as a premiere reformatory in the late 1910s and early 1920s, by the 1930s it had become a brutal institution led by incompetent superintendents. Chapter 6 examines how and why Whittier State School eventually became a repressive institution, with conditions that drove to two Mexican American boys to commit suicide in 1939 and 1940, respectively. Those incidents, as the chapter reveals, touched off a firestorm of controversy and conflicts that exposed the long-standing scientific beliefs about "defective delinquents"—many of them Mexicans, Mexican Americans, and African Americans—and the ways in which they were handled. Some advocated institutionalization and sterilization, while others suggested implementing culturally based, relevant programs aimed at assisting nonwhite, racial, and ethnic minorities. In the end, the boys' deaths were not in vain, for they led to a critical reexamination of the state's apparatus for controlling and containing delinquent youths and to the dismantling of the juvenile correctional system and establishment of the Youth Authority.

CHAPTER 6

The Legacy of Benny Moreno and Edward Leiva

"Defective Delinquents" or Tragic Heroes?

On the morning of August 11, 1939, Don C. Napper, a guard at Whittier State School, made a gruesome discovery in the solitary confinement unit of the Lost Privilege Cottage: Benny Moreno's lifeless body hanging from a leather belt. Moreno, a thirteen-year-old Mexican American boy, was in solitary for escaping from the institution the day before. School officials guessed that he had committed suicide sometime in the early hours of the morning. Eleven months later, Edward Leiva, a seventeen-year-old Mexican American ward, also in solitary, committed suicide as well. This time, the boy used torn bedsheets, which he had braided and looped through a vent on ceiling, to hang himself. According to his cellmates, Leiva had not intended to commit suicide but only to injure himself sufficiently so that he would be taken to the hospital from which he planned to escape. Leiva's plan went terribly wrong, however, when he stepped off the bed and the full weight of his body betrayed him, leading to his death.[1]

The suicides of Benny Moreno and Edward Leiva touched off a firestorm of controversies and conflicts over juvenile correctional practices in California. A series of public and private investigations as well as a flood of reports in the English and Spanish language media revealed that Whittier, once hailed as a premiere reformatory, had declined precipitously in the 1930s. The outcome of the hearings were the dismissal of key administrators and staff as well as the imprisonment of physically and sexually abusive personnel from Whittier State School, the dismantling of juvenile corrections in the state, and the creation of the Youth Authority in 1941.

This chapter investigates how and why Whittier State School, a premiere reformatory in the 1910s and 1920s, declined so significantly in the 1930s, creating conditions that led to the suicides of two Mexican American boys. It begins by examining the increasing challenges at Whittier State School in the 1930s, including political rivalries, cutbacks in state support, incompetent leadership, and increased neglect of the reformatory. Next, it looks into the boys' suicides and the investigations that followed, analyzing the ideas and ideologies that state officials held about delinquency, heredity, science, and race and how they were used to explain their deaths. Ultimately, state representatives argued, the delinquent boys' "defective" qualities contributed to their suicides, effectively absolving the state from much of the physical, sexual, and psychological abuse that the boys had endured. Family members and concerned Californians, on the other hand, blasted the state's findings and school's practices. The boys' deaths were not in vain: in the end, the tragedies brought long-overdue state and national attention to the needs of incarcerated minors, leading to the transformation of the juvenile correctional system and forming a legacy that continues to this day.

THE DECLINE OF WHITTIER STATE SCHOOL

The tragic suicides of Benny Moreno and Edward Leiva in 1939 and 1940, respectively, and the public uproar that ensued led state officials to take a hard look at correctional policies and practices at Whittier State School and across the state's juvenile justice system. Since the early 1930s, few politicians and members of the public had paid much attention to the school in particular or juvenile corrections in general. Political battles raging in the governor's office in Sacramento obscured the needs of the reformatory, though one battle in particular brought the school into the spotlight briefly. That incident was Governor James "Sunny" Rolph's dismissal of Whittier State School Superintendent Kenyon J. Scudder in 1931 and Rolph's appointment of Claude Smith, an inexperienced administrator, who quit shortly thereafter followed by the appointment of Dr. George Sabichi to the same post. That replacement of administrators, in turn, led to heated public battles over Rolph's political spoils system and the incompetency of Sabichi. Eventually, the pressure proved too much for Sabichi, and he resigned as Smith had done so earlier. In his stead, Rolph appointed Erastus J. Milne, a former juvenile court judge from Salt Lake City and former superintendent of industrial homes in Nevada and Utah. Though some contested Milne's credentials, he was recommended highly and ascended the post with little incident.[2]

When Milne arrived at Whittier State School in 1931, he encountered an increasingly austere, overcrowded, and brutal institution, and he did little to change it. For years, the state had neglected to provide inmates with a formal education, despite state compulsory laws. In 1939, the Osborne Association, a New York-based legal organization surveying reformatories throughout the United States, found that only about 10 of the 377 or so inmates at Whittier attended school full time, while the rest did so on a part-time basis. Newly admitted boys confined to the Receiving Cottage as well as recalcitrant inmates in the Lost Privilege Cottage received no education while in those units. Apparently, the school made some effort to meet the needs of youths "severely retarded in one or more subjects," for they had two "ungraded classrooms," composed of boys of different ages and levels. Those deemed beyond help—the "feeble-minded" or otherwise defective—received no schooling whatsoever.[3]

Individualized scientific attention was also in short supply. Much of the program Fred C. Nelles had built in the 1910s and 1920s was long gone. Norman Fenton, the current director of the California Bureau of Juvenile Research (CBJR), a shadow of its earlier manifestation, had relocated to Claremont College in the early 1930s after the funding all but dried up at Whittier. Much of the science-based, diagnostic work with inmates at the reformatory was limited to the fledgling Department of Research, which employed a part-time psychologist. As a result, few boys received attention, and those deemed "potentially psychotic or actually feeble-minded" remained at Whittier State School because transfer to state institutions was limited due to overcrowded conditions.[4]

The lack of an individualized program was, in some ways, a mixed blessing for those likely to perform poorly on the intelligence exams administered at the school, namely, the Mexican, Mexican American, and African American boys. Historically, youths of color sent to Whittier State School were more likely than white youths to perform poorly on the tests and to be identified as feebleminded; in many cases, they were transferred to Sonoma State Home where they were sterilized. A poorly funded scientific program at Whittier State School implied that these 'low performing' boys were no longer likely to be transferred to Sonoma or a similar place. Rather, they stayed at Whittier State School, leading to their increasing numbers at the reformatory.[5]

The reform school not only lacked individualized attention but also updated facilities. The Lost Privilege Cottage, for instance, a prison within a prison that was used for inmates who had committed serious infractions, was described as "drab" in the 1930s.[6] The solitary units, used for the boys who had violated policies within the cottage, were constructed of solid wood, barring visibility into or out of the rooms, leaving the inmates unsupervised for most of the day (Figure 8). Many other buildings, too, noted the Los Angeles County Grand Jury's Jails Committee in 1937, were run-down and overcrowded, including the dining quarters.[7] State cutbacks in the early 1930s, a result of the Great Depression, had forced school officials to cease serving meals in the individual cottages. Instead, they used a centralized dining hall, forcing the youths to take their meals in cafeterias like those found in adult penitentiaries.[8]

Public apathy and media indifference also contributed to the lack of interest in the conditions at Whittier as well as other reformatories around the state. For instance, in a span of nearly seven years, the *Los Angeles Times* produced no more than a small handful of stories on these institutions, and nearly all pertained to moments of "success" and "progress." Rarely did the paper or any member of the public report any transgressions or call for an investigation into the conditions at Whittier, which effectively gave the school administrators and staff carte blanche.[9]

The lack of oversight of Whittier State School, in turn, allowed Superintendent Milne to implement a code of silence that allowed staff members—many of them untrained and inexperienced—to carry out policies and practices as they saw fit. At the same time, Milne and his staff provided family members and the public with few details of what went on behind closed doors. To maintain that secrecy, staff warned inmates to keep quiet. "If you squawk," Guard Don V. Cavitt warned a boy who threatened to report the abuse of a deaf-mute ward to Superintendent Milne, "something will happen to you that you'll NEVER forget [emphasis in the original]."[10] At other times, when parents complained about the secrecy in the Lost Privilege unit, Cavitt admitted to one mother, "You see, we teach the boys, like the Army and Navy, not to tell, and [your son] has learned his lesson well."[11]

Secretive operations, lack of interest from the state and the public alike, incompetent leadership and staff, and severe cutbacks in state spending combined to contribute to the reform school's decline and, ultimately, to an environment that proved too much to endure for some boys. Not until the suicides of Benny Moreno and Edward Leiva in 1939 and 1940, respectively, did the brutal conditions at Whittier State School become

FIGURE 8. Solitary Confinement Units of the Lost Privilege Cottage. The solitary confinement units of the Lost Privilege Cottage at Whittier State School—where Benny Moreno and Edward Leiva committed suicide—were used for boys who had violated the rules of the cottage. The solid wood doors prevented visibility in and out of the cells, making it impos-´ sible to detect the boys' suicidal acts. Courtesy Los Angeles Herald-Examiner Collection, Los Angeles Public Library.

apparent to observers in and around the state and across the nation, lead-ing to drastic transformations in the making of California's juvenile justice system.

THE TRAGIC DEATH OF BENNY MORENO

On July 11, 1939, six months after arriving at the reformatory, Benny Moreno and his pal, Howard Doss, attempted to accomplish what many incarcerated youths before them had tried hundreds of times: escape. Since the school's founding in the 1890s, boys and girls had gone AWOL, the attempts only lessening when the living conditions improved, as they did during Fred C. Nelles's administration. After Nelles's death in 1927, however, the numbers slightly increased, then climbed steeply in the 1930s during Milne's administration. During that decade, at least 764 boys attempted to escape, with many of them going AWOL on more than one occasion (see Table 4). Regardless of when or how the youths attempted their escapes, most were caught; school officials sent out posses, alerted the local police, and sometimes asked nearby residents to assist in retrieving the boys. None of that seemed to matter much to Moreno, however, when he attempted to flee.[12]

With apparent determination, Moreno and Doss ran—and managed to elude the authorities for two days. Moreno was eventually caught and returned to the school, but Doss remained at large. Back at Whittier, Moreno ended up in the Lost Privilege Cottage, though it seemed to have little effect; within a month of his last escape, Moreno fled again, on August 10, 1939.[13] His taste of freedom was once again brief: officers caught up with him within thirty minutes and placed him in solitary in the Lost Privilege Cottage. Before entering the unit, Moreno removed his clothes, as was standard, including his undergarments, shoes, and belt, and was given a nightgown. Moreno seemed to take his confinement in stride. According to the guards, Moreno ate his lunch and dinner with little incident and conversed with "two other Mexican boys, his pals, who were in adjoining cells." That night, after the boys had turned in, supervisor Franklin E. Morrill reported that he inspected Moreno's cell "through the shutter on the door" at eight o'clock, midnight, and three o'clock in the morning, each time finding him "lying in his bed, apparently asleep."[14]

The next day, when morning guard Napper came on shift, he did not find Moreno asleep in his bed—he found him dead, hanging by his belt. Napper immediately notified the school's long-time physician, Doctor Tebbets, and Superintendent Milne, both of whom inspected the body and the cell. Milne, in turn, called the sheriff and informed Moreno's family. In the meantime, the Los Angeles County Coroner took the body to a funeral home in Whittier where a surgeon performed the autopsy.[15]

Two days later, the coroner ruled Moreno's death a suicide by "asphyxiation." That ruling, reported Aaron Rosanoff, Director of the Department of Institutions (responsible for the administration of state juvenile facilities and mental hospitals) to Governor Culbert L. Olson, "'completely exonerated' all officials and employees" from "any blame for the death."[16] The Board of Managers at Whittier State School agreed with the findings but suggested, nonetheless, further investigation to clear up any suspicions of foul play, for in recent days many civic and political organizations across the state had been demanding a thorough investigation. Governor Olson agreed, saying, "When a boy feels so strongly that the cards are so stacked against him that, at the age of 13, he hangs himself, there is something wrong somewhere."[17]

In response to the intense public scrutiny, Governor Olson appointed Dr. Rosanoff to investigate the school's disciplinary practices and the circumstances surrounding Moreno's death. Rosanoff agreed but did so reluctantly, believing the case had attracted unnecessary attention and the school was free from blame. "The boy was placed in what is known as the lost privilege cottage, and solitary confinement is merely being placed in a single room," he said.[18] That, Rosanoff contended, was "not harsh punishment."[19]

Despite his protests, Rosanoff carried out the inquiry hastily, examining school records and interviewing a small handful of administrators, employees, and inmates. His conclusion: Moreno's poor home environment and his personality were to blame. The family, noted Rosanoff, was extremely large—two parents and nine siblings with another child on the way—and largely impoverished, for the father, an agricultural worker, was unemployed and relied on public assistance to maintain the household. The home, admitted Rosanoff, was well kept, and no family member—save Benny—had a history of delinquency or criminality, a finding that likely surprised Rosanoff, a proponent of eugenics-based policies and practices who believed firmly in the links among heredity, delinquency, and race. Moreno's personality—as revealed through his childhood experiences, not the intelligence tests that had shown him to be "normal" with an IQ of 102—posed special difficulties for the family and for the boy. Ever since he was a young boy, Rosanoff explained, Benny had run away, played "hookey," stolen automobiles, and caused other problems.[20] Though Moreno's tests showed no evidence of a "*psychotic condition* [emphasis in the original]" or "*feeblemindedness* [emphasis in the original]," the boy had the signs of a "*psychopathic personality* [emphasis in the original]."[21] According to J. Harold Williams, the former psychologist at Whittier, psychopathic personalities, though normal in intelligence and often possessing alert minds, were excitable or neurotic, that is, "highly emotional, high strung, subject to fits of temper, [and] rage" as demonstrated through "some violent or near-violent act."[22] Psychopathic personalities also lacked sound judgment or individual responsibility and sometimes had suicidal tendencies, leading them to require permanent segregation.[23]

To remove the state's responsibility for the boy's death, Rosanoff explained that suicides rarely occurred in state reformatories. Instead, they were more common in the general society, especially during economic downturns and among "*institutionalized mental patients* [emphasis in the original]" as well as those afflicted with alcoholism and drug addictions. Moreover, he noted, Moreno's suicide was the first at the reformatory and under Superintendent Milne's watch in his thirty years of experience in Utah, Nevada, and California.[24]

To counter the claims that disciplinary measures, specifically the Lost Privilege Cottage, had contributed to Moreno's death, Rosanoff explained that those units were needed to deal with "mental defectives"—such as Moreno—needing special care and attention. The state had yet to establish an institution for "defective (feebleminded) and psychopathic (temperamentally abnormal) delinquents," a cause Rosanoff championed across the state. He concluded that, until the state segregated such individuals, isolation units must remain in use.[25]

Rosanoff's theories did little to quell the Moreno's family suspicions about their boy's death and the cursory investigation. The family's misgivings had begun the day they learned of Benny's death. That day, when his father, Domingo Moreno, had arrived at the funeral parlor to claim his son's body, the manager discouraged him from viewing the remains, warning him that doing so might "shock" him, "since the body 'looked horrible and was not prepared to be seen.'"[26] Shaken, Moreno agreed and returned home instead. At the wake, the family became increasingly doubtful about the situation: they noticed "blood on the back of the head" and on the "coffin pillow, and a swelling behind the right ear." The family then sent a letter to the probation officer, asking how, when, and if the boy had been beaten "unjustly" or if he had really taken his own life. To relieve their suspicions of foul play, Superintendent E. J. Milne arranged for a Spanish-speaking official to explain the autopsy report and coroner's inquest. That explanation in addition to the public allegations of abuse at the reformatory did little to ease their worries. Rather, they and the larger Mexican and Mexican American community grew even more dubious about the suicide and demanded further inquiry by an independent committee.[27]

The Moreno family and the larger Mexican and Mexican-American community's misgivings were not surprising given the blatant hostility and outright violence that Mexican-origin youths had been experiencing in recent years. In the 1930s and early 1940s, American-born Mexican American youths—largely the product of the massive wave of Mexican immigration in the early twentieth century—faced increased racial and ethnic discrimination and tension in their schools, neighborhoods, and many other sectors of society, despite their status as American-born citizens. To carve an oppositional identity to the larger American society and to that of their Mexican immigrant parents' generation, these youngsters adopted a *pachuco* and *pachuca* identity, which was characterized by alternative dress (the zoot suit), language (*caló*, a hybrid of Spanish and English), and cultural expressions that included increasingly popular, youth-inspired dance, music, and hairstyles. The authorities—particularly the police—and, later, United States servicemen on leave from their duties in World War II, would target male zoot suiters or pachucos for their alleged anti-American, unpatriotic, and criminal behavior as well as their gang affiliations. Nor did the young pachucas, their female counterparts, escape harassment. The zoot-wearing girls, with their tight skirts, coiffed hair, and pronounced make-up, were singled out for their perceived sexual immorality, a moral threat to the larger society. The hostility against Mexican American youth was most visibly expressed in the Sleepy Lagoon incident of 1942, in which seventeen Mexican American boys from Los Angeles were wrongfully accused and convicted of the murder of José Díaz, a peer who was killed mysteriously at a party in the unincorporated area of east Los Angeles. In the subsequent "zoot suit riots" in June 1943, a ten-day race riot in Los Angeles left many young people injured and family members fearful for their lives. Girls, too, were caught up in the melee, particularly the Sleepy Lagoon incident. For their involvement, some were sent to the Ventura School for Girls, while the boys did time in jail and prison. After two years, an appellate court overturned the boys' verdicts—with the court ruling the conviction a travesty of justice. So the men were exonerated though not before they had spent two years locked up, but the girls remained incarcerated at Ventura until their majority, twenty-one years of age, for refusing to identify the culprits in Díaz's death.[28]

In response to Benny Moreno's death, civil rights activists working with and on behalf of Mexican and Mexican American communities in California, namely, *El Congreso de Pueblos de Habla Española* (Congress of Spanish-Speaking Peoples), supported the family's fight. Formed only a year earlier in 1938 by notable leaders Eduardo Quevedo, Josefina Fierro, Luisa Moreno, and George I. Sánchez, El Congreso played a pivotal role in bringing national attention to Benny Moreno's death.[29] Less than two weeks after Moreno's death, over 1,000 *congresistas* marched to the governor's office to demand an investigation and seek justice for the Moreno family as well as the family of another Mexican American youth who had been unjustly gunned down by a policeman only days earlier. The protesters demanded an explanation for the state of Benny Moreno's body and, if necessary, an exhumation of the body to resolve "suspicions and even accusations" of brutality in Moreno's suicide and in the overt mistreatment of Mexicans in general. Sympathetic to their concerns, Governor Olson responded quickly, authorizing an investigation headed by an independent committee.[30]

Selected by El Congreso and the Moreno family, the Gallagher Committee (as it was known) included members of El Congreso, labor leaders, the Mexican Consul, and an attorney, Leo Gallagher, known for defending clients with left-leaning politics.[31] The committee's work was not easy, for it met stiff opposition, particularly from Superintendent Milne. He blasted it as "Communistic," intrusive, and disruptive. The "Spanish Speaking people's private interrogation of the boys," Milne charged, upset the inmates, leading them to "become panicky" and escape.[32] Within a thirty-six hour period, twenty-one boys had absconded. Superintendent Milne's fear of the Gallagher Committee's work was not unfounded because the group's work could expose the dire treatment and abusive conditions at the school. To deal with the potential for leaks, Milne invoked the reformatory's code of silence, sanctioning the punishment of any boys who spoke to the committee.

Despite Milne's efforts to guard the school's secrets, the Gallagher Committee managed to elicit incriminating details from several boys and from Moreno family members as well. Albert Burgueno, one of Benny Moreno's cellmates, testified that, on the night of his suicide, Moreno had been in good spirits, even joking around. Frank Ward, another cellmate, repeated a similar story, adding that Moreno told him he expected to "get out from the lock-up" really soon. When asked to explain how the belt came into Moreno's possession, the boys admitted that Supervisor Don V. Cavitt, another guard in the Lost Privilege Cottage, had given each of them their belts, though they could not explain why he had done so. Ray Valdez, Benny Moreno's friend, told the committee that the night before Moreno's death, he heard Cavitt say, "Just wait until I get a-hold of Moreno." Valdez also revealed a gruesome rumor about the boy's death: the mutilation of Moreno's testicles.[33] Family members, too, recounted to the committee stories of abusive practices at the school, as told to them by Benny.[34]

Not satisfied with the testimony alone, the Gallagher Committee and the family called for a reenactment of Benny Moreno's death as well as a disinterment and second autopsy. To simulate the suicide, Andres Gonzales, a Mexican man who shared Benny Moreno's height and weight, was asked to place a belt around his neck and tie it to the window frame to "permit his full weight to hang from it."[35] Although visibly uncomfortable, Gonzales agreed to do so, managing to suspend his weight with the belt, proving that Moreno had been capable of taking his life. Notwithstanding the reenactment, questions remained about how and why Moreno had access his belt, given the policies of the isolation unit. The subsequent disinterment and second autopsy answered some questions, particularly about the mutilation of the boy's body, but because of the severe decomposition, it was difficult to glean many other details. Nevertheless, the procedure determined that Moreno had "no broken or dislodged teeth, no broken or dislocated bones, and no cuts on the skin," barring those made by the surgeon or mortician, and no mutilation of the genitals, anus, or rectum. With the work completed and under pressure from state officials to finish the report, Leo Gallagher wrapped up the inquiry.[36]

Despite lingering questions, the Gallagher Committee exonerated the institution and individuals connected with the state reformatory of any responsibility or wrongdoing. The committee concluded that "[it is] beyond a reasonable doubt [that] Benny Moreno committed suicide." It continued, "there is not the slightest reason to believe that the deceased was physically mistreated" either "the day before or the day of his death."[37] Miscommunication between the family and the funeral parlor accounted for the family's misinformation, it decided. The committee could not explain, however, why Benny Moreno had ended his life because he had appeared "normal" and was "'a quiet, responsive boy, and not inclined to be morose.'" The committee ended its assessment by noting it was not "qualified to determine the psychological factors which induced [Moreno] to take his life."[38]

Not surprisingly, reform school and state administrators welcomed the Gallagher Committee's findings, though others remained deeply dissatisfied.[39] Indeed, Benny Moreno's family, individual members of the Gallagher Committee, and the larger Mexican American community questioned the final report for failing to probe the policies and practices at the reformatory and the broader social, economic, and political inequalities that had contributed to Moreno's imprisonment and death. The report, largely authored by Leo Gallagher alone, also left many other concerns unanswered, particularly the use of the solitary unit as well as the nature of the unequal power relations at the school, specifically those between staff and administrators, between staff and boys, and among boys of different races, ethnicities, and ages. Although some members of the committee, such as H. E. Lambert, disagreed with the findings, they nevertheless signed off. In challenging Gallagher's report, Lambert stated, "We [the committee] should have gone further and made certain criticisms" of the reformatory, though they apparently never did.[40]

THE SUICIDE OF EDWARD LEIVA: COINCIDENTAL OR CONNECTED?

Before the state investigation into Benny Moreno's death was complete, a second Mexican American boy—seventeen-year-old Edward Leiva—was found dead in solitary confinement (Figure 9). His death, only eleven months after Benny Moreno's hanging, was eerily familiar. According to the school's internal investigation, Leiva had died of self-asphyxiation, which he carried out by tearing his bedsheets, braiding them into a makeshift rope, and looping it through the ventilation unit in the ceiling. Fred Bennet, his cellmate, claimed Leiva had felt despondent in recent days: "[he said] he was going to end everything," for "he felt he was headed for San Quentin some day." "'I'll hang myself, I won't go through this again,'" Leiva reportedly said to Bennet. To that end, Leiva devised a ruse. He would hang himself just before the supervisor made his rounds so that he would be discovered unconscious but not dead. Then, Leiva believed, the supervisor would have to take him to the hospital, from which he would make his escape. Leiva planned to overpower a nurse, according to Bennet, then leave with her car. "I knew he couldn't drive a car, so I thought he was bluffing," Bennet told investigators. A short time later in the evening, Bennet said he heard "cot springs squeak in Leiva's cell, and shouted in chorus" with another "inmate in the 'solitary' block, but . . . nobody came until some minutes later," after it was too late.[41]

News of Leiva's death shocked and angered his family. His father, John Leiva, a cement worker from Lennox, California, reportedly "upbraided" Superintendent Milne for his son's death. Not satisfied with Milne's response to the way in which Edward had died, John Leiva attempted to question other boys at the school about what they knew. Milne, however, would not allow it. When finally given the opportunity to see his son's body, the *Los Angeles Times* reported, he "wept copiously as he made the identification of his dead son." Edward Leiva's mother appeared, too, and was equally distraught at the sight of her boy.[42]

Initially, neither Superintendent Milne nor Director of Institutions Rosanoff planned to investigate the matter any further, relying on the

FIGURE 9. Edward Leiva. First committed to Whittier State School in 1935 at the age of thirteen, Edward Leiva was released two years later on probation. Arrested three years later, in 1940, at the age of seventeen for theft, he was recommitted to the reformatory. He attempted to escape on several occasions and ended up in solitary, where he carried out his final attempt to flee the school. Photograph by Fred C. Nelles School for Boys (Whittier). Whittier, California. California State Archives, Office of the Secretary of State, Sacramento, California.

autopsy and coroner's inquest, both of which had determined that Leiva, like Moreno, had committed suicide. A day later, however, "public indignation mounted with revelations of cruelty, beatings, solitary imprisonment and other forms of torture assertedly inflicted on youthful inmates of the reformatory," reported the *Los Angeles Examiner,* a Hearst-owned daily known for its muckraking investigations. Governor Olson was moved to action. He ordered Rosanoff to make a full inquiry into Leiva's death and its relationship, if any, to Moreno's suicide.[43]

To Rosanoff, the investigation was misguided, for he believed Leiva's suicide was yet another instance of a defective boy confined to the wrong institution. Nevertheless, Rosanoff carried out the inquiry secretly and swiftly, concluding that Leiva's escape plan was not ingenious but a sign of a sick—mentally defective—individual. Suicides, he noted, were "vastly" increased with "defective and psychopathic delinquents" such as Edward Leiva and Benny Moreno before him. Leiva's "intelligence was not only subnormal, but also showed, in the course of years, a steadily deteriorating trend." The boy's fear of ending up at Preston or San Quentin, Rosanoff stated matter of factly, was "well-founded," for the boy had been unable to adjust at the reformatory or at home.[44]

To further absolve the state from responsibility, Rosanoff described the disciplinary practices at Whittier State School as relatively mild. Officers, he learned through interviews he conducted with boys who had spent time in solitary, forced inmates to scrub floors on their hands and knees and to "duck walk," which was "waddl[ing] while squatted on their [legs]." Guards in solitary also kicked or hit boys or whipped them with a belt or a strap. The punishments, though not sanctioned by the state, were not cruel, Rosanoff explained. Rather, they were carried out in a "fatherly fashion."[45] To free reform school officials, in particular, from any responsibility, Rosanoff argued that they had little knowledge of the abusive treatment meted in the Lost Privilege Cottage. Dr. Tebbetts, the twenty-year school physician, agreed as well, saying he had "never seen a case of injury in a boy resulting from abuse by employees." The hospital records, he continued, proved his point—apparently forgetting that he, the nurse, and other school officials closely monitored and guarded the content of the records.[46]

Rosanoff's report, while satisfactory to the state, did little to assuage the public's doubts about Leiva's death, especially given the recent death of Benny Moreno. Indeed, immediately following the news of Leiva's death, the *Los Angeles Examiner* began its own exhaustive inquiry into the suicides. Led by newspaper reporter Sid Hughes, the daily interviewed countless witnesses, interrogated numerous official reports, and printed over 150 articles and dozens of photographs investigating Leiva and Moreno's deaths as well as the secrecy of the state reformatory and state institutions more broadly. In contrast to the paper's reporting of Moreno's death a year earlier, which was limited to no more than a dozen articles, Leiva's suicide—the second in a year—prompted unabated front-page coverage for several months, bringing public attention to the dire conditions at the reformatory. In many ways, Leiva's death underscored the deeply rooted institutional troubles that Benny Moreno's suicide had suggested only months earlier, which the public and state officials had largely ignored and considered an anomaly.[47]

As soon as news of Leiva's suicide hit the airwaves, newspaper reporter Hughes began to interview family members, former inmates, and anyone who could speak to the abusive—physical, sexual, and psychological—conditions at the school. When questioned, Edward Leiva's family recounted months of physical abuse that Leiva had endured yet had refused to voice for fear of retaliation. The "guards 'pounded me with their fists,'" Leiva told his father during a visit, "'and put me in solitary confinement. I was there a whole month and lived mostly on bread and water.'"[48] When he walked out, he told his sister, Helen, "'I was so weak I fell down.'"[49] The father told the reporter, "I said, 'Eddie, I'm going to report this to the office.' 'Oh, no—don't!' [Leiva] said [to his father]. 'I am just going to be as good as I can, and take whatever they deal out and get out of here as fast as I can.'" So, John Leiva informed the paper, he let it drop. Despite the abuse, the family explained Leiva harbored no thoughts of suicide.[50]

Moreno's family recounted similar, troubling details about abuse, as told to them by Benny Moreno. His older sister told Sid Hughes that guards made boys punish each other for infractions. Boys sometimes beat each other with sticks or belts or they "sacked" the offending boy with a cloth sack over his head and beat him. Moreno was once beaten so badly he was sent to the hospital. In response to those incidents as well as to Benny being forced to eat cigarettes for carrying a cigarette butt in his back pocket, Domingo Moreno said to Hughes, "What could I do about such things? I am a poor Mexican laborer. I have no influence."

Sexual abuse was also rampant at the reformatory, according to the *Examiner*. For years, since the school's founding in the early 1890s, sexual abuse of inmates by other boys as well as by staff had gone largely unreported, officially and unofficially. Cruz Cruz, an impoverished fourteen-year-old Mexican American boy who had escaped from the reformatory and had been hiding in a secret location for nearly five months, informed the *Examiner* that he had suffered not only "merciless punishments and sadistic brutality" at the reformatory but also sexual indignities. Only a year ago, the *Examiner* reported, Cruz had been an upstanding student at his local school. Now, after having been sent to the reformatory for playing hooky, he was no more than "a ragged, hungry waif determined to take any risk rather than return to Whittier." "Hungry and in tatters, but still defiant, the Cruz boy told the *Examiner*: 'They'll have to shoot me before they take me back there.'"[51]

Such practices at Whittier State School were too much for some boys, including Benny Moreno and Edward Leiva, forcing them to run away. According to Benny Moreno's sister, when she asked him why he had run away, Moreno responded, "'I'm tired of all these punishments in here. I can't stand it—and there are a lot of other kids who feel the same way. Someday someone is going to find out what they do to us, then there will be plenty of trouble, because there are lots of boys who can tell things if they are not afraid.'"[52] Edward Leiva, too, "detested"

Whittier, for he was picked on and taunted. "Other boys were allowed to gang up and throw things at the Leiva boy," the *Examiner* indicated.[53] Moreover, for minor violations, as the family members described, guards locked boys in steel units—solitary confinement—"where instruments of self torture and suicide are available for use."[54]

The revelation of such sensationalistic conditions led the editors of the *Examiner* to go so far as to compare Whittier State School to concentration camps in Nazi Germany. "The public knows why men hang themselves in German concentration camps. But the public cannot understand why little boys hang themselves in an American institution designed to reform and correct them."[55] Something is wrong when a boy "who may be under powerful emotional stress" is confined "to solitary . . . where the means of self destruction are at hand." "New laws must be passed to end that."[56] "The Whittier School must be cleaned up," the editors demanded, "and cleaned up immediately."[57]

The *Examiner* revealed not only the physical and sexual abuse at the reformatory as well as the secrecy that accompanied it, but also the state's attempt to erase that mistreatment. The newspaper editors blasted Rosanoff's report, in which he described the Lost Privilege Cottage practices as "mild," "fatherly," and "fun," as "whitewash."[58] The paper questioned, too, Rosanoff's characterization of Whittier as "place of kindly and intelligent care," his justification of corporal punishment, and his attempt to place sole responsibility for Whittier State School on Superintendent Milne.[59] Ultimately, the *Examiner* sought to bring about a "formal indictment and trial of the persons involved." "No psychiatric lore or specialized methods can explain why two boys have committed suicide there," the paper noted, and it called Rosanoff's report "biased, ex-parte, [and] self-saving."[60]

National and local leaders in youth reformation issued scathing critiques as well. Father Edward Flanagan of the famed Boys Town in Nebraska—which had been the subject of several motion pictures—wrote a letter blasting the "system of unnecessary schools of torture and schools of crime."[61] "Suicide [w]as an escape from brutality!" He concluded that something must be done to clean up those institutions.[62] Closer to home, concerned citizens and political leaders around the state echoed Flanagan's call. To demonstrate mounting public indignation, the *Examiner* published letters from irate readers that supported the investigation as well as congratulated the paper for its "exposé of Whittier." Publishing the letters was a self-serving move on the newspaper's part, yet it nevertheless demonstrated the thoughts of some of its readership. "You are doing some brave work," wrote one man, comparing the newspaper to famous social critic and writer Charles Dickens "when he described the horrors of the Yorkshire school of 1840 in 'Nicholas Nickleby.' "[63]

Feeling pressure from the onslaught of the press, the public, and some politicians, and not wanting to repeat any mistakes made in the Moreno investigation, Governor Olson promptly responded to Leiva's suicide, demanding the suspension of the Lost Privilege Cottage, the replacement of the Board of Managers, and the appointment of a special citizen's commission to investigate the boys' death and the "alleged brutalities in the Lost Privilege Cottage" and at the reformatory more generally.[64] In response, Rosanoff agreed to perform an internal investigation. Olson scoffed at his suggestion, saying he would not allow such "'star chamber' procedure." "This will not be a routine investigation." Abuse in any form, Olson repeated, would not be tolerated—as Moreno and Leiva's suicides had revealed the state had turned a blind eye, allowing abusive practices to continue for years.[65]

Olson's appointment of a citizen's commission and its public nature was unsettling for Rosanoff and the other administrators and staff, who, over the previous ten years or so, had grown accustomed to working with little state oversight. Years later, Robert V. Chandler, the business manager at Whittier State School in the mid-1930s, echoed those sentiments when he recalled that the governor's "committee set up its investigation in the downtown area of Los Angeles and proceeded to call witnesses, including both staff and wards, with front page coverage from one of the large daily papers. The school became a place of fear for staff as their pictures and names were published with alleged charges of all kinds."[66]

As the public hearings uncovered, those charges were well founded: dozens of witnesses—in total more than 110 individuals, many of them previously interviewed by Sid Hughes and the *Examiner*—came before the new commission, repeating the stories of harrowing physical and sexual assaults, criminal neglect, gross mismanagement, and state complicity.[67]

In appointing the commission, Governor Olson did not select members of El Congreso, as he had in the Moreno inquiry, though they continued to play key roles. Instead, Olson chose California Superior Court Judge Ben B. Lindsey, a national leader and founder of the juvenile court movement in Denver, Colorado, to head a three-person board responsible for investigating the suicides and conditions at the school and for recommending changes (Figure 10). The Lindsey Commission, as it was

FIGURE 10. Ben B. Lindsey. Head of a state-appointed commission investigating the conditions at Whittier State School that led to the deaths of Benny Moreno and Edward Leiva, Ben B. Lindsey leans forward to hear the testimony of an inmate. When asked to recount the sexual abuse the boy suffered at the school, the inmate refused to do so in front of the women in the courtroom and only agreed to do so after Lindsey promised him discretion. Courtesy Los Angeles Herald-Examiner Collection, Los Angeles Public Library, Los Angeles, California.

known, included a civic leader and a minister, and it had the power to call witnesses, issue subpoenas, and ensure witnesses could speak freely without fear of reprisals. Although the commission covered much of the same ground as the articles by Sid Hughes—a "brilliant newspaper reporter," according to Lindsey—it also probed the school's history and unwritten policies and practices more deeply and more widely, indicting state administrators, staff, and the public.[68]

Over the course of several months, the Lindsey Commission questioned dozens of boys, family members, staff and administrators, political and civic leaders, and anyone associated or having knowledge of or covering up the suicides or conditions at Whittier State School. The Lindsey Commission paid particular attention to the possibility that Edward Leiva and Benny Moreno had been murdered or driven to suicide, thereby placing direct responsibility on Whittier State School, the Department of

Institutions, and the State of California more broadly. Among those who testified publicly to the likelihood of homicides at Whittier State School was John Leiva. Contrary to Rosanoff's theories, he said that his son, Edward Leiva, was not "a psychopathic delinquent." Nor, he insisted, was he "a drunkard and a tyrant in [my] own house." "Those are lies!" he stated emphatically. "My son didn't commit suicide. He was murdered!" The boy could not have reached the ventilator, he explained, even while standing on the bed. Curious about his claim, Lindsey called for a reenactment (much like Moreno's) of the boy's suicide at the Lost Privilege Cottage. Unlike Moreno's reenactment, which proved he could have caused his own death, Leiva's proved that no boy close to his height could have reached the vent alone or taken his life in that manner.[69]

Following the reenactment, the commission continued its inquiry and heard a litany of "cruelties that sound like descriptions of medieval inquisitions." Those included reports of physical and sexual abuse, some of which had not been revealed in Sid Hughes's investigation. Valdo Sánchez, an eighteen-year-old Mexican American boy, and several other boys testified about William Henry's regular "sexual inquisition." Sánchez said that Henry, a Euro-American guard in the Lost Privilege unit, often awoke him, Benny Moreno, and Cruz Cruz and "asked them many revolting questions." Another boy testified that a guard in the Wrigley Cottage, a unit for the youngest boys at Whittier, had been trying to do "evil things" to Moreno. "'I can't stand that evil man,'" Moreno told the boy, "'I am afraid of him, I am going to run away.'" Other boys told more explicit details of the widespread illicit sexual activity—namely, sodomy—that the administration knew about and allowed to continue. One boy, who preferred to remain anonymous, testified that it "all began with a supervisor [guard] at Whittier," who was later discharged, and that it included "many acts of perversion" with so many other boys that the boy could not count. When the boy complained to Milne, the superintendent said he was too busy and advised him to protect himself, saying that "if he didn't want to do those things they would not be done." When the boy turned to others for help, they too did nothing. The commission learned as well that wards who acquiesced to the guards' sexual advances were rewarded with better treatment. A former inmate, a youth from a wealthy family, said "boys willing to indulge in indecencies with the guards were better treated while we were brutally abused. It was out of this experience," he explained, "that I became bitter and vicious toward society and finally wound up in San Quentin."[70]

With more of the school's secret history of sexual and physical abuse exposed, the commission then heard about many of the irregularities involved in the investigation of Benny Moreno's death. Lost Privilege guard Don C. Napper admitted before the Lindsey Commission that the night of Moreno's death the guard on duty had failed to follow the policy of inspecting the boys every thirty minutes, contrary to what he had originally claimed. Such neglect, Lindsey believed, bordered on the criminal. "Don't you agree," he asked Napper, "that if [guard] Morrell had made his regular 30-minute inspection of the Moreno cell, the boy might not have died?" Napper conceded he might have intercepted the boy.[71]

The guard's lapse in inspecting the inmates in the solitary unit as well as the coroner's "botched" autopsy of Moreno raised further suspicions. Several doctors testified that the autopsy indicated undigested food in Moreno's stomach, which suggested he had not died the morning of August 11 but rather sometime the night before, a few hours after his dinner. Curiously, the presence of food had been noted during the original inquiry into Moreno's death, but because everyone believed he had died sometime in the morning and the coroner had accepted the presence of undigested food as routine, few paid attention to that detail. The Lindsey Commission's investigation into the timing of events the night of Moreno's death raised the suspicion that someone might have indeed killed him the night before and staged a suicide.[72]

The focus on the presence of undigested food did not go unnoticed. Rather, it proved so central to the Lindsey Commission's investigation that nearly all former members of the Gallagher Committee, who originally had exonerated the school and state officials, came forward recanting their group's final report. Even Leo Gallagher, the author of that report, repudiated their findings. "If I had known of the brutality testified to before your body and of the presence of undigested food in the Moreno boy's body," he told Lindsey, "indicating a question of the time of his death, I would not have declared his death to be suicide beyond all reasonable doubt." In separate testimony, other members had noted many of the irregularities at the reformatory, including the secrecy of school practices and harassment of witnesses, but they had not included those details in the final report. When Lindsey quizzed them about why they had omitted such findings, one responded, "If we had, the report would have filled a book."[73] Not amused, Lindsey criticized them severely for signing the report without reading it. Quevedo and Casares explained that they had signed under "force," yet who exactly forced them was not disclosed. It is likely they meant Gallagher, as he had a friendly relationship with reform school administrators, who, in turn, had pressured him to conclude the committee's work quickly.

The Lindsey Commission's probe of irregularities in the investigation of Moreno's death revealed more troubling practices at Whittier State School, including the transfer of boys 'who knew too much' about conditions at the school. The practice of removing boys to alternative state institutions was not a new development. Rather, it dated to the 1910s, with Fred C. Nelles's policy of weeding out the "defectives." The removal of potential witnesses, however, indicated an attempt to obstruct a state investigation. At least four individuals testified that they knew of at least three boys—Frank Ward, Howard Doss, and Alex Burgueno—who had been transferred to the Preston School of Industry and at least one boy—Felix Cordero—who had been sent to Camarillo State Hospital to keep them quiet about Moreno's death. "The Welfare and Institutions Code hardly gives Rosanoff that power [to transfer inmates]," noted one witness. "I believe it only allows him to transfer an insane patient from one asylum to another."[74]

Lindsey too was puzzled by that practice. "I don't know of any right they have to take boys directly to an insane asylum without a hearing," he said. The law did, in fact, allow Milne, with Rosanoff's approval, to send boys to insane asylums or state hospitals. Not until the Attorney General issued a new ruling a few days later, on August 20, 1940, were administrators banned from transferring youths from juvenile corrections to state hospitals. The new policy limited such transfers of patients or wards to "like institutions."[75]

The news of Cordero's transfer and diagnosis as mentally unsound disturbed members of the Lindsey Commission, leading Lindsey to question the process through which youths were "branded 'psychopathic' or 'defective' . . . and transferred to other institutions." Unbeknownst to Lindsey, in the 1910s and early 1920s, intelligence tests and eugenics fieldwork—as well as a host of racial, ethnic, and cultural biases in the scientific researchers' interpretation of those tools—were used to identify defective youths at Whittier State School and, to a limited extent, at Preston and the California/Ventura School for Girls. Those marked as mentally defective were then transferred to another institution, ideally Sonoma State Hospital but more frequently Preston or the juvenile court because the state hospital was backlogged and generally disliked accepting defective delinquents. In the late 1920s and 1930s, when the state refused to fund the scientific work at Whittier, school administrators carried out sporadic testing and relied on the opinions of the scientific researchers to determine who was normal and who was defective. More generally, few boys were diagnosed and transferred out of Whittier beyond that point. Nevertheless, under the law, the Director of Institutions had final say in making such transfers. Most parents were not aware of the statute, and some complained "that their sons had been arbitrarily transferred to institutions without any notice or consultation."[76]

Lindsey then turned his attention to the policies and practices of the Lost Privilege Cottage, questioning the reform school's officials about their efficacy. Do you consider that unit torture? Lindsey asked Milne. It "might be regarded as torture," Milne responded. "That's a confession," Lindsey retorted. "'Well, I'll tell you, Judge Lindsey,' Milne barked," reported a newspaper, "'I'll apologize to no man on earth for my treatment of these boys.'" Milne argued that he had never struck or mistreated a boy, overlooking the fact that neglect could be equally harmful. "Some of the guards might be abusing boys right now and I wouldn't know about it," he admitted, thus implicating himself in the abuse. Milne said he had dismissed four guards for brutality in the last four years at Whittier State School, but other than that he knew of no other transgressions at the reformatory.[77]

Unconvinced, the Lindsey Commission then interrogated Rosanoff about his knowledge of the practice of placing boys in the isolation unit for days at a time with no clothing, schooling, visits from parents, or other communication. Rosanoff refused to respond, saying instead that the testimony of "feebleminded, insane, psychopathic, anti-social and other types of irresponsibles, including not only adults, but also minors" before the Lindsey Commission had resulted in increased tragedies—suicide attempts—at other state institutions under his watch.[78]

Rosanoff and Milne's testimony as well as other staff members' admissions of abusive practices and other irregularities touched a raw nerve with the audience at the hearing (Figure 11). Throughout the process, family members, friends, and other onlookers—many of them Mexicans and Mexican Americans—cheered at the investigating committee and, alternatively, jeered at state personnel. The audience became particularly incensed when the part-time psychologist at Whittier State School offered to reveal the private records of the boys who had testified in the investigation so as to discredit their testimony. The staff member justified the revelations saying that the boys had waived their right to privacy when they became wards of the state. Angry, the audience

FIGURE 11. Leiva Family. The family of Edward Leiva—father, sister, mother, and other family members—attends the Lindsey Commission's hearings into the conditions at Whittier State School. Family members break down during the testimony of the abuse the boys suffered. Courtesy Los Angeles Herald-Examiner Collection, Los Angeles Public Library, Los Angeles, California.

booed at his suggestion. Judge Lindsey was not impressed either, calling it a "shameful act and utterly unfair."[79]

Soon after the state officials testified before the Lindsey Commission's hearings, another investigation got under way into the suicides, this time headed by Deputy District Attorney Eugene Williams and the Los Angeles County Grand Jury. Williams called the grand jury to determine whether criminal charges against staff and administrators were warranted in the boys' deaths. To enable the deputy district attorney to call witnesses, many of the same ones who had appeared before the Lindsey Commission, Judge Lindsey suspended the commission's work for a month. Before the grand jury, dozens of former Whittier State School boys recounted graphic testimony of physical and sexual abuse—the latter described as "sex torture" and "revolting orgies." Despite the testimony, the grand jury decided not to issue any indictments against school personnel. Undeterred by the news, Judge Lindsey explained that "technical aspects" of the case had prevented the grand jury from issuing formal charges, but the grand jury's "inaction" did not discredit the abuse and should not discourage other state and local officials from pressing criminal charges to "clean house" at the institution.[80]

In response, Deputy District Attorney Williams and John Leiva filed criminal charges in the Los Angeles Municipal Court against guards

Don V. Cavitt and Ivan B. McMillan for their role in the abuse. Throughout the trial, the men denied abusing Edward Leiva. McMillan claimed he had only "lectured the boy severely," although he admitted to using the duck walk and other forms of corporal punishment.[81] The court expressed little sympathy, however. It found both men guilty and ordered McMillan and Cavitt to jail for 165 days and 225 days, respectively. At same time, the State Personnel Board, which also had found the men guilty of "cruel and unusual punishment," dismissed the men from their posts at Whittier State School.[82]

In the meantime, the Lindsey Commission resumed its public hearing and completed its investigation, issuing an exhaustive 167-page report to the governor's office. In it, the commission denounced Whittier State School administrators for "gross inefficiency, mismanagement and irresponsibility" and demanded drastic reforms at the school. "The boys are sadly in need of guidance, training and understanding." Instead, "they are subjected to brutality, abuses and intimidation." Edward Leiva, it ruled, "had been beaten on a number of occasions" as had Benny Moreno, yet no one had expressed any responsibility in what happened at the school. "This apathy," wrote Lindsey, "and irresponsibility is the underlying cause of the abuses prevailing at Whittier."[83]

The Lindsey Commission concluded by recommending the appointment of a three-person panel of experts to develop a "workable program" for the school. Among those they identified as suitable included Father Flanagan, a member of the Osborne Association, and a representative of the United States Department of Justice who, preferably, resided in California. When completed with the work, the committee would then submit the recommendations to the governor's office and suggest one or more individuals to carry out the plan. That person would, in turn, serve a temporary, six-month appointment and be given broad power to implement the program. At the end of that term, the original three-person committee would then reexamine the school's condition and name a permanent superintendent with "training, qualifications, and experience, regardless of political affiliation."[84]

But before the state could implement those recommendations, the Lindsey Commission also implored state leaders to pay attention to the "racial problem" at the reformatory. According to the commission's estimates, about one-third of the population was of Mexican origin, a much larger proportion than that found across the state. "These boys," the commission found, "feel that they are definitely discriminated against." The committee believed them, "judging from the names they say they are called, and coupled with the social attitude of some of the [supervisors and teachers] in charge towards the Mexican boys." "'You dirty little greaser,'" Don Cavitt often said to Mexican boys, and "'you dirty little Mexican shote.' ('Shote' [wa]s an insulting word used for Mexican boys by some of the guards.)"[85] "Many racial quarrels and fights prevail at the school," according to the Commission, yet not a single staff person— not a single teacher or supervisor—was Spanish or Mexican or someone who could provide culturally relevant "counsel." This is surprising, Judge Lindsey continued, given that a member of the Gallagher Committee made that same suggestion a year ago. The failure to "eradicate racial antagonism" was also troubling, he noted, not only because it went against American principles but also because California had such a large Mexican population.[86] Despite those words, little more was said in public about the racial tensions in the school.

At the same time the Lindsey Commission made public its recommendations, Superintendent Milne faced the State Board of Personnel and charges of "flagrant and gross neglect of duty, misrepresentation, arbitrary conduct, and willful and deliberate absence from his post." That board did not take the matter lightly. It called numerous young witnesses, including "Americans and Mexicans, Negroes and whites" to testify about their experiences during Milne's tenure. The youths, in turn, described "staggering blows and kicks, whippings with leather straps, 'rabbit punches,'" as well as the practices of the "hot seat" and "pink belly."[87] The "hot seat," used to force confessions, involved a guard placing an electric heater under a table and forcing a boy to sit on the table for hours or until they owned up to a transgression.[88] Pink belly, on the other hand, was described as a "game" played among the boys, but it was no laughing matter—it was essentially the beating and rape of a boy by his peers.[89]

Superintendent Milne knew about these abuses, the board learned, but did little to stem them. Rather, he found ways to keep them secret. In some cases, he simply dismissed staff, as he did with Willis Root, a Wrigley Cottage guard who had forced a ten-year-old boy "to commit a degenerate act" on him. Rather than bring Root before the State Personnel Board, Milne simply "told him to take a vacation" and later dismissed him for "failing to return."[90] Milne also knowingly violated state policies, according to the board. From July 1938 to June 1940, Milne accepted forty-one boys with records of sex "perversion," likely homosexuality, even when such admissions were not allowed.[91]

Milne's reputation—what was left of it—was further tarnished a day before the State Board Personnel concluded its hearings. Driving while under the influence of alcohol, Milne lost control of his car and crashed into an orange grove in the City of Santa Ana. While he was attempting to flee the scene, the police arrested him for intoxication and drunk driving and jailed him for five hours until he produced bond. Later that same day, while still recovering from minor injuries, Milne learned that the State Personnel Board had found him guilty of "failure of good behavior, incompetency, inefficiency, inexcusable neglect of duty, [and] dishonesty," among other charges. Milne expressed surprise at the ruling, while continuing to deny any wrongdoing. "I have honestly tried to act and meet every situation honestly and fearlessly and if I have ever made a decision that may not have seemed what you had wished, I believe you all know I was at least honest and fair."[92] Three years later, in 1944, Milne sought his reinstatement by filing a petition in the Sacramento County Superior Court, alleging he had resigned "under duress, menace and pressure of the board (Personnel Board)." Milne's request was denied.[93]

Meanwhile, Aaron J. Rosanoff continued to defend the institution, the state, and his post as Director of Institutions, even after the Lindsey Commission had issued its final report. In a supplementary report submitted to Governor Olson in 1941, Rosanoff attempted to discredit much of the Lindsey Commission's findings, arguing they were biased and had failed to prove many theories, including the murder of Benny Moreno. He argued that, rather than using evidence, the commission had relied on "invective and other emotional pyrotechnics" from the testimony of many witnesses who "were of subnormal intelligence, insane, psychopathic, or criminal." Ultimately, Rosanoff concluded, the Lindsey Commission's findings changed little of what was known about the suicides and abuse at Whittier State School.[94]

Despite Rosanoff's opposition, the Lindsey Commission moved ahead with the appointment of the committee to make suggestions for overhauling the institution. That committee, which was headed by Father Flanagan, in turn, worked quickly and issued a number of drastic changes. First, it proposed the closure of the Receiving Cottage and Lost Privilege Cottage.[95] Next, it recommended the development of a child-centered, individualized program with well-trained, well-paid staff and urged the exclusion of "over-age children and those who are feeble-minded, crippled, tubercular or otherwise unable to participate in the full school program." The committee called for the presence of a physician, psychiatrist, psychologist, social worker, probation officer, educational director, and other professionals who could coordinate a special plan or program for each boy that could be updated as needed, similar to the program Fred C. Nelles had developed years earlier. The committee also suggested giving staff "psychological and psychiatric examinations to determine their fitness for handling children," reorganizing all academic and vocational departments, changing the name of the school to lessen the shame associated with the institution, and getting rid of all corporal punishment, the notorious monitor system, the merit system needed for parole, and the honor clubs. Instead of hiring more untrained and unprepared staff, they advocated assigning college-trained peer counselors to work with the youths, and they urged the establishment of a school-wide government, a library, house mothers in cottages, playground facilities, and other recreational activities such as the Catalina Camp (which had ended in the 1930s for reasons of "economy"), sports, scout troops, hobby clubs, dramatics, choir, religious services, and participation in community affairs. Finally, they urged follow-up attention after each boy's release.[96]

Soon after completing his work at Whittier State School, Father Flanagan returned to Boys' Town, leaving behind Patrick J. Norton, a colleague and the original founder of Boy's Town, who succeeded Milne as interim superintendent. Norton's stint as interim superintendent lasted but a few weeks, however, for he found the position too challenging in having to deal with boys who escaped from the institution on a daily basis and a bitter staff who was not willing to cooperate. When Norton left suddenly, two weeks after Flanagan's departure, Duffy, a well-respected Los Angeles high school teacher was appointed interim superintendent. Duffy, like Norton, lasted only a few weeks and was replaced by William B. Cox who was eventually appointed as the permanent superintendent.[97] Cox faced equally difficult conditions at the school, which led him to suggest the closure of the reformatory "until the notorious publicity had been forgotten."[98] The ill repute of the reformatory was so severe that few judges were willing to send boys to Whittier and parents pleaded with those same justices not to send their sons to that institution. As a result, within a matter of months, the population of inmates at Whittier plummeted from 350 to no more than 200. Within a few weeks of Cox's appointment, his status as a resident of New York also raised questions as to his eligibility, for the position was a state civil service appointment. In dire need of an experienced leader, state officials—with the governor's approval—selected the assistant superintendent to lead the institution on a temporary basis while state leaders mapped the reformatory's future plans.[99]

With the assistance of the American Law Institute's Model Youth Authority Act, created in 1940, a committee of concerned legislators, judges, lawyers, social workers, psychiatrists, and others across the state came together to propose legislation aimed at overhauling Whittier State School as well as Preston School of Industry and Ventura School for Girls. Rather than build the institutions on the principles of punishment and retribution, the new plan focused on rehabilitation and reform. When completed, the Youth Corrections Authority Act (later changed to the Youth Authority Act) went before the California legislature, where it passed nearly unanimously, and then to the governor's office, where it was signed promptly, establishing the Youth Authority in 1941, less than two years after the deaths of Edward Leiva and Benny Moreno. The Youth Authority specifically called for a three-person commission and mandated the acceptance of all commitments under twenty-three years of age, though initially, for the first three years, the Youth Authority could choose its wards. The law also granted the Youth Authority the power to establish delinquency prevention councils, though it lacked authority over the administration of Whittier, Preston, and Ventura, all institutions that fell under the purview of the Department of Institutions. To fund the Youth Authority, the law appropriated $10,000 for each of the three advisors and $100,000 to run the entire program for the next two years. It also renamed Whittier State School for Boys as the Fred C. Nelles School for Boys in honor of Nelles and in hopes of remaking the reformatory's image.

Initially, the Youth Authority consisted of Otto H. Close, Superintendent of the Preston School of Industry, Karl Holton, Chief Probation Officer of Los Angeles County, and Howard Slane, an appointee of the governor; its headquarters were in Sacramento, and it had branches in Los Angeles and San Francisco. A year later, in 1942, in an agreement between the governor and Aaron J. Rosanoff, authority over the juvenile correctional facilities was removed from the Department of Institutions and was placed with the Youth Authority—which, at that point, consisted of a run-down, poorly staffed diagnostic facility at Preston. Indeed, the process of building the Youth Authority lagged in the early 1940s primarily because of the outbreak of World War II and the U.S. involvement with the bombing of Pearl Harbor on December 7, 1941. By 1943, however, the Youth Authority had increased its status with the appointment of Karl Holton—a post he held for nearly ten years—and the formal transfer of the correctional facilities under its administration.

Paul J. McCusick, in turn, was selected as the superintendent for Nelles that same year. By then, the Youth Authority had a sizable population of 1,080 wards in the reformatories, 1,625 on parole, and 517 staff members.[100]

To proponents of the Youth Authority, and specifically Karl Holton, the Youth Authority's revolutionary approach held much promise in dealing with juvenile delinquency. On the eve of its launch, Holton wrote:

> It seems to me that for the first time we have an agency which can give an over-all picture of youth crime and youth delinquency; for the first time we have an agency which can make every facility, both public and private, which exists within the state available to every county, to every court, and to every young man and woman; for the first time we have an agency which can consistently promote standards of case work and of personnel and of institutional and agency programs; for the first time we have an agency which, with a minimum of red tape, can treat offenders as individuals; for the first time we have an agency which can promote a worth-while delinquency and crime prevention program on a *statewide* basis [emphasis in the original].[101]

The Youth Authority's ability to work successfully at preventing and handling juvenile delinquents—increasingly youths of color, namely, Mexicans, Mexican Americans, and African Americans—was yet to be seen in the second half of the twentieth century. Nevertheless, the development and implementation of such a program would not have been possible without the tragic deaths of Edward Leiva and Benny Moreno, two Mexican American boys who, in giving up their lives, called attention to the widespread abuse, incompetency, neglect, and public apathy plaguing the state's juvenile corrections. Their lives and deaths are a testament to the power and authority of the state in imposing notions or "states" of delinquency in confining and controlling alienated youths.

THE LEGACY OF BENNY MORENO AND EDWARD LEIVA

The tragic deaths of Benny Moreno and Edward Leiva and the numerous private and public investigations that followed not only exposed the decline of Whittier State School from a premiere reformatory in the 1910s and 1920s to an outdated, abusive institution in the 1930s but also blew the lid off the heinous practices at the reformatory and the juvenile correctional system more broadly. For nearly a decade, primarily during E. J. Milne's administration, a code of silence, unchecked physical and sexual abuse, gross mismanagement, and untrained and unrestrained staff with racial and ethnic prejudices ran rampant at the reformatory. However, state administrators and reform school personnel were not the only ones responsible for the school's sordid history, as this narrative has attested. The public's neglect and apathy of the reform school's financial and physical health also contributed to the school's decline. Ultimately, the youths sent to those institutions were the ones who suffered the most, not only for their own mistakes but also for those of adults. In the end, state leaders attempted to rectify past mistakes by appointing a body interested in providing individualized attention, a method tried and tested years earlier in the 1910s and 1920s, and brought back—albeit with modifications—once again in the 1940s, to handle contemporary problems, a cycle that would repeat itself in the second half of the twentieth century with mixed results.

Epilogue

Recovering Youths' Voices

In 2009, five years after the Fred C. Nelles Correctional Facility (formerly Whittier State School for Boys) closed after more than a century in operation, I had the good fortune of meeting Frank Aguirre, a sixty-nine-year-old Mexican American man and former inmate of Whittier State School. I met Frank through Mike Sprague, a newspaper reporter from the *Whittier News*, the local daily in Whittier, California, after he had learned of my interest in the institution. Frank, it seemed, had been in contact with Sprague about the state's future plans for the defunct reform school, a topic the reporter was covering in detail and Frank was following closely, for he had a personal history with the school.

As a young boy, Frank had been sent to the Fred C. Nelles Correctional in the early 1950s for "incorrigibility," a catchall phrase used to incarcerate youths considered beyond the care and control of the local authorities and often their parents as well (Figure 12). When I learned of Frank's history at Nelles and later the Preston School of Industry, I jumped at the opportunity to talk with him and learn more about his personal experiences before, during, and after the reformatory, for the written records I was investigating provided only muffled "voices" of youths. Initially, I had hoped to write a history of the reformatory using the oral histories of former juvenile offenders in California like Frank, but that project proved too lofty a goal, particularly for someone like myself who had not been trained as an oral historian. Nevertheless, my brief foray into the world of oral history provided the opportunity to

FIGURE 12. Frank Aguirre. Thirteen-year-old Frank Aguirre embraces his family during visiting day at Fred C. Nelles Correctional School for Boys (formerly Whittier State School) sometime in 1952. Frank was released shortly before his fourteenth birthday in 1954. Courtesy of Frank Aguirre, Personal Collection.

meet with him and with two other former inmates—Art Rodriguez, a well-known young adult writer, and Luis "Bato" Talamantez, a prison rights activist and former member of the San Quentin Six. I learned Frank's story and the ways in which his experience at the Nelles Correctional had impacted his life.[1]

In our conversations, Frank recalled his experience at Nelles with mixed feelings, suggesting it had improved some aspects of his life yet had done so at a heavy price. With his parents' consent, he said, he was first sent to Nelles for incorrigibility as a twelve-year-old boy; he eventually spent five years in the Youth Authority, finishing up his stint at the Preston School of Industry. "That was the last time I saw the inside of a prison," he told me proudly. "The [Nelles] school was tough and the discipline was tough," he recalled, and boys often escaped for those reasons. Yet few got away from Nelles, he also remembered. When caught and returned, escapees received harsh punishments, he told me. Upon their reentry to the school, boys landed in the discipline cottage—units used to segregate boys according to offense and age. There, Frank explained, youths spent fifteen to thirty days, depending on how long and how far they had run. Life in the cottage could be brutal, as he recalled. Three African American supervisors managed that cottage and made the boys take part in grueling exercises, he recalled. "Hey," he said, pointing to the few benefits of that experience, at least "you got into better physical condition." The escapees' troubles did not end there, however. Once these boys were returned to their unit or cottage, the "group supervisor [of the cottage] would conveniently leave the room . . . and the monitors and den leaders," who were wards themselves, "would beat the hell out of the boys for running away." This occurred, he explained, because when one boy ran, the entire unit lost time off and, ultimately, lost their early release: a single escape often meant that all the boys received an additional thirty to ninety days of confinement to their sentence.

Frank also recalled that he got into a lot of fights while at Nelles. As a light-skinned (*güero*) Mexican American, he had a difficult time integrating with the majority of youths of Mexican descent. Most of them rejected him for being "too white," and the whites rejected him for being "too brown," he said. Inevitably, fistfights ensued, which the supervisors rarely broke up. Instead, they would often let the youths fight it out "*mano a mano*" to let them "get it out of their system."

The discipline and regimentation—marching to and from their cottages and working in silence at vocational, agricultural, and husbandry trades—though rigorous, paid off, according to Frank. Youths learned self-control and manners, he said. Boys with good behavior earned time off for themselves, and those in the larger units and those with leadership skills were put in charge of overseeing the entire unit as monitors. Boys worked hard for what they had, Frank underscored: "No privileges were given to you." Following orders also earned his cottage special attention, he said. Indeed, Frank recalled proudly the accomplishments of his cottage, the Wrigley Cottage, which was known for housing the youngest boys, usually twelve years of age and under. Under the leadership of Frank O'Connell, Wrigley Cottage boys had a spectacular drill team. The team competed at the city and state level and against various branches of the United States armed forces, winning "more awards and trophies than any other [drill team] in the state," Frank stated. The highlight came in 1953 when they won the State Championship at Long Beach.[2] Reflecting on these bittersweet experiences, Frank lamented the closure of Nelles in 2004, because he felt the institution had taught self-restraint to the boys who needed it the most.

Frank's sense of injustice, however, tempered his nostalgia for Nelles Correctional Facility, especially given what happened to him after his release. After he left Preston, where he finished up his commitment,

Frank said he found himself labeled as a "bad boy from the other sides of the tracks." He recalled being treated like a leper in his own community. He believes that, by today's standards, his petty theft—the transgression that had landed him in Nelles in the first place—probably would have resulted in a reprimand at most. Instead, he said, the authorities in the early 1950s threw the book at him. As a result, his commitment to the Youth Authority turned him into a social outcast, a stigma that took years for him to overcome and one that he had not wanted to share publicly until recently.

Public educational administrators made matters worse for Frank when they refused him admittance to the local high school after he returned home at the age of seventeen. With only a ninth-grade education, Frank could not get a job, but he did manage to enlist in the military—an experience that ended fifteen months later when officials learned of his record and had him discharged. As a social outcast, Frank said he learned quickly how to survive. Instead of telling people about his past, "you [learned to] keep your mouth shut . . . You had to find your way." Indeed, Frank was resourceful. With schooling closed to him, Frank dug ditches while on an informal apprenticeship in the plumbing trade. After four years in that industry, he opened a plumbing, electrical, and air-conditioning business.

Despite his accomplishments, Frank was (and still is, in many ways) angry about his experience in the state institutions. Reflecting on his five years in and out of Nelles and Preston—from 1952 to 1957 and honorably discharged in 1961—he made a powerful confession: "I felt emotionally raped," he said. "They took my childhood!" His prospects for a better life had been ruined, all because of a minor transgression: "I wouldn't want to wish that experience on anyone." Frank's continuing resentment and palpable anger toward the juvenile correctional system, though tempered by time, reveals the complexity of "real life" experiences in weighing the benefits and costs of that system. Although Frank reaped the rewards of the discipline he could not get at home, he also sacrificed his innocence, youth, and future.

Since my interview with Frank, we have maintained a friendly personal and professional relationship peppered with periodic reminders of his interest in Nelles's past, present, and future. He calls or e-mails me occasionally to talk about my research and sends me newspaper stories about the latest developments in the reform school's situation. In many ways, Frank remains intimately tied to the past because of the limitations it placed on his present and his future.

The histories of many youths who passed through the reformatory system resembled Frank's experiences. Like Frank, many of the boys (and girls, for that matter) led productive lives after they left the reformatory, yet they also faced many challenges along the way. Many of them entered the armed forces, when permitted, and served in World War I and World War II; others went back to school or studied a trade or a profession that enabled them to find employment and make a decent wage. For instance, one young man, a Mexican American youth, found employment with a credit exchange company and juggled both that job and law school. Many other former inmates married and formed families, too. A significant proportion, however, quickly got into trouble after being released, and they landed back in the reformatory, in a local city or county jail, or in the state prison system at San Quentin or Folsom. Some of them spent many years in and out the penal system; others died from accidents and injuries sustained in those places. Some former delinquents also contracted contagious diseases such as tuberculosis, diphtheria, and syphilis; others developed drug addictions from which they eventually died; and a small handful took their own lives rather than live with the shame of being former delinquents. Others were forced to leave the state immediately, deported to their home states or countries of origin; others remained, roaming the territory and attempting to stay out of trouble for as long as possible.

Notwithstanding the challenges that confronted me in writing this book in recovering the voices of youths and of youths of color in particular, such as Frank Aguirre, I have attempted to give witness to their range of experiences in the formative years of California's juvenile justice system. Notions of science and scientific research as well as of race, heredity, and delinquency in the early twentieth century—and, before that, ideas about who or what was ultimately responsible for wayward or otherwise unwanted minors—shaped and continue to shape to a great extent the ways in which delinquent youths and youths of color in specific were and are handled by the state. State policies and practices aimed at dealing with the rising tide of delinquency—and its subsequent linking with feeblemindedness—resulted in the criminalization, racialization, and pathologization of youths of color. For some, this process meant segregation in a state institution, but for others it meant sterilization.

Despite the state's power over the young people in its custody, the youths and their family members found ways to negotiate and challenge the state apparatus. Some pitted their physical strength against the state by attempting to escape or to launch riots; others used more subtle forms of contestation—the "weapons of the weak"—such as dragging their feet, feigning interest in the scientific work at the institution, or, more boldly, writing letters of protest to the state institution administrators. Those pleas notwithstanding, the state flexed its power in exerting the full extent of the law to maintain its interests, which ultimately did more harm than good for many of California's most marginal members of society.

Notes

INTRODUCTION

1. For more on pachucos and pachucas of the 1940s, see, for instance, Luis Alvarez, *The Power of the Zoot: Youth Culture and Resistance during World War II* (Berkeley: University of California Press, 2009); Catherine C. Ramírez, *The Woman in the Zoot: Gender, Nationalism, and the Cultural Politics of Memory* (Durham, N.C.: Duke University Press, 2009); Eduardo Pagán, *Murder at the Sleepy Lagoon: Zoot Suits, Race, and Riot in Wartime Los Angeles* (Chapel Hill: University of North Carolina Press, 2003); Edward J. Escobar, *Race, Police, and the Making of a Political Identity: Mexican Americans and the Los Angeles Police Department, 1900–1945* (Berkeley: University of California Press, 1999); Mauricio Mazón, *The Zoot-Suit Riots: The Psychology of Symbolic Annihilation* (Austin: University of Texas Press, 1988); and Elizabeth Escobedo, "The Pachuca Panic: Sexual and Cultural Battlegrounds in World War II Los Angeles," *Western Historical Quarterly* 38, no. 2 (2007), 133–156.

2. I borrow from Eric Schneider's concept of "web"—interconnected relationships among private and public agencies and organizations influencing the lives of dependent and delinquent youths—to describe the juvenile justice system in California. Eric Schneider, *In the Web of Class: Delinquents and Reformers in Boston, 1830s to 1910s* (New York: New York University Press, 1993).

3. This book builds on and contributes to the literature on intelligence testing, which is vast and spans numerous fields. For this study, the following works were consulted: Paul Davis Chapman, *Schools as Sorters: Lewis M. Terman, Applied Psychology, and the Intelligence Testing Movement, 1890–1930* (New York: New York University Press, 1988); Chapman, "Schools as Sorters: Testing and Tracking in California, 1910–1925," *Journal of Social History* 14, no. 4. (Summer 1981), 701–717; David Tyack, *The One Best System: A History of the American Urban Education* (Cambridge, Mass.: Harvard University Press, 1974);

Leon J. Kamin, *The Science and Politics of the IQ* (New York: Halsted Press, 1974); Gilbert González, "Racism, Education, and the Mexican Community in Los Angeles, 1920–30," *Societas* 4, no. 4 (Autumn 1974), 287–301; Gilbert González, *Chicano Education in the Era of Segregation* (Philadelphia: Balch Institute Press, 1990); and Hamilton Cravens, *The Triumph of Evolution: The Heredity-Environment Controversy, 1900–1941*, 2nd ed. (Baltimore: John Hopkins Press, 1988).

4. For studies that influenced Nelles and the researchers he recruited to Whittier State School, see, for instance, Alfred Binet and Théodore Simon, *Mentally Defective Children*, trans. W. B. Drummond (London: Edward Arnold, [1914]); Charles B. Davenport, *Heredity in Relation to Eugenics* (New York: Henry Holt, 1913); E. A. Doll, *Clinical Studies in Feeblemindedness* (Boston: R. G. Badger, 1917); A. F. Tredgold, *Mental Deficiency* (London: Baillière, Tindall and Cox, 1922); H. H. Goddard, *Feeblemindedness: Its Causes and Consequences* (New York: MacMillan, 1914, reprinted 1920); and Pearce Bailey, "A Contribution to the Mental Pathology of Races in the United States," *Mental Hygiene* 1–2 (April 1922), 370–391.

5. This book also intersects with the study of eugenics, specifically in California and across the United States. The most relevant sources include: Alexandra M. Stern, *Eugenic Nation: Faults and Frontiers in Better Breeding in Modern America* (Berkeley: University of California Press, 2004). The literature on eugenics, like that on Progressivism, is rich. The following relevant works were consulted: Wendy Kline, *Building a Better Race: Gender, Sexuality, and Eugenics from the Turn of the Century to the Baby Boom* (Berkeley: University of California Press, 2001); Edward J. Larson, *Sex, Race, and Science: Eugenics in the Deep South* (Baltimore: John Hopkins University Press, 1995); Daniel Kevles, *In the Name of Eugenics: Genetics and the Uses of Human Heredity* (New York: Knopf, 1985); Steven Selden, *Inheriting Shame: The Story of Eugenics and Racism in the United States* (New York: Teachers College Press, 1999); Stephen J. Gould, *The Mismeasure of Man* (New York: W. W. Norton, 1981); James W. Trent, *Inventing the Feeble Mind: A History of Mental Retardation in the United States* (Berkeley: University of California Press, 1994); Ian Robert Dowbiggin, *Keeping America Sane: Psychiatry and Eugenics in the United States and Canada, 1880–1940* (Ithaca, N.Y.: Cornell University Press, 1997); Nancy Leys Stepan, *"The Hour of Eugenics": Race, Gender, and Nation in Latin America* (Ithaca, N.Y.: Cornell University Press, 1991); and Nathaniel Deutsch, *Inventing America's "Worst" Family: Eugenics, Islam, and the Rise and Fall of the Tribe of Ishmael* (Berkeley: University of California Press, 2009). A good overview is Frank Dikotter, "Recent Perspectives on the History of Eugenics," *American Historical Review* 103, no. 2 (April 1998), 467–478.

6. For more on the juvenile court in Chicago, see, for instance, David Tanenhaus, *Juvenile Justice in the Making* (New York: Oxford University Press, 2004); Michael Willrich, *City of Courts: Socializing Justice in Progressive-Era Chicago* (New York: Cambridge University Press, 2003); Anne Meis Knupfer, *Reform and Resistance: Gender, Delinquency, and America's First Juvenile Court* (New York: Routledge, 2001); Victoria Getis, *The Juvenile Court and Progressives* (Urbana: University of Illinois Press, 2000); and Anthony M. Platt, *The*

Child Savers: The Invention of Delinquency (New Brunswick, N.J.: Rutgers University Press, 2009, 3rd ed.).

7. The literature on the Progressives of the early twentieth century is vast. For this study, most of the works consulted are those that applied to California's early juvenile justice system. They include Mary Odem, *Delinquent Daughters: Protecting and Policing Adolescent Female Sexuality in the United States, 1885–1920* (Chapel Hill: University of North Carolina Press, 1995); Estelle Freedman, *Maternal Justice: Miriam Van Waters and the Female Reform Tradition* (Chicago: University of Chicago Press, 1998); Judith Raftery, *Land of Fair Promise: Politics and Reform in Los Angeles Schools, 1885–1941* (Palo Alto, Calif.: Stanford University Press, 1992); William Deverell and Tom Sitton, *California Progressivism Revisited* (Berkeley: University of California Press, 1994); Spencer C. Olin, *California's Prodigal Sons: Hiram Johnson and the Progressives, 1911–17* (Berkeley: University of California Press, 1968).

8. Michel Foucault, *Discipline and Punish: The Birth of the Prison*, trans. Alan Sheridan (New York: Pantheon, 1977).

9. Until the last few decades, the literature on females, sexuality, and juvenile delinquency in the early twentieth century was thin. Now, scholars pay significant attention to gender, sex, and sexuality, though in California few scholars have done the same. The notable exceptions are Odem, *Delinquent Daughters*, and Freedman, *Maternal Justice*. For more, see also Mary Odem, "Single Mothers, Delinquent Daughters, and the Juvenile Court in Early Twentieth-Century Los Angeles," *Journal of Social History* 25 (September 1991), 27–43; Mary Odem and Steven S. Schlossman, "Guardians of Virtue: The Juvenile Court and Female Delinquency in Early-Twentieth Century Los Angeles," *Crime and Delinquency* 37 (April 1991), 186–203; Steven S. Schlossman and Stephanie Wallach, "The Crime of Precocious Sexuality: Female Juvenile Delinquency in the Progressive Era," *Harvard Educational Review* 48 (February 1978), 68–95. Studies on delinquent males in late nineteenth and early twentieth century California are even more thin. Few if any published works exist. Most are dissertations and master's theses. See, for instance, Heather Allen Pang, "Making Men: Reform Schools and the Shaping of Masculinity, 1890–1920" (Ph.D. diss., University of California–Davis, 2000).

10. Under the Health Insurance Portability and Accountability Act of 1996 (HIPAA) and California Institutional Review Board rules and regulations, I cannot disclose the identity of youths associated with the state sterilization program in California hospitals. For the purposes of this study, all youths associated with the state sterilization program in California remain anonymous with the exception of the two boys who committed suicide at Whittier State School in 1939 and 1940, for their full names and identities appear in public sources. Names of other youths who appeared in the press are also disclosed. Elsewhere, too, I have disclosed identities of youths at Whittier State School. See Miroslava Chávez-García, "Intelligence Testing at Whittier State School, 1880–1920," *Pacific Historical Review* 76, no. 2 (May 2007), 193–228.

11. The silence and secrecy around sexual abuse and sexual activity in general in prisonlike institutions is not a new development or discovery. See, for instance, Tamara Myers, "Embodying Delinquency: Boys' Bodies, Sexuality, and

Juvenile Justice History in Early-Twentieth-Century Quebec," *Journal of the History of Sexuality* 14, no. 4 (October 2005), 383–414; and Regina G. Kunzel, *Criminal Intimacy: Prison and the Uneven History of Modern American Sexuality* (Chicago: University of Chicago Press, 2010).

CHAPTER 1

1. For the pertinent laws, see *Statutes of California and Amendments to the Codes* [hereafter *California Statutes*], 28th Session of the Legislature, 1889, chapter 108, sections 16–20, 115–116; and *California Statutes* (1893), chapter 222, sections 14–18, 332.

2. For Arthur C.'s case file, see Inmate Case File No. 32, vol. 99 (1891), 63–64, Inmate History Registers, Fred C. Nelles School for Boys (Whittier) Collection, Youth Authority Records, F3738, California State Archives, Sacramento [hereafter FNSB].

3. For more on Native Californian childrearing practices see, for instance, Robert F. Heizer and Mary A. Whipple, eds., *California Indians: A Source Book* (Berkeley: University of California Press, 1941); Sherburne Cook, *The Aboriginal Population of Alameda and Contra Costa Counties* (Berkeley: University of California Press, 1957); William McCawley, *The First Angelinos: The Gabrielino Indians of Los Angeles* (Novato, Calif.: Ballena Press, 1996), 2–3; Donald P. Jewell, *Indians of the Feather River: Tales and Legends of the Concow Maidu of California* (Menlo Park, Calif.: Ballena Press, 1987), 1. For the determination of a child's status in a southern California Native society, see Hugo Reid, "Letters," in Susanna Bryant Dakin, *A Scotch Paisano: Hugo Reid's Life in California, 1832–1852* (Berkeley: University of California Press, 1939), 227; for the chief's authority over adults in a tribe, see Vine Deloria Jr. and Clifford M. Lytle, *American Indians, American Justice* (Austin: University of Texas Press, 1983).

4. Delfina Cuero et al., *Delfina Cuero: Her Autobiography* (Menlo Park, Calif.: Ballena Press, 1991), 37–38.

5. Ibid., 38.

6. Reid, "Letters," 239–240.

7. On the Gabrieleños, see, for instance, McCawley, *The First Angelinos*, 105; and on the Cahuilla, see Harry C. James, *The Cahuilla Indians* (Banning, Calif.: Malki Museum Press, 1969), 59–84. McCawley's work is not without flaws: he relies primarily on Gerónimo Boscana's writings (see chapter discussion).

8. Elizabeth Colson, *Autobiographies of Three Pomo Women* (Berkeley: University of California Archeological Research Facility, Department of Anthropology, 1974).

9. Ruby Modesto and Guy Mount, eds., *Not for Innocent Ears: Spiritual Traditions of a Desert Cahuilla Medicine Woman* (Arcata, Calif.: Sweetlight Books, 1989), 54.

10. Jewell, *Indians of the Feather River*, 95. On Maidu childrearing, see Dunn, "The Maidu Indians," *Plumas County Historical Society Publication* 8 (1962), 20–30.

11. Reid, "Letters," 225.

12. Maynard Geiger and Clement Meighan, eds., *As the Padres Saw Them: California Indian Life and Customs as Reported by the Franciscan Missionaries, 1813–1815* (Santa Barbara, Calif.: Santa Barbara Mission Archive Library, 1976), 25.

13. Ibid., 23.

14. Ibid.

15. Gerónimo Boscana, *Chinigchinich: A Historical Account of the Beliefs, Usages, Customs, and Extravagancies of the Indians of this Mission of San Juan Capistrano, called the Acagchemem Tribe*, trans. Alfred Robinson (New York: Wiley and Putnam, 1846), 45.

16. Ibid.

17. Deloria Jr. and Lytle, *American Indians, American Justice*, xi.

18. Quote cited in Frederick Greenwald, "Treatment of Behavioral Problems of Children and Youth by Early Indigenous Americans," in *History of Juvenile Delinquency*, vol. 2, ed. Albert G. Hess and Priscilla F. Clement (Aalen, Germany: Scientia, 1993), 746. For more on the Aztecs, see ibid., 744. For more on the Jicarilla, see Morris Edward Opler, *Childhood and Youth in Jicarilla Apache Society*, vol. 5 (Los Angeles: Southwest Museum, 1946), 38–48.

19. Francis F. Guest, "An Inquiry into the Role of the Discipline in California Mission Life," *Southern California Quarterly* 71 (Spring 1989), 28; and Virginia M. Bouvier, *Women and the Conquest of California, 1542–1840: Codes of Silence* (Tucson: University of Arizona Press, 2001), 90–92.

20. Guest, "Inquiry into the Role of Discipline," 3; Geiger, *As the Padres Saw Them*, 39; and Sherburne F. Cook, *The Conflict between the California Indian and White Civilization* (Berkeley: University of California Press, 1976), 113–134.

21. Antonine Tibesar, ed. and trans., *Writings of Junipero Serra*, vol. 3, Academy of American Franciscan Historical Documentary Series, nos. 4–7 (Washington, D.C.: Academy of American Franciscan History, 1955–1966), 413.

22. Quote cited in Reid, "Letters," 275. Cook, *Conflict between the California Indian*, 122–123, also agrees that friars used the whip frequently.

23. Edward D. Castillo, "An Indian Account of the Decline and Collapse of Mexico's Hegemony over the Missionized Indians of California," in "The California Indians," special issue, *American Indian Quarterly* 13, no. 4 (Autumn 1989), 397.

24. Bouvier, *Women and the Conquest of California*, 94–106.

25. Rose Marie Beebe and Robert M. Senkewicz, eds., *Testimonios: Early California through the Eyes of Women, 1815–1848* (Berkeley: Heyday Books, Bancroft Library, 2006), 107.

26. Quote cited in Victoria Brady, Sarah Crome, and Lyn Reese, "Resist! Survival Tactics of Indian Women," *California History* 63 (Spring 1984), 142–144.

27. Guest, "Inquiry into the Role of the Discipline," 8.

28. Ibid.

29. For more, see Miroslava Chávez-García, *Negotiating Conquest: Gender and Power in California, 1770s to 1880s* (Tucson: University of Arizona, 2004); and Bouvier, *Women and the Conquest of California*.

30. Few cases remain focusing on Native children. For an example, see "*Civil Promovido por D[on] Felipe Villela contra Don Ygnacio Palomares,*" in *Alcalde Court Records,* vol. 8 (1843), 368–404, Seaver Center for Western History, Los Angeles County Museum of Natural History, Los Angeles, Calif.

31. Hubert H. Bancroft, *The Works of Hubert Howe Bancroft,* vol. 21 (San Francisco, Calif.: A. L. Bancroft, 1884–1886), 321.

32. Ibid, 329.

33. For more, see *Negotiating Conquest.*

34. For more on the violence, see, for instance, Sherburne F. Cook, *The Population of California Indians, 1769–1970* (Berkeley: University of California Press, 1979), 308–309; and Michael Magliari, "Free Soil, Unfree Labor: Cave Johnson Couts and the Binding of Indian Workers in California, 1850–1867," *Pacific Historical Review* 73, no. 3 (August 2004), 349–350.

35. Quote cited in Magliari, "Free Soil, Unfree Labor," 355.

36. Ibid.

37. Horace Bell, *Reminiscences of a Ranger, or Early Times in Southern California* (Los Angeles: Yarnell, Caystile and Mathes, 1881).

38. Magliari, "Free Soil, Unfree Labor," 355.

39. Ibid., 353.

40. Cook, *Population of California Indians,* 314–315.

41. Quote cited in Brady, Crome, and Reese, "Resist!" 146.

42. For culpability at the age of fourteen, see Diane Nunn and Christine Cleary, "From the Mexican California Frontier to Arnold-Kennick: Highlights in the Evolution of the California Juvenile Court, 1850–1961," *Journal of the Center for Families, Children and the Courts* 5 (2004), 4. For the statute, see *California Statutes* (1850), chapter 99, section 3, 229.

43. Francis Cahn, *Welfare Activities of Federal, State, and Local Governments in California, 1850–1934* (Berkeley: University of California Press, 1936), 53.

44. For evidence of Ysabel and Peralta's confinement, see "Ysabel (Indian Female)," Register No. 993, September 7, 1856, *San Quentin Prison Registers* (microfilm), Department of Corrections Records, F3717, California State Archives, Sacramento [hereafter SQPR]; and "Antonio Peralta (Indian)," Register No. 8148, April 17, 1878, SQPR. For more on the prison's early history, see Clare V. McKanna Jr., "The Origins of San Quentin, 1851–1880," *California History* 66, no. 1 (March 1987), 49–54; McKanna, "Ethnics and San Quentin Prison Registers: A Comment on Methodology," *Journal of Social History* 18, no. 3 (Spring 1985), 477–482; McKanna, *Race and Homicide in Nineteenth-Century California* (Reno: University of Nevada Press, 2002); Benjamin Justice, "'A College of Morals': Educational Reform at San Quentin Prison, 1880–1920," *History of Education Quarterly* 40 (Autumn 2000), 279–301; and Shelley Bookspan, *A Germ of Goodness: The Evolving California State Prison System, 1851–1944* (Lincoln: University of Nebraska Press, 1993).

45. These findings come from my analysis of the first forty years of the SQPR.

46. *Daily Alta California,* January 27, 1867, n.p. [1].

47. Ibid., August 9, 1868, n.p. [1].

48. Ibid.

49. For more on Native peoples in the aftermath of the conquest, see, for instance, Cook, *The Conflict between the California Indian,* and Albert Hurtado, *Indian Survival on the California Frontier* (New Haven, Conn.: Yale University Press, 1988). For more on Indian boarding schools, see, for instance, Matthew Sakiestewa Gilbert, *Education beyond the Mesas: Hopi Students at Sherman Institute, 1902–1929* (Lincoln: University of Kansas Press, 2010); Clifford E. Trafzer and Jean E. Keller, eds., *Boarding School Blues: Revisiting American Indian Educational Experiences* (East Lansing, Mich.: Bison Books, 2006); and Ward Churchill, *Kill the Indian, Save the Man: The Genocidal Impact of American Indian Residential Schools* (San Francisco: City Lights Publisher, 2004).

50. Magliari, "Free Soil, Unfree Labor," 367–376.

51. For more on the dispossession and violence experienced by Californios, Mexicans, and Indians in nineteenth-century California, see, for instance, Clifford E. Trafzer and Joel R. Hyer, eds., *Exterminate Them: Written Accounts of the Murder, Rape, and Slavery of Native Americans during the California Gold Rush, 1848–1868* (East Lansing: Michigan State University Press, 1999); Tomás Almaguer, *Racial Fault Lines: The Historical Origins of White Supremacy in California* (Berkeley: University of California Press, 1994); and Leonard Pitt, *Decline of the Californios: A Social History of the Spanish-Speaking Californians, 1846–1890* (Berkeley: University of California Press, 1966), 224–225.

52. For state population figures, see David J. Weber, *Foreigners in Their Native Land: Historical Roots of the Mexican Americans* (Albuquerque: University of New Mexico Press, 1973), 148; Sister M. Collette Standart, "The Sonoran Migration to California, 1848–1856: A Study in Prejudice," *Southern California Quarterly* 58 (1976), 333–358; and McKanna, "Ethnics and San Quentin Registers," 478.

53. See also Pitt, *Decline of the Californios,* 256–257.

54. For more on the Chinese, see Jean Pfaelzer, *Driven Out: The Forgotten War against Chinese Americans* (New York: Random House, 2007); Charles McClain, *In Search of Equality: The Chinese Struggle against Discrimination in Nineteenth-Century America* (Berkeley: University of California Press, 1996); and Alexander Saxton, *The Indispensable Enemy: Labor and the Anti-Chinese Movement in California* (Berkeley: University of California Press, 1975).

55. Details of life at San Quentin come from "San Quentin Daily Log, October 1, 1857 to June 30, 1861," San Quentin Prison, Department of Corrections Records, F3717, California State Archives, Sacramento. See also *Daily Alta California,* August 9, 1868, n.p. [1].

56. Cahn, *Welfare Activities,* 46.

57. Ibid., 47–48, 66; *Daily Alta California,* December 20, 1872, n.p. [1]; Nunn and Cleary, "From the Mexican California Frontier to Arnold-Kennick," 6–7; and George E. Miller, "Administrative History of California Institutions for Juvenile Offenders" (master's thesis, Sacramento State College, 1965), 5–20.

58. Quotes cited in R. J. Patti, "Child Protection in California, 1850–1966: An Analysis of Public Policy" (Ph.D. diss., University of Southern California, 1967), 58. See also Board of Commissioners, "Report of Commissioners, for the Establishment and Erection of State Reform School," in *Appendix to Journals of the*

State, Eleventh Session of the Legislature of the State of California (Sacramento: State Printing Office, 1860), 4.

59. *Daily Alta California*, March 13, 1858, n.p. [1].

60. For the 1864–1865 figures, see Board of Trustees, "First Biennial Report of the Trustees of the State Reform School for the Years 1864–65," in *Appendix to Journals of Senate and Assembly of the Sixteenth Session of the Legislature of the State of California*, vol. 2 (Sacramento: State Printing Office, 1866), 8; for the 1866–67 figures, see Board of Trustees, "Second Biennial Report of the Trustees of the State Reform School for the Two Years Ending October 31, 1867," in *Appendix to Journals of Senate and Assembly of the Seventeenth Session of the Legislature of the State of California*, vol. 1 (Sacramento: State Printing Office, 1868), 11.

61. Cahn, *Welfare Activities*, 47–50.

62. *Daily Alta California*, January 27, 1867, n.p. [1].

63. Ibid. See, also Nunn and Cleary, "From the Mexican California Frontier to Arnold-Kennick," 7.

64. Ibid., 5–6. For the school's closure, see "Report of Assembly Special Committee Appointed to visit the State Reform School at Marysville," in *Appendix to Journals of Senate and Assembly of the Sixteenth Session of the Legislature, of the State of California*, vol. 2 (Sacramento: State Printing Office, 1866), 1–5; and "Report of Assembly Committee on Education, in Relation to the State Reform School," in ibid., 1–4.

65. Information on child-saving institutions in Spanish-speaking communities in nineteenth-century California is sparse. See, for instance, Nicholas P. Beck, "The Other Children: Minority Education in California Public Schools from Statehood to 1890" (Ph.D. diss., University of California–Los Angeles, 1975), 16; and Pitt, *Decline of the Californios*, 224–225.

66. For more on the European institutions, specifically those in Germany and France, see Steven L. Schlossman, *Transforming Juvenile Justice: Reform Ideals and Institutional Realities, 1825–1920* (DeKalb: Northern Illinois University Press, 2005; originally published in 1977); and Steven L. Schlossman, "Delinquent Children: The Juvenile Reform School," in *Oxford History of the Prison: The Practice of Punishment*, ed. Norval Morris and David J. Rothman (New York: Oxford University Press, 1997), 329–349.

67. For population statistics for Los Angeles and San Diego, see Robert M. Fogelson, *The Fragmented Metropolis: Los Angeles, 1850–1930* (Berkeley: University of California Press, 1967), 56.

68. For figures for San Francisco, see ibid., 21.

69. Cahn, *Welfare Activities*, 41–45; and Patti, "Child Protection in California," 42–45.

70. For a listing of children's institutions founded in California, see Sara Elizabeth Reminger, "The Care of Dependent Children in California, 1850–1879" (master's thesis, Mills College, 1931), 4–5.

71. Patti, "Child Protection in California," 22; Cahn, *Welfare Activities*, 50; and Schlossman, *Transforming Juvenile Justice*, chapter 2. A statewide probation office was not established until 1929.

72. Cahn, *Welfare Activities,* 74–83, 97. See, also Nunn and Cleary, "From the Mexican California Frontier to Arnold-Kennick," 6.

73. "Address of Hon. W. C. Hendricks," in *The Laying of the Corner-Stone of the State Reform School at Whittier, Los Angeles County, California* (Sacramento: State Printing Office, 1890), 14.

74. Brainard F. Smith, "Report of Preston School of Industry," in *First Biennial Report of the Secretary of the Preston School of Industry, December 31, 1890* (Sacramento: State Printing Office, 1890), 6, Preston School of Industry Collection, Youth Authority Records, F3738, California State Archives, Sacramento.

75. "Petition of the Ladies' Protection and Relief Society, San Francisco, to the Legislature," in *Appendix to Journals of Senate and Assembly of the Eighteenth Session of the Legislature of the State of California,* vol. 2 (Sacramento,: State Printing Office, 1870), 17.

76. "Penology Report of the California State Penological Commission," in *Appendix to the Journals of the Senate and Assembly of the Twenty-Seventh Session of the Legislature of the State of California,* vol. 3 (Sacramento: State Printing Office, 1887), 6. Also see "Report of W. C. Hendricks to the Penological Commission of California," in *Appendix to the Journals of the Senate and Assembly of the Twenty-Seventh Session of the Legislature of the State of California,* vol. 3 (Sacramento: State Printing Office, 1887), 1–82.

77. For more on prison reform, see Justice, "'A College of Morals,'" 279–301; and Bookspan, *A Germ of Goodness.* For more on social reform in California in the 1880s, see, for instance, Mary E. Odem, *Delinquent Daughters: Protecting and Policing Adolescent Female Sexuality in the United States, 1885–1920* (Chapel Hill: University of North Carolina Press, 1995).

78. "Penology Report of the California State Penological Commission," 11–14.

79. For studies that take issue with the "novelty" of the nineteenth century reformatories in the United States, see, for instance, Schlossman, *Transforming Juvenile Justice*; and Anne Meis Knufper, *Reform and Resistance: Gender, Delinquency, and America's First Juvenile Court* (New York: Routledge, 2001).

80. "Penology Report," 14.

81. Ibid., 31–32.

82. *California Statutes* (1891), chapter 108, sections 1, 111; ibid., section 16, 115.

83. *California Statutes* (1891), chapter 108, section 13, 114–115; ibid., section 20, 116. For the lowering of the age limit, see *California Statutes* (1893), chapter 222, section 14, 332.

84. "Report of Board of Trustees of the Reform School for Juvenile Offenders, Located at Whittier, Los Angeles County for the Twenty Months Ending November 30, 1890," in *Biennial Report, Whittier State School, 1889–1890* (Sacramento, Calif.: State Office, 1890), 7, in FNSB.

85. Ibid., 8.

86. Ibid., 38.

87. Ibid.

88. Brainard F. Smith, "Report to the Honorable the State Board of Prison Directors," in "First Biennial Report of the Secretary of the Preston School of Industry (at Ione)," *Appendix to the Journals of the Senate and Assembly of the Twenty-Seventh Session of the Legislature of the State of California*, vol. 1 (Sacramento: State Printing Office, 1890), 9.

89. *California Statutes* (1890), chapter 103, section 15, 103; and ibid., section 20, 105.

90. Ibid., section 12, 102.

91. *Laying of the Corner-Stone*, 10.

92. *California Statutes* (1890), chapter 222, section 1, 328.

93. "Report of the Board of Trustees of the Reform School for Juvenile Offenders, Located at Whittier, Los Angeles County, . . . 1890," 7.

CHAPTER 2

1. For details on Nelle's personal life, see *Whittier News*, "Whittier Boys Lose Stanch [*sic*] Friend," August 27, 1917; O. H. Close, "Early-Day Practices and Changing Conceptions of Delinquency Treatment" (unpublished ms., ca. 1958), 36–37, in Preston School of Industry Collection, Youth Authority Records, F3738, California State Archives, Sacramento [hereafter PSIC]; and Steven L. Schlossman, "Delinquent Children: The Juvenile Reform School," in *The Oxford History of the Prison*, ed. Norval Morris and David J. Rothman, (New York: Oxford University Press, 1995), 379. For Governor Hiram Johnson's request, see Fred C. Nelles, "Superintendent's Report," in *Biennial Report: Whittier State School, 1913–1914* (Whittier, Calif.: Whittier State School, 1914) [hereafter *Biennial Report 1913–1914*], 14, in Fred C. Nelles School for Boys (Whittier), Youth Authority Records, F3738, California State Archives, Sacramento [hereafter FNSB]. For more on Johnson's party politics, see Spencer C. Olin, *California's Prodigal Sons: Hiram Johnson and the Progressives, 1911–17* (Berkeley: University of California Press, 1968).

2. Kenyon Scudder, "Between the Dark and the Daylight," undated ms., Regional Oral History Office, Bancroft Library, Berkeley, Calif., 142–143.

3. For the school's description, see Norman Fenton, *The Delinquent Boy and the Correctional School* (Claremont, Calif.: Claremont Guidance Center, 1935), 16; FNSB, F3738.

4. Nelles, "Superintendent's Report," *Biennial Report 1911–1912*, n.p., FNSB.

5. "State School Shake-Up to Be Investigated," *Los Angeles Times*, October 16, 1912, II, 1.

6. For more on the progressive movement, particularly in California, see Mary E. Odem, *Delinquent Daughters: Protecting and Policing Adolescent Female Sexuality in the United States, 1885–1920* (Chapel Hill: University of North Carolina Press, 1995); Estelle B. Freedman, *Maternal Justice: Miriam Van Waters and the Female Reform Tradition* (Chicago: University of Chicago Press, 1996); and William Deverell and Tom Sitton, eds., *California Progressivism Revisited* (Berkeley: University of California Press, 1994). For more on educational reform, see Lawrence T. Cremin, *The Transformation of the School: Progressivism in*

American Education, 1876–1957 (New York: Knopf, 1961); David Tyack, *The One Best System: A History of the American Urban Education* (Cambridge, Mass.: Harvard University Press, 1974); Herbert M. Kliebard, *The Struggle for the American Curriculum, 1893–1958,* 3rd ed. (New York: Routledge, 2004); and David Nasaw, *Schooled to Order: A Social History of Public Schooling* (New York: Oxford University Press, 1979).

7. For more on the evolution of the juvenile court law in California, see Diane Nunn and Christine Cleary, "From the Mexican California Frontier to Arnold-Kennick: Highlights in the Evolution of the California Juvenile Court, 1850–1961," *Journal of the Center for Families, Children and the Courts* 5 (2004), 3–27.

8. Nunn and Cleary, "From the Mexican California Frontier to Arnold-Kennick," 12–13.

9. Ibid., 5. For the statute establishing probation, see *Statutes of California and Amendments to the Codes* [hereafter *California Statutes*], 25th Session of the Legislature, 1883, chapter 91, section 1, 377–378; for the statute establishing the juvenile court, see *California Statutes* (1903), chapter 43, sections 1–13. For the amendments, see *California Statutes* (1915), chapter 631, section 1, 1225–1226. For more on juvenile court and probation officers in California, see Curtis D. Wilbur, "Juvenile Court," in *Report and Manual for Probation Officers of the Superior Court acting as Juvenile Court, Los Angeles County, California, 1912* (Los Angeles: Board of Supervisors, 1912), 11–16; and Odem, *Delinquent Daughters,* 74, 111–112. For more on the juvenile court system in other states, see Anthony M. Platt, *The Child Savers: The Invention of Delinquency,* 3rd ed. (New Brunswick, N.J.: Rutgers University Press, 2009); Steven L. Schlossman, *Transforming Juvenile Justice: Reform Ideals and Institutional Realities, 1825–1920* (DeKalb: Northern Illinois University Press, 2005; originally published in 1977); Anne Knupfer, *Reform and Resistance: Gender, Delinquency, and America's First Juvenile Court* (New York: Routledge, 2001); Elizabeth J. Clapp, *Mothers of All Children: Women Reformers and the Rise of Juvenile Courts in Progressive Era America* (University Park: Pennsylvania State University Press, 1998); and Paul Colomy and Martin Kretzmann, "Projects and Institution Building: Judge Ben B. Lindsey and the Juvenile Court Movement," *Social Problems* 42, no. 2 (May 1995), 191–215.

10. Nunn and Cleary, "From the Mexican California Frontier to Arnold-Kennick," 14–15.

11. Ibid., 15–17.

12. Nelles, "Superintendent's Report," *Biennial Report 1913–1914,* 31, FSNB.

13. Adina Mitchell, *Special Report to the Board of Trustees* (Whittier, Calif.: Whittier State School, 1896), 5, 8, FNSB.

14. For the ban of corporal punishment, see "Board of Trustees Report," in *Biennial Report 1897–1898,* 6, FSNB; for the superintendent's response, see T. B. Van Alstyne, "Superintendent's Report," in ibid., 34.

15. Quotes cited in "Whittier Whipping," *Los Angeles Times,* July 22, 1897, 5; for more, see "Unrest at Whittier," *Los Angeles Times,* July 22, 1897, 8.

16. See, for instance, "Trustees Shake Up Whittier School," *Los Angeles Times,* June 30, 1908; and "Mysterious Witness Out of Hiding Place," *Los Angeles Times,* July 19, 1908.

17. For more on the 1903 whipping of Mabel S., see Inmate Case File No. 1653, vol. 102 (1903), 509–510, Inmate History Registers, FNSB; and "Should Have Excluded Men," *Los Angeles Times*, December 15, 1905.

18. For illustration of straps used at the reformatory in the 1890s, see "Whittier Whipping," *Los Angeles Times*, November 17, 1896. For the 1911 riot, see "Rebel Girls Charge Back," *Los Angeles Times*, July 25, 1911, II, 2; and on the mismanagement of the Girl's Department, see "Girl's Department," *Amador Ledger*, December 7, 1906.

19. For the appointment of "trusties," see, for instance, Inmate Case File No. 205, vol. 98 (1894), 411–412, Inmate History Registers, FNSB; and Inmate Case File No. 531, vol. 99 (1894), 365–366.

20. For Nelles's policies, see Nelles, "Superintendent's Report," *Biennial Report 1915–1916*, 23–25, FNSB. For more on the changing conceptions of manhood, see Gail Bederman, *Manliness and Civilization: A Cultural History of Gender and Race in the United States, 1880 to 1917* (Chicago: University of Chicago Press, 1995), and Heather A. Pang, "Making Men: Reform Schools and the Shaping of Masculinity, 1890–1920" (Ph.D. diss., University of California–Davis, 2000).

21. On the Lost Privilege Cottage, see Scudder, "Between the Dark and the Daylight," 222–224. Nelles's approach in "disciplining" the mind rather than the body follows the processes Michel Foucault describes in *Discipline and Punish: The Birth of the Prison*, trans. Alan Sheridan (New York: Vintage Press, 1977).

22. Mitchell, "Reasons for Removing the Girls' Department," *Special Report to the Board of Trustees* (Whittier, Calif.: Whittier State School, 1896), Information File, FNSB; and *Los Angeles Times*, January 22, 1893, 10.

23. Details on the Girls' Department and later the California School for Girls are scant. See *California School for Girls, Biennial Reports, 1914–1920*, Bancroft Library, Berkeley, California; and Mary B. Perry, Oral History Interview, August 10, 1978, Ventura, California, p. 5, Administrative Records, Youth Authority, F3738, FNSB, California State Archives, Sacramento. For more on the school's appropriation, see Scudder, "Between the Dark and the Daylight," 147–149.

24. Quote cited in Elmer E. Knox and Norman Fenton, *Fred C. Nelles: An Appreciation* (Whittier, Calif.: Whittier State School, 1930), 4.

25. Quote cited in W. E. McVay, Ben. F. Pearson, and Prescott F. Cogswell, "Board of Trustees' Report," *Biennial Report 1911–1912*, 4.

26. For reform school officials' call for the cottage system, see *Los Angeles Times*, October 24, 1897, 22. Debate remains, however, on the merits of that system. See, for instance, Schlossman, *Transforming Juvenile Justice*; and Eric Schneider, *In the Web of Class: Delinquents and Reformers in Boston, 1810s–1930s* (New York: Oxford University Press, 1992).

27. *San Francisco Call*, July 2, 1909, 5.

28. Scudder, "Between the Dark and the Daylight," 218–220.

29. Nelles, "Superintendent's Report," *Biennial Report 1911–1912*, n.p.

30. *Los Angeles Times*, January 16, 1913, 11.

31. Scudder, "Between the Dark and the Daylight," 142.

32. *Los Angeles Times,* January 20, 1913; for a similar critique, see *Whittier News,* December 19, 1913, 1.

33. *Los Angeles Times,* November 6, 1912, II, 8; and ibid., October 16, 1912, II, 1. For more on the "shake-up" following his appointment, see *Los Angeles Times,* October 16, 1912, II, 1.

34. Nelles, "Superintendent's Report," *Biennial Report 1915–1916,* 23–25, 28–29; and Nelles, "Superintendent's Report," *Biennial Report 1913–1914,* 13.

35. Nelles, "Superintendent's Report," *Biennial Report 1917–1918,* 14.

36. For more on escapes, see Miroslava Chávez-García, "Youth, Evidence, and Agency: Mexican and Mexican American Youth at Whittier State School, 1890 to 1920," *Aztlán: A Journal of Chicano Studies* 32 (2006), 55–83.

37. *Whittier News,* January 23, 1914, 1, 4.

38. On the men's club, see ibid., March 3, 1916, 1; and ibid., May 19, 1920, 1.

39. Ibid., April 17, 1922, 1, 6.

40. *Los Angeles Times,* December 1, 1924, A2.

41. Ibid., December 3, 1924, A23. Nelles also hosted open houses. See, *Whittier News,* August 25, 1916, 1, 6; see also ibid., March 2, 1921, 8.

42. Ibid., December 14, 1920.

43. Nelles, "Superintendent's Report," *Biennial Report 1913–1914,* 21–22, 29.

44. J. Harold Williams, *A Study of 150 Delinquent Boys* (Palo Alto, Calif., 1915), FSNB; and Williams, "Defective, Delinquent, and Dependent Boys: Three Classes of State Wards," *Intelligence and Delinquency,* Department of Research Bulletin No. 2 (Whittier, Calif.: Whittier State School, 1915), FNSB.

45. For more on the Binet-Simon Intelligence Scale, see, for instance, Leila Zenderland, *Measuring Minds: Henry Goddard and the Intelligence Testing Movement* (New York: Cambridge University Press, 1998). For J. Harold Williams's belief in the ability of intelligence tests to produce efficient results, see Williams, "Report of the Department of Research," *Biennial Report 1917–1918,* 42. For more on the test contents, see Alexandra M. Stern, "An Empire of Tests: Psychometrics and the Paradoxes of Nationalism in the Americas," in *Haunted by Empire: Geographies of Intimacy in North American History,* ed. Ann L Stoler (Durham: University of North Carolina Press, 2006), 560–592. For the IQ scales and their meaning as used at Whittier State School, see Williams, "Report of the Department of Research," *Biennial Report 1915–1916,* 57–58, 62, 66.

46. According to Zenderland, *Measuring Minds,* 241–242, n54, Alfred Binet and Lewis Terman later modified their views. In a 1916 survey of adult inmates at San Quentin, Terman, for instance, admitted that "language handicaps" affected the testing process. See H. E. Knollin and Lewis S. Terman, "A Partial Psychological Survey of the Prison Population of San Quentin, California," in *Surveys in Mental Deviation in Prisons, Public Schools, and Orphanages in California,* ed. California State Board of Charities and Corrections (Sacramento: California State Printing Office, 1918), 8.

47. Fernald, "Report of the Psychological Work in the California School for Girls," *Journal of Delinquency* 1 (March 1916), 29, 21–22.

48. Quotes cited in Zenderland, *Measuring Minds,* 240–241.

49. Carlos Blanton, "'They Cannot Master Abstractions but They Can Often Be Made Efficient Workers': Race and Class in the Intelligence Testing of

Mexican Americans and African Americans in Texas During the 1920s," *Social Science Quarterly* 81 (2003), 1016. See also Daniel J. Kevles, "Testing the Army's Intelligence: Psychologists and the Military in World War I," *Journal of American History* 55 (1968), 574–576.

50. George I. Sánchez, "Bilingualism and Mental Measures," *Journal of Applied Psychology* 18, no. 6 (1934), 765–772. For similar critiques, see Sánchez, "Group Differences in Spanish-Speaking Children: A Critical View," *Journal of Applied Psychology* 16, no. 5 (1932), 549–558; and Sánchez, "Scores of Spanish-Speaking Children on Repeated Tests," *Journal of Genetic Psychology* 40 (1932), 223–233.

51. Goddard cited in Zenderland, *Measuring Minds*, 250.

52. Williams, "Report of the Department of Research," *Biennial Report 1915–1916*, 60–61.

53. Williams, "Psychological Survey of the Whittier State School," *Biennial Report 1913–1914*, 41.

54. Ibid., 15.

55. Quote cited in ibid., 32. For the literature Williams cited, see ibid., 30–33, 38–39; and Williams, "Feeble-Mindedness and Delinquency," in Fred C. Nelles et al., *Report of the 1915 Legislature Committee on Mental Deficiency and the Proposed Institution for the Care of the Feebleminded and Epileptic Persons, Pursuant to the Provisions of Chapter 729, Statutes of 1915* (Whittier, Calif.: Whittier State School, Department of Printing Instruction, 1917), 57–62, FNSB. For some of the "degenerate" family studies, see, for instance, Henry H. Goddard, *The Kallikak Family: A Study in the Heredity of Feeble-Mindedness* (New York: Macmillan, 1912), and Richard L. Dugdale, *"The Jukes": A Study in Crime, Pauperism, Disease and Heredity* (New York: Knickerbocker Press, 1877). For analysis of those works, see Nicole H. Rafter, ed., *White Trash: The Eugenic Family Studies, 1877–1919* (Boston: Northeastern University Press, 1988); and Nathaniel Deutsch, *Inventing America's Worst Family: Eugenics, Islam, and the Fall and the Rise of the Tribe of Ishmael* (Berkeley: University of California Press, 2009).

56. Williams, "Psychological Survey of the Whittier State School," 16.

57. Ibid., 15–16.

58. Ibid., 47.

59. Ibid., 25.

60. For more on the "Mexican problem" of the early 1900s and its connection to immigration restrictions, see, for example, David Gutiérrez, *Walls and Mirrors: Mexicans, Mexican Americans, and the Politics of Ethnicity* (Berkeley: University of California Press, 1995); and Mae M. Ngai, *Impossible Subjects: Illegal Aliens and the Making of Modern America* (Princeton, N.J.: Princeton University Press, 2004).

61. Blanton, "'They Cannot Master Abstractions,'" 1014–1026.

62. J. Harold Williams, "Quotations: The Present Status of Juvenile Delinquency in California," *Journal of Juvenile Delinquency* 5, no. 5 (September 1920), 188.

63. Williams, "Psychological Survey of the Whittier State School," 35. For more on Gosney and Popenoe's work, see E. S. Goseny and Paul Popenoe, *Sterilization for Human Betterment: A Summary of Results of 6,000 Operations in California, 1909–1929* (New York: MacMillan, 1929).

64. Quote cited in Lewis M. Terman, Virgil Dickinson, and Lowry Howard, "Backward and Feeble-Minded Children in the Public Schools of 'X' County, California," 19–45, in *Surveys in Mental Deviation*.

65. Williams, "Psychological Survey of the Whittier State School," 40, 47.

66. Ibid., 40–41.

67. Nelles, "Wards of the State: Suggestions Regarding their Scientific Segregation and Re-Distribution into Proper Groups for Effective Treatment," *Biennial Report 1913–1914*, 11–12. See also Nelles, "Report of Superintendent," *Biennial Report 1915–1916*, 6–8.

68. Ibid., 14.

69. Fred C. Nelles et al., *Report of the 1915 Legislature Committee*, FNSB.

70. For Fernald's opinion, see *Whittier News*, February 27, 1916, 1, 6.

71. Nelles, "Superintendent's Report," *Biennial Report 1913–1914*, 8–10; Nelles, "Superintendent's Report," *Biennial Report 1917–1918*, 10; and Knox and Fenton, *Fred C. Nelles*, 7.

72. Alexandra M. Stern, *Eugenic Nation: Faults and Frontiers of Better Breeding in Modern America* (Berkeley: University of California Press, 2005), 99–104.

73. Ibid., 84, 103–110.

74. Nelles, "Changes in the Nature of the Population at Whittier State School," *Journal of Delinquency* 9 (1925), 231–232.

75. Williams, "Report of the Department of Research," *Biennial Report 1915–1916*, 52; Nelles, "Superintendent's Report," *Biennial Report 1917–1918*, 4–6.

76. Williams, "Report of the Department of Research," *Biennial Report 1915–1916*, 54.

77. Ibid., 89.

78. Lewis M. Terman, *Measurement of Intelligence: An Explanation of and a Complete Guide for the Use of the Stanford Revision and Extension of the Binet-Simon Intelligence Scale* (Boston: Houghton Mifflin, 1912), 91–92.

79. For a sample of Walter Lippmann and Terman's exchange, see Lippman, "A Future for the Tests," *New Republic*, 29 (November 1922), 9–11; and for Terman's response, see "The Great Conspiracy; or the Impulse Imperious of Intelligence Testers Psychoanalyzed and Exposed by Mr. Lippmann," *New Republic*, December 27, 1922, 1–15. For more, see Paul D. Chapman, *Schools as Sorters: Lewis M. Terman, Applied Psychology, and the Intelligence Testing Movement, 1890–1930* (New York: New York University Press, 1988), 135–139. For evidence Nelles's researchers were aware of such questions, see Julia Mathews, "321 Girls," *Journal of Juvenile Delinquency* 8 (1923), 200: "There has been a tendency of late to decry somewhat the value of the I.Q. as a diagnostic index."

80. For more on the Army tests, see, for instance, Kevles, "Testing the Army's Intelligence," 565–581; John L. Rury, "Race, Region, and Education: An Analysis of Black and White Scores on the 1917 Army Alpha Intelligence Tests," *Journal of Negro Education* 57 (1988), 51–65; and Henry L. Minton, "Terman and Mental Testing: In Search of the Democratic Ideal," in *Psychological Testing and American Society, 1890–1930*, ed. Michael M. Sokal (New Brunswick, N.J.: Rutgers University Press, 1987), 95–112.

81. On the testing of children, see Gilbert González, "Racism, Education, and the Mexican Community in Los Angeles," *Societas* 4 (1974), 293–294; and Nelles, "Superintendent's Report," *Biennial Report 1917–1918*, 4–9.

82. González, "Racism, Education and the Mexican Community," 295–296. For examples of the analyses derived from the tests given to students, see, for instance, Franklin C. Paschal, "Racial Differences in the Mental and Physical Development of Mexican Children," *Comparative Psychology Monographs* 3 (1926), 1–76.

83. For Nelles's contact with Davenport, see Williams, *Defective, Delinquent, and Dependent Boys,* 3–4. For public statements about the school's "world class" stature, see "Reform at Whittier," *Sacramento Bee,* June 10, 1917, in Miscellaneous Records, Newspapers Clippings, Youth Authority Records, F3738, California State Archives, Sacramento; and *Los Angeles Times,* December 1, 1924, A2: "Mr. Fred C. Nelles has earned a nation-wide reputation in his work . . . changing an old-fashioned 'house of corrections' or 'reform school' into one of the most successful educational institutions in the country." Years later, in 1943, following the decline of the school, criminologists characterized Whittier as the former "show place of the nation in the juvenile correctional field." Quote cited in John R. Ellingston, *Protecting Our Children from Criminal Careers* (New York: Prentice-Hall, 1948), 87.

84. For more on the CBJR, see Williams, "Early History," 213.

85. For Mathews's communication with Terman, see Julia Mathews, CBJR, Whittier, California, to Lewis Terman, Stanford University, Palo Alto, California, January 23, 1923, Terman Papers, Special Collection, Stanford University, Stanford [hereafter Terman Papers]. For Terman's response to Mathews, see Terman to Mathews, January 25, 1923, Terman Papers.

86. State of California, *Third Biennial Report, Department of Institutions of the State of California, Two Years Ending June 30, 1926* [hereafter *Biennial Report*] (Sacramento: State Printing Office, 1926), 9.

87. Ibid., 3–8, 16.

88. Kenyon J. Scudder, "Report of the Superintendent of the Whittier State School in State of California," in State of California, *Biennial Report 1928,* 80.

89. State of California, *Biennial Report 1928,* 80, Youth Authority Records, F3738, California State Archives, Sacramento.

90. Scudder, "Between the Dark and Daylight," 180.

91. State of California, *Biennial Report 1928,* 80.

92. Ibid., 80–87.

93. Letter, Miriam Van Waters, Referee, Juvenile Court, Los Angeles County, to Lewis S. Terman, Stanford, July 3, 1928, Terman Papers; and Letter, Lewis S. Terman, to Miriam Van Waters, Los Angeles, July 9, 1928, Terman Papers.

94. State of California, *Biennial Report 1928,* 88.

95. Quote cited in Kenyon Scudder, "Between the Dark and the Daylight," 332; for more on Scudder's removal, see ibid., 303–329.

96. For criticisms of Sabichi's administration, see "Angeleno Gets Whittier Post," *Los Angeles Times,* April 26, 1933.

97. Orin Bell, "Superintendent of Southern Reception Center Clinic, 1953–1965, Oral History Interview," Oral Histories, Administrative Records, Youth Authority Records, F3738, California State Archives, Sacramento, 58.

CHAPTER 3

1. For Pedro C.'s social case history, see State of California, Bureau of Juvenile Research, Social Case History (SCH), "Family of Pedro C., No. 351, #3850," 1–20, Eugenics Records Office (ERO), American Philosophical Society Library (APS). All social case histories are found in ERO, APS; all identities of youths and their family members have been removed in this study for privacy. For more on Covert, see J. Harold Williams, "Early History of the California Bureau of Juvenile Research," *Journal of Juvenile Research* 28, no. 4 (October 1934), 212. Little else remains on Covert's personal life or on the lives of other eugenics fieldworkers. For contemporary beliefs about the inheritance of dysgenic traits and eugenics more broadly and about how they played out in the juvenile and criminal justices system, see, for instance, Amy LaPan and Tony Platt, "'To Stem the Tide of Degeneracy': The Eugenic Impulse in Social Work," in *Mental Disorders in the Social Environment: Critical Perspectives,* ed. Stuart A. Kirk, 139–164 (New York: Columbia University Press, 2005); Alexandra M. Stern, *Eugenic Nation: Faults and Frontiers of Better Breeding in Modern America* (Berkeley: University of California Press, 2005); Michael Willrich, "The Two-Percent Solution: Eugenic Jurisprudence and the Socialization of American Law, 1900–1930," *Law and History Review* 16, no. 1 (Spring, 1998): 63–111; Michael Willrich, *City of Courts: Socializing Justice in Progressive Era Chicago* (Cambridge: Cambridge University Press, 2003); Daniel J. Kevles, *In the Name of Eugenics: Genetics and the Uses of Human Heredity,* rev. ed. (Cambridge, Mass.: Harvard University Press, 1995); James W. Trent, *Inventing the Feeble Mind: A History of Mental Retardation in the United States* (Berkeley: University of California Press, 1994); Phillip Reilly, *The Surgical Solution: A History of Involuntary Sterilization in the United States* (Baltimore: Johns Hopkins Press, 1991); Steven Selden, *Inheriting Shame: The Story of Eugenics and Racism in America* (New York: Teachers College Press, 2001); and Edward J. Larson, *Sex, Race, and Science: Eugenics in the Deep South* (Baltimore: Johns Hopkins University Press, 1995).

2. SCH, "Family of Pedro C., No. 351, #3850," 2. For the claim that Mexicans were "less active temperamentally than the Whites, Negroes, or Chinese," see Williams, "Early History," 199.

3. J. Harold Williams, "The Homes They Come From," *California Bulletin of Social Work,* 15–17, J. Harold Williams Papers, box 7, Special Collections, UCLA, Los Angeles.

4. SCH, "Family of Pedro C., No. 351, #3850," 11.

5. For assertions that mothers' intelligences were lower than fathers', see Williams, "Early History," 206–207.

6. SCH, "Family of Pedro C., No. 351, #3850," 12–15.

7. Ibid., 18.

8. The records indicate that the fieldworkers carried out at least 400 histories on wards at Whittier State School. Half of those, however, were lost prior to their arrival at the ERO, APS. The remaining 203 are of histories carried out on 127 Euro-American, 44 Mexican and Mexican American, and 33 African American youths.

9. Quoted in Stern, *Eugenic Nation,* 11.

10. Stern, *Eugenic Nation,* 14, 16, 87, 90; and Mark B. Adams, Garland E. Allen, and Sheila Faith Weiss, "Human Heredity and Politics: A Comparative Institutional Study of the Eugenics Record Office at Cold Spring Harbor (United States), the Kaiser Wilhelm Institute for Anthropology, Human Heredity, and Eugenics (Germany), and the Maxim Gorky Medical Genetics Institute (USSR)," *Osiris* 20, no. 1 (2005), 233–235. For more on the ERO, see the work of Garland E. Allen, including "The Eugenics Record Office at Cold Spring Harbor, 1910–1940: An Essay in Institutional History," *Osiris* 2 (1986), 225–264. For more on positive and negative eugenics, see Wendy Kline, *Building a Better Race: Gender, Sexuality, and Eugenics from the Turn of the Century to the Baby Boom* (Berkeley: University of California Press, 2001).

11. Quoted in Adams et al., "Human Heredity and Politics," 234.

12. Ibid., 236–237.

13. Quoted in ibid., 238.

14. Quote is from Mae M. Ngai, *Impossible Subjects: Illegal Aliens and the Making of Modern America* (Princeton, N.J.: Princeton University Press, 2004), 3. Emphasis in the original quote. See also, ibid., 7, 9; and Stern, *Eugenic Nation,* 9, 57–81. For more on immigration restrictions and links to feeblemindedness in the United States, see, for instance, Alexandra M. Stern, "Buildings, Boundaries, and Blood: Medicalization and Nation-Building at the U.S.-Mexico Border, 1910–1930," *Hispanic American Historical Review* 79, no. 1 (1999), 41–81.

15. Quoted in Amy Sue Bix, "Experiences and Voices of Eugenics Field Workers: 'Women's Work' in Biology," *Social Studies of Science* 27 (1997), 644.

16. Ibid., 627–628.

17. Henry H. Goddard, *Feeblemindedness; Its Causes and Consequences* (New York: MacMillan, 1914); Goddard, *The Kallikak Family: A Study in the Heredity of Feedble-Mindedness* (New York: Macmillan, 1914); G. Stanley Hall, *Adolescence: Its Psychology and Its Relations to Physiology, Anthropology, Sociology, Sex, Crime, Religion and Education, I–II* (New York: D. Appleton, 1904); and Arthur Estabrook, *The Jukes in 1915* (Washington, D.C.: Carnegie Institution of Washington, 1916). The fieldworkers' activities were publicized in the Eugenics Society's journal, *Eugenical News.*

18. Bix, "Experiences and Voices of Eugenics Field Workers," 632.

19. Ibid., 636.

20. Quoted in "Qualities Desired in a Eugenical Field Worker," 1921, no. 1011, Harry H. Laughlin Papers, Truman State University, Papers, C-2-4, 8 (www.eugenicsarchive.org/html/eugenics/static/images/1101.html, accessed February 15, 2010).

21. Quoted in Bix, "Experiences and Voices of Eugenics Field Workers," 650. See also ibid., 626, 641.

22. "Meeting Notes," 331–339, Field Worker Files, MSC 77, series 7, box 1, 334.7, ERO, APS.

23. Cold Spring Harbor, Eugenics Records Office, "The Position of Field Workers," *Eugenical News* 4 (1919), 41.

24. Adams, "Human Heredity and Politics," 237–239; and Bix, "Experiences and Voices of Eugenics Field Workers," 656. It is unclear precisely how many

social case histories fieldworkers completed, for the records are incomplete. For a sample, see ERO, APS.

25. Adams, "Human Heredity and Politics," 238–239. For early criticism of "slipshod" fieldwork, see J. E. Wallace Wallin, "The Hygiene of Eugenic Generation," *Psychological Clinic* 8 (October 1914), 124; and ibid., "Conclusion," 170–179.

26. For more on the transformation of eugenics in the postwar period, see, for instance, Stern, *Eugenic Nation*.

27. Williams, "Individual Case History Outline," 72.

28. For evidence of the influence of the ERO in the CBJR, see, for instance, J. Harold Williams et al., *Whittier Social Case History Manual*, CBJR Bulletin no. 10 (Whittier, Calif.: Whittier State School, 1921), Fred C. Nelles School for Boys (Whittier), Youth Authority Records, F3738, California State Archives, Sacramento [hereafter FNSB], 16, 36.

29. For more on the classes at the CBJR, see Williams, "Early History," 209–210; and on the fieldworkers, see ibid., 211–212.

30. For more on the nature of their work, see Williams, *Whittier Social Case History Manual*, 17–38.

31. For more on the symbols used in the research, see Williams et al., *Whittier Social Case History Manual*, 41–43. For samples of published family trees, see ibid., 42, 51.

32. Ibid, 3.

33. Ibid., 4–7. That publication included the work of previous studies published by Williams and fieldworkers, including: J. Harold Williams, *A Guide to the Grading of Homes*, Department of Research, Bulletin no. 7 (Whittier, Calif.: Whittier State School, 1918), FNSB; and Williams and Willis S. Clark, *A Guide to the Grading of Neighborhoods*, Department of Research, Bulletin no. 8 (Whittier, Calif.: Whittier State School, 1919), FNSB. Other guides included Williams, "Individual Case History Outline," *Journal of Delinquency* 5, no. 3 (May 1920), 71–82; Williams, *Outline for the Study of Mental Deficiency* (Whittier, Calif.: CBJR, 1922), FNSB; and Williams, "The Homes They Come From." For more on the professionalization of social work in particular and its relation to fieldwork, see LaPan and Platt, "'To Stem the Tide of Degeneracy,'" 139–164.

34. Williams cited these works, among many others from the ERO, as foundational to the CBJR. See Williams et al., *Whittier Social Case History Manual*, 44. See, for instance, Charles Davenport, *Trait Book* (Cold Spring Harbor, N.Y.: ERO, 1912), and *How to Make a Eugenical Family History* (Cold Spring Harbor, N.Y.: ERO, 1915).

35. Quoted in SCH, "Family of James Edward F., No. 199," 5. For Goddard's views, see Goddard, *Feebleminded Causes and Consequences*; and Trent, *Inventing the Feeble Mind*, 163–164.

36. Wallin, "The Hygiene of Eugenic Generation," 124.

37. For physical markers, see, for instance, SCH, "Family of Bernie S., No. 239, #3530," 4; SCH, "Family of Jose M., No. 240, #3610, Mex-Ind," 3; and SCH, "Family of Fred M., No. 214, #3411," 28–30.

38. SCH, "Family of Harold H., No. 255, #3658," 2.

39. SCH, "Family of Lee Theodore S., No. 200, #3375," 20.

40. SCH, "Family of Walter & Marcus J. (Negro), No. 207, #3536 & #3560," 7–9, 17.

41. Ibid., 19–20.

42. For the role of photographs in the social case histories, see Williams et al., *Whittier Social Case History Manual,* 12.

43. SCH, "Family of Thomas H. W., No. 201, #3367," 21.

44. Ibid., 10. See also SCH, "Family of Ernest S. (Mexican-Indian), No. 168, #3445," 2.

45. For Williams's work establishing a race-based intelligence hierarchy, see J. Harold Williams, "The Intelligence of the Delinquent Boy," *Journal of Delinquency,* Monograph 1 (Whittier, Calif.: Whittier State School, Department of Research, 1919). For more on racial hierarchies, see, for instance, Williams, "Early History"; and Williams, "Racial Problem of Mexicans," *Journal of Delinquency* 5 (September 1920), 1.

46. For more on nineteenth-century terminology, see, for instance, Leon Litwack, *Been in the Storm So Long: The Aftermath of Slavery* (New York: Vintage, 1979), esp. 252–255.

47. SCH, "Family of Victor R., No. 322," 2.

48. Ibid.

49. Ibid., 3–4.

50. SCH, "Family of Manuel C. (Unnumbered)," 1; and SCH, "Family of Jesus G., No. 131, #3283 (Mex-Ind)," 1.

51. SCH, "Family of Arthur and John A., No. 305," 25.

52. SCH, "Family of Pedro T., No. 129, #2766 (Mex-Ind)," 13. For another similar case, see SCH, "Family of Jose M., No. 240, #3610, Mex-Ind," 14.

53. SCH, "Family of Louis A., No. 227 #3483, (Mexican Indian)," 1, 12.

54. SCH, "Family of Jose Magbaleno F. [*sic*], No. 275, #3587," 1, 13.

55. SCH, "Family of Arthur and Henry, No. 294," 14.

56. SCH, "Family of Ernest S. (Mexican-Indian), No. 168, #3445," 18; for a similar case, see SCH, "Family of Albert R., No. 299," 17.

57. SCH, "Family of Nathan Tom M. (Negro), No. 268," 1–2.

58. Ibid., 3.

59. Ibid., 8.

60. SCH, "Family of John W. (Negro), No. 221, #3399," 2–3, 5, 8, 13, 22, 31–32.

61. SCH, "Family of Oscar K., No. 137, #3327 (Colored)," 1–2, 7.

62. SCH, "Family of Joe F., No. 312," 4, 12.

63. SCH, "Douglas W. (Negro), No. 278," 5–6.

64. Ibid., 11.

65. Ibid. For similar cases, see SCH, "Family of Carl H., No. 249, #3566," 3; and SCH, "Family of Joseph M., No. 277, #3567," 4.

66. For classic studies examining the Euro-American dominant views of African Americans in slavery, see, for instance, George M. Frederickson, *The Black Image in the White Mind* (New York: Harper & Row, 1971). For studies on African Americans in reconstruction and the Jim Crow era, see Leon Litwack, *Trouble in Mind: Black Southerners in the Age of Jim Crow* (New York: Vintage, 1999); Eric Foner, *Reconstruction: America's Unfinished Revolution, 1863–1877* (New

York: Harper, 2002); and David Oshinsky, *Worse Than Slavery: Parchman Farm and the Ordeal of Jim Crow Justice* (New York: Free Press, 1997).

67. SCH, "Family of Johnny G., No. 318, #3741," 3.

68. For studies on the stereotypes of Mexicans and Mexican Americans in the nineteenth century, see, for example, Antonia I. Castañeda, "The Political Economy of Nineteenth-Century Stereotypes," in *Between Borders: Essays on Chicana/Mexicana History,* ed. Adelaida del Castillo (Encino, Calif.: Floricanto Press, 1990), 213–238; Reginald Horsman, *Race and Manifest Destiny: Origins of American Racial Anglo-Saxonism* (Cambridge, Mass.: Harvard University Press, 1981); and Tomas Almaguer, *California Fault Lines: The Historical Origins of White Supremacy in California* (Berkeley: University of California Press, 1994).

69. SCH, "Family of Louis A. P. (Mexican Indian), No. 227, #3423," 3.

70. SCH, "Family of Xavier [sic] V., No. 333," 1, 10.

71. SCH, "Family of Jacob V., No. 231 #3481," 1, 8.

72. SCH, "Family of Arthur and John A., No. 305," 24.

73. SCH, "Family of Joe M. (Mex-Ind), No. 240, #3610," 2.

74. SCH, "Family of Armando T. (Mex-Ind), No. 211, #3475," 2.

75. SCH, "Family History of Edward B., Colored, No. 164, #3360," 2, 10.

76. SCH, "Family of Jacob V., No. 231, #3481," 3.

77. SCH, "Family of Fred G., No. 218, #3434, Mexican-Indian," 2.

78. SCH, "Family of Timothy D., No. 236, #3290, Mexican-Indian," 3.

79. SCH, "Family of Victor R., No. 322, #3857, Mexican-Indian," 16.

80. For more on the "new" and "old negroes," see Litwack, *Trouble in Mind,* 179–216. For the size of the African American community in California in the early twentieth century, see Chapter 2.

81. SCH, "Family of Walter J. (Negro), No. 153, #3419," 2.

82. SCH, "Family of Julius J. (Negro), No. 237, #3488," 3–4.

83. SCH, "Family of Nathan Tom M. (Negro), No. 268, #3535," 3.

84. Ibid., 15.

85. Williams, "The Homes They Come From," 15, 17.

86. SCH, "Family of Paul B. (Unnumbered), #3265, Colored," 7.

87. SCH, "Family of Christobal M. [sic], No. 192, #3302," 5.

88. SCH, "Family of Armando T. (Mex–Ind), No. 211, #3475," 10.

89. Williams, "Early History," 203.

90. Ibid., 204.

91. SCH, "Family of William V., No. 210, #3369," 4–5.

92. For more on the Irish, see SCH, "Family of Joseph C. O., No. 208, #3408," 2–3, 22; and SCH, "Family of James Edward F., No. 199," 40–41.

93. For the Slovenian family's characterization, see SCH, "Family of Frank L., No. 244, #3494," 3; and for the Armenian family, see SCH, "Family of Harry S., No. 262, #4098," 16–17.

94. SCH, "Family of John S., No. 301," 12, 13, 20.

95. For the Swedish family, see SCH, "Family of Harold C., No. 254, #3511," 21–23.

96. James L. Scott, *Weapons of the Weak: Everyday Forms of Peasant Resistance* (New Haven, Conn.: Yale University Press, 1985), xvi, 29–31, 35–36, 284–286.

97. SCH, "Family of Ernest S., (Mexican-Indian), No. 168, #3445," 3–4.

98. Ibid., 7.

99. SCH, "Family of Oscar K., No. 137, #3327 (Colored)," 7.

100. SCH, "Family of Walter & Marcus J. (Negro), No. 207, #3536 & #3560," 1–3.

101. SCH, "Family of [Arthur and] John A., No. 21, #3752," 15.

102. For John A.'s case, see ibid., 5–6.

103. See Peggy Pascoe, *What Comes Naturally: Miscegenation Law and the Making of Race in America* (New York: Oxford University Press, 2009); and Peggy Pascoe, "Miscegenation Law, Court Cases, and Ideologies of 'Race' in Twentieth-Century America," *Journal of American History* 83, no. 1 (June 1996), 44–69.

104. SCH, "Family of Nathan Tom M. (Negro), No. 268," 6, 8.

105. Ibid., 17.

106. For the Cristobal M. case, see SCH, "Family of Christobal M. [*sic*], No. 192, #3302," 16.

107. SCH, "Family of James Edward F., No. 199," 41.

108. Ibid., 43–44.

109. Ibid., 45.

110. Ibid., 30, 47–48.

CHAPTER 4

1. State of California, Bureau of Juvenile Research, Social Case History (SCH), "Family of Christobel M. [*sic*], No. 192, #3302," 3, Eugenics Record Office (ERO) records, American Philosophical Society Library, Philadelphia, Pennsylvania (APS). See also SCH, "Family of Christobel, Fred, Tony, and Albert M. [*sic*], Supplementary Report of Social Case History, No. 192, 1." All social case histories are found in ERO, APS; all identities of youths and their family members have been removed in this study for privacy.

2. SCH, "Family of Christobel M. [*sic*], No. 192, #3302," 12.

3. For more on the girls, see Chapter 1.

4. See also Steven Schlossman and Stephanie Wallach, "The Crime of Precocious Sexuality: Female Juvenile Delinquency in the Progressive Era," *Harvard Educational Review* 48, no. 1 (1978), 65–94.

5. Among the 622 females who ended up at the school, whites were the largest group (513; 82 percent), followed by Mexicans (75; 12 percent), and blacks (34; 5 percent).

6. Whittier State School, *Biennial Report: Whittier State School, 1913–1914* (Whittier, Calif.: Whittier State School, 1914), Fred C. Nelles School for Boys (Whittier), Youth Authority Records, F3738, California State Archives, Sacramento [hereafter *Biennial Report 1914* and FNSB, respectively], 24.

7. Nelles's quote cited in "Whittier State School," *Riverside Enterprise*, December 23, 1915.

8. For more on the anti-Mexican, restrictionist trend of the 1920s and 1930s, see, for instance, David Gutiérrez, *Walls and Mirrors: Mexican Americans, Mexican Immigrants, and the Politics of Ethnicity* (Berkeley: University of California

Press, 1995), 69–116; Mark Reisler, *By the Sweat of Their Brow: Mexican Immigrant Labor in the United States, 1900–1940* (Westport, Conn.: Greenwood Press, 1976); and Abraham Hoffman, *Unwanted Mexican Americans in the Great Depression: Repatriation Pressures, 1929–1939* (Tucson: University of Arizona Press, 1974).

9. For the girls' population figures at Whittier State School, see FNSB, vols. 98–108 (1891–1912). After 1912, the state transferred the girls to the California (and later Ventura) School for Girls. Those population records are woefully incomplete.

10. Orin Bell, "Superintendent of Southern Reception Center Clinic, 1953–1965, Oral History Interview," Oral Histories, Administrative Records, Youth Authority Records, F3738, California State Archives, Sacramento, 41; and Ben B. Lindsey, "Whittier State School Report/Investigation, 1940–1941," Ben Lindsey Papers, box 6, folder 7, UCLA Special Collections, Los Angeles.

11. *Biennial Report 1914*, 24.

12. Robert M. Fogelson, *The Fragmented Metropolis: Los Angeles, 1850–1930* (Cambridge, Mass.: Harvard University Press, 1963), 76.

13. For more on the incarceration of young of people of color, see Chapter 2.

14. Whittier State School, *Biennial Report 1914*, 12.

15. For Holton's observation, see Karl Holton, "Development of Juvenile Correctional Practices," Earl Warren Oral History Project (UCB, Bancroft, 1972, interview date: June 24, 1971), 54–57. For more on the forest labor camps in California, see Volken Janssen, "When the 'Jungle' Met the Forest: Public Work, Civil Defense, and Prison Camps in Postwar California," *Journal of American History* 96, no. 3 (December 2009), 703–726.

16. SCH, "Family of Christobel M. [*sic*], No. 192, #3302," 13–14. In addition to the Sherman Institute, many Whittier State School inmates had also spent time at the St. Francis Orphanage in Watsonville, the Spanish American Institute in Gardena, and the Home of the Good Shepherd in Los Angeles.

17. See, for instance, the conditions found at the Juilly Home in Los Angeles. See SCH, "Family of Ernest (Juilly) F., No. 206," 9–10. For other similar places, see "Living Proof in Refutation," *Los Angeles Times*, February 25, 1913, II, 12; and Holton, "Development of Juvenile Correctional Practices," 53.

18. These findings come from my investigation of the Inmate History Registers, vols. 98–137 (1890–1940), FNSB.

19. Mary E. Odem, *Delinquent Daughters: Protecting and Policing Adolescent Female Sexuality in the United States, 1885–1920* (Chapel Hill: University of North Carolina Press, 1995).

20. SCH, "Family of Christobel, Fred, Tony, and Albert M. [*sic*], Supplementary Report of Social Case History, No. 192," 5–6, 15.

21. The data on nativity (place of birth) comes from my analysis of the Inmate History Registers, vols. 98–137 (1890–1940), FNSB.

22. Studies on African American youths in California of the early 1900s are limited. See, for instance, Lawrence B. De Graff, Kevin Mulroy, and Quintard Taylor, eds., *Seeking El Dorado: African Americans in California* (Seattle: University of Washington Press, 2001); Quintard Taylor, *In Search of the Racial Frontier: African Americans in the West, 1528–1990* (New York: W. W. Norton,

1999); and Quintard Taylor and Shirley Anne Moore, *African American Women Confront the West, 1600–2000* (Norman: University of Oklahoma Press, 2008).

23. Holton, "Development of Juvenile Correctional Practices," 54–57.

24. These details come from Inmate History Registers, vols. 98–137 (1890–1940), FNSB.

25. Emily Huntington, Leona Jones, Donna Moses, and Ruth Turner, "The Juvenile Court: A Study of the Organization and Procedure of the Juvenile Court with Special Reverence to Seven Counties of California," (bachelor's thesis, University of California–Berkeley, 1917), Bancroft Library, Berkeley, California, 111.

26. For more on syphilis, see, for instance, Ann R. Gabbert, "Prostitution and Moral Reform in the Borderlands: El Paso, 1890–1920," *Journal of the History of Sexuality* 12, no. 4 (October 2003), 581–582; and Allan M. Brandt, *No Magic Bullet: A Social History of Venereal Disease in the United States since 1880* (New York: Oxford University Press, 1985), 12, 41, 130, 161.

27. For the photographs, see Inmate History Registers, vols. 98–137 (1890–1940), FNSB. For more on photography in the justice system, see Anna Pegler-Gordon, *In Sight of America, Photography and the Development of U.S. Immigration Policy* (Berkeley: University of California Press, 2009); and Jonathon Finn, *Capturing the Criminal Image: From Mug Shot to Surveillance Society* (Minneapolis: University of Minnesota Press, 2009).

28. For more details of daily life, see Inmate History Registers, vols. 98–137 (1891–1940), FNSB.

29. For more on sexual assaults, see Chapters 3 and 6.

30. For more on the surgical procedure, see Edward J. Larson, *Sex, Race, and Science: Eugenics in the Deep South* (Baltimore: Johns Hopkins University Press, 1995), 27; and Alexandra M. Stern, *Eugenic Nation: Faults and Frontiers of Better Breeding in Modern America* (Berkeley: University of California, 2005), 7, 83–84.

31. For the results of Cristobal's exam, see SCH, "Family of Christobel M. [*sic*], No. 192, #3302," 2–3.

32. For the results of Fred and Tony's exams, see ibid., 6–7, 9.

33. For the results of Albert's exams, see SCH, "Family of Christobel, Fred, Tony, and Albert M. [*sic*], Supplementary Report of Social Case History, No. 192," 1–2.

34. SCH, "Family of Christobel M. [*sic*], No. 192, #3302," 1.

35. SCH, "Family of Christobel, Fred, Tony, and Albert M. [*sic*], Supplementary Report of Social Case History, No. 192," 2.

36. SCH, "Family of Christobel M. [*sic*], No. 192, #3302," 17.

37. Ibid., 15–16.

38. For Albert's exam, see SCH, "Family of Christobel, Fred, Tony, and Albert M. [*sic*], Supplementary Report of Social Case History, No. 192," 1–2.

39. Ibid., 2, 7.

40. For Albert's sterilization, see Fred O. Butler, Medical Superintendent, Sonoma State Home, Eldridge, California [FOB], to Earl E. Jensen, Director, Department of Institutions, Sacramento, California [EAJ], August 23, 1927, in "Sterilization Authorizations and Related Documents for Patients Admitted to California State Mental Institutions," Department of Mental Hygiene, State of

California, Sacramento [hereafter "Sterilization Authorizations"], reel 115, n.p. For more on the "stigmata of degeneracy," see Chapter 3 and the "Recommendation and Approval for Vasectomy or Salpingectomy for the Purpose of Sterilization," in "Sterilization Authorizations," June 6, 1937, reel 120, n.p.

41. *Statutes of California and Amendments to the Codes* [hereafter *California Statutes*], Thirty-Eighth Session of the Legislature, 1909, chapter 720, section 1, 1093–1094.

42. *California Statutes* (1913), chapter 363, sections 1–4, 775–776.

43. *California Statutes* (1917), chapter 489, section 1, 571–572; and Stern, *Eugenic Nation*, 99–100.

44. Stern, *Eugenic Nation*, 99–100; Wendy Kline, *Building a Better Race: Gender, Sexuality, and Eugenics from the Turn of the Century to the Baby Boom* (Berkeley: University of California Press, 2005), 50–51; and Alex Wellerstein, "States of Eugenics: Institutions and the Practices of Compulsory Sterilization in California," in *Reframing Rights: Bioconstitutionalism in the Genetic Age*, ed. Sheila Jasanoff (Cambridge, Mass.: MIT Press, 2011), 22.

45. Stern, *Eugenic Nation*, 83–84, 104–108.

46. For contemporary views of the diseases, particularly epilepsy, see Thomas F. Joyce, Medical Superintendent, Pacific Colony, Spadra, California (TJ), to Harry Lutgens, Director, Department of Institutions, Sacramento, California (HL), July 3, 1935, in "Sterilization Authorizations," reel 119, n.p. The patient, wrote Joyce will "never be able to maintain a family should he ever leave the institution and marry." For more on the state hospitals, see Wellerstein, "States of Eugenics," 9–11; and Joel Braslow, *Mental Ills and Bodily Cures: Psychiatric Treatment in the First Half of the Twentieth Century* (Berkeley: University of California Press, 1997).

47. Segregating defective patients, according to Paul Popenoe and Roswell Hill Johnson, the leading advocates of eugenics in California and across the country, was "the policy of isolating feebleminded and other antisocial individuals from the normal population into institutions, colonies, etc., where the two sexes are kept apart." Quote cited in, Larson, *Sex, Race, and Science*, 23.

48. For more on the feebleminded, see Chapter 3; James W. Trent Jr., *Inventing the Feeble Mind: A History of Mental Retardation in the United States* (Berkeley: University of California Press, 1994), 141–42; and Kline, *Building a Better Race*, 37, 51.

49. Kline, *Building a Better Race*, 33.

50. Quote cited in Wellerstein, "States of Eugenics," 15–16.

51. Quoted in ibid., 4.

52. Larson, *Race, Sex, and Science*, 32–39.

53. For more on *Buck v. Bell*, see Paul A. Lombardo, *Three Generations, No Imbeciles: Eugenics, the Supreme Court, and* Buck v. Bell (Baltimore: Johns Hopkins University Press, 2008).

54. FOB to HL, June 20, 1936, in "Sterilization Authorizations," reel 119, n.p.

55. Kline, *Building a Better Race*, 33, 52, 101–102, 106. Alex Wellerstein argues that individual administrators at state hospitals had more power over daily operations than state officials in Sacramento. My research confirms those findings. For an opposing view, see Larsen, *Sex, Race, and Science*, 26. For more

on Butler's advocacy work around the country, see Butler, "Sterilization in California," *Eugenical News* 12, no. 3 (March 1927), 28–29.

56. Philip Reilly, *Surgical Solution: History of Involuntary Sterilization in the United States* (Baltimore: Johns Hopkins University Press, 1991), 98; and Allison C. Carey, "Gender and Compulsory Sterilization Programs in America, 1907–1950," *Journal of Historical Sociology* 11, no. 1 (March 1998), 74–105.

57. For more on *pachucos* and *pachucas* (zoot suiters) of the 1930s and 1940s, see the Preface and Chapter 6.

58. Close is quoted in "Interview with Mr. Close," 4 pp., in "Investigation Reports," Preston School of Industry, 1889–1994, Youth Authority Records, F3738, California State Archives, Sacramento [hereafter PSI]. On the compulsory nature of Sonoma State Home, see E. S. Gosney and Paul Popenoe, "Eugenics Sterilization in California," in *Eugenical News* 12, no. 8 (August 1927), 113–114. For more on Gosney and Popenoe's work, see the E. S. Gosney Papers and the Human Betterment Foundation, 1880–1945, University Archives, California Institute of Technology, San Marino.

59. For evidence of surrogate families, see SCH, "Family of Luke L., No. 130, #3333," 14. For more on the "overcrowded condition" at Sonoma State Home, see FOB to EAJ, April 18, 1932, in "Sterilization Authorizations," reel 117, n.p. For the long waiting lists at Sonoma, see Huntington et al., "The Juvenile Court," 113.

60. For the law enabling superintendents to transfer wards, see *California Statutes* (1915), chapter 631, section 8, 1232.

61. For the statute allowing the transfer of a ward from a state school to a state hospital, see *California Statutes* (1917), chapter 776, section 34, 1630.

62. For Urback's statements, see "Ex-Whittier Man to Tell of Torture," *Los Angeles Examiner*, August 7, 1940, 1, 5, section 1.

63. See, for instance, FOB to EAJ, May 12, 1938, in "Sterilization Authorizations," reel 120, n.p.

64. Quote cited in Amy LaPan and Tony Platt, "'To Stem the Tide of Degeneracy': The Eugenic Impulse in Social Work," in *Mental Disorders in the Social Environment: Critical Perspectives,* ed. Stuart A. Kirk (New York: Columbia University Press, 2005), 148.

65. LaPan and Platt, "To Stem the Tide," 149.

66. I would like to thank Alexandra Stern for pointing out the "farce" of consent.

67. For the officer's exchange with Benito S.'s father, see J. C. Geiger, Health Officer, per Mary S. Scally, Department of Public Health, San Francisco, to FOB, November 24, 1931, in Inmate Case Files, Inmate #13694 (Confidential), PSI.

68. For evidence of social workers visiting homes to secure consent, see TJ to FOB, May 9, 1938, in "Sterilization Authorizations," reel 120, n.p.

69. FOB to HL, July 30, 1936, in "Sterilization Authorizations," reel 120, n.p. For a harsher assessment of a Mexican family and their refusal to provide consent, see FOB to HL, November 4, 1936, in "Sterilization Authorizations," reel 120, n.p.

70. FOB to EAJ, August 23, 1927, in "Sterilization Authorizations," reel 115, n.p.

71. FOB to Aaron J. Rosanoff, M.D., Director, Department of Institutions, Sacramento, California (AJR), January 18, 1940, in "Sterilization Authorizations," reel 121, n.p. For evidence of the clinical conference, see Elizabeth Hoyt, M.D., Pacific Colony, Spadra, California (EH) to TJ, February 12, 1940, in "Sterilization Authorizations," reel 122, n.p.

72. For more on the Catholic Church's opposition to sterilization and the eugenics movement, see Christine Rosen, *Preaching Eugenics: Religious Leaders and the American Eugenics Movement* (New York: Oxford University Press, 2004), 139–164; and Sharon Leon, "'A Human Being, Not a Mere Social Factor': Catholic Strategies for Dealing with Sterilization Statutes in the 1920s," *Church History* 72, no. 3 (2004), 383–411. For the church's opposition, see, for instance, E. J. Mahoney, "The Morality of Sterilization," *The Catholic Mind* 34, no. 10 (May 1936), 205–216; and Kevin O'Rourke, "An Analysis of the Church's Teaching on Sterilization," *Hospital Progress* vol. 55, no. 5 (1976), 68–75. Others who opposed eugenics included Franz Boas and his followers as well as Dr. Abraham Myerson. See Hamilton Cravens, *The Triumph of Evolution: The Heredity-Environment Controversy, 1900–1941* (Baltimore: Johns Hopkins Press, 1988), 172–180. For more on Myerson, see Albert Deutsch's work, which credits Myerson with throwing "the lid open on the sterilization of defective delinquents." For more on Myerson's work, see Abraham Myerson, "Certain Medical and Legal Phases of Eugenic Sterilization," *The Yale Law Journal* 52, no. 3 (June 1943), 618–33; for Deutsch's comments, see *Our Rejected Children* (Boston: Little, Brown, 1947), 66. See also LaPan and Platt, "To Stem the Tide," 151.

73. TJ to HL, January 3, 1935, in "Sterilization Authorizations," reel 119, n.p.

74. For more on the Mexican consulate in Los Angeles, see Francisco E. Balderrama, *In Defense of La Raza: The Los Angeles Mexican Consulate and the Mexican Community, 1929–1936* (Tucson: University of Arizona Press, 1982); and Natalia Molina, *Fit to Be Citizens? Public Health and Race in Los Angeles, 1879–1939* (Berkeley: University of California Press, 2006).

75. EH to TJ, February 12, 1940, in "Sterilization Authorizations," reel 122, n.p.; and TJ to AJR, February 13, 1940, ibid.

76. *Sara Rosas García, Petitioner*, v. *State Department of Institutions, et al., Respondents*, Civ. no. 12533, Court of Appeal of California, Second Appellate District, Division One, 36 Cal. App. 2d 15; 97 P.2d 264; December 18, 1939. The case is also cited briefly in "Constitutionality of State Laws Providing Sterilization for Habitual Criminals," *Yale Law Journal* 51, no. 8 (June 1942), 1380–1387.

77. For more on sterilizations in the 1950s, see Wellerstein, "States of Eugenics," 23; and Stern, *Eugenic Nation*.

CHAPTER 5

1. O. H. Close, "Life with Youthful Offenders," unpublished ms. [ca. 1958], 83–84, Preston School of Industry, Youth Authority Records, F3738, California State Archives, Sacramento [hereafter PSI].

2. Ibid., 4–5, 37, 83–85.

3. Ibid, 84; and, State of California, *Fourteenth Biennial Report of the Board of Trustees of the Preston School of Industry, at Ione, July 1, 1918 to June 30,*

1920 (Ione, Calif.: Preston School Print Shop, 1920) [hereafter *Fourteenth Biennial Report*], PSI, 10.

4. State of California, *First Biennial Report of the Board of Trustees of the Preston School of Industry, at Ione, July 1, 1892 to June 30, 1894* (Ione, Calif.: Preston School Print Shop, 1920) [hereafter *First Biennial Report*], PSI, 10–11.

5. E. M. Preston, "Report of the Preston School of Industry," in *First Biennial Report*, 5–7; Carl Bank, "Report of Superintendent," in ibid., 11. For more on Bank, see John F. Lafferty, *The Preston School of Industry: A Centennial History*, 2nd ed. (Ione, Calif.: Preston School of Industry Print Shop, 1997), 19.

6. Bank, "Report of Superintendent," *First Biennial Report*, 12.

7. Ibid., 14.

8. Lafferty, *The Preston School of Industry*, 90–91.

9. "Education Reformation," *Los Angeles Times*, December 8, 1906, I12.

10. For Bank's comments, see State of California, *Second Biennial Report of the Board of Trustees of the Preston School of Industry, at Ione, July 1, 1894 to June 30, 1896* (Ione, Calif.: Preston School Print Shop, 1920) [hereafter *Second Biennial Report*], PSI, 14, 16. For comments on boys going hungry, see "A Mismanaged School," *Los Angeles Times*, April 5, 1895, 3.

11. "Preston School Scandal," *Los Angeles Times*, November 17, 1897, 3.

12. For more, see "Brutality at Ione," *Los Angeles Times*, November 28, 1897, 3; "Ione School Investigation," *Los Angeles Times*, December 4, 1897, 3; "Paddled the Boys, Dr. O'Brien Has Not Spared the Rod at Ione," *Los Angeles Times*, December 5, 1897, A3; and "O'Brien's Successor," *Los Angeles Times*, December 18, 1897, 3.

13. Dexter A. Clement, "A History of the Preston Band" (master's thesis, Sacramento State College, 1965), 8–9.

14. Lafferty, *Centennial History*, 52–56. For the *Sacramento Bee* report, see "Rottenness," *The Sacramento Bee*, October 12, 1900; and for the *Los Angeles Times* article, see "Big Scandal at Ione, Reform School Run by Debased Boys," *Los Angeles Times*, October 13, 1900, I, 4.

15. Kenyon J. Scudder, "Between the Dark and the Daylight," undated ms., p. 32, Regional Oral History Office, Bancroft Library, Berkeley, California.

16. Close, "Life with Youthful Offenders," 2–5, 91; Scudder, "Between the Dark and the Daylight," 51. For more on the George Junior Republic, see Jack M. Holl, *Juvenile Reform in the Progressive Era: William R. George and the Junior Republic Movement* (Ithaca, N.Y.: Cornell University Press, 1981).

17. *Sacramento Bee*, January 18, 1915.

18. Scudder, "Between the Dark and the Daylight," 66–69.

19. Ibid., 62–66.

20. For Scudder's comments, see State of California, *Thirteenth Biennial Report of the Board of Trustees of the Preston School of Industry, at Ione, July 1, 1916 to June 30, 1918* (Ione, Calif.: Preston School Print, 1918) [hereafter *Thirteenth Biennial Report*], PSI, 70. For more evidence of corporal punishment, see "Lashes for Boys Who Escaped from Preston," *Sacramento Bee*, June 18, 1915, Miscellaneous Records, Newspapers Clippings, PSI. The following also appear in that collection: "Preston Flogging Cases under Probe," *Sacramento Bee*, June

20, 1915; and "Charge Brutal Treatment of Ione Boys," *Los Angeles Herald*, June 5, 1917. For the abolishment of corporal punishment, see "Flogging at Ione School Abolished," *Los Angeles Record*, December 22, 1917.

21. "Boy Suicide Charges He Was Abused," *San Francisco Daily News*, February 13, 1917.

22. For Derrick's explanation of the program, see State of California, *Eleventh Biennial Report of the Board of Trustees of the Preston School of Industry, at Ione, July 1, 1912 to June 30, 1914* (Ione, Calif.: Preston School Print Shop, 1914) [hereafter *Eleventh Biennial Report*], PSI, 18.

23. For more on self-government at Preston, see *Thirteenth Biennial Report*, 54–58. For opposition, see Close, "Life with Youthful Offenders," 2.

24. Kenyon J. Scudder, "Criminologist and Social Engineer, 1967," 32, Oral Tapes and Transcripts, Administrative Records, Youth Authority, F3738, California State Archives, Sacramento.

25. *Eleventh Biennial Report*, 18–21.

26. State of California, *Twelfth Biennial Report of the Board of Trustees of the Preston School of Industry, at Ione, July 1, 1914 to June 30, 1916* (Ione, Calif.: Preston School Print, 1916) [hereafter *Twelfth Biennial Report*], 76–79.

27. On staff neglect of duties, see Close, "Life with Youthful Offenders," 2–3; and *Thirteenth Biennial Report*, 55. On the failure of self-government, see *Fourteenth Biennial Report*, 4; and O. H. Close, "Early-Day Practices and Changing Conceptions of Delinquency Treatment" (unpublished ms., ca. 1958), PSI, 49.

28. "Charge Brutal Treatment of Ione Boys," *Los Angeles Herald*, June 5, 1917, PSI.

29. See Close, "Life with Youthful Offenders," 38, 91; and Scudder, "Between the Dark and the Daylight," 61–62, 115–123, 146. For Gains' shooting, see "Inmate Records, Investigation Reports, Samuel Gains," 1919, PSI.

30. Scudder, "Criminologist and Social Engineer," 77.

31. "Would Restore Ione Corporal Punishment," *Los Angeles Times*, January 16, 1920, I, 2.

32. For Sears's findings, see "Retiring Head of Preston School 'Roasts' Atkinson in a Letter," *Stockton Record*, February 17, 1920, PSI.

33. For the resolution, see *Fourteenth Biennial Report*, PSI, 12. For more on the abolishment of corporal punishment, see, for instance, Leslie Davies, "Ione Residents Claim Preston Morale Is Low," *Free Press*, November 22, 1919, PSI.

34. See *Fourteenth Biennial Report*, 3; and Scudder, "Criminologist and Engineer," 147–149, 163–167.

35. Scudder, "Between the Dark and the Daylight," 58.

36. *Fourteenth Biennial Report*, 101; and Close, "Life with Youthful Offenders," 11, 34.

37. Scudder, "Between the Dark and the Daylight," 129.

38. Close, "Life with Youthful Offenders," 88.

39. Ibid., 31. For population statistics, see State of California, *Fourth Biennial Report, Department of Institutions of the State of California, Two Years Ending June 30, 1928* (Sacramento: State Printing Office, 1928), 54.

40. Close, "Life with Youthful Offenders," 6–7.

41. Margaret F. Sirch, State Board of Charities and Corrections, "Report of Medical Care and Treatment Preston School of Industry, April 26–27, 1920," *Investigation Reports*, PSI, 1.

42. State of California, *Tenth Biennial Report of the Board of Trustees of the Preston School of Industry, at Ione, July 1, 1910 to June 30, 1912* (Ione, Calif.: Preston School Print Shop, 1912) [hereafter *Tenth Biennial Report*], 39.

43. Ibid., 28–29.

44. Ibid., 28.

45. On segregating inmates, see ibid., 39; on the hiring the researchers, see *Twelfth Biennial Report*, 7.

46. Ibid., 8.

47. Lafferty, *Centennial History*, 81; and William B. Cox and Joseph A. Shelly, eds., *Handbook of American Institutions for Delinquent Juveniles*, vol. 3, *Pacific Coast States* (New York: Osborne Association, 1940), 85.

48. *Eleventh Biennial Report*, 14–16.

49. Ibid., 12–17.

50. *Twelfth Biennial Report*, 23.

51. Ibid.

52. Ibid., 24.

53. "Twenty Percent Normal at Ione," *Sacramento Bee*, June 24, 1916.

54. Scudder, "Between the Dark and the Daylight," 51.

55. *Twelfth Biennial Report*, 25.

56. Scudder, "Between the Dark and the Daylight," 92; Preston School of Industry, *Twelfth Biennial Report*, 26.

57. Ibid., 30, 33.

58. Ibid., 21–22, 36–37.

59. *Twelfth Biennial Report*, 39.

60. Ibid., 30–34. For more on home conditions, see *Eleventh Biennial Report*, 15.

61. Scudder, "Between the Dark and the Daylight," 74.

62. "Delinquency Caused by Bad Homes," *Oakland Tribune*, December 31, 1916, PSI.

63. *Twelfth Biennial Report*, 27.

64. Ibid., 28; *Thirteenth Biennial Report*, 64; and Scudder, "Between the Dark and the Daylight," 52.

65. *Thirteenth Biennial Report*, 64.

66. Ibid., 59–61.

67. *Twelfth Biennial Report*, 28–29; and *Thirteenth Biennial Report*, 15. For more on Company M, see Hugh Montgomery, Preston, to Fred Allen, Berkeley, January 24, 1915, Superintendent Records, PSI.

68. *Thirteenth Biennial Report*, 64–65; and Scudder, "Between the Dark and the Daylight," 92.

69. See Chapter 4 for more on Fred O. Butler and Sonoma State Home.

70. *Thirteenth Biennial Report*, 60, 64–65.

71. Ibid., 15–16; and Scudder, "Between the Dark and the Daylight," 93.

72. *Thirteenth Biennial Report*, 15.

73. Ibid., 2.

74. "Board of Trustees Minutes," March 1919, Trustees' Minutes, 1919–1921, PSI.

75. Scudder, "Between the Dark and the Daylight," 92, 107. Contrary to Scudder's statement, limited testing was carried out at Preston in 1920 before Close's arrival. See *Fourteenth Biennial Report*, 16, 19–21.

76. For Close's authorization, see "Board of Trustees' Minutes," October 8, 1920, PSI.

77. Close, "Life with Youthful Offenders," 21–22. That process was confirmed in 1939 by the Osborne Association's investigation of Preston. See Cox and Shelly, eds., *Handbook of American Institutions*, 76.

78. For the creation of the Department of Institutions, see Elsey Hurt, *California State Government: An Outline of Its Administrative Organization from 1850 to 1936* (Sacramento: State Printing Office, 1936), 104–105.

79. For the transfer of twenty-six Preston inmates to Sonoma, see Sonoma State Hospital, "Register of Applications, 1884–1949," 9 vols., Sonoma State Hospital Records, Department of Mental Hygiene Records, F3607, California State Archives, Sacramento [hereafter SSH, "Register of Applications"].

80. Scudder, "Between the Dark and the Daylight," 92.

81. Fred O. Butler, Sonoma, to Mrs. Mary S. Scally [*sic*], San Francisco, November 4, 1931, in Inmate Case Files, "Inmate #13694 (Confidential)," 1931–47, PSI.

82. Quote cited in "Interview with Mr. Close," 4, in Inmate Records, Investigation Reports, PSI.

83. Scudder, "Between the Dark and the Daylight," 93. For Close's transfer of one boy, see "Register of Applications," vol. 7 (1937–1940). My research indicates that another four boys, all of them former inmates, were also sent to Sonoma. They were not sent directly from the school but from the juvenile court. See "Sterilization Authorizations and Related Documents for Patients Admitted to California State Mental Institutions," Department of Mental Hygiene (Health), State of California Archives, Sacramento [hereafter "Sterilization Authorizations"], reels 114–121.

84. This finding comes from my investigation of the "Register of Applications" and "Sterilization Authorizations."

85. State of California, *Second Biennial Report, Department of Institutions of the State of California, Two Years Ending June 30, 1924* (Sacramento: State Printing Office, 1924) [hereafter *Second Biennial Report, Department of Institutions*], 38.

86. V. Pierpont Husband, "Truancy as a Factor in the Delinquency of Boys: A Case-Study of 300 Boys in the Preston School of Industry at Ione, California and Comparisons with the Truancy Problem of the Sacramento City Schools" (master's thesis, College of the Pacific 1930), 51–54.

87. Ibid., 78–79. The Biennial Reports confirm that Mexican-origin boys constituted at least 20 percent of the population in the 1920s. See *Second Biennial Report, Department of Institutions*, 43; and State of California, *Fourth Biennial Report, Department of Institutions of the State of California, Two Years Ending*

June 30, 1928 (Sacramento: State Printing Office, 1928), 72–73. For Close's statements about the Mexican population in 1928, see *Fourth Biennial Report, Department of Institutions*, 1928, 58.

88. Close, "Life with Youthful Offenders," 29–30.

89. Leon Adams, "Boys Learn Crime," *Daily News*, July 10, 1923; Adams, "Notorious Crooks 'Graduates' of Preston," *Daily News*, July 11, 1923; Adams, "Lessons in Burglary Are Given by Boys at Preston," *Daily News*, July 12, 1923; Adams, "School Guards 'Bad' Examples," *Daily News*, July 13, 1923; Adams, "No Work for Preston Boys," *Daily News*, July 14, 1923; Adams, "Torture Use on 'Bad Boys,'" *Daily News*, July 16, 1923; Adams, "Reform School Up to Women," *Daily News*, July 17, 1923; Adams, "Only Two Per Cent of Boys are Reformed at Preston," *Daily News*, July 18, 1923; Adams, "Many Preston 'Boys' in Pen," *Daily News*, July 20, 1923; Adams, "Disease of Body and Mind Easily Spread at Preston," *Daily News*, July 17, 1923; and Adams, "Reform School Fine as Start," *Daily News*, July 21, 1923.

90. O. H. Close, Waterman, California, to Cornelia McKinney Stanwood, San Francisco, California, April 27, 1923, PSI.

91. Quotes cited in Scudder, "Between the Dark and the Daylight," 100.

92. Scudder noted that the monitor system was "finally done away with in 1959." Ibid., 99–100.

93. O. H. Close, "Early-Day Practices," PSI. For more on the migration of youths during the Depression, see Karl Holton, "Development of Juvenile Correctional Practices," Earl Warren Oral History Project (Berkeley, Calif., Bancroft Library, 1972; date of interview, June 24, 1971), 54–57.

94. Close, "Early-Day Practices," 49.

95. The praise from the association is found in Cox and Shelley, eds., *Handbook of American Institutions*, 4, 17, 98, 62, and 52, respectively. For similar comments, see ibid., 14, 23–24, 27, 39, 93.

96. For the association critiques, see ibid., 98–101. The credit system was used to track the inmates' "good behavior" and to determine their release date, while the silent bench was used to punish inmates who transgressed the school's policies. The use of the "V" mark on the inmates' soles of their shoes, on the other hand, was used to deter them from escaping.

97. George E. Miller, "Administrative History of California Institutions for Juvenile Offenders" (master's thesis, public administration, Sacramento State College, 1965), 83–108, PSI.

98. Quoted in John R. Ellingston, *Protecting Our Children from Criminal Careers* (New York: Prentice-Hall, 1948), 85. Information about the association's study—"Report on Administration and Program of Preston," California Taxpayers' Association, April 1945—comes from ibid., 84–85. After many searches, I could not locate the association's original report.

99. Karl Holton, "Development of Juvenile Correctional Practices," 93.

100. Ibid.

101. Ibid., 94.

102. Ibid.

103. George Tonzi, "Oral Interview, Preston School Employee, 1934–36," April 5, 1978, 2–3, 13–14, PSI.

104. Ibid., 20.

105. Scudder, "Between the Dark and the Daylight," 367–368.

106. Alfred Deutsch, *Our Rejected Children* (Boston: Little, Brown, 1947), 111–113.

CHAPTER 6

1. Dozens of accounts detailing the boys' suicides and subsequent investigations appear in a variety of sources. For English- and Spanish-language newspaper accounts, see, for instance, "Boy, 13, Hangs Himself at State School," *Los Angeles Examiner* [hereafter *LAE*], August 12, 1930, sect. 1, 5; "Boy Hangs Self in Cell," *Los Angeles Times* [hereafter *LAT*], July 24, 1940, A1; "He Did Not Hang Himself, She Repeats in Dull Agony," *People's World*, August 19, 1939, 1, in Leo Gallagher Papers, box 2, folder 9, Southern California Regional Library, Los Angeles [hereafter *LGP*]; "Un Niño Mexicano Preso Se Ahorco," *La Opinion*, August 12, 1939, 1; "Se Suicida Otro Niño Mexicano en Whittier," *La Opinion*, July 24, 1940, 1; "Another Reform Boy Hangs Self," *Daily News*, July 23, 1940, n.p., in LGP, box 2, folder 9.

2. For views over Milne's appointment, see, for instance, "Angeleno Gets Whittier Post," *LAT*, April 26, 1933, 3; and "Milne Ouster Hearing Opens in North Today," *LAE*, August 5, 1940, section 1, 7.

3. William B. Cox and Joseph A. Shelly, eds., *Handbook of American Institutions for Delinquent Juveniles*, vol. 3, *Pacific Coast States* (New York: Handbook of American Institutions for Delinquent Juveniles, 1940), 170.

4. Ibid., 161–166, 179–180.

5. Ibid., 153–167.

6. Ibid., 181–183.

7. "'Jails Committee' Report to the Foreman and Members of the 1937 Grand Jury of the County of Los Angeles," Final Report of the 1937 L.A. County Grand Jury, December 31, 1937. Minutes, vol. 237, 104 (unpublished). Thanks to Natalia Molina for bringing this source to my attention.

8. Cox and Shelley, eds., *Handbook of American Institutions,* 155–162. Robert V. Chandler, a former Whittier employee and business manager between 1933 and 1937, noted, too, in 1954 in an oral history that "the program slowly deteriorated along with the overall plant, both as a result of improper attention. Curtailed funds during the 1930s also hindered any new programs for progress." Quoted in George E. Miller, "Administrative History of California Institutions for Juvenile Offenders" (master's thesis, public administration, Sacramento State College, 1965), 65, in Fred C. Nelles School for Boys (Whittier), Youth Authority Collection, F3738, Secretary of State, California State Archives, Sacramento [hereafter *FNSB*].

9. For a sample of the limited reporting, see, for instance, "Honors Bestowed at Placement Breakfast," *LAT*, August 23, 1935, 7; and "Council Speaker Outlines to Women Chief Delinquency Causes," *LAT*, March 10, 1936, A6.

10. "Whittier Honor Graduate Reveals Beating by Guard," *LAE*, August 8, 1940, section 1, 8.

11. "Whittier Horror Told under Oath, Beatings, Starvation, Tortures Bared by Lindsey Committee," *LAE*, August 13, 1940, section 1, 1, 6. Record keeping

of abuses during Milne's administration was also poor. Details of abuse were rarely, if ever, recorded.

12. For the state's account of Moreno's suicide, see Aaron J. Rosanoff, Director, Department of Institutions, Sacramento, to Culbert L. Olson, Sacramento, August 21, 1939, Investigation, Superintendent's Records, FNSB [hereafter Rosanoff, Investigation I], 1–14. Not surprisingly, few details of Moreno's escapes and suicide remain in the Whittier State School Case Files. See FNSB Case Files, vol. 134, no. 7649 (1939), 4–5.

13. Rosanoff, Investigation I, 3.

14. For Rosanoff's account, see ibid., 3–4; and Rosanoff, Director of Institutions, Sacramento, to Culbert L. Olson, Sacramento, August 9, 1940, 1–30, in Superintendent's Records, FNSB, [hereafter Rosanoff, Investigation II]. For more details, see "Report of [Gallagher] Committee Appointed by Governor Culbert L. Olson," 1–11, Superintendent Records, FNSB. The original report appears in LGP, box 2, folder 9.

15. Rosanoff, Investigation I, 4; "Inquiry Opened in Boy Suicide," *LAT,* August 29, 1939, A1; "Boy, 13, Hangs Himself at State School"; and Letter, Karl Holton, Los Angeles, California, to Leo Gallagher, Los Angeles, California, October 11, 1939, in LGP, box 2, folder 8.

16. Rosanoff, Investigation II, 4.

17. Quoted in "Boys' School Suicide Probed," *LAE,* August 12, 1930, section 1, 4; and "Jury Hears Details of Boy's Suicide," *LAE,* August 15, 1939, section 1, 5.

18. "Youth at State School Suicide," *LAT,* August 12, 1939, A1.

19. "Boy, 13, Hangs Himself at State School."

20. Rosanoff, Investigation I, 1–2.

21. Ibid., 3–5.

22. For more on psychopathic personalities, see J. Harold Williams, *Whittier Social Case History Manual* (Whittier, Calif.: California Bureau of Juvenile Research, 1921), 43, FNSB; and Mildred S. Covert, "Excitability in Delinquent Boys," *Journal of Juvenile Research* 5, no. 6 (November 1920), 224–239.

23. Rosanoff, Investigation I, 6. For Rosanoff's statements, see, for instance, "Changes Urged at Reformatory, Defectives Should be Recognized, says Rosanoff," *LAE,* August 24, 1939, section 1, 5.

24. Rosanoff, Investigation I, 6–8.

25. Ibid., 10–14.

26. For details on the boy's autopsy and a summary of what transpired, see Gallager Committee Report, 5–6, FNSB.

27. For what the family saw at the wake, see Gallagher Committee Report, 6, FNSB. For details of the probation officer's meeting with the family, see Karl Holton, Probation Office, Los Angeles, to Leo Gallagher, Attorney, Chairman of Citizens' Committee, October 11, 1939, in LGP, box 2, folder 8. For public doubts about the suicide, see, for instance, "He Did Not Hang Himself, She Repeats in Dull Agony," *People's World,* August 19, 1939, 1, LGP, box 2, folder 9; "New Charges Made in Boy's 'Suicide,' " ibid., 2; and "State Starts Probe of Reform School Today," *People's World,* ibid., 1.

28. For more on *pachucos* and *pachucas,* see the Preface of this book. For a similar miscarriage of justice, against Faustino Sánchez, who was killed by a po-

liceman a week after Moreno was found dead, see "Manifestacion por La Muerte de F. Sánchez, Se Llevo a Cabo Ayer en un Mitin," *La Opinion*, August 17, 1939, 1, 8; and Laura Mihailoff, "Protecting Our Children: A History of the California Youth Authority" (Ph.D. diss., University of California–Berkeley, 2008), 46–50.

29. For more on *El Congreso*, see David G. Gutiérrez, *Walls and Mirrors: Mexican Americans, Mexican Immigrants, and the Politics of Ethnicity in the Southwest, 1910–1986* (Berkeley: University of California Press, 1995), 110–116; Geroge J. Sánchez, *Becoming Mexican American: Ethnicity, Culture, and Identity in Los Angeles, 1900–1945* (New York: Oxford University Press, 1993); and Vicki L. Ruiz, "Una Mujer sin Fronteras: Luisa Moreno and Latina Labor Activism," *Pacific Historical Review* 73, no. 1 (February 2004), 1–20.

30. For evidence of the mass rallies and manifestations, see "Mientras Se Investiga al Sonado Caso, el Gobierno del Estado ha Prometido Intervenir," *La Opinion*, August 18, 1939, 1. For Fierro's role in the investigation, see "Probe Sought of Boy Suicide," *LAE*, August 18, 1939, section 1, 28; and J. Frank Burke, "A Thoughtless and Unwise Investigation," A Talk, Radio Station KFVD, October 9, 1939, FNSB.

31. Governor Culbert L. Olson, Sacramento, California, to Manuel Caqares [*sic*], Mrs. John Bright, Mr. Eduardo Quevedo, et al., September 13, 1939, FNSB. For more details of El Congreso's involvement in the investigation, see Kenneth C. Burt, *The Search for a Civic Voice: California Latino Politics* (Claremont, Calif.: Regina Books, 2007), 22–24.

32. For Milne's red-baiting of the committee, see E. J. Milne, Whittier State School, Whittier, California, to David [Milne], Chicago, Illinois, September 14, 1939, Superintendent's Records, FNSB. For the Gallagher Committee's attempt to hold private meetings with the boys, see Milne to Board of Managers, October 13, 1939, 1–3, Superintendent's Records, FNSB.

33. Gallagher Committee Report, 8. For more on Cavitt's involvement, see "Belt Missing in Whittier Case Found, Allegedly Used by Moreno to Hang Himself, *LAE*, September 9, 1940, section 1, 1, 3.

34. See, for instance, "Mother of Boy Who Took Life in State School Testifies," *LAT*, October 8, 1939, A2.

35. Quoted in Gallagher Committee, 3, FNSB.

36. Gallagher Committee, 2–10, FNSB; "Boy's Body to Be Exhumed, *LAT*, November 1, 1939, 15; and, "State School Death Depicted," *LAT*, November 3, 1939, 14.

37. Gallagher Committee Report, 10.

38. Ibid. For more on the Gallagher's Report and its reception, see "Report Made in Boy Death," *LAT*, November 29, 1939, A22.

39. For Milne's positive response to the outcome, see Letter, Milne to Board, Whittier, October 13, 1939, 1–3, Superintendent's Records, FNSB.

40. For evidence that members of the Gallagher Committee took issue with the final report, see Gallagher Committee Report, 10–11, FNSB. For Lambert's belief that they should have "gone further" with the investigation, see Gallagher to Milne, Whittier, California, December 4, 1939, LGP, box 2, folder 8. Josefina Fierro also apparently opposed the report. See Rosanoff to Gallagher, November 29, 1939, and Gallagher to Rosanoff, December 4, 1939, all in LGP, box 2, folder 8.

41. "Boy Hangs Self in Cell"; "Boy Hanging Held Suicide," *LAT,* July 26, 1940, 10; and "Whittier School Inquiry Opens," *LAT,* October 2, 1940, 19. For details of Leiva's early life, see Rosanoff, Investigation II. For Leiva's case file, see Whittier State School Case Files, vol. 126, no. 6758 (1935), 113–114.

42. "Boy Hanging Held Suicide."

43. For the uproar over the second suicide, see, for instance, "Grand Jury Probe of School Ordered by Fitts, Public Aroused over Boy's Death in Reformatory at Whittier," *LAE,* July 27, 1940, section 1, 1, 8; "Whittier Horror Told under Oath, Beatings, Starvation, Tortures Bared by Lindsey Committee," *LAE,* August 13, 1940, section 1, 1, 6. Not everyone supported the investigation; some Californians worried about the political and economic fallout. See, for instance, "California's Shame, the Whittier Hangings," editorial cartoon, *LAE,* August 12, 1940, section 1, 14; and "Civil, Legislative Leaders Hit Rosanoff Whitewash," *LAE,* August 12, 1940, section 1, 7.

44. Rosanoff, Investigation II, 4.

45. Ibid., 7.

46. Ibid., 6–7.

47. My investigation of the *Los Angeles Examiner* indicates that while the paper gave Moreno's death little attention, Leiva's death brought unprecedented coverage. For the first of several dozens reports, see, for instance, "Another Boy Hangs Self at Whittier, *Los Angeles Examiner,* July 24, 1940, 5, section 1. This pales in contrast to the *Los Angeles Times* coverage: Fifty stories. *The People's World,* known as a radical press, and *La Opinion* also weighed in on the investigation: they ran nearly thirty articles in three months in 1940. For examples of some of the sensational photos and editorial cartoons, see "Administration under Fire, Time to Act!" *LAE,* July 29, 1940, section 1, 9; and, "'Crime School!' Witnesses Tell Whittier Evils," *LAE,* August 12, 1940, section 1, 7. For Sid Hughes's role in the investigation, see Letter, Ben B. Lindsey, Los Angeles, California, to William Allen White, Esq., Emporia, Kansas, March 18, 1941. The letter is a loose document found in "Whittier State School Report/Investigation, 1940–1941," Ben Lindsey Papers, box 6, folder 7 [hereafter Lindsey, WSS Report/Investigation], UCLA Special Collections, Los Angeles.

48. "Grand Jury Probe of School Ordered by Fitts," LAE, July 27, 1940, section 1, 1, 8.

49. "Leiva Boy's Kin Tell of Beatings," *LAE,* July 27, 1940, section 1, 8.

50. "Boy's Sister Reveals His Last Letter," *LAE,* July 27, 1940, section 1, 8. Edward Leiva's suicide led other parents to fear that their sons would contemplate suicide as well. See, for instance, "Father Wires Olson to Save Son's Life, Young Inmate Threatens to Kill Himself," *LAE,* July 27, 1940, section 1, 8. For more on demands for a full investigation, see "Civic Group Protest Boys Ill Treatment," *LAE,* July 27, 1940, section 1, 8; and "Letters Back Institutional Probe," *LAE,* August 12, 1940, section 1, 7.

51. For Cruz Cruz's stories, see "Escaped Boy (Cruz) Tells Horror at Whittier," *LAE,* July 30, 1940, section 1, 8; for similar details from *La Opinion,* see "El Procurador le Presenta Sus Pruebas," *La Opinion,* July 30, 1940, 8. For more, see "Ex-Whittier Man to Tell of Torture," *LAE,* August 7, 1940, section 1, 1, 5; "Ex-Official Tells of Terrorism at Whittier School, *LAE,* July 31, 1940, section 1, 1, 10. For

accounts of abuse recounted by visitors, see "School Brutality Told by Witness," August 1, 1940, section 1, 13. In that piece, Frank L. Sage, a visitor to the school, said he witnessed a guard say to a boy: "Now you little— . . . get over there by that tree (pointing) and rub your dirty face into the ground until I tell you to stop."

52. "Sister Quotes Dead Youth on Punishment," *LAE*, July 28, 1940, section 1, 12–13. For other cases of abuse, see "Parents of Whittier Inmate Charge Boy's Mistreatment, Sworn Statement Brings No Reply," *LAE*, July 29, 1940, section 1, 1, 8.

53. "Full Probe in Reformatory Suicide Asked," *LAE*, July 26, 1940, section 1, 1.

54. Ibid.

55. Editorial: "Whittier State School for Boys Must Be Cleaned Up," *LAE*, July 28, 1940, section 1, 1, 2.

56. "Grand Jury Probe of School Ordered by Fitts, Public Aroused over Boy's Death in Reformatory at Whittier," *LAE*, July 27, 1940, section 1, 1, 8.

57. "Whittier State School for Boys Must Be Cleaned Up." For more evidence of abuse, see, for instance, "Boy Suicide Tortured Months, Parolee Says, Youth Bares Terror Reign at Whittier," *LAE*, August 1, 1940, section 1, 13; "Parolee Tells of Whittier's Mock Hanging," *LAE*, August 6, 1940, section 1, 1, 7; "Boy's Testimony Reveals Brutal Rule at Whittier, Youth Discloses Vicious Discipline, Hard Labor Declared Demanded of Ill and Weak," *LAE*, August 3, 1940, section 1, 6.

58. For a sensational political cartoon, see "Whitewash!" *LAE*, August 16, 1940, section 1, 12.

59. "Rosanoff Endorses School Terror Room, Punishment by Whittier Guards Gets Whitewash [*sic*]," *LAE*, August 11, 1940, 1, 3, section 1. The *Examiner* scrutinized Rosanoff's report and conclusions, comparing his findings to the statements of abuse issued by the boys: "Charges by Whittier Boys and Defense by Rosanoff," *LAE*, August 11, 1940, section 1, 3.

60. Editorial: "Whittier Probe Should Bring Indictments," *LAE*, August 12, 1940, section 1, 1. For other current and state officials who criticized Rosanoff's report, see "Kepple Accuses Rosanoff in School Suicide Storm," *LAE*, July 30, 1940, section 1, 8. In that article, Assemblyman Gerald C. Kepple of Whittier, a vocal critic of the Department of Institutions, denounced Aaron J. Rosanoff's proposed state institution for defective delinquents "as 'cheap political trickery.' " That project had nothing to do with juveniles, Kepple explained. Rosanoff was trying "to deflect attention [of the boys' deaths] from his department, where it belongs." For the *Examiner*'s critique of Milne's administration and distortion of "facts," particularly his claim that the school "reformed" a significant number of boys, see "Whittier 'Grads' Repeaters," *LAE*, July 31, 1940, section 1, 10; and "Rehabilitation Fails in 303 of 545 Cases, Survey of Boys Released from 1932 to 1936 Contradicts Claims of Superintendent," *LAE*, August 3, 1940, section 1, 6.

61. "New Brutalities at Whittier Told; Full Inquiry Set," *LAE*, July 30, 1940, section 1, 1, 8.

62. "Abolish Reform Schools, Pleads Flanagan," *LAE*, July 30, 1940, section 1, 7.

63. For more of those letters, see "Irate Citizens Seek Thorough Torture Quiz, Whittier Operation Declared 'Disgrace to Our State' by Writer, Others Back Injury," *LAE*, August 11, 1940, section 1, 3.

64. Osborne Investigation, 213; for Olson's decision to close solitary confinement, see "Public's Ire Forces Whittier Death Quiz, Suicide Tries by 6 Other Boys Bared," *LAE,* July 28, 1940, section 1, 1, 13. For evidence of the pressure mounted on Olson, see "Mr. Olson, What Are You Going to Do about This? What Governor Olson Says about Whittier," *LAE,* July 28, 1940, section 1, 12; "What Governor Olson Said Last August," *LAE,* July 28, 1940, section 1, 12; and "Leiva Suicide Angers Citizens to Whiter Heat," *LAE,* July 28, 1940, section 1, 12. For more on the "public pressure" for the inquiry, see Editorial: "Letters Praise *Examiner* Disclosures at School," *LAE,* August 4, 1940, section 1, 9; and "Citizens Urge Full Probe of Whittier, Santa Barbara Woman Asks Check of All Such Schools," *LAE,* August 5, 1940, section 1, 8 (that woman asked for attention to the Ventura School). For Olson's suspension of the board, see "Trustees Shifted to Spur Whittier Probe, Judge Lindsey Will Preside at Special Inquiry," *LAE,* August 1, 1940, section 1, 1, 12. By late August, the School Board of Managers, contrary to Milne's suggestions, had closed solitary confinement; see "Probe into Whittier to Resume Today," *LAE,* August 26, 1940, section 1, 3; and "[Elmer] Murphey Announces Potential Ban on LP," *LAE,* August 25, 1940. In response, Rosanoff stated that they would do it "as soon as we can make other arrangements"; "'Solitary' Ban on Way, Rosanoff Declares," *LAE,* August 30, 1940, section 1, 3.

65. "Olson Orders Open Probe of Whittier School Conditions, Governor Bans Secrecy, Calls Rosanoff 'Excited,'" *LAE,* July 29, 1940, section 1, 1, 8. For Rosanoff's refusal of public hearings, see "Rosanoff Tells Discipline Need."

66. Quote cited in Lawrence B. McVicar, "A History of the California Youth Authority" (master's thesis, California State University–Sacramento, 1972), 66, Youth Authority, California State Archives, Sacramento.

67. For the number of witnesses—over 110—called, see, "Dr. Rosanoff Faces Whittier Quiz Today," *LAE,* October 14, 1940, 5.

68. For Lindsey and the Committee's formal appointment, see "Trustees Shifted to Spur Whittier Probe"; and "Lindsey Will Open Whittier Hearings Soon," *LAE,* August 5, 1940, section 1, 1, 7; for Olson's formal appointment of the Committee, see "Olson's Letter Authorizing Thorough Whittier Inquiry," *LAE,* August 7, 1940, section 1, 5. For more on the work of Judge Ben B. Lindsey, see Paul Colomy and Martin Kretzmann, "Projects and Institution Building: Judge Ben B. Lindsey and the Juvenile Court Movement," *Social Problems* 42, no. 2 (May 1995), 191–215; and D'Ann Campbell, "Judge Ben Lindsey and the Juvenile Court Movement 1901–1904," *Arizona and the West* 18, no. 1 (Spring 1976), 5–20.

69. For John Leiva's allegations of murder, see "Son Was Murdered, Father Cries at Whittier Hearing," *LAE,* August 17, 1940, section 1, 5; and "New Terror Stories Due in Whittier School Inquiry," *LAE,* August 18, 1940, section 1, 20. For allegations of cover-ups at the school, see "Whittier Hospital Records Called Brutality Aid, No Data Available about Causes of Boys' Injuries," *LAE,* December 18, 1940, section 1, 10. In that piece, the nurse admitted she never recorded the injuries the boys described because she believed they were lying. She also noted that it was not her job to find out how the boys had been injured. For more details on how the medical personnel covered up the boys' injuries, see Lindsey, WSS Report/Investigation, 74–76. See also ibid., 118–128, where

Lindsey blasts the Bar Association for their work. For more details, see "Whittier Terror Bared by Secret Court Records," *LAE*, August 2, 1940, section 1, 1, 6; "Juvenile Court Records Bare Torture at Whittier, Boys Beaten until Backs Livid, Bruised," *LAE*, August 2, 1940, section 1, 6; and "Whittier Horror Told under Oath, Beatings, Starvation, Tortures Bared by Lindsey Committee," *LAE*, August 13, 1940, section 1, 1, 6. See also "Wide Reforms Urged by Whittier Committee, *LAT*, April 19, 1941, 3. For the abuse uncovered by the Lindsey Commission, see "Moreno Boy's Death by Beating Hinted in Quiz," *LAE*, August 29, 1940, section 2, 1; "Whittier Youths Accuse Guards," *LAE*, August 29, 1940, section 2, 1, 7. For more on the theory that Cavitt drove Moreno to commit suicide, see "Two Boys Blame Guard Cavett [*sic*] for Whittier Hanging, Warned to Keep His Mouth Shut, Released Lad Tells Probers," *LAE*, August 20, 1940, section 1, 1, 9.

70. For Valdo Sánchez's testimony, see "Removal of Youths to Block Whittier Death Quiz Charged, Lindsey Reports on 'Serious Situation' to Olson," *LAE*, August 14, 1940, section 1, 1, 8. For Benny's complaints of the "evil man," see "Lindsey Probers Reveal Brutal Whittier Beatings," *LAE*, December 10, 1940, section 1, 11. For the boy's testimony of widespread sodomy, see Lindsey, WSS Report/Investigation, 139–143. For the wealthy boy's testimony, see "School Pushed Boys into Crime," *LAE*, August 15, 1940, section 1, 10.

71. See "Events on Night of Hanging Amaze Whittier Probers, Light Burned Out in Boy's Death Cell," *LAE*, August 21, 1940, section 1, 3. For more irregularities, see "Doubt Case by Lindsey on Whittier Death Story, Guard Denies Slugging of Inmates," *LAE*, August 22, 1940, section 2, 1, 8. That article also demonstrates that few, if any guards, had any training or former experience in working with youths. Don C. Napper, for instance, had been a former kitchen helper at Norwalk, and Cavitt formerly had been an orderly at Norwalk. For similar accounts of abuse, see, for instance, "Ex-Official Tells of Terrorism at Whittier School, *LAE*, July 31, 1940, section 1, 1, 10.

72. For details of the doctor's testimony, see "Whittier State School Report," 11–12.

73. For more on these details, see "State Aide Hints at Foul Play in Hanging of Young Prisoner at Whittier School," *LAE*, August 23, 1940, section 1, 3; "Slaying Hinted in Whittier Quiz," *LAE*, August 16, 1940, section 1, 1, 7; and "Science Bares Sinister Clews [*sic*] in Whittier Quiz, Believe Moreno Boy Dead for 10 Hours," *LAE*, August 30, 1940, section 1, 3. For more on the secrecy at the school, see "Removal of Youths to Block Whittier Death Quiz Charged"; also see "Olson Warns School Heads at Whittier," August 15, 1940, section 1, 1, 10. For Quevedo and Casares's testimony, see "Boy Explains Suicide Belt," *LAT*, September 4, 1940, A3; and Lindsey, WSS Report/Investigation, 56–58. For the fallout of Gallagher's recantation of the report, see LGP, box 2, folders, 8, 9.

74. For Lindsey's questioning of the transfers, see "Removal of Youths to Block Whittier Death Quiz Charged." That article also states that Quevedo testified that boys told him they were threatened with transfer if they spoke about what had happened. See also "Slaying Hinted in Whittier Quiz."

75. For evidence of the Attorney General's ruling, see Cox and Shelly, eds., *Handbook of American Institutions*, 194, n1, letter dated August 29, 1940.

76. "Whittier Probe to Center on Suicide, Murder Point," *LAE*, August 19, 1940, section 1, 7. The scientific research at Whittier in the late 1930s was haphazard, as was evident in Edward Leiva's treatment or lack thereof at Whittier. See "Probers Flay Rosanoff's Report," *LAE*, December 19, 1940, section 1, 8.

77. For Milne's testimony, see "Whittier Head Guarded from Angry Crowds," *LAE*, September 6, 1940, section 1, 1, 10. For more details on Milne's stance on the Lost Privilege Cottage, see, for instance, "Boy Hangs Self in Cell"; and "Police Rescue Whittier School Superintendent from Attack by Mob at Boys' Suicide Hearing," *LAT*, September 6, 1940, A1. On conflicts over the use of the LP, see "Officials Disagree on 'Solitary Cells,'" *LAE*, July 29, 1940, section 1, 1, 8.

78. For Rosanoff's testimony, see "Rosanoff Insists Suicide Cottage Stay at Whittier, Barred Chamber Upheld by Director," *LAE*, August 23, 1940, section 1, 3.

79. "Police Rescue Whittier School Superintendent." Later, the psychologist revealed that Rosanoff's daughter had instructed him to reveal the boys' personal records. See Lindsey, WSS Report/Investigation, 108–109.

80. "Boy Charges Sex Torture at Whittier, Perverted Practices, Revolting Orgies Blamed on Guards by Escapee, Jury Will Act," *LAE*, September 14, 1940, section 1, 6; "Woes at Whittier Told by 4 Lads to Grand Jury, 21 Others Yet to Testify in Inquiry," *LAE*, October 2, 1940, section 1, 3; and "7 Youths Tell Grand Jury of Brutality at Whittier, Boy Deaf Mute 'Heard,'" *LAE*, October 3, 1940, section 1, 5. For continued efforts to prosecute guards, see "Whittier Case Prosecutions Considered, DA's Office May Issue Complaints Despite Failure of Grand Jury to Act," *LAE*, October 23, 1940, section 1, 1, 5.

81. "Denial Made Boys Beaten," *LAT*, December 28, 1940, 3.

82. "Two Whittier Guards Face Arrest," *LAE*, October 25, 1940, 1; "Whittier Head Accuses Aid of Cruelty," *LAE*, November 16, 1940, 1; Editorial: "Dead End Kids?" *LAE*, January 4, 1941, section 1, 12; "Whittier Officials Deny Suit Charges," *LAE*, January 15, 1941, 3; and "Cavitt Given 225 Days for Boy Brutality," *LAE*, January 30, 1941, 3. John Leiva also brought charges against reform school administrators soon after learning of his boys' death. See "Hanged Boys' Father Sues for $100,000," *LAE*, August 13, 1940, section 1, 6.

83. For details of the Lindsey Commission's final report, see "Report Calls for Shake-up at Whittier," *LAT*, December 8, 1940, 1; and Lindsey, WSS Report/Investigation, 158–163.

84. Lindsey, WSS Report/Investigation, 164–165.

85. For Cavitt's statements, see "Lindsey Probers Reveal Brutal Whittier Beatings," *LAE*, December 10, 1940, section 1, 11.

86. For discussion of the racial problem, see Lindsey, WSS Report/Investigation, 144–145, 160. The *LA Examiner* also reprinted portions of the Lindsey Report. See, for instance, "Whittier Horrors Bared in Reports of Lindsey Probe," *LAE*, December 9, 1940, section 1, 1; and "Lindsey Body Refutes Rosanoff Whittier Report, Conclusions Hit in School Deaths," *LAE*, December 9, 1940, section 1, 10. For the recommendations in Lindsey's report, see "Humane Group Will Demand Milne Ouster Today, Personnel Board to Hold Hearing," *LAE*, December 9, 1940, section 1, 11; and "Olson Praises Lindsey Views on Whittier," *LAE*,

December 24, 1940, 1, 9. For Flanagan and Cox's appointment, see "Speed Urged in Reforms at Whittier," *LAE*, February 11, 1941, 17.

87. "New Brutalities at Whittier Told; Full Inquiry Set," *LAE*, July 30, 1940, section 1, 1, 8. For more charges against Milne, see "Gross Neglect Laid to Whittier Head," *LAE*, July 30, 1940, section 1, 8.

88. "Whittier School Aide Faces Ouster Charges," *LAE*, July 23, 1941, 11.

89. "Accused Officials at State School Hearing," *LAE*, August 12, 1941, A1.

90. "Milne Tells Whittier Story," *LAE*, August 14, 1941, 1A.

91. "Row Breaks Up Whittier Hearing," *LAE*, December 10, 1940, B3. For the "defense" of the institution, see "Whittier Rule Defended," *LAT*, October 15, 1940, A3. For charges against Milne for allowing the boys into the school, see "Dismissal of Milne and Others Asked," *LAT*, May 14, 1941, 2. For the charges against him, see "Guards' Immoralities Concealed, Is Charge," *LAE*, May 14, 1941, section 1, 13. For more of the testimony of boys before the State Personnel Board, see "Boys School Inmates Recount Cruelties," *LAT*, July 21, 1941, 2.

92. "Milne Arrested as Drunk Driver, Dismissal Asked, Whittier School Head Faces Suspension after Wild Night Ride," *LAE*, May 5, 1941, section 1, 1, 13; "Milne Suspended from School Job," *LAE*, May 15, 1941, section 1, 6; "Milne Ouster Hearing Opens in North Today," *LAE*, August 5, 1940, section 1, 7; and "Moves in Whittier School Inquiry Declared Political," *LAT*, July 28, 1940, 16.

93. "Milne Seeks Reinstatement," *LAT*, August 16, 1944, 14.

94. For the supplementary report, see California, Department of Institutions, Aaron J. Rosanoff, Director, Supplementary Report on Whittier State School, to His Excellency, Culbert L. Olson, Governor, 3. January 15, 1941, Youth Authority Records, F3738, California State Archives, Sacramento [hereafter Rosanoff, Investigation III], 1–30. Also see "Hearing Ends in Boy Deaths," *LAT*, September 7, 1940, A3.

95. "Change Made at Whittier," *LAE*, April 16, 1941, A8.

96. "Priest Blasts School Rule," *LAT*, April 20, 1941, A1; "Wide Reforms Urged by Whittier Committee," *LAE*, April 19, 1941, 3; and "Whittier School Troubles Told," *LAT*, April 20, 1941, A2.

97. For Duffy's appointment, see "Boys' School Head Named," *LAT*, April 18, 1941, 14; and for his difficulties, see, for instance, "Duffy Scolds Whittier Boys," *LAT*, April 22, 1941, 1A.

98. "Sixty Boys Escape at Whittier School," *LAT*, April 21, 1941, 1.

99. "Action Asked for Whittier," *LAT*, April 22, 1941, 1.

100. For the original law, see California, *Welfare and Institutions Code* (Deering 1941 Supplement), 1700–1873. This discussion draws from Karl Holton, "Youth Correction Authority in Action: The California Experience," *Law and Contemporary Problems* 9, no. 4 (Autumn 1942), 655–666; and Holton, "California Youth Authority: Eight Years of Action," *Journal of Criminal Law and Criminology* 41, no. 1 (May–June, 1950), 1–23. For a thorough history of the Youth Authority, see Mihailoff, "Protecting Our Children." I would like to thank Laura Mihailoff for sharing her work with me.

101. Holton, "Youth Correction Authority in Action," 662.

EPILOGUE

1. Phone interviews and correspondence took place in July and August 2007. We finally met in person in late August 2007 and again in September 2010. We continue to communicate.

2. I have not been able to verify this through newspaper research.

Bibliography

ARCHIVAL AND MANUSCRIPT COLLECTIONS

Alcalde Court Records Collection. Seaver Center for Western History, Los Angeles County Museum of Natural History. Los Angeles, Calif.

Beam, Kenneth S. Papers. Bancroft Library, Berkeley, Calif.

California. Appendix to the Journals of the Senate and Assembly. California State Library, Sacramento, Calif.

———. Statutes of California and Amendments to the Codes. California State Library, Sacramento, Calif.

California Department of Corrections. California State Archives, Sacramento, Calif.

California Department of Mental Hygiene (Health), Secretary of State, California State Archives, Sacramento, Calif.

California Newspapers Collection. California State Library, Sacramento, Calif.

California Youth Authority Records. California State Archives, Sacramento, Calif.

Eugenics Records Office Records. American Philosophical Society Library, Philadelphia, Penn.

Gallagher, Leo. Papers. Southern California Library for Social Studies and Research, Los Angeles, Calif.

Gosney, E. S. and Human Betterment Foundation Records. California Institute of Technology Archives, Pasadena, Calif.

Lindsey, Ben B. Collection. UCLA, Special Collections. Charles E. Young Research Library, Los Angeles, Calif.

Los Angeles Herald Photographs. Los Angeles Public Library, Los Angeles, Calif.

Olson, Culbert L. Papers. Bancroft Library, Berkeley, Calif.

Proceedings of the California Governor's Investigating Committee on Penal Affairs, December 4, 1943–January 18, 1944. Bancroft Library, Berkeley, Calif.

Regional Oral History Office. Bancroft Library, Berkeley, Calif.

Terman, Lewis S. Papers. Stanford University Archives, Stanford, Calif.

Williams, J. Harold. Papers. UCLA, Special Collections. Charles E. Young Research Library, Los Angeles, Calif.

PUBLISHED PRIMARY SOURCES

Bailey, Pearce. "A Contribution to the Mental Pathology of Races in the United States." *Mental Hygiene* 1–2 (April 1922): 370–91.

Binet, Alfred, and Théodore Simon. *Mentally Defective Children*, trans. W. B. Drummond. London: Edward Arnold, 1914.

Bogardus, Emory S. *The City Boy and His Problems: Survey of Boy Life in Los Angeles.* Los Angeles: House of Ralston, 1926.

———. "Exploring for the Causes of Crime." *Journal of Social Forces* 3, no. 3 (March 1925): 464–466.

———. "Gangs of Mexican-American Youth." *Sociology-Social Research Journal* 28 (1943): 55–66.

———. *Methods of Training Social Workers.* Los Angeles: South California Sociological Society, 1921.

———. "The Mexican Immigrant and Segregation." *The American Journal of Sociology* 36, no. 1 (July 1930): 74–80.

———. *The Mexican in the United States.* Los Angeles: University of Southern California Press, 1934.

———. "Second Generation Mexicans." *Sociology-Social Research Journal* 13 (1928): 276–283.

———. "A Study of Juvenile Delinquency and Dependency in Los Angeles County for the Year 1912." *Journal of Criminal Law and Criminology* (September 1914): n.p. [10 pp.].

Breckinridge, Sophonisba Preston, Edith Abbott, and Julia Lathrop. *The Delinquent Child and the Home: A Study of the Delinquent Wards of the Juvenile Court of Chicago.* Rev. ed. Whitefish, Mont.: Kessinger Publishing, 2008. Originally published in 1916.

Butler, Fred O. "Sterilization in California." *Eugenical News* 12, no. 3 (March 1927): 28–29.

Butler, Fred O., and Leo L. Stanley. "Bedside Medicine: Human Sterilization." *California and Western Medicine* 39, no. 3 (September 1933): 199–203.

California Department of Social Welfare. "Health, Relief and Delinquency Conditions among the Mexicans of California." In *Mexicans in California. Report of Governor C. C. Young's Mexican Fact-Finding Committee.* San Francisco: State Building, 1930.

Cold Spring Harbor, Eugenics Records Office. "The Position of Field Workers." *Eugenical News* 4 (1919): 41.

"Constitutionality of State Laws Providing Sterilization for Habitual Criminals." *Yale Law Journal* 51, no. 8 (June 1942): 1380–1387.

Covert, Mildred S. "Excitability in Delinquent Boys." *Journal of Juvenile Research* 5, no. 6 (November 1920): 224–239.

Cox, William B., and Joseph A. Shelly, eds. *Handbook of American Institutions for Delinquent Juveniles.* Vol. 3. *Pacific Coast States.* New York: Osborne Association, 1940.

Davenport, Charles B. *Heredity in Relation to Eugenics.* New York: Henry Holt, 1913.

———. *How to Make a Eugenical Family History.* Cold Spring Harbor, N.Y.: Eugenics Record Office, 1915.

———. *Trait Book.* Cold Spring Harbor, N.Y.: Eugenics Record Office, 1912.

Deutsch, Alfred. *Our Rejected Children.* Boston: Little, Brown, 1947.

Doll, E. A. *Clinical Studies in Feeblemindedness.* Boston: R. G. Badger, 1917.

Ellingston, John R. *Protecting Our Children from Criminal Careers.* New York: Prentice-Hall, 1948.

Estabrook, Arthur. *The Jukes in 1915.* Washington, D.C.: Carnegie Institution of Washington, 1916.

Fernald, Grace M. "Report of the Psychological Work in the California School for Girls." *Journal of Delinquency* 1 (March 1916): 22–31.

Goddard, Henry. *Feeblemindedness: Its Causes and Consequences.* New York: Macmillan, 1914.

———. *The Kallikak Family: A Study in the Heredity of Feeble-Mindedness.* New York: Macmillan, 1914.

Gosney, E. S., and Paul Popenoe. "Eugenics Sterilization in California." *Eugenical News* 12, no. 8 (August 1927): 113–114.

Hall, G. Stanley. *Adolescence: Its Psychology and Its Relations to Physiology, Anthropology, Sex, Crime, Religion, and Education.* Vol. 1. New York: D. Appleton, 1904.

Hendricks, W. C. "Address of Hon. W. C. Hendricks." In *The Laying of the Corner-Stone of the State Reform School at Whittier.* Sacramento, Calif.: State Printing Office, 1890.

Hiller, Francis H. *The Juvenile Court of Los Angeles, County, California.* Los Angeles: Rotary Club of Los Angeles, 1928.

Holton, Karl. "California Youth Authority: Eight Years of Action." *Journal of Criminal Law and Criminology* 41, no. 1 (May–June 1950): 1–23.

———. "Youth Correction Authority in Action: The California Experience." In "The Correction of Youthful Offenders," special issue. *Law and Contemporary Problems* 9, no. 4 (Autumn, 1942): 655–666.

Hurt, Elsey. *California State Government: An Outline of Its Administrative Organization from 1850 to 1936.* Sacramento: State Printing Office, 1936.

Lippman, Walter. "A Future for the Tests." *New Republic,* November 29, 1922: 9–11.

Mahoney, E. J. "The Morality of Sterilization." *Catholic Mind* 34, no. 10 (May 1936): 205–216.

Mathews, Julia. "A Survey of 341 Delinquent Girls in California." *Journal of Delinquency* 8, nos. 3–4 (Mary–July 1928): 196–231.

Myerson, Abraham. "Certain Medical and Legal Phases of Eugenic Sterilization." *Yale Law Journal* 52, no. 3 (June 1943): 618–633.

Nelles, Fred C. "Changes in the Nature of the Population at Whittier State School." *Journal of Delinquency* 9, no. 6 (1925): 231–232.

O'Rourke, Kevin. "An Analysis of the Church's Teaching on Sterilization." *Hospital Progress* 55, no. 5 (1976): 68–75.

Paschal, Franklin C. "Racial Differences in the Mental and Physical Development of Mexican Children." *Comparative Psychology Monographs* 3 (1926): 1–76.

Popenoe, Paul, and E. S. Gosney. *Sterilization for Human Betterment: A Summary of Results of 6,000 Operations in California, 1909–1929*. New York: Macmillan, 1929.

———. *Twenty-Eight Years of Sterilization in California*. Pasadena, Calif.: Human Betterment Foundation, 1938.

Sánchez, George I. "Bilingualism and Mental Measures." *Journal of Applied Psychology* 18, no. 6 (1934): 765–772.

———. "Group Differences in Spanish-Speaking Children: A Critical View." *Journal of Applied Psychology* 16, no. 5 (1932): 549–558.

———. "Scores of Spanish-Speaking Children on Repeated Tests." *Journal of Genetic Psychology* 40 (1932): 223–233.

Terman, Lewis M. "Expert Testimony in the Case of Alberto Flores." *Journal of Delinquency* 3, no. 4 (July 1918): 145–164.

———. "The Great Conspiracy; or the Impulse Imperious of Intelligence Testers Psychoanalyzed and Exposed by Mr. Lippmann," *New Republic*, December 27, 1922: 1–15.

———. *The Measurement of Intelligence: An Explanation of and a Complete Guide for the Use of the Stanford Revision and Extension of the Binet-Simon Intelligence Scale*. Boston: Houghton Mifflin, 1912.

Terman, Lewis M., Virgil Dickinson, and Lowry Howard. "Backward and Feeble-Minded Children in the Public Schools of 'X' County, California." In *Surveys in Mental Deviation in Prisons, Public Schools, and Orphanages in California*, edited by California State Board of Charities and Corrections, 19–45. Sacramento: State Printing Office, 1918.

Tibesar, Antonine, ed. and trans. *Writings of Junipero Serra* 3. Washington, D.C.: Academy of American Franciscan History, 1955–1966.

Tredgold, A. F. *Mental Deficiency (Amentia)*. London: Baillière, Tindall and Cox, 1922.

Wallin, J. E. Wallace. "The Hygiene of Eugenic Generation." *The Psychological Clinic* 8, no. 5 (October 1914): 121–137, 170–179.

Wilbur, Curtis D. "Juvenile Court." In *Report and Manual for Probation Officers of the Superior Court acting as Juvenile Court, Los Angeles County, California, 1912*, ed. City of Los Angeles, 11–16. Los Angeles: Board of Supervisors, 1912.

Williams, J. Harold. "Early History of the California Bureau of Juvenile Research." *Journal of Juvenile Research* 28, no. 4 (October 1934): 187–214.

———. "Individual Case History Outline." *Journal of Delinquency* 5, no. 3 (May 1920): 71–82.

———. "The Intelligence of the Delinquent Boy." *Journal of Delinquency*, monograph no. 1. Whittier, Calif.: Whittier State School, Department of Research, 1919.

———. "Quotations: The Present Status of Juvenile Delinquency in California." *Journal of Juvenile Delinquency* 5, no. 5 (September 1920): 183–189.

———. "Racial Problem of Mexicans." *Journal of Delinquency* 5 (September 1920): 1–15.

———. *A Study of 150 Delinquent Boys*. Palo Alto, Calif.: Stanford University, 1915.

SECONDARY SOURCES

Adams, Mark B., Garland E. Allen, and Sheila Faith Weiss. "Human Heredity and Politics: A Comparative Institutional Study of the Eugenics Record Office at Cold Spring Harbor (United States), the Kaiser Wilhelm Institute for Anthropology, Human Heredity, and Eugenics (Germany), and the Maxim Gorky Medical Genetics Institute (USSR)." *Osiris* 20, no. 1 (2005): 232–262.

Allen, Garland. "Eugenics and American Social History, 1881–1950." *Genome* 31, no. 2 (1989): 885–889.

———. "The Eugenics Record Office at Cold Spring Harbor, 1919–1940." *Osiris*, 2nd ser. (1986): 225–264.

Almaguer, Tomás. *Racial Fault Lines: The Historical Origins of White Supremacy in California*. Berkeley: University of California Press, 1994.

Alvarez, Luis. *The Power of the Zoot: Youth Culture and Resistance during World War II*. Berkeley: University of California Press, 2009.

Balderrama, Francisco E. *In the Defense of La Raza: The Los Angeles Mexican Consulate and the Mexican Community, 1929–1936*. Tucson: University of Arizona Press, 1982.

Bancroft, Hubert H. *The Works of Hubert Howe Bancroft*. San Francisco: A. L. Bancroft, 1884–1886.

Bederman, Gail. *Manliness and Civilization: A Cultural History of Gender and Race in the United States, 1880 to 1917*. Chicago: University of Chicago Press, 1995.

Beebe, Rose Marie, and Robert M. Senkewicz, eds. *Testimonios: Early California through the Eyes of Women, 1815–1848*. Berkeley, Calif.: Heyday Books, Bancroft Library, 2006.

Bell, Horace. *Reminiscences of a Ranger, or Early Times in Southern California*. Los Angeles: Yarnell, Caystile and Mathes, 1881.

Bix, Amy Sue. "Experiences and Voices of Eugenics Field-Workers: 'Women's Work' in Biology." *Social Studies of Science* 27 (1997): 625–668.

Blanton, Carlos. "'They Cannot Master Abstractions but They Can Often Be Made Efficient Workers': Race and Class in the Intelligence Testing of Mexican Americans and African Americans in Texas during the 1920s." *Social Science Quarterly* 81 (2003): 1014–1027.

Bookspan, Shelley. *A Germ of Goodness: The Evolving California State Prison System, 1851–1944*. Lincoln: University of Nebraska Press, 1993.

Bouvier, Virginia M. *Women and the Conquest of California, 1542–1840: Codes of Silence*. Tucson: University of Arizona Press, 2001.

Brandt, Allan M. *No Magic Bullet: A Social History of Venereal Disease in the United States since 1880*. New York: Oxford University Press, 1985.

Braslow, Joel. *Mental Ills and Bodily Cures: Psychiatric Treatment in the First Half of the Twentieth Century.* Berkeley: University of California Press, 1997.

Burt, Kenneth C. *The Search for a Civic Voice: California Latino Politics.* Claremont, Calif.: Regina Books, 2007.

Cahn, Francis. *Welfare Activities of Federal, State, and Local Governments in California, 1850–1934.* Berkeley: University of California Press, 1936.

Campbell, D'Ann. "Judge Ben Lindsey and the Juvenile Court Movement 1901–1904." *Arizona and the West* 18, no. 1 (Spring 1976): 5–20.

Carey, Allison C. "Gender and Compulsory Sterilization Programs in America, 1907–1950." *Journal of Historical Sociology* 11, no. 1 (March 1998): 74–105.

Castañeda, Antonia I. "The Political Economy of Nineteenth-Century Stereotypes." In *Between Borders: Essays on Chicana/Mexicana History,* edited by Adelaida del Castillo, 213–238. Encino, Calif.: Floricanto Press, 1990.

Castillo, Edward D. "An Indian Account of the Decline and Collapse of Mexico's Hegemony over the Missionized Indians of California." *American Indian Quarterly* 13, no. 4 (Autumn 1989): 391–408.

Chapman, Paul D. *Schools as Sorters: Lewis M. Terman, Applied Psychology, and the Intelligence Testing Movement, 1890–1930.* New York: New York University Press, 1988.

———. "Schools as Sorters: Testing and Tracking in California, 1910–1925." *Journal of Social History* 14, no. 4 (Summer 1981): 701–717.

Chávez-García, Miroslava. "Intelligence Testing at Whittier State School, 1880–1920." *Pacific Historical Review* 76, no. 2 (May 2007): 193–228.

———. *Negotiating Conquest: Gender and Power in California, 1770s to 1880s.* Tucson: University of Arizona, 2004.

———. "Youth, Evidence, and Agency: Mexican and Mexican American Youth at Whittier State School, 1890 to 1920." *Aztlán: A Journal of Chicano Studies* 32 (2006): 55–83.

Churchill, Ward. *Kill the Indian, Save the Man: The Genocidal Impact of American Indian Residential Schools.* San Francisco: City Lights Publisher, 2004.

Clapp, Elizabeth J. *Mothers of All Children: Women Reformers and the Rise of Juvenile Courts in Progressive Era America.* University Park: Penn State University Press, 1998.

Colomy, Paul, and Martin Kretzmann. "Projects and Institution Building: Judge Ben B. Lindsey and the Juvenile Court Movement." *Social Problems* 42, no. 2 (1995): 191–215.

Colson, Elizabeth. *Autobiographies of Three Pomo Women.* Berkeley: University of California Archeological Research Facility, Department of Anthropology, 1974.

Cook, Sherburne F. *The Aboriginal Population of Alameda and Contra Costa Counties.* Berkeley: University of California Press, 1957.

———. *The Conflict between the California Indian and White Civilization.* Berkeley: University of California Press, 1976: 113–134.

———. *The Population of California Indians, 1769–1970.* Berkeley: University of California Press, 1979.

Cravens, Hamilton. "Applied Science and Public Policy: The Ohio Bureau of Juvenile Research and the Scientific Prevention of Juvenile Delinquency." In

Psychological Testing in American Society, edited by Michael M. Sokal, 158–194. New Brunswick, N.J.: Rutgers University Press, 1987.

———. *The Triumph of Evolution: The Heredity-Environment Controversy, 1900–1941.* Baltimore: Johns Hopkins Press, 1988.

Cremin, Lawrence T. *The Transformation of the School: Progressivism in American Education, 1876–1957.* New York: Vintage, 1961.

Dakin, Susanna Bryant. *A Scotch Paisano: Hugo Reid's Life in California, 1832–1852.* Berkeley: University of California Press, 1939.

De Graff, Lawrence B., Kevin Mulroy, and Quintard Taylor, eds. *Seeking El Dorado: African Americans in California.* Seattle: University of Washington Press, 2001.

Deutsch, Nathaniel. *Inventing America's Worst Family: Eugenics, Islam, and the Fall and the Rise of the Tribe of Ishmael.* Berkeley: University of California Press, 2009.

Deverell, William, and Tom Sitton, eds. *California Progressivism Revisited.* Berkeley: University of California Press, 1994.

Dikotter, Frank. "Recent Perspectives on the History of Eugenics." *American Historical Review* 103, no. 2 (April 1998): 467–478.

Dowbiggin, Ian Robert. *Keeping America Sane: Psychiatry and Eugenics in the United States and Canada, 1880–1940.* Ithaca, N.Y.: Cornell University Press, 1997.

Dugdale, Richard L. *"The Jukes": A Study in Crime, Pauperism, Disease and Heredity.* New York: Knickerbocker Press, 1877.

Fass, Paula. "The IQ." *American Journal of Education* 88 (August 1980): 431–458.

———. *Outside In, Minorities and the Transformation of American Education.* New York: Oxford University Press, 1989.

Fenton, Norman. *The Delinquent Boy and the Correctional School.* Claremont, Calif.: Claremont Guidance Center, 1935.

Escobar, Edward J. *Race, Police, and the Making of a Political Identity: Mexican Americans and the Los Angeles Police Department, 1900–1945.* Berkeley: University of California Press, 1999.

Escobedo, Elizabeth. "The Pachuca Panic: Sexual and Cultural Battlegrounds in World War II Los Angeles." *Western Historical Quarterly* 38, no. 2 (2007): 133–156.

Fernald, G. M. "Report of the Psychological Work in the California School for Girls." *Journal of Delinquency* 1 (1916): 21–29.

Finn, Jonathon. *Capturing the Criminal Image: From Mug Shot to Surveillance Society.* Minneapolis: University of Minnesota Press, 2009.

Fogelson, Robert M. *The Fragmented Metropolis: Los Angeles, 1850–1930.* Berkeley: University of California Press, 1967.

Foner, Eric. *Reconstruction: America's Unfinished Revolution, 1863–1877.* New York: Harper, 2002.

Foucault, Michel. *Discipline and Punish: The Birth of the Prison.* New York: Pantheon Books, 1977.

Frederickson, George M. *The Black Image in the White Mind.* New York: Harper & Row, 1971.

Freedman, Estelle B. *Maternal Justice: Miriam Van Waters and the Female Reform Tradition.* Chicago: University of Chicago Press, 1996.

Gabbert, Ann R. "Prostitution and Moral Reform in the Borderlands: El Paso, 1890–1920." *Journal of the History of Sexuality* 12, no. 4 (October 2003): 575–604.

Gilbert, Matthew Sakiestewa. *Education beyond the Mesas: Hopi Students at Sherman Institute, 1902–1929.* Lincoln: University of Kansas Press, 2010.

Goddard, Henry H. *The Kallikak Family: A Study in the Heredity of Feeble-Mindedness.* New York: Macmillan, 1912.

González, Gilbert. *Chicano Education in the Era of Segregation.* Philadelphia: Balch Institute Press, 1990.

———. "Racism, Education, and the Mexican Community in Los Angeles." *Societas* 4 (1974): 287–301.

Gould, Stephen. *The Mismeasure of Man.* New York: Norton, 1981.

Greenwald, Frederick. "Treatment of Behavioral Problems of Children and Youth by Early Indigenous Americans." In *History of Juvenile Delinquency,* Vol. 2, 735–755, edited by Albert G. Hess and Priscilla F. Clement. Aalen, Germany: Scientia, 1993.

Guest, Francis F. "An Inquiry into the Role of the Discipline in California Mission Life." *Southern California Quarterly* 71 (Spring 1989): 1–67.

Gutiérrez, David G. *Walls and Mirrors: Mexicans, Mexican Americans, and the Politics of Ethnicity.* Berkeley: University of California Press, 1995.

Heizer, Robert F., and Mary A. Whipple, eds. *California Indians: A Source Book.* Berkeley: University of California Press, 1941.

Hoffman, Abraham. *Unwanted Mexican Americans in the Great Depression: Repatriation Pressures, 1929–1939.* Tucson: University of Arizona Press, 1974.

Hogeveen, Bryan. "'The Evils with Which We Are Called to Grapple': Elite Reformers, Eugenicists, Environmental Psychologists, and the Construction of Toronto's Working-Class Boy Problem, 1860–1930." *Labour/Le Travail* 55 (Spring 2005): 37–68.

Holl, Jack M. *Juvenile Reform in the Progressive Era: William R. George and the Junior Republic Movement.* Ithaca, N.Y.: Cornell University Press, 1981.

Horsman, Reginald. *Race and Manifest Destiny: Origins of American Racial Anglo-Saxonism.* Cambridge, Mass.: Harvard University Press, 1981.

Hurtado, Albert. *Indian Survival on the California Frontier.* New Haven, Conn.: Yale University Press, 1988.

Janssen, Volken. "When the 'Jungle' Met the Forest: Public Work, Civil Defense, and Prison Camps in Postwar California." *Journal of American History* 96, no. 3 (December 2009): 703–726.

Jewel, Donald P. *Indians of the Feather River: Tales and Legends of the Concow Maidu of California.* Menlo Park, Calif.: Ballena Press, 1987.

Justice, Benjamin. "'A College of Morals': Educational Reform at San Quentin Prison, 1880–1920." *History of Education Quarterly* 40 (2000): 279–301.

Kamin, Leon J. *The Science and Politics of the IQ.* New York: Halsted Press, 1974.

Kevles, Daniel J. *In the Name of Eugenics: Genetics and the Uses of Human Heredity.* Rev. ed. Cambridge, Mass.: Harvard University Press, 1995.

———. "Testing the Army's Intelligence: Psychologists and the Military in World War I." *Journal of American History* 55 (1968): 565–581.

Kliebard, Herbert M. *The Struggle for the American Curriculum, 1893–1958.* New York: Routledge, 1986.

Kline, Wendy. *Building a Better Race: Gender, Sexuality, and Eugenics from the Turn of the Century to the Baby Boom.* Berkeley: University of California Press, 2001.

Knollin, H. E., and Lewis S. Terman. "A Partial Psychological Survey of the Prison Population of San Quentin, California." In *Surveys in Mental Deviation in Prisons, Public Schools, and Orphanages in California,* edited by California State Board of Charities and Corrections, 6–18. Sacramento: State Printing Office, 1918.

Knox, Elmer E., and Norman Fenton. *Fred C. Nelles: An Appreciation.* Whittier, Calif.: Whittier State School, 1930.

Knufper, Anne Meis. *Reform and Resistance: Gender, Delinquency, and America's First Juvenile Court.* New York: Routledge, 2001.

Kunzel, Regina G. *Criminal Intimacy: Prison and the Uneven History of Modern American Sexuality.* Chicago: University of Chicago Press, 2010.

Lafferty, John F. *The Preston School of Industry: A Centennial History.* 2nd ed. Ione, Calif.: Preston School of Industry Print Shop, 1997.

LaPan, Amy, and Tony Platt. "'To Stem The Tide of Degeneracy': The Eugenic Impulse in Social Work." In *Mental Disorders in the Social Environment: Critical Perspectives,* edited by Stuart A. Kirk, 139–164. New York: Columbia University Press, 2005.

Larson, Edward J. *Sex, Race, and Science: Eugenics in the Deep South.* Baltimore: Johns Hopkins University Press, 1995.

Leon, Sharon. "'A Human Being, Not a Mere Social Factor': Catholic Strategies for Dealing with Sterilization Statutes in the 1920s." *Church History* 72, no. 3 (2004): 383–411.

Litwack, Leon. *Been in the Storm So Long: The Aftermath of Slavery.* New York: Vintage, 1979.

———. *Trouble in Mind: Black Southerners in the Age of Jim Crow.* New York: Alfred A. Knopf, 1998.

Lombardo, Paul A. *Three Generations, No Imbeciles: Eugenics, the Supreme Court, and Buck v. Bell.* Baltimore: Johns Hopkins University Press, 2008.

Magliari, Michael. "Free Soil, Unfree Labor: Cave Johnson Couts and the Binding of Indian Workers in California, 1850–1867." *Pacific Historical Review* 73, no. 3 (2004): 349–389.

Mazon, Mauricio. *The Zoot-Suit Riots: The Psychology of Symbolic Annihilation.* Austin: University of Texas Press, 1988.

McCawley, William. *The First Angelinos: The Gabrielino Indians of Los Angeles.* Novato, Calif.: Ballena Press, 1996.

McClain, Charles. *In Search of Equality: The Chinese Struggle against Discrimination in Nineteenth-Century America.* Berkeley: University of California Press, 1996.

McKanna, Clare V., Jr. "Ethnics and San Quentin Prison Registers: A Comment on Methodology." *Journal of Social History* 18, no. 3 (Spring 1985): 477–482.

———. "The Origins of San Quentin, 1851–1880." *California History* 66, no. 1 (1987): 49–54.

———. *Race and Homicide in Nineteenth-Century California*. Reno: University of Nevada Press, 2002.

Minton, Henry L. "Terman and Mental Testing: In Search of the Democratic Ideal." In *Psychological Testing and American Society, 1890–1930*, edited by Michael M. Sokal, 95–112. New Brunswick, N.J.: Rutgers University Press, 1987.

Molina, Natalia. *Fit to Be Citizens? Public Health and Race in Los Angeles, 1879–1939*. Berkeley: University of California Press, 2006.

Myers, Tamara. "Embodying Delinquency: Boys' Bodies, Sexuality, and Juvenile Justice History in Early-Twentieth-Century Quebec." *Journal of the History of Sexuality* 14, no. 4 (October 2005): 383–414.

Ngai, Mae M. *Impossible Subjects: Illegal Aliens and the Making of Modern America*. Princeton, N.J.: Princeton University Press, 2004.

Nunn, Diane, and Christine Cleary. "From the Mexican California Frontier to Arnold-Kennick: Highlights in the Evolution of the California Juvenile Court, 1850–1961." *Journal of the Center for Families, Children and the Courts* 5 (2004): 3–27.

Nunn, Ruby, and Guy Mount, eds. *Not for Innocent Ears: Spiritual Traditions of a Desert Cahuilla Medicine Woman*. Arcata, Calif.: Sweetlight Books, 1989.

Odem, Mary E. *Delinquent Daughters: Protecting and Policing Adolescent Female Sexuality in the United States, 1885–1920*. Chapel Hill: University of North Carolina Press, 1995.

———. "Single Mothers, Delinquent Daughters, and the Juvenile Court in Early Twentieth-Century Los Angeles." *Journal of Social History* 25 (September 1991): 27–43.

Odem, Mary E., and Steven S. Schlossman. "Guardians of Virtue: The Juvenile Court and Female Delinquency in Early-Twentieth Century Los Angeles." *Crime and Delinquency* 37 (April 1991): 186–203.

Olin, Spencer C. *California's Prodigal Sons: Hiram Johnson and the Progressives, 1911–17*. Berkeley: University of California Press, 1968.

Opler, Morris Edward. *Childhood and Youth in Jicarilla Apache Society*. Los Angeles, Calif.: Southwest Museum, 1946.

Oshinky, David. *Worse Than Slavery: Parchman Farm and the Ordeal of Jim Crow Justice*. New York: Free Press, 1997.

Pagan, Eduardo. *Murder at the Sleepy Lagoon: Zoot Suits, Race, and Riot in Wartime Los Angeles*. Chapel Hill: University of North Carolina Press, 2003.

Pascoe, Peggy. "Miscegenation Law, Court Cases, and Ideologies of 'Race' in Twentieth-Century America." *Journal of American History* 83, no. 1 (June 1996): 44–69.

———. *What Comes Naturally: Miscegenation Law and the Making of Race in America*. New York: Oxford University Press, 2009.

Paul, Diane. *Controlling Human Heredity: 1865 to the Present*. Atlantic Highlands, N.J.: Humanities Press, 1995.

Pegler-Gordon, Anna. *In Sight of America: Photography and the Development of U.S. Immigration Policy*. Berkeley: University of California Press, 2009.

Pfaelzer, Jean. *Driven Out: The Forgotten War against Chinese Americans*. New York: Random House, 2007.

Pitt, Leonard. *Decline of the Californios: A Social History of the Spanish-Speaking Californians, 1846–1890*. Berkeley: University of California Press, 1966.

Platt, Anthony M. *The Child Savers: The Invention of Delinquency*. 3rd ed. New Brunswick, N.J.: Rutgers University Press, 2009.

Rafter, Nicole H., ed. *White Trash: The Eugenic Family Studies, 1877–1919*. Boston: Northeastern University Press, 1988.

Raftery, Judith Rosenberg. *Land of Fair Promise: Politics and Reform in Los Angeles Schools, 1885–1941*. Stanford, Calif.: Stanford University Press, 1992.

Ramirez, Catherine S. *The Woman in the Zoot: Gender, Nationalism, and the Cultural Politics of Memory*. Durham, N.C.: Duke University Press, 2009.

Reilly, Phillip. *The Surgical Solution: A History of Involuntary Sterilization in the United States*. Baltimore: Johns Hopkins Press, 1991.

Reisler, Mark. *By the Sweat of Their Brow: Mexican Immigrant Labor in the United States, 1900–1940*. Westport, Conn.: Greenwood Press, 1976.

Rosen, Christine. *Preaching Eugenics: Religious Leaders and the American Eugenics Movement*. New York: Oxford University Press, 2004.

Ross, Dorothy. *G. Stanley Hall: The Psychologist as Prophet*. Chicago: University of Chicago Press, 1972.

Ruiz, Vicki L. "Una Mujer Sin Fronteras: Luisa Moreno and Latina Labor Activism." *Pacific Historical Review* 73, no. 1 (February 2004): 1–20.

Rury, John L. "Race, Region, and Education: An Analysis of Black and White Scores on the 1917 Army Alpha Intelligence Tests." *Journal of Negro Education* 57 (1988): 51–65.

Sánchez, George J. *Becoming Mexican American: Ethnicity, Culture, and Identity in Los Angeles, 1900–1945*. New York: Oxford University Press, 1993.

Saxton, Alexander. *The Indispensable Enemy: Labor and the Anti-Chinese Movement in California*. Berkeley: University of California Press, 1975.

Schlossman, Steven L. "Delinquent Children: The Juvenile Reform School." In *Oxford History of the Prison: The Practice of Punishment*, edited by Norval Morris and David J. Rothman, 329–349. New York: Oxford University Press 1997.

———. *Transforming Juvenile Justice: Reform Ideals and Institutional Realities, 1825–1920*. DeKalb: Northern Illinois University Press, 2005. Originally published in 1977.

Schlossman, Steven, and Stephanie Wallach. "The Crime of Precocious Sexuality: Female Juvenile Delinquency in the Progressive Era." *Harvard Educational Review* 48, no. 1 (1978): 65–94.

Schneider, Eric. *In the Web of Class: Delinquents and Reformers in Boston, 1830s to 1910s*. New York: New York University Press, 1993.

Scott, James C. *Weapons of the Weak: Everyday Forms of Peasant Resistance*. New Haven, Conn.: Yale University Press, 1985.

Selden, Steven. *Inheriting Shame: The Story of Eugenics and Racism in America*. New York: Teachers College Press, 2001.

Sontag, Susan. *On Photography*. New York: Farrar, Straus, and Giroux, 1977.

Standart, Sister M. Collette. "The Sonoran Migration to California, 1848–1856: A Study in Prejudice." *Southern California Quarterly* 58 (1976): 333–358.

Stepan, Nancy Leys. *"The Hour of Eugenics": Race, Gender, and Nation in Latin America*. Ithaca, N.Y.: Cornell University Press, 1991.

Stern, Alexandra M. "Buildings, Boundaries, and Blood: Medicalization and Nation-Building at the U.S.-Mexico Border, 1910–1930." *Hispanic American Historical Review* 79, no. 1 (1999): 41–81.

———. "An Empire of Tests: Psychometrics and the Paradoxes of Nationalism in the Americas." In *Haunted by Empire: Geographies of Intimacy in North American History*, edited by Ann L. Stoler, 560–592. Durham: University of North Carolina Press, 2006.

———. *Eugenic Nation: Faults and Frontiers in Better Breeding in Modern America*. Berkeley: University of California Press, 2004.

Tanenhaus, David. *Juvenile Justice in the Making*. New York: Oxford University Press, 2004.

Taylor, Quintard. *In Search of the Racial Frontier: African Americans in the West, 1528–1990*. New York: W. W. Norton, 1999.

Taylor, Quintard, and Shirley Anne Moore. *African American Women Confront the West, 1600–2000*. Norman: University of Oklahoma Press, 2008.

Trafzer, Clifford E., and Joel R. Hyer, eds. *Exterminate Them: Written Accounts of the Murder, Rape, and Slavery of Native Americans during the California Gold Rush, 1848–1868*. East Lansing: Michigan State University Press, 1999.

Trafzer, Clifford E., and Jean E. Keller, eds. *Boarding School Blues: Revisiting American Indian Educational Experiences*. East Lansing, Mich.: Bison Books, 2006.

Trent, James W. *Inventing the Feeble Mind: A History of Mental Retardation in the United States*. Berkeley: University of California, 1994.

Tyack, David. *The One Best System: A History of the American Urban Education*. Cambridge, Mass.: Harvard University Press, 1974.

Vine, Deloria, Jr., and Clifford M. Lytle. *American Indians, American Justice*. Austin: University of Texas Press, 1983.

Weber, David J. *Foreigners in the Their Native Land*. Albuquerque: University of New Mexico Press, 1973.

Wellerstein, Alex. "States of Eugenics: Institutions and the Practices of Compulsory Sterilization in California." In *Reframing Rights: Bioconstitutionalism in the Genetic Age*, 29–58, edited by Sheila Jasanoff. Cambridge, Mass.: MIT Press, 2011.

Willrich, Michael. *City of Courts: Socializing Justice in Progressive Era Chicago*. Cambridge, United Kingdom: Cambridge University Press, 2003.

———. "The Two-Percent Solution: Eugenic Jurisprudence and the Socialization of American Law, 1900–1930." *Law and History Review* 16, no. 1 (Spring 1998): 63–111.

Zenderland, Leila. *Measuring Minds: Henry Goddard and the Intelligence Testing Movement*. New York: Cambridge University Press, 1998.

UNPUBLISHED DISSERTATIONS, MASTER'S THESES, AND
PAPERS

Beck, Nicholas P. "The Other Children: Minority Education in California Public Schools from Statehood to 1890." Ph.D. diss., University of California–Los Angeles, 1975.

Clement, Dexter A. "A History of the Preston Band." M.A. thesis, Sacramento State College, 1965.

Culp, Alice Bessie. "A Case Study of the Living Conditions of 35 Mexican Families of Los Angeles with Special Reference to Mexican Children." M.A. thesis, University of Southern California, 1922.

Huntington, Emily, Leona Jones, Donna Moses, and Ruth Turner. "The Juvenile Court: A Study of the Organization and Procedure of the Juvenile Court with Special Reverence to Seven Counties of California." B.A. thesis, University of California–Berkeley, 1917.

Husband, V. Pierpont. "Truancy as a Factor in the Delinquency of Boys: A Case-Study of 300 Boys in the Preston School of Industry at Ione, California and Comparisons with the Truancy Problem of the Sacramento City Schools." M.A. thesis, College of the Pacific, 1930.

Matthews, George Edwards. "The Development of the California Youth Authority: With Special Reference to the Fred C. Nelles School." M.A. thesis (history), California State University–Fullerton, 1973.

McVicar, Lawrence B. "A History of the California Youth Authority." M.A. thesis, California State University–Sacramento, 1972.

Mihailoff, Laura. "Protecting Our Children: A History of the California Youth Authority." Ph.D. diss., University of California–Berkeley, 2008.

Miller, George E. "Administrative History of California Institutions for Juvenile Offenders." M.S. thesis (public administration), Sacramento State College, 1965.

Pang, Heather A. "Making Men: Reform Schools and the Shaping of Masculinity, 1890–1920." Ph.D. diss., University of California–Davis, 2000.

Patti, R. J. "Child Protection in California, 1850–1966: An Analysis of Public Policy." Ph.D. diss., University of Southern California, 1967.

Reminger, Elizabeth. "The Care of Dependent Children in California, 1850–1879." M.A. thesis, Mills College, 1931.

Shackelford, R. "To Shield Them from Temptation: Child Saving Institutions and the Children of the Underclass in San Francisco, 1850–1910." Ph.D. diss., Harvard University, 1991.

Sundwick, Karen S. "Schools for Crime: Juvenile Reformatories in Porfirian Mexico, 1876–1911." Ph.D. diss., University of New Mexico, 1986.

Index

AMERICAN CROSSROADS

Edited by Earl Lewis, George Lipsitz, George Sánchez, Dana Takagi, Laura Briggs, and Nikhil Pal Singh

TEXT
10/13 Sabon

DISPLAY
Sabon

COMPOSITOR
Westchester Book Group

INDEXER

PRINTER AND BINDER
Maple-Vail Book Manufacturing Group